POLITICAL ECONOMY IN NINETEENTH-CENTURY AMERICA

Selected and Introduced by
Morgen Witzel

Volume 6

History of American Thought

Political Economy in Nineteenth-Century America

Selected and Introduced by **Morgen Witzel**

Volume 1
Mathew Carey
Essays on Political Economy, 1822

Volume 2
Francis Wayland
The Elements of Political Economy, 1837

Volume 3
George Tucker
Political Economy for the People, 1859

Volume 4
Amasa Walker
The Science of Wealth: A Manual of Political Economy, 1866

Volume 5
William Graham Sumner
Problems in Political Economy, 1884 and
Essays on Political Economy, 1885

Volume 6
Francis A. Walker
Political Economy, 1892

Printed in England by Antony Rowe Ltd, Chippenham

POLITICAL ECONOMY

Francis A. Walker

THOEMMES PRESS

Published by Thoemmes Press, 2003

Thoemmes Press
11 Great George Street
Bristol BS1 5RR, England

http://www.thoemmes.com

Political Economy in Nineteenth-Century America
6 Volumes : ISBN 1 84371 048 X

British Library Cataloguing-in-Publication Data
A CIP record of this title is available from the British Library

This book is printed on acid-free paper, sewn, and
cased in a durable buckram.

AMERICAN SCIENCE SERIES.—ADVANCED COURSE.

POLITICAL ECONOMY

BY

FRANCIS A. WALKER

President of the Massachusetts Institute of Technology,

AUTHOR OF "THE WAGES QUESTION," "MONEY," "MONEY, TRADE AND INDUSTRY," "LAND AND ITS RENT," ETC.

THIRD EDITION, REVISED AND ENLARGED.

London

MACMILLAN AND CO.

1892

THE MERSHON COMPANY PRESS,
RAHWAY, N. J., U. S. A.

CONTENTS.

PART I.

PAGE.

CHARACTER AND LOGICAL METHOD OF POLITICAL ECONOMY, - - - - 1

PART II.

PRODUCTION.

CHAPTER I. LAND AND NATURAL AGENTS, - - - - - - - 33
" II. LABOR, - - - - - - - - - - - - - 44
" III. CAPITAL: ITS ORIGIN AND OFFICE, - - - - - - 61
" IV. THE PRODUCTIVE CAPABILITY OF A COMMUNITY - - - 69

PART III.

EXCHANGE.

CHAPTER I. THE THEORY OF VALUE, - - - - - - - - - 78
" II. THE THEORY OF INTERNATIONAL EXCHANGES, - - 111
" III. MONEY AND ITS VALUE, - - - - - - - - - 120
" IV. MONEY AND ITS VALUE—(*Continued.*)—
DEBASED COIN: SEIGNIORAGE - - - - - 143
" V. INCONVERTIBLE PAPER MONEY, - - - - - - - 152
" VI. BANK MONEY, - - - - - - - - - - - 166
" VII. THE REACTION OF EXCHANGE UPON PRODUCTION. - - - 171

PART IV.

DISTRIBUTION.

CHAPTER I. THE PARTIES TO THE DISTRIBUTION OF WEALTH, - - - 187
" II. RENT, - - - - - - - - - - - - - - 193
" III. INTEREST, - - - - - - - - - - - - - 218

CHAPTER IV. PROFITS, - - - - - - - - - - - - - - 232
" V. WAGES, - - - - - - - - - - - - - - - - 245
" VI. WAGES CONTINUED: THE CONDITION OF THE LABORING CLASS, AS AFFECTED BY IMPERFECT COMPETITION, 258
" VII. TWO OTHER SHARES IN DISTRIBUTION, - - - - - 272
" VIII. THE REACTION OF DISTRIBUTION UPON PRODUCTION, - 279

PART V.

CONSUMPTION.

CHAPTER I. SUBSISTENCE: POPULATION, - - - - - - - - - 292
" II. THE APPEARANCE OF NEW ECONOMIC WANTS, - - - - 305
" III. CONSUMPTION; THE DYNAMICS OF WEALTH; THE REACTION OF CONSUMPTION UPON PRODUCTION, - - - - - 314

PART VI.

SOME APPLICATIONS OF ECONOMIC PRINCIPLES.

1. USURY LAWS, - - - - - - - - - - - - - - - - 330
2. INDUSTRIAL CO-OPERATION, - - - - - - - - - - - - - 341
3. POLITICAL MONEY, - - - - - - - - - - - - - - - 351
4. PAUPERISM, - - - - - - - - - - - - - - - - . 359
5. THE DOCTRINE OF THE WAGE FUND, - - - - - - - - - 364
6. THE MULTIPLE OR TABULAR STANDARD, - - - - - - - - 371
7. TRADES UNIONS AND STRIKES, - - - - - - - - - - - 375
8. THE KNIGHTS OF LABOR, - - - - - - - - - - - - - 384
9. ATTACKS ON THE DOCTRINE OF RENT, - - - - - - - - - 394
10. NATIONALIZATION OF THE LAND, - - - - - - - - - - 407
11. THE BANKING FUNCTIONS, - - - - - - - - - - - - 433
12. THE NATIONAL BANKING SYSTEM OF THE UNITED STATES, - - 439
13. FOREIGN EXCHANGES, - - - - - - - - - - - - - - 448
14. BI-METALLISM, - - - - - - - - - - - - - - - 463
15. THE REVENUE OF THE STATE, - - - - - - - - - - - 475
16. TAXATION, - - - - - - - - - - - - - - - - - 488
17. "PROTECTION" VS. FREEDOM OF PRODUCTION, - - - - - - 505
18. SOCIALISM, - - - - - - - - - - - - - - - - 517

POLITICAL ECONOMY

POLITICAL ECONOMY.

PART I.

CHARACTER AND LOGICAL METHOD OF POLITICAL ECONOMY.

1. What Political Economy is.—Political Economy, or Economics, is the name of that body of knowledge which relates to wealth.

Political Economy has to do with no other subject, whatsoever, than wealth. Especially should the student of economics take care not to allow any purely political, ethical or social considerations to influence him in his investigations. All that he has, as an economist, to do is to find out how wealth is produced, exchanged, distributed and consumed. It will remain for the social philosopher, the moralist, or the statesman, to decide how far the pursuit of wealth, according to the laws discovered by the economist, should be subordinated to other, let us say, higher, considerations. The more strictly the several branches of inquiry are kept apart, the better it will be for each and for all.

The economist may also be a social philosopher, a moralist, or a statesman, just as the mathematician may also be a chemist or a mechanician; but not, on that account, should the several subjects be confounded.

2. Political Economy does not Inculcate Love of Wealth.—Because political economy confines itself to discovering the laws of wealth, it has by some been called, derisively, the Gospel of Mammon. In reply to this sneer it would be enough to say that, while wealth is not the sole interest of mankind, it is yet of vast concern, of vital concern, to individuals and to communities. As such, it deserves to be studied. Now, if it is to be studied at all, it will best be studied by itself. The easiest and surest way to increase our knowledge of any subject is to isolate it, and investigate it, to the strict exclusion, for the time, of all other subjects.

But more may be said. Political Economy does not inculcate love of wealth. It simply inquires how that passion, or propensity, in the degree in which it exists, does, in fact, influence the actions of men. Political Economy has no quarrel with passions or propensities which may, in a greater or less degree, supplant the love of wealth. It does not assume to sit in judgment on human conduct ; It exercises no choice among human motives ; It simply undertakes to follow causes to their effects in one single department of human activity, *viz.*, the pursuit of wealth.

3. Political Economy Tempers the Passion for Wealth.—So far from ministering to greed, it would be easy to prove that the study of Political Economy has tended, by showing how wealth is really best gained and kept, to banish a ravening, ferocious greed which seeks to snatch its objects of desire by brutal violence, at whatever cost of misery to others, and to replace this by an enlightened sense of self-interest, which seeks its objects through exchanges mutually beneficial, and which supports social order and international peace as the conditions of general well-being.

Political Economy does not plant the love of wealth in human minds. It finds it there, a strong, native passion, which, but for enlightened views, is likely to break out into private rapine and public war. A little more than one hundred years ago, before Adam Smith published his great work, "The Wealth of Nations," it was a maxim of public policy, that only one party to trade could profit by a transaction, and that all which one party might gain, the other must lose. Out of this root grew wars and commercial restrictions which set man against man, and nation against nation, making the intercourse of even the most civilized states a game of deceit and violence. Adam Smith left the love of wealth in human minds, not rebuked but enlightened. Little more than a century has elapsed, yet mankind have made greater progress toward humane and mutually advantageous international relations in that time than during all the other centuries of human history.

4. But What is Wealth?—Economists have found much difficulty in defining Wealth; and not a few writers, especially of late, have chosen to abandon the word altogether.

Several of these have called Political Economy the Science of Exchanges. But the use of this term only removes the essential difficulty of the subject one stage further away. Exchanges of what? All human life, in society, is made up of exchanges, in feeling, word and act. The family relation, the neighborhood, the State, the Church, imply an unceasing exchange of sympathies, activities and incentives, only a portion of which are within the view of the economist.

If we say exchanges of wealth, we have not escaped the difficulty of defining Political Economy, since we have, all the same, to tell what wealth is. If we say exchanges of services, we must further explain what sort of services we mean, since there is an infinitude of services of man to man, in a great variety of relations, with which Political Economy can claim to have nothing to do. The services of parents to children, of children to parents, of children to each other, of friend to friend, do not form any part of the subject matter of Political Economy.

If we say economic services, we have still to define the scope of the word economic: that is, we are back again at the point from which we started.

5. The Term a Popular One.—The substitute offered for the term wealth, in describing the field of Political Economy, proving thus defective, let us see what we can do with the word so long in use.

Wealth is, as Prof. Price justly observes, "the word which belongs to the world which Political Economy addresses." It would, therefore, be a matter of regret, were it to be abandoned unnecessarily. When the man of business, the laboring man, even the man of leisure, is told that Political Economy is the science of wealth, he at once feels drawn to the subject. No one is above, few are below, an interest in the subject. But the term, science of exchanges, is not especially attractive. A banker, deeming that "foreign exchanges" are meant, may at first think himself concerned; but will discover his misapprehension when he opens the book. The great majority of people will doubt, on hearing the title, whether they care much or any thing about the science of exchanges.

Since, then, so great popular interest attaches to the word, wealth, it would be a pity to lose the use of it without good reason.

6. Yet Subject to Scientific Uses.—And we note that the conception of wealth formed by men who are not students of Political Economy, is clear and well-defined. It is only scholars, when they begin to talk and write about wealth, who find any difficulty in the use of the word. Stop a dozen men in succession, and ask them what constitutes wealth, and you will find an almost perfect agreement. "Every one," says Mr. John Stuart Mill, "has a notion sufficiently correct for common purposes of what is meant by wealth. The inquiries which relate to it are in no danger of being confounded with those relating to any other of the great human interests."

Moreover, if we inquire what is the difficulty attributed to the use of the term, we find that it relates, not so much to the definition of wealth, as to the formation of a catalogue of the articles which make up the wealth of an individual or community.

Now, it is not important that such a catalogue should be formed. It would not even be fatal to a definition of wealth that certain objects should be found which seemed to fall across the line of demarkation. All definitions in Political Economy, as, indeed, in the natural sciences, are subject to this condition. Few naturalists will presume to say just where the vegetable kingdom ends and the animal kingdom begins. There are objects in nature concerning which it would puzzle the most learned scholar to say whether they are animal or vegetable. Yet we do not, on that account, hesitate to say that a tree belongs to the vegetable, and an elephant to the animal kingdom.

7. Relation of Wealth to Value.—Wealth comprises all articles of value and nothing else. If any thing have not value, it does not belong to this category. It may conceivably be better than wealth; but it certainly is other than wealth. It may become a means of acquiring wealth; but it is not wealth itself. In the language of Prof. N. W. Senior, "the words wealth and value differ as substance and attribute. All those things, and those only, which constitute wealth, are valuable."

8. But What is Value?—Value is the power which an article confers upon its possessor, irrespective of legal authority or personal sentiments, of commanding, in exchange for itself, the labor, or the products of the labor, of others. Briefly and somewhat elliptically speaking: Value is power in exchange.

We say: irrespective of legal authority. The Emperor of Germany can, by a word, call two millions of men from their homes and send them to distant fields, even to foreign lands, to work, to watch, to march, to fight and to die. Yet these services are not economic, because not voluntary. On the other hand, the services of a soldier in the British army are economic, as they are rendered under the terms of a voluntary enlistment, the result of a fair and open bargain between the crown and the subject.

We say also: irrespective of personal sentiments. The mother hangs over the sick bed, day and night, draining her very life blood to save her child. Her services are not economic, because dictated by a purely personal sentiment. On the other hand, the work of the hired nurse and of the feed physician comes fairly within the view of the economist.

9. Transferability Essential to Value.—We note that exchange implies two exchangers. Value is, then, a social phenomenon.

But exchange implies, also, the capability of detaching from the present possessor the articles to be exchanged, and making them over to another.

Do health, strength, intelligence, skill, possess this capability? Are they wealth? Have they value?

Not a little of the difficulty which has attended the use, in economics, of the word wealth, has arisen from attributing value to such properties or possessions as these. Prof. Alfred Marshall, in his admirable work, "The Economics of Industry," even includes honesty in the "personal wealth" of a country.

But let us apply the test of our definition. Can these possessions or properties be exchanged? Can health, strength, intelligence, skill, be detached and become the property of another? No; they can be taken away from one, as by sickness or death; but they can not be made over to any one else. The gouty millionaire can not, with all that he has, purchase the robust health of the laborer by the wayside, or buy for his empty-headed son the learning or the trained faculties of the humblest scholar. Hence, all that which some economists have called intellectual capital, and all that which, by analogy, might be called physical capital, are to be excluded from the category of wealth.

10. Better than Wealth, but not Wealth.— Those possessions or properties have seemed to be things so desirable in themselves, so much to be preferred, in any right view of human welfare, that excellent writers have not been able to bring themselves to leave them out of the field of economics. But Political Economy is the science, not of welfare, but of wealth. There may be many things which are better than wealth, which are yet not to be called wealth. A good name is rather to be chosen than riches, and loving favor than silver and gold; yet a good name is not riches, and loving favor is neither silver nor gold.

Here the popular understanding of the word coincides with the definition given for scientific purposes. Plain men do not speak of such qualities, or endowments, as being wealth. No merchant or manufacturer or laboring man would include any one of these items in an account of his wealth, however precious he might esteem them.

And it is to be noted that it does not matter whether the

incapacity to detach and make over a possession to another, arises from the nature of things, as in the case of personal health and strength, skill and intelligence, or from the constraints of law or public opinion. In Circassia, a beautiful daughter is wealth, and is popularly so accounted. No one in making up the list of his wealth would omit this item, any more than he would leave out his horses or his fields. In Christian countries, a daughter is not wealth, though she is far better than wealth. The Proclamation of Emancipation, in the United States and in Russia, annihilated a vast mass of wealth ; it created what was better than much wealth—a body of free men.

But while strength, skill and intelligence can not be detached, and transferred, and thus can not be said to be wealth, the present use of them can be assigned to another, and hence may become the subject of exchange. The rich valetudinarian may command the services of the robust laborer, in waiting on his person ; he may hire the poor scholar to be tutor to his son. The usufruct of all such qualities and endowments, therefore, properly constitutes an item of wealth, and, by the force of contract, the capability of transferring this species of wealth may be extended beyond the present moment to considerable periods of time, as when a man is hired by the month or year.

11. Relation of Wealth to Community of Goods.—But it may be objected that, inasmuch as exchange implies a present individual possessor, were community of goods or of labor to be universally established, there would no longer be such a thing as wealth, or such a department of human inquiry as Political Economy.

To this it is sufficient to reply, that community of labor or of enjoyment is simply impossible, from the very nature of mankind.

Were a hundred persons to unite in such a society, each would have to work by himself : the exertion must be his ; the pain and weariness would be all his. On the other hand, what he received from the common stock, would be his own ; the food would nourish him alone ; the clothing and the food would warm only him ; none of his fellows would share in the pleasure or the benefit of what he consumed.

The so-called community of labor and of goods, then, amounts simply to a mode of roughly apportioning exertion and enjoyment, on the basis of an assumed equality of abilities and of needs. Subject to all the injustice involved in such an assumption, each one of the hundred members would still part with his services to his fellows, and receive from them his remuneration, in the form of food, clothing, fuel and shelter.

12. Relation of Value to Gratuity.—It will have been gathered from what has been said respecting value, that wealth and well-being are not synonymous. Much which is essential to the latter is no element of the former. Wealth may be increased at the expense of well-being, as in the case of the reduction of free laborers to the grade of chattel slavery. Wealth may be diminished temporarily by causes which minister to the advancement of the community and the State, as in the case of inventions which throw out of use large amounts of material and apparatus, or of ameliorating changes in nature which allow costly contrivances to be dispensed with.

" If," wrote Prof. Senior, " the climate of England could suddenly be changed to that of Bogota, and the warmth which we extract imperfectly and expensively from fuel were supplied by the sun, fuel would cease to be useful, except as one of the productive instruments employed by art ; we should want no more grates or chimney-pieces in our sitting-rooms ; what had previously been a considerable amount of property, in the fixtures of houses, in stock in trade and materials, would become valueless ; coals would sink in price ; the most expensive mines would be abandoned ; those which were retained would command smaller rents."

13. Continuous Displacement of Value by Gratuity.—We are now called further to notice that there is a constant tendency to this diminution of the sum of wealth, and even to the annihilation of individual items, from age to age. So rapid and persistent is that tendency that, but for the increase of population, and the multiplication and diversification of human desires, due to increasing civilization and refinement, the subject matter with which Political Economy has to deal would be continually diminishing.

How small the sum of wealth which would suffice for a community, in our stage of knowledge and skill, which should aspire to live only as well as a tribe of savages! The boats, the nets, the huts, the clothing and the domestic utensils of a primitive community represent an incredible amount of exertion and sacrifice; possess a vast amount of purchasing power. A like outfit would require but an insignificant part of the labor power of a modern community, and would have but little purchasing power.

The tendency which has been noted arises out of the progress of mankind in the chemical and mechanic arts, by which operations formerly difficult are made easy; by which materials naturally scarce are made plentiful; by which human necessities once urgently felt are wholly obviated, and, finally, by which things once costing labor are made to produce themselves spontaneously.

14. Growth of Human Wants.—In fact, however, while, in any community, this displacement of value by gratuity is continually in progress, the increase of population and the multiplication and diversification of human wants may be operating as steadily and strongly in the other direction. The labor that is made free by discoveries and inventions is applied to overcome the difficulties which withstand the gratification of newly-felt desires. The hut is pulled down to make room for the cottage; the cottage gives way to the mansion; the mansion to the palace. The rude covering of skins is replaced by the comely garment of woven stuffs; and these, in the progress of luxury, by the most splendid fabrics of human skill. In a thousand forms wealth is created by the whole energy of the community, quickened by a zeal greater than that which animated the exertions of their rude forefathers to obtain a scanty and squalid subsistence.

15. Distinction between Wealth and Property.—A further distinction is that between wealth and property. The neglect of this has caused great confusion, especially in discussions of the principles and methods of taxation.

Mr. J. S. Mill affords an example of the confusion of these terms when he says, respecting a mortgage on a landed estate, "this is wealth to the person to whom it brings in a revenue, and who could, perhaps, sell it in the market for the full amount of the debt. But it is not wealth to the country; if the engagement were annulled, the country would be neither poorer nor richer."

A more accurate statement of the case would be this: The landed estate is wealth, that is, possesses value; that is, confers upon its possessor the power of commanding, in exchange for itself, the labor, or the products of the labor, of others. The mortgage is property, or a right to wealth; in this case, a right to an undivided portion of the landed estate. The amount of the property of the owner of the estate is the value of the estate less the mortgage. There is but one body of wealth; there are two properties, that of the owner, and that of the mortgagee. The wealth of the community is no greater and no less, whether the ownership of the estate be entire, or divided into two or half a dozen properties.

Indeed, we might say that "property" is not a word with which the political economist has any thing to do. It is legal, not economic, in its significance.

"The wealth," says Prof. Senior, "which consists merely of a right or credit, on the part of A., with a corresponding duty or debt on the part of B., is not considered by the Political Economist. He deals with the things which are the subjects of the right, or the credit, not with the claims or liabilities which may affect them. In fact, the credit amounts merely to this: that B. has in his hands a part of the property of A."

16. The Premises of Political Economy.—What are the proper premises of Political Economy? that is, what facts and principles should the economist take to reason from? Are they many or few? Shall the economist take into account all the facts, mental or physical, which influence the phenomena of wealth; or shall he confine himself to certain principal facts?

Shall we take man, for the purpose of economic reasoning, precisely as he is found to be, with all his appetencies and characteristics, so far as they affect the power and the disposition to labor, or so far as they increase or impair the ability of individuals to secure their share in the distribution of the product of industry? or shall we create, for the purposes of our reasoning, an economic man, assumed to be impelled by certain motives in respect to wealth, from whose actions men in general, knowing themselves to be more or less fully controlled by similar motives, may derive instruction?

Instead of seeking to extend our knowledge of the actual conditions under which wealth is produced by man, shall we content ourselves with certain leading conditions, such as that food is produced without human labor only in small quantities and very precariously; that the soils of every country vary widely in fertility; and that of no soil can the produce be increased indefinitely without a more than proportional expenditure of labor and capital?

Shall we take account of the various endowments, in the way of soil and climate, mineral resources and water power, of different countries? Shall we study their institutions and the predominant traits of character manifested by their people, so far as these appear to influence their actions in respect to wealth? Or shall we, on the other hand, disregard all that makes one nation to differ from another, caring to learn nothing of any which would not hold good of all.

Upon the answer to these questions depends the character and logical method of Political Economy. Upon that answer depends also much of the usefulness of this department of inquiry and the interest it may be expected to arouse in the public mind.

17. Two Schools of Political Economy.—The differences of opinion which exist regarding the proper extent of the premises of Political Economy have given rise to two schools which are commonly called the English and the German school.

The economists of the former school insist that the proper premises of pure Political Economy consist of a few certain facts of human nature, of human society, and of the physical constitution of the earth. That these, not more than five or six in number, constitute all the premises proper to the inquiry.

That the scope of economic reasoning can not be extended beyond these without destroying the purity and simplicity of the science, and introducing error and confusion.

The economists of the latter school hold that it is the province of Political Economy to explain the phenomena of wealth. That, in order to do this, the economist must inquire how men do, in fact, behave in regard to wealth, constituted as they are, and under the conditions and circumstances in which they are placed.

In this view, nothing that importantly influences the production and distribution of wealth can be neglected by the economist. All human history becomes his domain. The other sciences, alike the physical and the moral, become tributary to the science he cultivates.

With its premises thus enlarged, Political Economy ceases to be something which one man of superior intellect could, with a definite exertion of his faculties, work completely out at a sitting, as Beckford wrote "Vathek"; and that too without having visited any community beyond the one in which he was born, or knowing a page of history. Political Economy, as thus comprehended, becomes a work to which many men and successive ages must contribute; the material of which is accumulated in human experience, and is thus continually on the increase. It becomes a work which never is, but is always to be done, growing with the growing knowledge of the race.

18. Prof. Cairnes' Statement.—It has been said that the two schools of Political Economy are known as the English and the German school. The terms are not fortunate, inasmuch as some of the economists who have labored most fully in the spirit of the so-called German school, have been natives of the British Isles. The best statement known to me of the true scope of economic inquiry is that given by Prof. Cairnes, from whose admirable lectures* I abridge the following paragraphs, preserving the author's phraseology:

The desires, passions and propensities which influence man-

* "On the Character and Logical Method of Political Economy," first published in 1857; reprinted, revised and enlarged in 1875, just before the lamented author's death.

kind in the pursuit of wealth are almost infinite. Yet among these are some principles of so marked and paramount a character as both to admit of being ascertained, and when ascertained, to afford the data for determining the most important laws of the production and distribution of wealth. To possess himself of these is the first business of the political economist. He has then to take account of some leading physiological facts connected with human nature; and, lastly, to ascertain the principal physical characteristics of those natural agents of production on which human industry is exercised.

But it must not be thought that when these cardinal facts have been ascertained, and their consequences duly developed, the labors of the political economist are at an end. Many subordinate influences will intervene to disturb, and occasionally to reverse, the operation of the more powerful principles, and thus to modify the resulting phenomena.

19. Subordinate Causes in Economics.—The next step, therefore, in his investigations will be to endeavor to ascertain the character of those subordinate causes, whether mental or physical, political or social, which influence human conduct in the pursuit of wealth. These, when he has found them, and is enabled to appreciate them with sufficient accuracy, he will incorporate among the premises of the science.

Thus, the political and social institutions of a country, in particular, the laws affecting the tenure of land, will be included among such subordinate agencies. It will be for the political economist to show in what way causes of this kind modify the operation of more fundamental principles. Again, any great discovery in the arts of production, such, *e. g.*, as the steam engine, will be a new fact for the consideration of the political economist. It will be like the discovery of a new planet, the attraction of which, operating on all the heavenly bodies within the sphere of its influence, will cause them more or less to deviate from the path which had been previously calculated for them.

In the same way, also, those motives and principles of action which may be developed in the progress of society, so far as they may be found to affect the phenomena of wealth, will also be taken account of by the political economist. He will consider, *e. g.*, the influence of custom in modifying human conduct in the pursuit of wealth. He will consider how, as civilization advances, the estimation of the future in relation to the present is enhanced, and the desire for immediate enjoyment is controlled by the increasing efficacy of prudential restraint. He will also observe how ideas of decency, comfort and luxury are developed as society progresses, modifying the natural force of the principle of population, influencing the mode of expenditure of different classes, and affecting thereby the distribution of industrial products. Even moral and religious considerations are to be taken account of by the economist precisely in so far as they are found, in fact, to affect the conduct of men in the pursuit of wealth.

20. Remarks on Prof. Cairnes' Statement.—Nothing could be added to this statement of the logical method of Political Economy, as it is pursued by those who hold that it is the province of the science to explain the phenomena of wealth; and that, to this end, all causes which, whether primarily, or principally social, ethical, physical or physiological, do, in fact, enter to affect the actions of men respecting wealth, should be identified and determined, so far as may be, both in their direction and in the degree of their influence.

In this view the economist who omits any cause, structural or dynamic, physical or moral, which affects the production, exchange, distribution or consumption of wealth, must justify himself, not by the plea that such a cause has no relevancy to his investigation, but by some plea which would excuse an admittedly less than complete treatment of the subject, *e. g.*, the lack of information, the limitations of the human faculties, or the need, for popular instruction, of very brief and very general statements of principle.

21. Mr. Mill on the Economic Man.—On the other hand, perhaps the best statement of the view taken by the economists of the so-called English school, as to the proper premises of Political Economy, is that given by Mr. J. S. Mill, in his work published in 1844.

"Political Economy," says Mr. Mill, "is concerned with

man solely as a being who desires to possess wealth and who is capable of judging of the comparative efficacy of means to that end. * * * It makes entire abstraction of every other human passion or motive, except those which may be regarded as perpetually antagonizing principles to the desire of wealth, namely, aversion to labor and desire of the present enjoyment of costly indulgences. These it takes, to a certain extent, into its calculations, because these do not merely, like other desires, occasionally conflict with the pursuit of wealth, but accompany it always, as a drag or impediment, and are, therefore, inseparably mixed up in the consideration of it. Political Economy considers mankind as occupied solely in acquiring and consuming wealth." *

We have here all the elements of the economic man. He is taken as a being perfectly capable of judging of the comparative efficacy of means to the end of wealth. That is, he will never fail, whoever he may be, or wherever he may live, whether a capitalist or a laborer, rich or poor, taught or untaught, to know exactly what course will secure his highest economic interest, that is, bring him the largest amount of wealth.

Moreover, that end of wealth he never fails to desire, with a steady, uniform, constant passion. Of every other human passion or motive, Political Economy "makes entire abstraction." Love of country, love of honor, love of friends, love of learning, love of art, pity, shame, religion, charity, will never, so far as Political Economy cares to take account, withstand the effort of the economic man to amass wealth.

There are, however, two human passions and motives, of which Political Economy takes account, as "perpetually antagonizing principles to the desire of wealth," namely, "aversion to labor and desire of the present enjoyment of costly indulgences," that is, indolence and gluttony.

As by this view of Political Economy all men are taken as equally absorbed in the passion for wealth, so all men are

* In his great work, subsequently published, Mr. Mill did not confine himself to the method here described; but professedly dealt with Political Economy in many of its "Applications to Social Philosophy."

taken as equally lazy and self-indulgent. The South Sea Islander and the large-brained European are equally averse to exertion; equally subject to the impulses of immediate appetite.

22. Ricardo the Master of the English School.—Such are the features of the economic man, as delineated by Mr. Mill. Not a few treatises have been written mainly according to this method. The ablest body of doctrine ever composed from this point of view is that of David Ricardo. Hence this school of Political Economy may not inaptly be called the Ricardian. Mr. Ricardo, indeed, modified those assumptions so far as to recognize the difference in economic quality existing between men of different countries, not only between the East Indian and the Englishman, but also between the Englishman and the Portuguese. Within the same country, however, he recognized no such differences; but held rigorously to the few and simple postulates which have been stated. The acuteness of his intellect, the tenacity of his logical grasp, make him easily the master of all the economists of this school.

23. Relations of the Two Schools.—It need not be a matter of surprise that so wide a difference of opinion as to the proper scope of economic inquiry should have led to much passionate controversy. The economists of the so-called German school have been disposed to deny, not only the universality of principles deduced from assumptions so arbitrary and falling so far short of the real facts of life and society, but also the significance, for any purpose whatever, of conclusions thus obtained. The economists of the so-called English, or Ricardian school, have treated the method of their opponents as unscientific, giving scope to charlatanry, and at the best tending to mere sentimentality.

The mutual contempt entertained by the two schools is not justified by a large view of the progress of economics in the past, or by a consideration of the history of other social sciences. Political Economy should begin with the Ricardian method. A few simple assumptions being made, the processes of the production, exchange and distribution of wealth should be traced out and be brought together into a complete system, which may be called pure Political Economy, or arbitrary Political Economy, or, *a priori* Political Economy, or by the name of its greatest teacher, Ricardian Political Economy. Such a scheme should constitute the skeleton of all economic reasoning; but upon this ghastly frame-work should be imposed the flesh and blood of an actual, vital Political Economy, which takes account of men and societies as they are, with all their sympathies, apathies, and antipathies; with every organ developed, as in life; every nerve of motion or of sensibility in full play.

24. The True Labor of Philosophy.—On this subject what could be more pregnant with meaning than the aphorism of Bacon, "Those who have treated of the sciences have been either empirics or dogmatical.

"The former, like ants, only heap up and use their store; the latter, like spiders, spin out their own web.

"The bee, as a mean between both, extracts matter from the flowers of the garden and the field; but works and fashions it by its own efforts.

"The true labor of philosophy resembles hers; for it neither relies entirely or principally on the powers of the mind, nor yet lays up in the memory the matter afforded by the experiments of natural history and mechanics, in its raw state, but changes and works it in the understanding."

25. Is Political Economy indeed a Science?—The answer to this question depends rather upon the definition imposed on the word science, than upon the view we take of Political Economy itself. If we give the word no wider extension than Dr. Whewell gave it, when he spoke of "those bodies of knowledge which we call sciences," Political Economy indubitably ranks as a science. It forms a body of knowledge, constantly growing, it is true, from the outside, and undergoing not a little change from time to time within, yet still embracing, in the present, a vast collection of related facts, with the reason of their succession, one to another, more or less clearly seen, and allowing many practical rules and precepts of great importance in determining human conduct to be deduced with all needed assurance. In this sense, then, Political Economy is a science.

Whether it be a science in the highest sense given that word, may be disputed. M. Comte, the great positivist philosopher, denied the claim of Political Economy to this title. In his view, it is an attribute of a true social science that it results in establishing a rational filiation between events, so as to allow of systematic prevision respecting their occurrence in a certain succession. Prediction—forecast of the future—is, according to M. Comte, the fruit of all true science. Of this, he asserts, political economy has not shown itself capable.

Prof. Cairnes rejoins that the economic prevision is a prevision not of events, but of tendencies. Admitting the incapacity of forecasting events, Prof. Cairnes urges that "it argues no imperfection in economic science. The imperfection is not here, but in those other cognate sciences, to which belongs the determination of the non-economic quantities in the problem, etc. * * Meanwhile it is no slight gain, in speculating on the future of society, to have it in our power to determine the direction of an order of tendencies exercising so wide, constant and potent an influence on the course of human development, as the conditions of wealth. * * * So much for the highest form of scientific fruit, 'forecast of the future.' The principle, however, of establishing a filiation in events may take the more modest form of explaining the past. * * That political economy, assuming that it fulfills its limited purpose of unfolding the natural laws of wealth, is capable of throwing light on the evolutions of history, will scarcely be denied."

26. The Practical Importance of Political Economy.—We can not stay to discuss the question. Whether Political Economy be or be not a science in the high sense attributed to that word by M. Comte, it assuredly is, as a branch of social inquiry, worthy the earnest attention of every publicist and every citizen. It deals with some of the most important subjects which concern society. Whether the degree of assurance that may be attained in the study of these questions be higher or be lower, the questions can not but be more justly decided by reason of such study.

If Political Economy have not yet reached the standing of a true science, in the high sense in which that word is used by M. Comte; if political economists are still at disagreement on many points of theoretical or practical importance, it can not be denied that the investigation of the conditions of wealth by Adam Smith and his successors has already resulted in the removal of monstrous delusions which a century ago profoundly affected the legislation of every civilized country, to the inexpressible injury of the commonwealth of nations. The first fruits of Political Economy have been worth a million times the intellectual effort that has been bestowed upon the subject.

27. Distinction between a Science and an Art.—Before proceeding to inquire whether Political Economy should be dealt with as a science or as an art, it seems desirable strongly to emphasize the distinction between a science and an art. This is the more needed because of the strangely persistent habit of economic writers in confusing these two things, which should be kept clearly distinct.

A science, whether the science of mathematics, or physics, or mechanics, or chemistry, or geology, or physiology, or economics, deals only with the relations of cause and effect within its own field. It assumes nothing to be a good and nothing to be an evil. It does not start with the notion that something is desirable or undesirable; nor does it arrive at any such conclusion as its result. It has no business to offer precepts or prescriptions. Its sole single concern is to trace effects back to their causes; to project causes forward to their effects.

An art, on the other hand, starts with the assumption that a certain thing is desirable or that a certain other thing is undesirable; that something is a good or that something is an evil. The object it seeks is to ascertain how the good may be attained, or the evil avoided. In pursuing this inquiry, it makes use of the principles, or laws, governing the relations of cause and effect, which have been ascertained in the cultivation of any and all sciences that have in any way to do with its own subject matter. As a result, it issues with certain precepts and prescriptions for the guidance and assistance of those who would gain the good or avoid the evil which that particular art has in contemplation, whether it be the art of navigation, or of cookery, of painting, of gunnery, of architecture, of mining, or of weaving.

28. The Distinction Illustrated.—This distinction between a science and an art ought to be sufficiently clear; but the inveterate disposition of economic writers, which has been referred to, will perhaps justify an illustration which I shall make familiar, even at the risk of appearing coarse.

Suppose I am in my laboratory and a man enters who says that he desires to consult me, as a professor of chemistry, as to whether he had better swallow the contents of a vial which he holds in his hand. I reply to him: "Sir, I have no advice, as a professor of chemistry, to offer you as to what you shall swallow or refrain from swallowing. I perceive that the liquid contained in your vial is prussic acid. I will cheerfully state to you the action of prussic acid on any substance about which you may choose to inquire; but probably you had better, for your apparent purpose, go to Prof. S., the physiologist, who can more fully and readily than myself explain the precise action of prussic acid when taken into the stomach of a living being."

The inquirer now goes to Prof. S., and says that he desires to consult him, as a professor of physiology, as to whether he had better swallow the liquid which the chemist has told him is undilute prussic acid. Prof. S. replies: "Sir, should you consult me as a fellow being, I would not stand on ceremony, but frankly advise you to empty the contents of your vial into the sink. But if you insist on consulting me as a professor of physiology, I must reply that I have no advice to give. Physiology, sir, is a science; as such, it has nothing to do with precepts or prescriptions, but only with the relations of cause and effect within the field of animal life. As a student of that science, I inform you that, if you swallow the liquid, you will experience such and such sensations, and, at about such a time, you will be dead. Since you still insist upon having advice as to whether you had better do this or not, I refer you to my neighbor, Dr. G., who is the professor, not of a science, but of an art. As such, it is his business to give advice regarding conduct. As such, he has a right to entertain the notion that certain things are good, and certain things evil ; that the means calculated (as shown by the appropriate science or sciences) to bring about the good, are desirable ; that the courses which (as shown by the appropriate science or sciences) lead to the evil, are undesirable. He would not be a physician unless he held that pain and death were evil ; life and the absence of pain, good. What he is a physician for is to help his patients to avoid the evil and obtain the good. In doing this he will naturally seek to apply the largest and latest results of the *science* of physiology to the *art* of healing."

29. Distinction between Political Economy as a Science and as an Art.—"If," says Prof. Senior, "Political Economy is to be treated as a science, it may be defined as the science which states the laws regulating the production and distribution of wealth, so far as they depend on the action of the human mind. If it be treated as an art, it may be defined as the art which points out the institutions and habits most conducive to the production and accumulation of wealth ; or, if the teacher ventures to take a wider view, as the art which points out the institutions and habits most conducive to that production, accumulation and distribution of wealth which is most favorable to the happiness of mankind."

30. Prof. Senior goes on to remark that, in the eighteenth century, political economy was treated as an art, a branch of statesmanship. Sir James Steuart so treated it. The French Physiocrats so regarded it. Even with Adam Smith, "the scientific portion of his work is merely an introduction to that which is practical."

Oddly enough, the statesman Turgot must be made an exception to the remark respecting the French Physiocrats. "It is remarkable," says Prof. Senior, "that the only man among the disciples of Quesnay* who was actually practicing

*See paragraph 48.

political economy as an art, is the only one who treated its principles as a science. His 'Réflexions sur la formation et la distribution des richesses,' published in 1774, is a purely scientific treatise. It contains not a word of precept, and might have been written by an ascetic, who believed wealth to be an evil."

Prof. Senior continues: "The English writers who have succeeded Adam Smith have generally set out by defining political economy as a science, and proceeded to treat it as an art. Mr. Ricardo is, however, an exception. His great work is little less scientific than that of Turgot. His abstinence from precept, and even from illustrations drawn from real life, is the more remarkable, as the subject of his treatise is 'Distribution,' the most practical branch of political economy, and 'Taxation,' the most practical branch of Distribution. The modern economists of France, Germany, Spain, Italy and America, so far as I am acquainted with their works, all treat political economy as an art."

31. We shall deal with Political Economy as a Science. —The inveterate disposition, which Prof. Senior thus notes, to abandon the investigation of principles for the formulation of precepts, has doubtless retarded greatly the progress of political economy. It can not be too strongly insisted on, that the economist, as such, has nothing to do with the questions, what men had better do; how nations should be governed; or what regulations should be made for their mutual intercourse. His business simply is to trace economic effects to their causes, leaving it to the philosopher of everyday life, to the moralist or the statesman, to teach how men and nations should act in view of the principles so established. The political economist,* for example, has no more

* A distinguished English Economist, quoting this remark, in the *Contemporary Review*, asks with some asperity, "What, then, should the political economist preach?" I answer, nothing. His business is to teach and not to preach. He acquits himself of his duty when he shows the relations of cause and effect within the field of industry, leaving it to statesmen, moralists and men of affairs to act for themselves, or to preach to others, with reference to what the political economist teaches.

call to preach free trade, as the policy of nations, than the physiologist to advocate monogamy as a legal institution.

Throughout this work until we reach Part VI, which will be in terms devoted to Some Applications of Economic Principles, the effort will be made to treat political economy strictly as a science. If at any point the writer lapses into expressions only suitable to the teacher of an art, it will be partly because of that strong predisposition which has been noted in almost all writers on this subject, and partly to the influence of example.

32. Is There a National Political Economy?—This is a question which has been much debated. The so-called protectionists have favored the view that each country has a political economy of its own. One writer of our own country has entitled his work "American Political Economy."

The controversy over this question arises out of the confusion produced, first, by the failure to distinguish between the science of political economy and the use of political economy in the art of statesmanship ; secondly, by the different views taken of the proper premises of the science of political economy by the two schools (Par. 17) before referred to.

Those who say that there is an American Political Economy, for example, mean that the precepts derived from political economy, whether addressed to the legislator, or to the body of the people, should not be applied to America without reference to the peculiar constitution, conditions and needs of America. But a science has nothing to do with precepts or prescriptions. Rules of conduct belong to an art.

33. National and Race Characteristics.—Moreover, the notion that there is a political economy for each race of men, and even for each nation, has been fostered by the arbitrary character of the assumptions of what we have called the Ricardian school, and by the refusal to pay a reasonable regard to some of the most characteristic features of human nature and some of the most prominent facts of industrial society, embracing institutions and laws which vitally affect the production and distribution of wealth.

Thus, the *à priori* economist, in discussing the question

of wages, assumes, for the purposes of his reasoning, a body of laborers who are wholly intent on getting the largest remuneration ; who will, for any advantage, however slight, change their occupation, and with equal readiness their place of abode, at least within their own country ; who, moreover, are so intelligent and well-informed that no preference, economically, can exist on behalf of any other occupation or place of abode, without their knowing it, and, of course, acting at once upon it. The economist having created such a race of beings, whose likeness is found nowhere upon earth, proceeds to point out,' it may be with great acuteness and accuracy, what the individual members thereof would do in various supposed cases, under the impulse of this or that economic force. His conclusions are put forth as "laws" of political economy.

Is it strange that an intelligent East Indian, reading these conclusions, should say, if this is political economy, it must be European political economy, and there should be a separate political economy for the East, since here, over vast regions, social and religious feelings absolutely prohibit multitudes of workmen from changing their occupation, for any reason ; while the almost uniform penury of the laboring class, their ignorance, superstition, and fear of change, combine to render movement from place to place tardy and difficult, if not, as in most cases, practically impossible ?

34. Relation of Political Economy to other Sciences.—Political Economy does not ascertain for itself a single one of the facts which form the premises of the economist. These are all derived from other sciences as data, *i. e.*, things given. From the physiologist, for instance, is obtained the fact of man's need of food to sustain life, from which is deduced the economic doctrine of minimum wages. From the physiologist, again, is obtained the fact of a strong disposition, arising from the sexual passion, to carry population beyond the limits of decent or comfortable subsistence, from which is deduced the much-abused doctrine known as Malthusianism. From the agricultural chemist is obtained the fact that, beyond a certain point, the application of capital and labor to land yields a continually diminishing return, from which is deduced the doctrine of Rent. None of these facts does the economist ascertain for himself. He takes them, as the realized results of other sciences, and makes them the premises, the starting point, of his own.

Even the fact of the indisposition of men to strenuous exertion, from which is deduced the principle that they will, so far as they are intelligent and are left free to act, always buy in the cheapest market, is not found by the economist. It is furnished, ready to his hand, by the moral philosopher. The economist takes from all sciences, by turns, all facts which bear upon the one subject, wealth; considers them only so far as they bear thereon; and puts them together and builds them up into a "body of knowledge" which he calls the Science of Wealth, or Political Economy. Even in the field of prices and wages, the distinction should always be observed between the economic statistician, who finds the facts, and the economist, who puts the facts into their place in the industrial system.

35. Political Economy and Natural Theology.—Prof. Cliffe Leslie has shown the powerful influence exerted upon the economic views of Adam Smith, who, as Professor of Moral Philosophy in the University of Glasgow, had occasion to teach both Political Economy and Natural Theology, by the assumption of a beneficent natural order of society, to the disturbance of which by human institutions are due all the economic evils that afflict mankind. To this order-of-nature it should, according to Dr. Smith, be the unceasing effort of mankind to return; and the political economist will fully discharge himself of his mission as an investigator and teacher when he points out the path by which mankind may make their way back to that state in which all things economic will work together for the good of the race.

Now, this subjection of political economy to the interests of natural theology is wrong. I do not say that good natural theology will make bad political economy. I content myself with asserting that political economy has just as much right to be independent of natural theology, as have astronomy and geology. There was a time when the students of those sciences were deemed to be bound to restrain themselves within the supposed requirements not only of natural theology, but also of revealed religion. We know how mischievous were the consequences of that subjection.

Political economy owes nothing to natural theology. The economist is under no obligation to any assumptions derived from that source. He has no more right to start with the theory of an order of nature which is purely beneficent, than he would have to start with the opposite theory of an order of nature wholly maleficent. As economist, he has no mission to "vindicate the ways of God to man." He is to investigate the laws of wealth. That duty he will best discharge by reasoning as justly as his mental powers enable him to do, from economic premises which have been established by adequate induction, and from such only.

36. Political Economy and Political Equity.—The boundary line between ethical and economic inquiry is perfectly clear, if one will but regard it. Great confusion has been engendered by writers in economics wandering off into discussions of political equity. The economist, as such, has nothing to do with the question whether existing institutions, or laws, or customs, are right or wrong: why right, or how far right: why wrong, or how far wrong. His only concern with them is to ascertain how they do, in fact, affect the production and distribution of wealth.

It is true that if the sense of injustice be awakened in the mass of the people, or in any considerable class in the community, industry, frugality, and sobriety are likely to be in a greater or less degree impaired, and thus the production and distribution of wealth will be affected. But it is wholly because of the effect last indicated, and not at all because of its ethical character, that any social arrangement or political institution comes within the consideration of the economist.

Indeed there is reason to believe that such arrangements and institutions do not necessarily produce economic evils in proportion to the degree in which they violate political equity. A custom or law might conceivably be inequitable in the degree to be flagrantly iniquitous, yet exert only a slight influence upon the production or distribution of wealth. Another, presenting so great an array of reasons in its favor that many ethical writers would strongly approve it, might, by crossing popular prejudices, or through some wholly adventitious feature of its own, become a mighty economic force for mischief. Indeed, it is not at all because a social arrangement or political institution is wrong, but because people think it wrong, that it does harm in the domain of wealth. The system of land tenure against which the peasantry of Ireland are so largely in revolt does an amount of mischief which is wholly independent of the consideration whether the Irish people or the English Parliament be at fault in the matter.

37. Respect the Limits of Economic Inquiry.—Hence we say that the limits of strictly economic inquiry should be scrupulously respected. The writer on ethics who deems the greatest good of the greatest number the ultimate rule of right, may make excursions into economics, in order to judge of the moral quality of an act, or a system, by its effects on the production and distribution of wealth ; but the economist, on his part, has no occasion to cross the boundary line. The French writers, who have, in general, been singularly just in their apprehension of the character and logical method of political economy, have, more than all others, erred on this side. Many of them write throughout with a side glance at the existing social system. They profess to be intent on the solution of economic problems, while directing their efforts toward the vindication of political arrangements. The writings of the admirable Frederic Bastiat are deeply infected with this error. He strives incessantly to prove that the institution of property is just ; whereas the only concern which, as an economist, he has with that institution, is to inquire how it influences the action of mankind in respect to wealth.

38. Sentiment and Political Economy.—Holding rigidly to the same view of the nature and scope of economic inquiry, we see that those who allow their opinions to be in any degree shaped by what is called sentiment, are equally wrong with those who sneer at any recognition of sentiment by the economist. The economist's own sentiments should be put completely out of sight; he has only to do with the sentiments of others, and with these only so far as they affect the actions of men in respect to wealth.

We shall have occasion to observe that feelings of justice, of compassion, of respect, of kindly regard, may greatly influence the rents paid in any country, by tenants to landlords, or the wages paid by employers to workingmen or workingwomen. So far as such sentiments produce these effects, they require to be recognized as economic forces.

39. Relation of Political Economy to Sociology.—M. Comte, whom we have already quoted, as denying to political economy the character of a true science, because its history did not, as he esteemed it, bear the tests of continuity and fecundity, also held that the phenomena of wealth should not, and could not advantageously, be considered apart from the facts of the intellectual, moral and political order with which they are closely interwoven. Society, he held, must be considered in the totality of its elements. All isolated theory of a particular aspect of social life, such as wealth, or of a single order of relations, *e. g.*, the economic, he regarded as essentially vicious. The laws and conditions of wealth, in the view of this writer, are a single thread in a closely knit web of social interests and concerns, from which no one can be disconnected, to be contemplated by itself alone.

To this opinion, Mr. J. S. Mill has made what seems to be a conclusive reply:

"Notwithstanding," he says, "the universal *consensus* of the social phenomena, whereby nothing which takes place in any part of the operations of society, is without its share of influence on every other part, and notwithstanding the paramount ascendency which the general state of civilization and social progress in any given society must hence exercise over all the partial and subordinate phenomena, it is not the less true that different species of social facts are, in the main, dependent, immediately, and in the first resort, on different kinds of causes, and, therefore, not only may with advantage, but must be studied apart, just as, in the natural body, we study separately the physiology and pathology of each of the principal organs and tissues, though every one is acted on by the state of all the others, and though the peculiar conditions and general health of the organism co-operate with and often predominate over, the local causes, in determining the state of any particular organ."

40. Obstacles which Political Economy Encounters.— It is worth while to note certain obstacles which the economist encounters in his efforts to secure the popular recognition and acceptance of the laws of wealth, as he discerns them in his study of man and society. Two of these may be regarded as wholly peculiar in kind, or highly peculiar in the degree in which political economy encounters them.

The first is well expressed by Prof. Cairnes: "Its close affinity to the moral sciences brings it constantly into collision with moral feelings and prepossessions, which can not fail to make themselves felt in the discussion of its principles; while its conclusions, intimately connected as they are with the art of government, have a direct and visible bearing upon human conduct, in some of the most exciting pursuits of life." Archbishop Whately had the same in view when he remarked that the demonstrations of Euclid would not have commanded universal assent had they been applicable to the pursuits and fortunes of individuals.

41. Another of the obstacles referred to is found in the fact that political economy has to do with affairs so ordinary and familiar that men, in general, feel themselves competent, irrespective of study or of special experience, to form opinions regarding them. The more closely men are concerned with any matter, the harder it is to maintain the authority of the learned body which assumes to engross scientific knowledge on the subject.

Few are presumptuous enough to dispute with the chemist or mechanician upon points connected with the studies and labors of his life; but almost any man who can read and write feels at liberty to form and maintain opinions of his own upon trade and money.

Now, this is not wholly of evil. The plain common-sense of unlettered men has not infrequently served as a corrective to economic doctrines too finely drawn for the purposes of legislation, perhaps based upon a partial and disparaging view of human nature. But while thus, in the application of political economy to the art of statesmanship, the self-assertion of the uninstructed mind has not been without its advantages, this disposition has certainly hindered the development of political economy as a science. The economic literature of every succeeding year embraces works conceived in the true scientific spirit, and works exhibiting the most vulgar ignorance of history and the most flagrant contempt for the conditions of economic investigation. It is much as if astrology were being pursued side by side with astronomy, or alchemy with chemistry.

42. A third obstacle which political economy encounters arises from the use of terms derived from the vocabulary of every-day life, such as value, exchange, wealth, rent, profits—with some of which are associated in the popular mind conceptions inconsistent with, or, at times, perhaps antagonistic to, those which are in the view of the writer on economics. Thus, as we have seen, the economist uses the word, value, in the single sense of power-in-exchange. Common speech makes every thing valuable which is useful, desirable or meritorious, irrespective of the consideration whether, by reason of its scarcity or the difficulty of securing it, this or that article so spoken of confers upon its possessor the power of commanding in exchange the labor, or the products of the labor, of others.

The chemist, the geologist, the botanist, on the other hand, invents terms for the classes of objects or the classes of phenomena which he is to discuss. The reader carries with him into the discussion only the idea of the thing which the author has created for the purpose. If the writer be clear, and the reader be careful, there is no danger of a failure of understanding. But, no matter how precise the one may be in definition, or how close the attention of the other, it is inevitable that the use, in economic discussion, of terms taken from the vocabulary of common life, should engender confusion, from the practically irresistible tendency of the mind of the reader, and even, in a degree, of the writer, to slip back to the habitual meanings of the words employed.

43. So strongly has this last disadvantage pressed upon some writers, that they have been impelled to resort to strange and foreign terms to obviate the difficulty. Thus, Archbishop Whately, treating political economy as the science of exchange, introduced the Greek word, Catallactics, to express the scope of his inquiry ; and Prof. Hearn has given to his admirable book the name, Plutology, to escape the vagueness of meaning which he thought he saw in the popular use of the word wealth.

44. The Departments of Political Economy.—All the questions of political economy are both conveniently and appropriately discussed under four titles : Production, Exchange, Distribution and Consumption.

Of late, a disposition has been manifested, on the part of many writers, in England and America, to drop these familiar titles ; to decline to admit any departments in political economy ; and to treat of production and distribution, *e. g.*, as not separable in economic discussion.

This has unquestionably been stimulated, if, indeed, it has not been generated, by the wish to bring political economy into a strictly scientific form, with which the recognition of distinct departments has been deemed incompatible. It may be doubted whether our knowledge of the laws of wealth has yet reached the degree of completeness and assurance which would allow a science to be constituted after the lofty ideal of these writers. Meanwhile there seems reason to believe that the abandonment of the familiar and useful terms, production, exchange, distribution and consumption, has caused some very important considerations to be overlooked. "Nothing," said Edmund Burke, "is so great an enemy to accuracy of judgment as a coarse discrimination ; a want of such classification and distribution as the subject admits of."

Now, clearly the subject, wealth, admits of being considered, first, with respect to the motives which lead to its production and the conditions under which production takes place ;

secondly, with respect to the laws which govern the exchange of products in the market ; thirdly, with respect to the forces which distribute the product of industry, in larger or smaller shares, among the several classes of persons who take part in production ; fourthly, with respect to the influences which the different modes of consumption exert upon the disposition and the ability to take part in the future production of wealth.

And if wealth admits of being considered in these several aspects, it seems to me clear that such a classification will conduce both to completeness of view and to accuracy of judgment. We shall have occasion to note (Pars. 247-249), a very striking instance of the mischief that has arisen from the neglect of this classification by recent writers in economics.

PART II.—PRODUCTION.

CHAPTER I.

LAND AND NATURAL AGENTS.

45. What is the Production of Wealth?—By this term we signify all those acts and courses through which it comes about that an article confers upon its possessor the power, irrespective of legal authority or personal sentiments, to command, in exchange for itself, the labor, or the products of the labor, of others. Briefly and somewhat elliptically, we may say, the production of wealth means the creation of values.

This, of course, does not imply the creation of matter; it does not, of necessity, imply even a change of form in the thing which before had not value but now becomes possessed of it.

46. Modes of Production.—A distinguished German professor has classified values, in respect of their origin, as time-value, place-value, and form-value. Thus, a cake of ice which has no value in the winter may acquire value through being kept over into the following summer. The preservation of the ice, whatever of effort and care and expenditure that may involve, is the production of wealth to that extent. The value thus created would be, in the phrase of Prof. Knies, time-value.

Again, a cake of ice which has in summer a certain value in the region where it was first formed, say, Maine, would have a much higher value in a semi-tropical region, where water is seldom frozen at any season of the year, say, Louisiana. The transportation of the ice, and its protection from the melting heat of the climate, would be a further production of wealth. The value thus created would be, in the phrase of the writer already quoted, place-value.

In neither this nor the former case has human effort effected the formation of the ice, which work was the gratuitous operation of nature. The vast bodies of values created by commerce are mainly what would be termed place-values, the value created in giving form to the articles concerned being but small in comparison.

In the creation of form-value, there is the widest possible range of operations, mechanical or chemical, from that of the agriculturist, by whose intervention the black earth of the prairie is transmuted into golden grains, to that of the lace-maker, whose whole industry is to arrange his gossamer into fantastic shapes. However little the material may be wrought, and by whatever agencies that little may be effected, we say that wealth is produced whenever value is added or acquired through any act or any process.

47. The Agents of Production.—The three primary agents in the production of wealth are Land, Labor and Capital.*

48. Land.—The school of economists in France, prior to the revolution, who were known as the Physiocrats, insisted upon regarding land as the sole source of wealth. According to this school, of which the physician Quesnay was the founder, labor is incapable of creating value except as employed upon the soil. Agriculture is, therefore, the sole means of increasing the wealth of a nation. All applications of labor or capital in manufacture, in transportation, or in trade, must be barren, since there is no net produce remaining, as in agriculture,† after the expenses of cultivation have been met.

There was this much of truth in the physiocratic theory,

---

* Labor will form the subject of Chapter II of the present book; Capital, the subject of Chapter III. We shall necessarily speak of labor and of capital before reaching those topics, in their due order, but what we shall thus say will be confined within limits which will allow no misunderstanding on the part of the reader.

† That there is a surplus in agriculture, over the cost of production, is sufficiently proved by the payment of rent to the owner of land. (See Chapter on Rent.)

that the raw material of all manufactures, the subject matter of all trade and transportation, comes originally from the soil ; and its value can not escape the influence of the great, comprehensive principle to which we give the name, "the law of diminishing returns in agriculture," the principle, namely, that after a certain stage of cultivation has been reached, the soil fails to yield a proportionally increased return to new applications of labor and capital. Since, then, this law is so far-reaching and all-embracing that even the operations of trade and manufacture do not escape its influence, it requires to be stated here with great precision and fullness of illustration. There is no use in the reader going on if he does not master this principle in all its bearings. He might just as well stop short here, for, as Prof. Cairnes has said, if this principle did not exist, "the science of political economy would be as completely revolutionized as if human nature itself were altered."

49. The Great Law of Agricultural Production.—In any given condition of the art of agriculture, there is a limit to the amount of labor and of capital which can advantageously be employed or expended upon a given area of land. If, after this limit has been reached, more laborers are employed, each will have to be content with a smaller quantity of produce at harvest. And, in the same way, if more capital be expended upon the land, each dollar of capital—whether in the form of hoes or carts or oxen, will make a smaller addition to the crop of the year than a dollar expended before the point of diminishing returns was reached. We shall sufficiently illustrate the principle if we confine our view to applications of labor, assuming the amounts of capital to increase correspondingly with the number of laborers.

50. Increasing Returns.—Let us suppose that ten laborers, with a certain outfit of tools and implements, are engaged in cultivating, in common, a tract of land of a hundred acres, producing 2,000 bushels of wheat a year, being twenty bushels per acre, and two hundred bushels per capita. Now, let it be supposed that two new laborers appear and join themselves to this company. What will be the crop of that year for the united twelve, assuming agricultural conditions constant? Will it be 2,400 bushels, or more, or less? The answer to this question will depend upon whether the point of diminishing returns has been reached with the original ten laborers, or not. If not, the crop of the new year may be not merely 2,400 bushels, but even more, say, 2,500 bushels, since, the limit of the chemical capabilities of the soil not being reached, the mechanical advantages which result from the division of labor, to be explained under a subsequent title, will enable the twelve laborers to raise more, per man, than the ten could do.

51. Diminishing Returns.—But if the limit indicated in paragraph 49 had been reached when the ten were laboring together upon the land, the new crop will fall short, much or little, of 2,400 bushels; and consequently, each of the twelve laborers will have to be content with less than 200 bushels. Let us suppose the crop to amount to 2,280 bushels, each acre producing 22.8 bushels. Each man will, then, receive 190 bushels as his share.

Now, let it be supposed that three additional laborers are received into the company. Will the crop now be 3,000 bushels, or 200 bushels per man of the fifteen? Clearly not. Will it prove to be 2,850 bushels, 28.5 bushels per acre, giving each man 190 bushels as his share, as before? Not if the industrial character of the laborers and the knowledge of the art of agriculture undergo no change. If twelve laborers make the land yield but 22.8 bushels per acre, the fifteen can not make the same amount of land yield 28.5 bushels per acre. The crop will be something less than that: say, 27 bushels per acre, which would give each man 180 bushels.

If, again, we suppose five additional laborers to join the company, the crop will not be 40 bushels per, acre; as would be necessary in order to give each man 200 bushels, which the original ten received; or 38 bushels per acre, as would be necessary in order to give each man 190 bushels which the first twelve received; or even 36 bushels per acre, as would be necessary in order to give each man 180 bushels, which the first fifteen received; but the crop could not be forced by the labor of twenty laborers above, say, 32 bushels per acre, which would give each of the laborers 160 bushels.

No. of laborers.	No. of bushels per acre.	Total No. bushels on the whole tract.	Each laborer's share.
10	20	2000	200
12	22.8	2280	190
15	27	2700	180
20	32	3200	160

In like manner, it would be found that, however far the accession of new laborers were carried, each new arrival would result in reducing the quantity of grain which each laborer of the entire body could obtain by a year's work. This reduction of the *per capita* produce would go forward, at first slowly and afterwards rapidly, until the result would be reached, that, whereas the original company lived comfortably, or even luxuriously, the forty or fifty who had come to work on the same area would be found living wretchedly, perhaps reduced to the verge of starvation.

52. This Condition is Universal.—About the universal application of this condition there can be no intelligent question. There is not an acre of land on the face of the earth on which 60 and afterward 120 bushels of wheat can be raised by the application, first of twice, and afterward of four times, the amount of labor needed to produce 30 bushels. At some time in the progressive cultivation of every field, sooner or later, according to the state of agriculture, a stage will be reached after which every successive increment of the product will be obtained only through a more than proportional expenditure of labor. This condition applies, not only to the cultivated field, but to grazing lands, to the mine, the forest and the sea. It governs the cost of producing fish and whale oil; fuel and timber for manufactures; coal, iron and copper, for the furnace and the forge; wool for clothing, and the carcasses of cattle and sheep for food. The operation of the principle is in some of these cases obscured by the accident of great discoveries of natural stores and resources, or important inventions in the chemical or mechanical arts involved in the extraction of these articles for the use of man.*

53. The Law of Diminishing Returns in Application to Manufactures.—Such is the law of diminishing returns in agriculture. As has been stated, no part of the field of production but is overshadowed by this great dominating condition of human life and labor. Not only is the whole body of agricultural produce subject to its influence, but the raw material of all manufactures, and the subject matter of all trade and transportation, coming originally from the soil, are affected in value by the increasing difficulty which attends each successive increment of product.

But while no part of the field of production lies beyond the shade of this primary condition, various classes of products are affected by it in very different degrees, according as they stand nearer to, or further from, agriculture or the purely "extractive" industries. Thus, every product of iron, is in some measure, subject to the influence of this condition. If a greater and still greater quantity of iron ore is to be derived from a given number of known mines, this involves mining at a lower and still lower depth, which, in turn, involves a greater expenditure of labor in hoisting, ventilating, pumping, etc.

But it is only the iron, as ore, or as an ore product, which is subject to this condition. If a hundred weight of ore be rendered into pig iron, the cost of the latter will be very much increased by the necessity of mining at an increasing depth. If the pig iron be taken to the forge or foundry, and there rendered into plate iron or stove castings, the cost of the latter will be enhanced but little if any more, since the production of wealth, (*i. e.*, the creation of values) by mechanical pro-

* It has been shown that this principle of increasing difficulty, or of diminishing returns, applies even to the harvesting of crops. Roscher quotes from Von Thünen a table showing the experience of agricultural laborers in attempting to glean all the potatoes of a field. Supposing 100 scheffels to represent the quantity grown on a given area, a single laborer could gather 30 in a day, while the average of the first four laborers would be 20. But the fifth man would only gather 6.6; the sixth man only 4.4; the seventh man only 3, and so on.

cesses, is not subject to the law of diminishing returns. Ten men in mechanical pursuits can produce ten times as much as one. If, again, the iron be rendered by successive processes into fine screws, knife-blades or watch springs, the first cost of the material becomes small, in comparison with the cost of the labor expended in working and perfecting it.

Mr. Babbage, in 1832, estimated that bar iron of the value of $1 became worth when manufactured into—

Slit iron for rails	$ 1.10
Horseshoes	2.55
Wood saws	14.28
Scissors, best	446.94
Penknife blades	657.14

It is evident that the only part of the cost of the $657 worth of knife blades, here, which is affected by the condition of diminishing returns, is the original dollar's worth of bar iron, and the cost of the bushel or two of coal necessary to produce the mechanical power and the melting and tempering heat for the successive processes of manufacture. An increase of the difficulty of mining which should double the price of bar iron might affect the price of scissors very slightly.

54. So far, then, as human wants can be met through the elaboration of the raw materials taken from the soil, there is a constant tendency to a greater and still greater satisfaction of those wants, through the perfection of mechanical and chemical processes. But, after all, the chief concern of the masses of the people is with the cost of the raw materials of food, clothing and shelter. The bulk of their consumption is of coarse forms of agricultural produce, simply prepared. It is of no advantage to the laborer that at a small additional expense he can have his cotton wrought into forms which a century ago would have excited the admiration of a court, if all the cotton he can procure is not enough to keep him warm.

55. The Soil, a Fund for the Endowment of the Human Race.—Subject always to the condition which has been described in the foregoing paragraphs, the soil, consisting of rock pulverized at one period or another of the world's existence, constitutes the sole original endowment of the human race. The different varieties of soil possess the capability of rewarding human labor in very different degrees; but every kind of decomposed rock will, if treated with due quantities of water, yield vegetables, grains or fruits for man's food, fibers for his clothing, timber to construct his house, fuel to warm it. Even the undecomposed rock which forms the crust of the earth, constitutes a store from which human wants may be supplied, though in smaller degree and with greater pains. Metals and minerals, of an almost infinite number of uses, mechanical, chemical, physiological, are extracted by the aggressive enterprise of man from the very rock which has withstood unbroken all the effects of fire and frost, earthquake and torrent. It is wholly upon this natural endowment that the race have lived in the past; and it is the extent of this endowment which is to determine the maximum number the race can reach, aud the longest period of time through which the race can survive. Now, of this fund with which mankind are endowed, we note, in addition to the limited capability of production within a given season, upon a given area, already dwelt upon, that the fund, in the present state of the art of agriculture, is subject to waste and possible ultimate exhaustion.

56. Exhaustion of the Soil.—Those writers who advocate what is known as the policy of Protection, have made great use of the fact that the soil is subject to exhaustion; that its productive capabilities are, in the strict sense of the word, a fund, from which so much and no more can be taken. Besides the outright destruction of fertility due to wanton abuse of nature, the ordinary prudent use of the soil steadily diminishes the fund of productive essences from which future generations must draw their supplies of food, clothing and shelter. "For every fourteen tons of fodder carried off from the soil," says Prof. Johnston, "there are carried away two casks of potash, one of soda, a carboy of vitriol, a large demijohn of phosphoric acid and other essential ingredients."

But what becomes of the materials thus taken away?

Surely, if the doctrines of modern physical science are true, no force can be lost out of nature ; consumption must be followed by production in other forms ; or, rather, consumption is nothing but the production of new forms.

It is true that no force can be lost out of nature ; yet force may be transmuted from forms in which it ministers to human wants into forms in which it serves no purpose useful to man, as, for example, when your house burns down and goes off into the air, in sudden heat and with a great smoke ; or a certain amount of force may be so dissipated that men can no longer employ it for their advantage. The productive essences taken from the soil, in the form of food for man and beast, may, without being diminished in actual amount, be so scattered as to be unavailable for the nourishment of vegetable life in the future.

"Whenever," says Prof. R. E. Thompson, "the products of the soil are consumed in the vicinity of the farm, the farmer will have at hand the means of making such a return to the soil as will keep up and even increase its fertility. But whenever they are transported to a considerable distance for consumption, the power to make an adequate return to the soil is seriously diminished, if not absolutely destroyed. The richest soil can not long sustain such a process of exhaustion, if its proprietors are engaged in sending its natural wealth over land and sea to a distant market".

57. Free Trade and Exhaustion of the Soil.—It is upon this the protectionist bases his chief argument. He claims that local markets should be everywhere created to prevent what he calls "earth-butchery." The tendency to make new countries the magazines from which older countries draw their supplies of raw materials should be crossed and checked by legal impositions, not so much upon the exportation of the raw materials from the former, as on the importation of finished products from the latter. Every considerable community should be driven, against the impulses of immediate interest, to fashion for its own consumption the materials produced from its own soil.

Now, the most obvious and natural answer to this is, that

men are the best judges of their own interests, and that producers and consumers should be left to make their bargains unhindered. But it will appear, in the further progress of our inquiry, that the interests of individuals do not always consist with the interests of the community. This is clearly seen, in the case of the felling of the forests, where immense injury may be done to the soil, an injury perhaps that is practically irreparable, through the selfish action of a few persons seeking their own immediate advantage.

If the same is not true in an equal degree of the abuse of the soil through an excessive drain upon its productive essences, due to the passion for sudden gain inducing the cultivators to take much from the ground and put back little, this is due to two facts. First. The arable land of a country is generally owned by a larger number of persons than the wood land, so that more of those who would suffer by the effects of an abuse of nature are in a position to prevent abuse. Secondly. The consequences of "earth-butchery" in the destruction of forests are more instant and less remediable than in the waste of the soil in cultivation.

58. Some Waste Unavoidable.—The liability to exhaustion of the soil, through exportation of its produce, is a fact properly to be taken into account. The importance which should be attributed to the fact is a matter of question. I believe the protectionist writers generally give it more weight than it deserves, chiefly through omitting two considerations.

First. Even the building up of manufacturing and commercial towns would not prevent a large part of the waste.

In nearly all such towns, when of considerable size, the excreta of men and even of animals, and, also, to a great extent, the refuse of kitchens and of manufactures, are thrown into the streams and carried out to sea. The utilization of sewage, on any large scale, has never yet been made profitable. It has been done as a matter of experiment, as a matter of sentiment, or to prevent the defilement of rivers; but almost invariably it costs, in the present state of the arts, more than a hundred cents on the dollar's worth of soil-dressing obtained. Some waste of this kind seems inseparable from the human occupation of the earth.

59. Natural Renewal of the Soil.—Secondly. The protectionist's argument overlooks the consideration that, in addition to the progress of invention, postponing, though it may not avert, exhaustion, a continuous addition is being made to the soil available for the raising of food, through the decomposition of rocks and the formation of rockdust (weathering). The mountain loses of its substance by the force of frosts and floods, and the valleys are enriched with the material thus worn away. Even the stones that lie in the earth, a mere encumbrance to cultivation, yield to the unceasing action of the elements that surround them and give up to the soil the same properties to which its pristine fertility was due. Moreover, the conversion of the nitrogen of the atmosphere into nitrates (nitrification), is continually going on. "In rare cases," writes one of the most eminent of agricultural chemists, "these agencies alone maintain a high state of fertility, as where red-rock easily disintegrates and is exceptionally rich in plant food, or where plains are fertilized by the matter brought from mountains and deposited by streams. More commonly, these natural causes maintain a moderate productiveness only, and require tillage, irrigation and manuring to raise the production to a high pitch: tillage, irrigation and manuring all operating to accelerate and intensify rock-disintegration and nitrification; irrigation and manuring acting also by replacing removed matters.

"Any region that has once been fertile for a period of fifty years, under a given system of management, may remain fertile under that system forever, unless the soil is removed or buried by flood, or unless the climate becomes unpropitious."*

---

*Prof. S. W. Johnson, of Yale College, Director of the Connecticut Agricultural Experiment Station.

Prof. Johnson further remarks: "The crops that astonish us by their heavy acreage-yield are not the crops that feed the nations. The wheat fields and corn fields of 'the West' yield but 15 bushels of wheat and but 40 to 50 bushels of corn. The hay, the pasturage, which make up the grand total of our forage, are obtained at an average rate of one ton,

CHAPTER II.

LABOR.

60. The Hunter State.—The second great agent in the production of wealth is human labor. Up to a certain low point, the grosser human wants are supplied by the bounty of nature. So long as this continues, value does not emerge; wealth is not produced. Man may live like the squirrels or the monkeys, from the spontaneous fruits of shrubs and trees; or, like other large and fierce animals, he may prey upon smaller and weaker species, which, in their turn, are nourished without care by grasses or nuts. So long as races of men subsist in this fashion, they are doomed to remain few in numbers, low in character, subject to occasional visitations of famine, the victims of ferocious enemies among the higher orders of animals, or of internecine war in the unceasing struggle for existence. Political economy has no more to do with men in such a state than with the monkeys who compete with each other for cocoanuts and bananas.

61. The Pastoral State.—Labor, in the economic sense, first clearly appears in the pastoral state. Here men no longer subsist on the bounty of nature, or perish miserably and helplessly when that bounty fails. They no longer hunt for nuts and roots and fruits which have grown without care and without labor, or for casual animals nourished upon the spontaneous products of the soil, bred and reared without human intervention. In the pastoral state, tribes tame the cattle and sheep and goats and asses which once ran wild, training them to be easily guided, handled and controlled, caring for their

---

per acre. The 40 bushels of wheat, 90 of corn, 2½ tons of hay, that good farmers, in long cultivated regions, gather, per acre, from small areas, are exceptional. For these exceptional natural fertility, or natural manuring, or else exceptional artificial fertilization are required; but for the agricultural production of the world "*im grossen und ganzen*" small crops per acre, fed mostly by natural disintegration of the soil and natural nitrification, as by natural rainfall and natural supplies of carbonic acid and solar energy, are the rule."

subsistence, driving them to fresh pastures, digging wells or diverting streams to give them a constant supply of water, even cutting the abundant food of summer and curing and storing it against the season of scarcity. The hunter protects the animals he has tamed against those that still remain savage, and folds or houses them against severe storms and protracted cold; he bleeds, blisters and physics them in sickness; superintends their breeding after their kind, and cares for the young far beyond the power or the wisdom of the dam. By all these forms of labor, men in the pastoral condition make that to be wealth which in a state of savagery was no wealth.

62.—And of this social condition we note two things: First, population increases largely. It requires many thousands of acres to support a family of hunters; as many hundreds will support a family of shepherds. The animal that in the one condition yielded, once for all, a carcass of three or four hundred pounds net, now returns, for the little care given her, five hundred gallons of milk every year, making, if the owner pleases to expend some additional labor, three hundred pounds of cheese. Another animal that once yielded a carcass of fifty pounds, covered with a pound of coarse stiff hair, now parts every year with four or five pounds of soft, flexible wool, susceptible of being wrought into forms of the greatest beauty and usefulness.

Secondly, the subsistence derived by communities in the pastoral state is not only more ample; it is also far more secure. Men are no longer subject to be swept by famine, as by a hurricane, from the face of the earth. In the main, subsistence, and with it existence, has ceased to be precarious; it has become constant and calculable.

63. Agriculture.—The next economic state is reached in agriculture. Man no longer skims the surface of the land; he plows into the depths of the soil, and brings up the productive energies that lay hidden far below the roots of the grass on which the cattle were wont to graze. And now, where hundreds of acres were required to support a family, as many score suffice. Population rapidly increases. Man and beast no longer wander to seek their food. Food is brought to them. Tribes cease to shift their place from season to season as the exigencies of pasture demand. The cottage replaces the tent. New wants are felt, now that men are not obliged to carry around with them all they own. New and varied forms of wealth appear.

To do only the things which formerly were done, would require less exertion, and consequently values tend to diminish, since value measures, speaking roughly, the difficulty of attainment ; but more things now require to be done ; there are more who feel wants, and each of them feels more wants, than formerly, and hence the body of values increases, in the face of improvements in the arts which tend to substitute gratuity for value.

64. Two Factors of Labor Power.—The labor power of any community, whether in the pastoral or in the agricultural state, or in the higher state where manufactures and commerce enter, is compounded of two factors, that derived from the efficiency of the individual laborer, and that derived from what we call by the somewhat unsatisfactory term, the division of labor, which embraces the joint action of men in production, the differentiation of productive processes, the specialization of trades and the organization of productive forces.

65. The Efficiency of the Individual Laborer.—The degree in which the labor of an individual shall be efficient in the creation of values, *i. e.*, the production of wealth, depends upon several causes.

First : His inherited strength, his original endowment of physical force. This endowment varies greatly, not only as between individuals of the same community, but as between communities, races and nations. Into the causes of the differences in this respect existing, it is not necessary to enter. That inquiry belongs to the physiologist and the ethnologist. The economist has to do only with the fact. In the matter of sheer lifting-strength alone, the individuals of one race may, on the average, surpass those of other races by fifty, one hundred or two hundred per cent.; while in the matter of the use of that strength, in operations at once difficult and delicate, the range of existing differences is very much wider.

66. Relation of Food to Industrial Efficiency.—A second reason for the higher industrial efficiency of the laborers of one class or nation than belongs to those of another, is found in the quantity and quality of the food consumed by the laborers of the two classes or nations, respectively. The human stomach bears much the same relation to the whole frame as the furnace to the steam engine. In the one, as in the other, must all the forces which are to drive the machine be generated. In the one, as in the other, the force generated will, within certain limits, increase with the material supplied. With more fuel, the engine will do more work. With more food, the man will do more work.

But not proportionally more. To a great extent the return made, in force, to the introduction of new fuel into the furnace varies according to a principle which is strongly analogous to that which governs the returns made, in crops, to the application of new labor to land. Thus, if we suppose that, with a furnace of a given height of chimney, 3 lbs. of coal to the square foot of grate surface, are supplied, we should have, resulting from the consumption, a certain amount of force available to do the engine's work. But that amount would be small. A great part of all the heat generated would be lost by radiation in the tubes and through the cooling effect of the water in the boilers. Now, suppose that, instead of 3 lbs., 6 are consumed. Will the efficiency of the engine be doubled merely? No, the engine will do easily three times as much work. If 9 lbs. are used, the power will be still further increased, not only positively but proportionally, that is, there will not only be more power, but more power for each pound of coal. If 12 lbs. are consumed, there may be a still further addition to the force generated, not only positively but proportionally. It might be easily found that, with this amount of fuel, the resulting force would be, not four times as much as with 3 lbs., but eight or ten.

The parallelism which exists between the economy of applying labor to land and the economy of supplying fuel to the furnace, is broken at one point. Labor may be applied to land indefinitely with an increase of absolute, though not always of relative, production. But coal can not be added indefinitely to the fire beneath the boiler.

67. The economy of supplying food to the human machine is in a high degree analogous. If, for example, a laborer were supplied with only 100 oz., per week, of a certain kind of food, the laboring power which would be generated by the digestion and assimilation of that food would be very slight. After a course of such diet, the man would crawl feebly to his task; would work with a very slight degree of energy when he first started out, and would soon become exhausted. Were 125 oz. given to the laborer, he would be able, with no greater strain on his constitution, to accomplish an amount of work which would be not merely one quarter more, but largely in excess of it. He would perhaps be able to do one-half as much more. Were his subsistence to rise to 150 oz. there would be a still further gain. His efficiency would be to his efficiency when receiving 125 oz., not as 6 to 5, but as 7, or perhaps 8, to 5. With 150 oz., the laborer's diet might be regarded as sufficient for comfort, health and a reasonable development of muscular strength. Let the amount of food be carried up to 200 oz., and we should have a liberal, generous diet, ample to supply all the waste of the tissues, and to keep the fires of the body burning briskly, generating force enough to allow the laborer to put forth great muscular exertions through long periods of time.

Up to a certain limit, then, with food as with fuel, the true economy of consumption is found in increasing the supply. Niggardliness is waste, and waste of the worst sort. But, just as there is a maximum limit with the fuel, so there is with food. After that limit is reached, the increase of food does not imply a proportional increase of force, if, indeed, any increase at all; and after a certain still higher point is reached, the increase of food brings mischief.

68. Under-fed Laborers.—The consideration here presented is of great importance in explaining the varying efficiency of labor. Probably the inhabitants of the United States constitute the only large population in the world who are thoroughly well-nourished; that is, who have enough of wholesome food to secure the greatest economy of consumption. "Many a French factory hand," writes Lord Brabazon, "never has any thing better for his breakfast than a large slice of common sour bread, rubbed over with an onion, so as to give it a flavor." "Meat," says a careful observer, "is rarely tasted by the working classes in Holland. It forms no part of the bill of fare, either for the man or his family." Of the laborers of Belgium, an official report states: "Very many have for their entire subsistence but potatoes, with a little grease, brown or black bread, often bad; and for their drink a tincture of chicory." Even through large portions of happy England, the fabled land of the beef-eater, there is a mass of unimpeachable testimony to show that the working classes are able to obtain less nourishment by far than is necessary to the highest efficiency of their labor. "In the west of England," wrote Prof. Fawcett, in 1864, "it is impossible for an agricultural laborer to eat meat more than once a week." Of the peasantry of Devonshire, Canon Girdlestone wrote: "The laborer breakfasts on tea-kettle broth—hot water poured on bread and flavored with onions—dines on bread and hard cheese, at 2d. a pound, with cider very washy and sour; and sups on potatoes or cabbage, greased with a tiny bit of fat bacon. He seldom more than sees or smells butcher's meat."

Now, as to the want of true economy in thus reducing the consumption of food among the working classes, there can not be a moment's question. The case may perhaps be best put by saying that if cattle were not kept better nourished than are the majority of laborers in the world, it would not "pay" to have cattle at all. It would be better to do without them entirely. Barely to keep them alive would require a large expenditure of food, and to give them, in addition to this, only enough to secure a low grade of muscular strength and activity, would not make them worth their keep.

69. Influence of Sanitary Conditions on the Efficiency of Labor.—A third reason for the higher industrial efficiency of the laborers of one class or nation than of another, is found in different sanitary conditions, especially those which concern the quality of the air. The food which is taken into the animal system is converted into blood which is kept in a state of purity by being oxydized in the lungs, through the process of breathing. In this process, the foul and stupefying element, carbon, is thrown off into the atmosphere, and the life-giving element, oxygen, is taken into the system. That this may be done, there should be, in all inclosed habitations, a sufficiency of space to each person and a free access of fresh air. Human beings confined in small, unventilated rooms inevitably lose vigor; the process of the oxidization of the blood being checked, the process of making blood, through the digestion and assimilation of the food taken into the stomach, is checked. With foul air, therefore, a smaller amount of muscular force is generated from the same amount of food. Not only so, but the food taken into the system may become an actual obstruction and cause of disease, through the failure of digestion and assimilation. Moreover, in close rooms, unventilated and uncleaned, the germs of certain diseases, known as filth-diseases, *viz.*, typhus and typhoid fevers, scarlet fever, diphtheria and others, are preserved and readily communicated, to the impairment of health and the destruction of life.

70. The cause here adduced is not of slight importance in accounting for the differences in the labor power of different communities and nations of men.

As the people of the United States are the best nourished, so they are, by a long interval, the best sheltered people in the world. It is impossible for an American who has not traveled widely, to form an adequate conception of the manner in which the laborers of other countries are housed. "Hovels, cellars, mere dark dens," wrote Mr. Inglis of the city homes of Ireland, in 1834, "damp, filthy, stagnant, unwholesome places."

In 1861, one-third of the population of Scotland lived in houses of one room only; another third in houses of two rooms. In England the character of the country cottages and of the dwellings of the poorer classes in the cities is even worse than in Scotland. Cases are not infrequent where families of 7 to 13 members occupy a single bedroom.

Of the cottages of Devonshire, Canon Girdlestone says : "They are, as a rule, not fit to house pigs in." The cottages of the County of Durham were thus described by the Poor Law Commissioners of 1842. "The average size of these sheds is about 24 by 16 feet. They are dark and unwholesome ; the windows do not open, and many of them are not larger than 20 feet by 16 ; and into this space are crowded eight, ten, or even twelve persons."

71. If this is the way Englishmen have to live in the country, we might expect to hear worse things of the towns, where land is sometimes worth as many silver crowns as would cover its surface. Some years ago Mr. Edwin Chadwick declared that more filth, worse physical suffering and mental disorder than John Howard described in his account of the prisons of his day, were to be found among the cellar populations of the working people of Liverpool, Manchester, or Leeds, and in large portions of the Metropolis. Much has of late been done, both by private philanthropic effort and under the authority of law, to cure the evils described ; yet still much that is hideous remains.

It is in such homes that the greater part of the present laborers of the world were born and reared. And it is in homes like these, that, in their estate as laborers, they have to live, to eat, to rest and to sleep after the exhausting toil of the day. It is not to be wondered at that children grow up puny and deformed ; that scrofula and rheumatism become deeply seated in the constitution ; that the blood grows foul and the pulse feeble ; that the efficiency of the laborer falls to a low point, while his power to labor at all becomes liable to be prematurely terminated.

72. The Laborer's Intelligence.—A fourth reason for the superior efficiency of the laborers of one class or nation over those of another, is found in their higher intelligence. Intelligence is a powerful factor in industrial efficiency. I speak not now of technical knowledge, but of clearness of mind, quickness of apprehension, strength of memory, and the power of consecutive thought, in no more than the degree in which these may fairly be expected to be found in a nation where popular education has existed for generations; in the degree, for instance, in which they are found in New England, in Saxony, in parts of Scotland.

The intelligent is more useful than the unintelligent laborer:

(*a*) Because he requires a far shorter apprenticeship. He can learn his trade in a half, a third, or a quarter the time which the other requires. (*b*) Because he can do his work with little or no superintendence. He is able to carry instructions in his mind, and to apply them with discretion to the varying conditions of his work. (*c*) Because he is less wasteful of materials. In some branches of manufacture the value of the materials used is equal to the amount paid in wages. In others it is twice, thrice, and even ten times as much. A very little difference in the degree of thoughtfulness, foresight and regard for instructions, on the part of the laborer, may make a great difference in the net product.

73. (*d*) Because he readily learns to use machinery, however delicate or intricate. The extent to which labor is saved and power increased by the use of machinery hardly needs illustration here. It is only the intelligent workman who can freely avail himself of this great help. Brains are not alone required for the invention of machines; they are wanted for their adjustment, their ordinary use, and their occasional repair. He who is to use a machine need not be the same man as he who made it; but, to a great extent, he should be the same kind of man.

74. Race Characteristics Regarding Machinery.—The capability of dealing with costly and delicate machines varies greatly between different races and nations of men. Notwithstanding the prodigious increase in the power of producing cotton goods, through the inventions of Watts, Arkwright, and Sitgreaves, vast quantities of cotton are still spun or woven by hand. In some of the countries of Europe, as Turkey and Greece, the ordinary "mechanical powers," the screw, the lever, the inclined plane, etc., are used but little, or not at all, the lifting or pulling being done by direct physical force, at, of course, the expenditure of a vast amount of animal strength. Even in highly civilized nations the application of agricultural machinery is limited by the inability of the peasantry to use it. The Judges of the World's Fair of 1852 reported that there was probably as much sound, practical labor-saving invention and machinery unused, at that time, as was used; and that it was so far unused, "solely in consequence of the ignorance and incompetence of the work-people."

75. Machinery in the United States.—The United States is the only country in the world, excepting some of the English colonies, in which it can be safely assumed of the average laborer that, after a reasonable period of experiment and trial, he will be able to use delicate and costly machinery to the advantage of his employer.* In all other countries, even the most civilized, it is only picked laborers who can use intricate machinery without doing more damage than their labor is worth.

76. Cheerfulness and Hopefulness in Labor.—A fifth reason for the higher efficiency of the laborers of one class or nation than of another, is found in greater cheerfulness and hopefulness, growing out of higher self-respect and social ambition, and a more direct and certain interest in the product of industry.

---

* A remarkable illustration of the strong natural aptitude of the American for the use of machinery, has come to my notice during the present year, 1887. A boot and shoe manufacturer, employing eleven hundred hands, had occasion, during a great and long-protracted strike, to replace considerably more than half of the old operatives by new hands. This branch of industry is well known for the vast variety of highly intricate and delicate machinery which it uses. Yet at the end of five months, during which this substitution had been carried through to completion, the machines in this factory were found, on careful inspection, to be in absolutely as good condition, as at the beginning of the strike.

Had an English manufacturer carried through such a replacement of old by new hands, his machinery at the end of that time would have been worth just what it would have sold for, by the pound, as old iron.

The first three causes which have been adduced are purely physical, affecting the laborer's muscular force and capability of endurance. The fourth cause adduced, *viz.:* the laborer's general intelligence, determines his intellectual qualification for his work, his ability to direct his bodily powers, such as they are, to the production of wealth, with the maximum of effect and the minimum of waste. The cause now adduced is moral, affecting the will.

The importance of this cause is most conspicuously seen in the wastefulness and inefficiency of slave labor. Always and everywhere, that labor has been found to be vastly inferior to the labor of freemen. Even the stimulus of the lash fails to command the faculties which instantly spring into activity under the inspiration of an ample reward. Fear is far less potent than hope in evoking the energies of mind or body; while efforts made under the influence of the former passion are far more exhausting than those made under the influence of the latter.

77. Nearness and Directness of the Reward.—Even among free laborers, the degree in which the physical and intellectual powers may be engaged in the production of wealth depends greatly on the directness and certainty of the reward. This is proved by the difference everywhere observed between the exertions of wage laborers and those of men working on their own account. The wage laborer necessarily becomes, in a great degree, a time server, an eye pleaser. He saves himself as much as he can; he counts his hours; he measures the work he does. But more than this, a laborer not merely will not, he can not, the laws of human nature remaining the same, work as hard for another as he would if working as his own man.

On the other hand, he who is working for himself keeps no grudging account of his time or exertion. If the proprietor of land, he knows that every stroke of his arm is creating wealth which he and his children are to enjoy; that every straw saved is his own. He watches against waste with unfailing eagerness. His vines, his plants, his animals, his fences, his buildings, are borne upon his mind; and no care or pains are withheld to guard them against the almost infinite forms of injury which beset these species of wealth. He is early afield, for the day is not long enough for all he wishes to do; and when night falls, he still lingers, tying up his vines, tinkering his sheds, tending his cattle, bringing home the harvest.

Even beyond the mere love of wealth, of what can be bought and sold, enters the love of his land, which is his own, which was his father's, which shall be his son's after him; and he works upon it, sparing himself little more than does the mother caring for her child. "Give a man the secure possession of a bleak rock," said Arthur Young, "and he will turn it into a garden." The vineyards of the Rhine, built up, in many cases, of earth brought in baskets up the sides of the mountains, are speaking witnesses to the truth of this saying; while many of the richest fields of Holland and Belgium, once drifting wastes, illustrate that other saying of the eminent traveler: "The magic of property turns sand into gold."

78. Influence of Bad Laws in Producing Idleness.— Doubtless much of the indolence we have been accustomed to regard as constitutional with certain races and nations, and as indicating lack of physical endurance or feebleness of will, is due simply to the absence of incentive, resulting from unjust laws or bad social institutions. It would be enough to make one laugh to hear the Scotch spoken of as lazy. The energy and perseverance of that people have been illustrated in every quarter of the globe. Yet, three or four generations ago, the Scottish people, says Prof. Hearn, "were conspicuous for their incorrigible indolence." The ample explanation was found in the almost universal system of short leases or of tenancy at will. A single wise action of legislation cured this defect; and with it disappeared the laziness of the Scotchman.

Not half so long ago as that, the Irish were a proverb over Europe, for indolence and shiftlessness. Arthur Young describes them as "lazy to an excess at work," but "spiritedly active at play." The Irishman of that day was spiritedly active at play, because the fun was sure to be all his own. There were no laws or institutions which robbed him of his sport. He was lazy to an excess at work, because invidious laws, social proscription and the customs relating to land kept from him a large part of the natural fruits of his labor. Every country of the globe has witnessed, since 1850, the indomitable pluck and energy of the Irish at work under equal laws and with "a fair chance."

79. The Varying Efficiency of Labor.—I have indicated the chief causes which influence the efficiency of the individual laborer in the production of wealth. The joint effect of all these is very considerable. Industrial operations conducted upon a large scale have shown that wide differences exist in the working power of men of different nations. In comparing the cost of constructing railroads in India and in England, for instance, it was found that, though the Indian laborer received but 4½ to 6d. a day, and the English laborer, 3s. to 3s.6d., the sub-contracts in the two countries were let at the same prices. The English cotton spinner is paid as many shillings as the East India spinner gets pence ; yet the cotton cloth of England undersells that of India in Indian markets. As between England and Russia, it is found that a weaver in the former country tends from two to three times as many looms as in the latter, the English looms, moving, moreover, at a higher rate of speed.

As between England and France, the superiority of the labor of the former country has been repeatedly shown in great competitive experiments. Mr. Brassey states that, in the construction of certain French railways, it was found that the working capacity of the Englishman was to that of the Frenchman as five to three. Superior as are the workmen of England to those of other countries of Europe, they are, in turn, surpassed, on the average, by those of the United States, in the respects of strength, intelligent direction of force, and ability to use machinery to advantage.

80. The Division of Labor.—The second factor of the labor power of a community is that which is commonly called by the unsatisfactory term, division of labor, embracing, as was said on an earlier page, the joint action of men in production, the differentiation of productive processes, the specialization of trades, and the organization of industrial forces. The term, organization of labor, is perhaps the best single term that can be used to cover all this ground.

In primitive society the division of labor does not exist, or is found only in a rudimentary state. Each able-bodied man does all which any one does. Each builds his wigwam or hut, shapes his bows and arrows ; cares for his horses, if he have any, and hunts or fishes in his own right and name. Yet, even here, the division of labor as between the sexes is in some degree carried out. The women make the nets, weave the blankets and cook the food, as duties suitable to their powers.

Soon, however, emerges a division of labor founded on differences of capability less fundamental than those of sex. The smith appears, working at first alike in iron, wood and stone. He does all the work of this class which the community requires ; and, in return, receives flesh and fish from those whose spears and hooks are sharpened and pointed at his forge. As the amount of this class of work to be done increases, three smiths, instead of one, come to be employed ; one working in iron, one in wood, and one in stone, known respectively as the blacksmith, the carpenter and the mason. As the wants felt by the community are multiplied, as modes and fashions appear, new classes of artisans come into existence, each working on some one class of substances, or making some one class of articles. The cabinet-maker follows the carpenter ; the jeweler the blacksmith ; the sculptor, in time, the mason. Finally, the operations of each trade come to be distributed among several distinct classes of laborers.

81. How the Division of Labor Increases Production.— It is difficult adequately to appreciate the increase of production which results from the application of this principle.

(*a*) It shortens apprenticeship. If each man had to learn the whole of a trade, much more to learn several trades, he would have to take a great deal of time and spoil a great deal of material and many tools in doing so. But when each workman is required to learn but a single trade, and, within that trade, to practice only one simple operation, the period of instruction becomes very brief. The end of a few months finds him intelligent, if not expert, in his business.

(*b*) It develops dexterity. Long after the workman has so far mastered his trade as to be able to perform its operations without mistake, he continues to gain in productive power, through the incessant repetition of his task. The sense especially concerned in his work, be it sight, or touch, or hearing, becomes preternaturally acute. The muscles brought especially into play gain in size and activity. Even certain organs may become involved in the operations of the trade, and undergo changes which, whether favorable to the general health and symmetry, or not, are of a nature to facilitate the customary work. Any one who watches a cashier counting notes, a telegraph operator sending messages, can see how wonderfully practice must come into industry, to make perfect the workman.

82. (*c*) It obviates the loss of time and the distraction of thought which would be involved in passing from place to place, and in laying down the tools of one trade to take up those of another. In agriculture, where the division of labor can be carried but a little way, we know a great deal of time is thus lost.

(*d*) It facilitates invention and leads to the discovery of improved processes and new materials. Practiced thus in detail, every art or trade is studied in detail, and, one by one, here a little and there a little, its mechanical possibilities come to be seen and realized. Some of the most conspicuous discoveries in the history of industry have, indeed, come through scientific research, or by casual suggestion ; but an infinite multitude of inventions and improvements in processes, accomplishing, in their aggregate effect, an incredible gain to productive power, have been the result of the minute study of the operations of industry, in detail, by men each of whom was dealing with a single class of substances, performing a single operation, with the aid, perhaps, of a single tool.

(*e*) It allows women and children, as well as men who are suffering from some partial disability, to find places in the industrial order where they can labor to advantage ; while among men of full powers it assigns to each that work which is best suited to his individual capacity.

83. The Territorial Division of Labor.—This is a phrase devised by an English economist during the great popular agitation which preceded the repeal of the Corn Laws,* to express the carrying out of the principle of the division of labor, which we have thus far contemplated in operation among the individuals of a community, to communities and to nations. The phrase intimates that the vast industrial advantages which attend the application of that principle within the hamlet and throughout the country, will accompany that principle in its extension over the whole field of the world's production.

This is the main, indeed, we may say the sole, economic argument in favor of Free Trade, as opposed to what is called Protection. The claim to freedom of trade as a "natural right" is not one of which the economist can properly take account. On the other hand, the arguments of the protectionist, based on the political importance of the industrial self-sufficiency of the nation, and on the alleged social and intellectual advantages resulting from a diversification of national industry, are equally out of his view.

Inasmuch as the protectionist plea for limiting the territorial extension of the principle of the division of labor, includes a claim that the creation by law of industrial entities corresponding to existing political entities, has an influence, not only upon the production, but also upon the distribution of wealth (which department of our inquiry we have not yet reached), and as the whole question of protection or free-trade is bound up with political and sociological considerations, it has seemed best to postpone the remarks we have to make upon that question to Part VI, "Some Applications of Economic Principles."

84. The Organization of Industry.—But the advantages

* Imposing high duties on foreign grain imported into England. These laws were repealed by Parliament in 1846, under the leadership of Sir Robert Peel. The study of the history of the Repeal movement affords an admirable economic exercise.

derived immediately from the division of labor, are but a part of the total advantage which is attributable to what we have termed the organization of industry. In addition to those already indicated, we find, under the larger title, a vast gain of productive power resulting from the introduction of the principle of competition, the creation of *esprit de corps*, and the direction given to the mass of laborers by the few clear, strong spirits, which, under such a system, dominate the industrial operations of the community.

(*a*) Competition can only be introduced as an active force where the opportunity for exact and easy comparison of results exists. Where each one of a number of persons is performing every day a large number of miscellaneous duties, now a little of this, then a little of that, it is difficult or impossible to measure the achievements of the several persons so employed, bring them to a scale, and assign credit or blame. But when those duties are so distributed that each person is charged with the performance of a certain, definite task, comparison becomes possible.

(*b*) The creation of *esprit de corps* within trades and professions becomes a tremendous force in industry. Competition operates upon the laborer, through the employer's desire to get the most out of each workman, and through the laborer's desire to obtain and retain employment. The principle now invoked operates on the laborer, perhaps not less powerfully, through the public sentiment of the craft, establishing standards of workmanship and laws of conduct which tend to lift each workman to the level of the best.

85. (c) Mastership in Industry.—But the most important of the sources of gain in productive power, now under consideration, is found in that mastership of industry which is created by the division of labor. That division can not proceed to its natural limits without giving rise to the subordination of the mass of the laboring population to a select and comparatively small body of employers, who assume the responsibilities and direct the agencies of production.

Whether this gain is accomplished at a certain social and political cost, is a question the economist is not called upon to discuss. That question belongs to the social philosopher or the statesman. The economist, as such, is guilty of an unwarrantable presumption if he undertake to measure the quantity of economic advantage which would offset the smallest ethical or physiological injury. He does all that he is called upon to do, all that he can undertake to do without impairing the scientific value of his results, when he traces causes to their effects within the field of economics alone.

Looking at the matter in its purely economic aspect, it is clear that the gain in question is not realized without an initial loss, inasmuch as the laborer, under the wages system, necessarily has a less direct and certain interest in the product of his industry, than the man who labors on his own account. But this loss is compensated, many times over, by the gain to production which results from the impulse and direction given to industry by the thought-power and will-power of the ablest minds in the community.

CHAPTER III.

CAPITAL: ITS ORIGIN AND OFFICE.

86. THE third great agent in the production of wealth is Capital. The capital of a community is that part of its wealth (excluding land and natural agents, considered as unimproved*) which is devoted to the production of wealth.

Some writers, indeed, insist that the climate of a country, so far as it especially favors production, is to be reckoned as a part of the capital of that country. I prefer to say that the beneficent distribution of heat and moisture, by the gratuitous action of nature, is a favorable condition of production, but is not capital. A sound system of jurisprudence, which secures the impartial administration of justice; a sound organization of the political body, which maintains peace

* The reason for this exception will appear when we come to treat of the rent and price of land.

and order, are most favorable conditions of production; they lead to a vast creation of values; they are better than much capital to the people enjoying them; but they are not capital.

87. The Origin of Capital.—The origin of capital is so familiar that it need not be dwelt upon at length. A simple illustration may suffice. Let us take the case of a tribe dwelling along the shore, and subsisting upon fish caught from the rocks which jut into the sea. Summer and winter together, good seasons and bad, they derive from this source a scanty and precarious subsistence. When the fish are plentiful, the people live freely, even gluttonously. When their luck is bad, they submit to privations which involve suffering, sometimes famine.

Now let us suppose that one of these fishermen, moved by a strong desire to better his condition, undertakes to lay by a store of fish. Living as closely as will consist with health and strength, he denies himself all superfluity, even at the height of the season, and by little and little accumulates in his hut a considerable quantity of dried food. This is wealth. Whether it shall become capital or not depends upon the use which is to be made of it.* If destined to be merely a reserve against hard times, it remains wealth, but does not become capital.

But our fisherman, in laying by his store of fish, has higher designs than to equalize the food consumption of the year. As the dull season approaches, he takes all the food he can carry and goes into the hills, where he finds trees whose bark can be detached by sharp stones. Again and again he returns to his work in the hills, while his neighbors are painfully striving to keep themselves alive. At the end of the dull season he brings down to the water a canoe, so light that it can be borne upon his shoulders, so buoyant that he can paddle in it out to the "banks," which lie two or three miles from shore, where in one day he can get as many fish as he could catch from off the rocks in a week.

* "All labor expended for a distant end falls under the head of capital."—ROSCHER.

88. The Professional Boat-Builder.—The canoe is capital; the fisherman is a capitalist. He can now take his choice of three things. He may go out in his canoe and bring home supplies of fish which will allow him to marry and rear a family in comfort, and with his surplus hire some of his neighbors to build him a hut, their women to weave him blankets, and their children to bring water from the spring and wait upon his family. Secondly, he may let out the canoe to some one who will be glad to get the use of it on payment of all the fish which one family could fairly consume, and himself stay at home in complete idleness, basking in the sun, and on stormy days seeking refuge in his hut. Thirdly, he may let out the canoe and himself turn to advantage the knowledge and experience acquired in its construction by making more canoes.

The last is the course he decides to take. Again and again he reappears upon the shore, bringing a new canoe, for the use of which a score of his neighbors clamorously compete. And later canoes, be it noted, are made with a smaller effort and sacrifice on the part of the builder. He has become familiar with the groves where the trees are largest and the trunks most clear of branches. He has acquired a knack which makes it almost a pleasure to strip off the vast rolls of tough elastic bark. He never spoils his half-completed work, now, by an ill-directed blow. Moreover, his toil is reduced to a minimum, for he has hired men to carry his burdens and do the heavy labor.

89. The Increase of Capital.—But soon the canoe-builder's profits are threatened. Thus far, in the possession of exceptional skill and knowledge, he has been a monopolist, and has reaped a monopolist's gains. Now, however, stimulated by the sight of such great wealth gathered (that is, so great a *command of other people's labor* acquired) by one man, others begin to enter the field.

As an essential condition, each must save and accumulate enough food to support him while making his first boat, that is, must accumulate a certain amount of capital. This, however, is less difficult than it was in the case of the original builder, first, because fish have come, through the multiplication of boats, to be much more easily obtained; secondly, because there are fewer experiments to make; thirdly, because certainty and nearness of success will inspire the labors of ten men where one will be moved to great sacrifice and exertion by a prospect that is distant and doubtful. Moreover, some of the shrewdest of the assistants of the old boat-builder, who have watched him at work, and whom he has trusted more and more to do even the nicer parts of his task, begin to desert him and to set up for themselves. The rent of boats falls rapidly; the old master, who has become rich and self-important, and perhaps a little lazy with years, goes out of the business.

90. First Effects of Competition.—For a time, while the number of boats increases rapidly, the quality suffers deterioration; two fishermen are drowned upon the banks by the breaking up of boats in a sudden squall. The boat-builders in fault are condemned by the general assembly of the tribe to support the widows and orphan children. The rage for mere cheapness is checked. Boats are now tested before they are used, and some ambitious builders find themselves driven out of the trade by the failure of their work.

And it is important to be noted that the profits of boat-building are rapidly reduced. The first boat built repaid the cost of its construction in a few weeks. The boats now made only repay the cost of their construction in the course of months. Yet, the men who make boats still get a better livelihood than those who use them; while those who use boats get a better livelihood, even after paying the rent, than those who still fish off the rocks.

91. What Will They Do with It?—Now let us suppose that the manufacture of boats has proceeded so far that there is one serviceable boat for every four adult males of the tribe. At this point, one of two widely divergent courses may be adopted, with very important results to the future of the community.

First, the multiplication of boats goes forward until each man is provided with a boat in which he can catch enough fish, in two or three hours a day, to keep him and his family, summer and winter, good seasons and bad. The creation of capital has at least led to this result : it has put famine out of the question. There is always an abundance of fresh fish, on the banks, and of cured fish even in the meanest hut. The rest of the time is spent in idleness or sport.

Secondly, the manufacture of boats stops at the point where fish for the whole tribe can be provided by one-fourth of its members, toiling early and late upon the banks. The remaining members, those who, through youth or self-indulgence, have failed to provide themselves with boats, those who through misfortune have lost their boats and have become discouraged, those who by physical weakness or natural or acquired infirmity are least fitted to undertake the rugged duty of the fisherman, and those who have been intimidated by tales or by experience of hardships, or by the sight of the bodies of drowned fishermen rolled ashore after a storm—these all betake themselves, in one capacity or another, to the service of the fishermen, the capitalist-employers (Par. 304) of the tribe. Only so many boat-builders remain as are needed to repair and keep up the existing stock. The house-builder now takes the place of the boat-builder. No one is satisfied to live in the sort of hut which would once have been thought good enough for the chief. Menial servants become numerous. The fashioning of ornaments and trinkets takes up a vast amount of labor.

92. New Economic Desires.—Soon a new want emerges. A plant with bright flowers is discovered among the hills and brought home as a curiosity. It is raised, as a rather distinguished thing, in front of houses of especial pretension. By cultivation it undergoes more or less change, particularly in the development of large tubers which are found to be highly palatable and nutritious. The absurd name, potatoes, is applied to these tubers. As affording a change from the everlasting sea-food of the fathers, they are relished greatly, and soon a number of persons are breaking up ground to plant and cultivate these tubers, which are exchanged, on liberal terms, for fish taken on the banks.

The introduction of a vegetable diet marks the beginning of a revolution in the life of the community. After this, any thing is possible. The taste for a diversified diet, once felt, knows no limits. Agriculture has begun, involving the necessity of capital in a hundred forms. New foods are followed by new fibers; manufactures spring into being, and all the potentiality of the modern nation now resides in a tribe which a generation ago lived wholly on fish caught from rocks along the shore.

93. The Law of Capital.—It is not necessary to trace further the increase of capital. At every step of its progress, capital follows one law. It arises solely out of saving. It stands always for self-denial and abstinence. At the first beginning, savings are made slowly and painfully; and the first items of capital have a power in exchange (an ability, that is, to command the labor of those who have not capital), corresponding to the difficulty with which they are secured. The bow, the spear, the canoe, the spade, much as they cost, pay for themselves in a few days. Subsequent increments of capital are gained at a constantly diminishing sacrifice,* and receive a constantly diminishing remuneration, until, in the most advanced countries, buildings are erected and machines constructed which only pay for themselves in ten, twelve or even twenty years.

At every stage, we note, too, that capital releases labor power which was formerly occupied in providing for the wants of the community according to its then prevailing standard of living. At every stage, the members of the community make their choice, whether they will apply the labor power, thus released, to the production of wealth, in other branches, or will content themselves with living as well as before, upon easier terms, giving up the newly acquired leisure to idleness or sport.

94. Subsistence.—The office of capital has been perhaps abundantly shown in the account given of its origin. Capital, as

* Prof. Marshall remarks that the whole continent of Asia, with its thousand millions of inhabitants, has less power of saving than England has.

we have seen, is that portion of wealth* which is employed in the production of new forms of wealth.

At first, capital is limited to the means of subsistence for the producer. It was not easy in the first stage of industrial progress, to lay by enough of the game or the fish of one season to last until the next. For want of such a store of food many a tribe perished. Many another was kept in a low, miserable condition, unable to shift its seat to more promising localities, and continually depleted by famine and disease. But when once a tribe, by exceptional good fortune, or through prudence and self-control, acquired a reserve sufficient for a full year's subsistence, it became in a degree master of its conditions. It could shift its seat to better hunting or fishing grounds. It could pursue its avocations systematically and economically, doing that which should be esteemed most productive in the long run, not, as before, hurriedly and wastefully, under the stress of immediate want. The physical strength of its members was kept at the highest point by ample and regular diet.

An ample year's subsistence forms the most important advance which a people ever make in their progress towards industrial prosperity. No subsequent step costs one-half, or a tithe as much. Many peoples never find themselves able quite to accomplish this. The people of British India can hope for no more, in good years, than to be carried through into the next; while, once in every four or five years, a famine following a short crop sweeps away millions by sheer starvation, or by the fevers which feed upon half-famished populations. Even in Ireland, there was known, half a century ago, a period two or three months long, preceding harvest, which was called by the peasantry "the starving season."

95. Tools.—The next purpose, in logical, and generally, also, in historical order, for which capital is accumulated, is the acquisition of tools. I use the word here in its largest sense, including all apparatus, utensils and machinery. The knife, the bow, the spear, the canoe, the net, are the tools of a cer-

* Excluding land and natural agents, considered as unimproved.

tain stage of industrial society. The spade, the cart, the plow, the distaff, the forge, are the tools of a later stage. The loom, the lathe, the printing press, the trip-hammer, the railroad and the ship, may, with equal propriety, be called the tools of to-day. The buildings which protect machinery from the weather, and the shops in which trade and manufactures are carried on, are, in this sense, tools.

96. Materials.—The third form which capital takes is that of Materials. The word, as here used, covers all kinds of wealth which are devoted to the production of wealth in any other way than as subsistence for the laborer, or as tools to increase his power in production. In a primitive state, materials play a small part. The bait for the hook among the tribe of fishermen ; the corn saved for seed in a planting community, are the most prominent materials of early industry. In a later age a large part of all the accumulated wealth of a community exists in this form.

Ultimately, indeed, these materials will be wrought partly into tools, partly into the means of subsistence. A part, also, may come to be devoted to purposes of luxury or display, and, hence, cease to be capital at all. But at any given time, the capital of a community may be classed under these three heads : Subsistence, Tools, Materials.

97. The Three Forms of Capital.—In a certain sense these three may be resolved into one, Subsistence ; as, indeed, all the forms of subsistence itself may be resolved into one, Food. Thus, the first simple tools of the barbarous community may be said to be exactly represented by the subsistence required by the laborers engaged in making the tools. The first materials produced by the aid of these tools may be said to be represented by the subsistence of the laborers using the tools, added to that of the laborers who made the tools. And so of the more elaborate tools and the more various and costly materials of after ages : all may be said to represent the subsistence of the laborer while engaged in the act of production.

Likewise all the forms of subsistence, food, clothing, shelter and fuel, may, in theory, be reduced to one, food. The clothing of the laborer, for example, represents the food which he consumed while he was gathering the fibers of the wild grasses and weaving them into a blanket. The hut represents the food consumed during its erection. The fuel represents the food consumed while the laborer was gathering fagots in the forest.

98. One of the advantages of this classification is, that it directs the attention to the part performed by tools, machinery and apparatus, in the production of wealth. Look into many text books on Political Economy, and you will find capital spoken of as if its main, or even its sole office, were to furnish subsistence to the laborer. Yet two nations may be equally provided with subsistence, while the superiority of one of them in the possession of tools may give it a prodigious advantage over the other in the power of producing wealth. One man with simple tools may do the work of ten men equally well fed, but having only their hands to work with. Ten men with the wood-working, cotton and wool-working, or metal-working machinery of to-day, run by steam or water power, may easily do the work of a thousand, with distaff, chisel, saw and axe.

CHAPTER IV.

THE PRODUCTIVE CAPABILITY OF A COMMUNITY.

99. We have spoken, in succession, of land power, labor power and capital power. The productive capability of any community is determined by these three elements, in the degrees in which they are severally found to exist there.

While the land remains in the condition of increasing returns (Par. 50), as in the Eastern States of the American Union during their earlier history, production may be large, per head of population, with but a small amount of capital available. Even after cultivation has reached the condition of diminishing returns (Par. 51), the energy, intelligence and skill of the laboring class, and the thorough organization of industry, may wrest a comparatively high rate of produce from the reluctant soil; or, in spite of an ignorant, clumsy and spiritless population, as in the west of England, the concentration of a vast capital upon a naturally rich soil may yield large returns, long after the same stage of cultivation has been reached.

100. Where all three conditions are found favorable to production, *i. e.*, fertile lands not yet fully taken up, an intelligent and energetic laboring population, with abundant capital, as in the opening up of parts of our Western States within the last thirty years, and notably in the development of Minnesota and Dakota now going on, the rate at which wealth grows appears almost fabulous. Surely, inevitably, however, the increase of population will bring about the condition when an increasing labor power and capital power must struggle with a decreasing capability of the soil. Mechanical inventions, chemical discoveries, may long postpone the diminution of the per-capita product ; all improvements in the industrial character of the working classes, or in the organization of labor, enable a larger population to be supported without reduction in the quality of their subsistence ; but not the less is the power of one of the factors of production steadily on the decline.

This principle applies, be it observed, only to the per-capita product. The absolute quantity produced increases constantly with every increment of labor or capital judiciously applied to the land. There never comes a time when more laborers will not produce larger harvests. There never comes a time when additional capital introduced into agriculture cannot secure for itself some return.

101. Such is the condition under which the earth is cultivated by human labor, for the supply of human wants. The production of wealth by mechanical processes is, however, as we have seen (Par. 53.), subject to this condition only so far as relates to the materials employed in manufactures, all of which are derived from agriculture. The mechanical processes themselves are subject to no such drawback. On the contrary, the increase of population for a considerable period allows the division of labor to take place more fully, with the result of enlarged production. Hence the multiplication and diversification of conveniences and refinements, so far as they involve no increase in the amount of material consumed, may be carried forward literally without limit.* Labor and capital here act with prodigious force, not, as we might say, by addition, but by multiplication, each step rendering every successive step easier, as the force of habit and invention give to production a constantly accelerating rate of movement.

102. Productive Capability not fully Realized.—Productive capability being thus determined by the three elements which have been stated, the greatest question which the economist has to answer, the most difficult, the most important question in economics, is, why the actual production of wealth falls so far short of its productive capability. But this is a question which cannot be finally answered till the reader has been taken through all the departments, by turns, of economic science. It is not until the economist reaches the department of consumption, that he can show how the use which is made of wealth may waste the capital power of a community, or may impair its labor power through the effects of vicious indulgence upon muscular strength and upon the will of the laborer. In the department of distribution, again, we shall see how the division of the product of industry, among the several persons and classes of persons engaged, may work great and permanent injury to those who are at disadvantage in making their claim ; and how disputes and contests over that division may seriously reduce the amount to be divided. In the department of exchange, the economist meets the question in a special form, namely, what is the cause of those occasional stoppages of production which are known as crises, or "hard times," when the wheels of industry move with painful slowness, and the wealth which has been gathered in preceding periods is wasted in an inactivity from which all classes suffer, and yet for which no one seems accountable, since all are, or profess to be, ready and

* The important mistake committed by Mr. Henry George, through overlooking this point, will be indicated in Par. 515–7.

desirous to work. Under each of these titles, thus, we shall find something by which to explain the phenomenon that the actual production of every commercial and manufacturing country, taking a term of years together, falls far below the possible production.

103. Industrial Structure.—Even under the present title, we have to note a liability which besets the productive power of a community arising from what we may term its industrial structure. By this term is intended that organization of the capital power and the labor power of a community, which makes the productive capability of the whole depend, in a greater or less degree, upon the character of individuals or classes of individuals, and, in consequence, upon accidents affecting the fortunes of such individuals or classes. This is a matter far too little regarded in reasoning about the wealth of nations and communities. Writers in economics are apt to speak of the labor power and the capital power of a community as if they were aggregates of pure force. No reference is made to structural organization. Complete homogeneity and the highest mobility are assumed for the whole labor-mass and the whole capital-mass.

In such a way of looking at the subject we lose sight of the possibilities of great loss to production arising out of two conditions.

104. (a) Partial Immobility of Capital and Labor.—In all advanced industrial societies, labor and capital become committed to certain courses, from which they can only depart after much delay, against great resistance, at heavy cost. We have seen how vast is the increase in productive power caused by the division of labor, the differentiation of industrial functions, the specialization and localization of trades and the organization of the productive forces.

Precisely according to the chances of gain resulting herefrom, is the risk of loss, in the case of mistake or misadventure. The artisan who has learned a trade becomes comparatively helpless if the opportunities for working at that trade are taken away. The factory hand who has learned to perform only one operation out of the multitude that go to the spinning of a single yard of cloth, can do little if he be thrown out of the place where that operation is to be performed in immediate connection with all the others. In theory, the artisan or the factory hand may turn to some other field of production, and soon acquire the knowledge and the manual skill required in some new art or trade. The observation of large populations, through long periods, shows that such readjustments of specialized labor demand more energy and more enterprise than are possessed by most laborers, occupy a great deal of time, at the best, and involve no small waste of labor power.

Not infrequently that readjustment is not fully accomplished in the generation that first feels the necessity for it. The population or class of laborers upon whom this demand is made, prove unequal to the task, lose hopefulness, courage and self-respect, and by a slow decline sink into pauperism, squalor, vagabondage and vice, too often transmitting tainted blood and tainted minds to the generation that follows.

105. (b) Misdirection of Labor and Capital.—Capital power and, in perhaps a greater degree, labor power are in the hands of individuals whose peculiarities of character, of habitude, of station, seriously modify the application of capital and labor to production; whose mistaken aims, whose erroneous impulses, may divert these forces from the object which we have supposed them to be seeking with an unremitting and an unmistaking attraction; whose accidents of fortune may impair the energy of the industrial movement, or for a time arrest it completely.

The most familiar illustration we could use is that of a factory whose master has suddenly died. The labor power remains; the capital power remains; but the spring that set them in motion is broken. It may happen that a son, or a partner, of equal ability, will at once step forward and take up the burden that has fallen from the nerveless hands. It may be, on the other hand, that a long period of embarrassment will result, during which labor and capital will stand idle. Perhaps the loss will never be made good. An incompetent person succeeds by right of relationship. Bad management dissipates both the accumulated wealth and the reputation of the establishment. After a dreary struggle, the stock and fixtures are sold, the factory is dismantled, and the operatives go forth to find employment elsewhere as they may. There is many a thriving town in New England, whose only reason for growth, through fifty years, from small beginnings, has been found in the accident of the birth there, and the long life, of a single energetic, able, careful man of business. There is many a "deserted village" whose decay dates from the sickness or death of one man, out of the many hundreds who thronged its streets.

So difficult is the control and direction of capital and labor, that a distinct class is called into being, in all industrially advanced communities, to undertake that function. This class is known as the employing class, or, to adopt a word from the French, the *entrepreneur* class.

106. The Entrepreneur Class.—Mastership is essential to a large and varied production. The industrial enterprises of the civilized states could not have been brought to their present height without mastership, and could not be maintained at that height one year without it. Whatever may be true of politics, the industry of the world is not tending toward democracy, but in the opposite direction.

In its first stages, the division of labor does not necessarily imply the introduction of the master-class. When the forms of production are few; when materials are simple; when only hand-tools are used; when each artisan working at his bench makes the whole of the article to be marketed; when styles are standard, and the consumers of the product are found in the immediate neighborhood, the need of the master is not felt. But when the hand-loom gives way to the power-loom; when the giant factory absorbs a thousand petty shops; when many persons, of all degrees of skill and strength, contribute to a result which perhaps not one of them comprehends perfectly or at all; when machinery is introduced which deals with the gauzy fabric more delicately than the human hand, and crushes stone and iron with the force of lightning; when costly materials require to be brought from the four quarters of the globe, and the products are distributed by the agencies of commerce through every land; when fashion enters, demanding incessant changes in form or substance to meet the caprices of the market, then the master becomes a necessity of the situation.

His work is not alone to enforce discipline through the body of laborers thus brought under one roof; not alone to organize these parts into a whole and keep every part in its place, at its proper work; not alone to furnish technical skill, and exercise a general care of the vast property involved. Beyond these and far more than these, he is called upon to assume the responsibilities of production; to decide what shall be made, after what patterns, in what quantities, at what times; to whom the product shall be sold, at what prices, and on what terms of payment. The armies of industry can no more be raised, equipped, held together, moved and engaged, without their commanders, than can the armies of war.

107. Those conditions of production which bring to the laborer the necessity of finding a master under whom he can work, bring to the man of superior abilities and acquirements the opportunity to employ his powers for the greatest economic advantage of society and for the greatest profit to himself. In a community where division of labor has proceeded but a little way, the man of intellect moves but one pair of arms. In a highly organized industrial system, he moves a thousand.

One man who has the genius to plan finds a host of helpers, each of whom can execute his schemes nearly if not quite as well as he himself individually could, who yet would have been wholly helpless and amazed in the presence of the exigencies, the difficulties, the dangers, which only arouse the spirit of the master, stimulate his faculties, and afford him the keenest zest of enjoyment.

108. Whether we regard this as the ideal state or not, whether we rejoice or repine at the extension of the principle of mastership in industry, it is the most characteristic fact of the industrial system of to-day. It is likely to gain rather than to lose importance in the years to come.

During the great moral and political fermentation which

brought on the Revolution of 1848, the attention of social reformers in France was called to the possible benefits of Co-operation, being an industrial system in which mastership should disappear. Not a few of the English economists, and, following them, American economists generally, have been led to take up co-operation as a practicable scheme, which only needs to be tried in order to work the most beneficent results.

So far from it being true that the abolition of mastership is at present feasible,* there never was a time when the distance between the man and the master was so wide as it is to-day. Nay, the distance between the mere superintendent, or overseer, on the one hand, who thoroughly understands the technicalities of production, and has all the ability required for executing orders, for enforcing discipline among the working force, and for keeping the machinery of the mill smoothly running, and the real master, the organizer and energizer, on the other, is greater to-day than it ever was before. That distance, so far as I can judge, tends continually to increase. The possibilities of gain or of loss were never so great as now. The choices and decisions essential to the conduct of business were never so frequent or so difficult. The difference in the product, which results from the difference between the able and the inferior management of affairs, was never so great. The toleration offered to the commonplace in industry was never so small.

109. Possibilities of Industrial Damage Involved in the Entrepreneur System.—While the entrepreneur system is, thus, an agency of the highest efficiency in increasing the productive power of a community; becomes, indeed, the condition without which the industrial enterprises of modern society could not exist, it will be seen that it involves the possibility of industrial disasters commensurate with the forces it sets in motion. Just as the accidents of the railway are more

---

* I speak here of industry as a whole, and especially of the largest branches, supplying general markets. When we come to speak of Industrial Co-operation, in Part VI, I shall note certain possible exceptions, in the case of smaller branches of industry suppiying narrower markets.

destructive and fearful than those of the wagon road, so do the catastrophes of modern production exceed, in their wreck of fortune and waste of capital, all that is possible under the less ambitious organization of productive agencies. The mistakes of the man who controls a thousand workmen are multiplied a thousand fold.

And those mistakes will not be infrequent. While the entrepreneur class in any community consists generally of strong men, that class contains many persons who by the accident of fortune have come into the control of the agencies of production without the necessary qualifications, and who habitually mismanage and misdirect these agencies, to the lowering of the general scale of productiveness in the community. Moreover, the ablest men of business themselves fall far short of the ideal standard. Not to speak of intellectual failings, infirmities of the will are such as to make it a matter of course that no small part of the industrial power placed in the hands of the entrepreneur class will be misdirected. The perfect temper of business is found in few men: oscillations between recklessness, on the one hand, and over-cautiousness, on the other, constitute the rule, while absolute self-poise is the rare exception. In paragraphs 313 to 314, are indicated certain causes which tend to multiply the proportion of incompetent employers.

110. Destruction of Wealth.—Another cause which requires to be mentioned, as in a degree accounting for the failure of industrial society to accumulate wealth and maintain a productive capability corresponding to the theoretical efficiency of the three primary agents of production, land, labor, and capital, is the actual destruction of wealth by accident or convulsions of nature. The losses by fire, alone, in the United States probably exceed a hundred millions of dollars a year, if structures only are considered; while were we to add the damage to crops and forests, the sum of wealth consumed by this fearful agent would be greatly increased. Hurricanes, and storms, and floods, and accidents by rail, annually waste and destroy no inconsiderable portion of the products of human skill and toil.

PART III.—EXCHANGE.

CHAPTER I.

THE THEORY OF VALUE.

111. Exchange as a Department of Political Economy.— We have seen that there is a tendency among recent writers to abolish the familiar departments of political economy, severally known as production, exchange, distribution and consumption, as interfering unduly with the simplicity and perhaps with the dignity of the science they have chosen to cultivate. Even of those who have retained certain of these titles, there is a general consent at least to abandon exchange, as a department of political economy.*

I am disposed to think that this general abandonment of exchange, as a distinct title in political economy, is due to a confusion of exchange with trade or commerce, viewed as productive agencies. It is seen that the most of what is done in trade or commerce pertains to the production of wealth. The labor employed in packing or baling goods, in transporting them to market, in opening and exposing them for sale, is engaged in the production of wealth, equally with that employed in raising the raw materials from the ground, or fashioning them into merchantable shapes. Values are created as truly in the one case as in the other. Even the labor of the clerks and salesmen is productive labor as much as that of the artisan or the agriculturist. The horses and wagons, the locomotives and cars, the shops and warehouses, of trade and commerce are strictly productive agencies.

---

* To this Mr. Mill forms a conspicuous exception. He makes exchange, as distinguished from production and from distribution, the subject of one of the books of his Political Economy.

What is it, then, that need be considered under the title, exchange? What is left, after production has been fully treated? Why should this department of political economy be retained?

Under the title, exchange, in a systematic treatise on political economy, I would consider the Ratios of Exchange, the terms on which goods, commodities, articles possessing value, items in the sum of wealth, exchange for one another. We are here called to answer the question: Why does so much of this commodity exchange for so much of that? Why not for more? Why not for less?

Such a question, it appears to me, can best be treated apart from the exposition of the physical conditions under which wealth is produced (as, for instance, the efficiency of the division of labor, or the diminishing productiveness of land); apart from the discussion of the forces by which the product of industry is distributed in wages, interest, profits, rent; apart, also, from the question, what effects upon the future production of wealth will be wrought by giving one direction, or another, to the consumption of the existing body of wealth.

112. Exchange Arises out of the Division of Labor.—The occasion for exchange arises out of the division of labor. Were all persons engaged in the same productive avocations, there would be no inducement to exchange. To barter fish for fish, or bread for bread, would be simply a waste of time and energy. It is because men first divide in production that they afterward unite in exchange. It would be easy to conceive a community in which each producer should be engaged in precisely the same work as every other, each raising from the ground or making by the labor of his hands all that he were to eat, drink or wear. In such a situation, all that has been said of the causes of the varying efficiency of individual laborers would hold good; all that has been said concerning "diminishing returns in agriculture," all that has been said of the origin and office of capital, would still hold good. But there would be no actual exchange, because there would be no division of labor.

Let, however, the production of the individuals of a community be varied by ever so little, the occasion for exchange will arise. If one agriculturist raise wheat, another rye, another potatoes; and if others raise, some cattle, some sheep, some swine, the products will soon begin to be exchanged. Then the question will arise, how much wheat shall be given for a bushel of rye or potatoes; how many sheep or swine for an ox?

Let the principle of the division of labor be carried further, until a score or a hundred of mechanical arts and trades and half a dozen learned professions come to be recognized, and the occasions for exchange will rapidly extend to a large part of the entire production of the community. The farmer may still consume a half * of his own corn and beef and potatoes, but the smith will scarcely consume the product of his own labor for three days in the year; the boot-maker will be content with one out of fifty pairs of boots he makes in the same time; the physician will probably take none of his own medicines.

113. An Exchanging Class.—And it will result, either that these persons, having occasion to exchange their products for those of others, will have to give up an appreciable portion of their time to making those exchanges in person, or else, the work of making exchanges will become the subject matter of a new profession or avocation.

If the smith can in one day make as many horseshoes as the farmer could in ten; and if the farmer can in one day do as much in raising wheat as the smith could in two or three, it is evident that the peddler or shopkeeper who enables the farmer to keep steadily at work raising wheat and yet have shoes for his horses, and the smith to keep making shoes and

* In England, says Prof. Roscher, it is 38.8 per cent. of the supply that comes to the market; in Belgium, 40; in Saxony, at least 50 per cent. In Germany, the farmers consume on an average, two-thirds themselves.

The ratio between the portion of the crop marketed and the portion consumed at home, is, of course, not the same for any two countries. or for the same country, at any two dates. It is continually changing with changes in the habits of living among the people, with changes in the facilities of transportation, etc.

nothing else, and yet have bread to live upon, is a productive agent as truly as smith or farmer.

Just as the division of labor between the individuals of a community gives rise to exchange, so the extension of the same principle to the communities of any country, or still further, to all the countries of the world, creates new occasions for exchange and rapidly multiplies the objects to be exchanged. In all these successive cases the agencies by which exchanges are effected : the labor of the men engaged in trade or transportation ; the horses and wagons, the steam-cars and ships ; the services of the clerks who write orders for goods and keep account of sales and payments, of the bankers who advance the requisite capital or remit the proceeds of commercial ventures, even of the shipping reporters and financial editors who supply the information upon which merchants and bankers alike must act, all these agencies are as truly productive of wealth as the labor of mechanics or miners or agriculturists, and are to be treated under the title, production.

We have, under the title exchange, only to investigate the principles which determine that so many dozens of wood screws made in Providence or so many pounds of horseshoe nails made in Troy, shall purchase so much of the wheat of Illinois, the tobacco of Kentucky, the sugar or molasses of Cuba, the tea of China.

114. Value.—Whence comes this power-in-exchange? What are its conditions, and what its limitations?

We have defined value as the power which an article confers upon its possessor, irrespective of legal authority or personal sentiments, of commanding, in exchange for itself, the labor, or the products of the labor, of others.

But let us go further, and inquire how it is that one article confers on its possessor such a power, while another does not; why it is that, of two articles of value, one confers the power of commanding the labor of others for weeks or years, while another is parted with for the service of a day or an hour.

115. Value and Price.—But, first, let us introduce a term, the use of which is not absolutely necessary at this point, but which will, nevertheless, save much circumlocution, and perhaps avoid a liability to misunderstanding—that term is Price. Value is, briefly speaking, purchasing power, or power in exchange. Price is purchasing power expressed in terms of some one article; power-in-exchange-for-that-article, be the same wheat, or beef, or wool, or gold, or silver. In common speech the word price brings up the idea of money-value, the purchasing power of an article expressed in terms of money. Yet it is equally correct to say that the price of a horse is seventy-five bushels of wheat, as to say that it is one hundred dollars. Inasmuch as we have not yet introduced the money function into our discussion, the word price, throughout the present chapter, will be understood in its more general sense, as the purchasing power of a commodity expressed in terms of some other article.

116. Distinction between Value and Utility.—In setting out upon our search for the law of value, a distinction of great importance requires to be made. Value must be severely distinguished from utility. Many economists of merit have stumbled at this point. Even of those who have observed the distinction between the two conceptions, some have resorted to unfortunate terms for their characterization, and have written of value in use and value in exchange. Now, value in use is utility, and nothing else, and in political economy should be called by that name and no other. Value is power-in-exchange, and, therefore, the term value-in-exchange is seen to be a bad one, at once clumsy and misleading.

Nor must it be thought that value and utility have any such necessary and constant relation to each other that one may safely be used for the other. On the contrary, an article may have the highest conceivable utility, yet no value.

The utility of atmospheric air is inexpressible. Atmospheric air has usually no value, because it is supplied naturally, in such abundance that any one can have as much of it as he has occasion to use without giving for it either his labor or the products of his labor. Even atmospheric air may, however, acquire value and be sold at a regular, definite price, so much per cubic foot, as when delivered through pipes to a diver beneath the surface of the ocean.

The utility of water is also beyond expression, yet ordinarily water has no value. In cities, however, water is delivered to householders at fixed rates, supposed to represent the cost of the service by which the fluid is stored, conducted and delivered. Water, though ordinarily to be had gratuitously, may thus acquire value. On the other hand, something may even be paid for merely getting rid of it. A party may enter into a contract for pumping it out of a mine, or a swamp, or a cellar, at so much a gallon. A much higher price is often paid for removing the fluid from the place where it is not wanted, than is commonly paid for bringing it to the place where it is wanted.

But while utility and value must not, in economic reasoning, be used interchangeably, as they so often are in ordinary speech, *utility is everywhere one of the elements of value. It is always present, where value is present.* It can not be assumed that a man will give his labor or the products of his labor for that for which he has no use.

117. Useful does not mean Beneficial. — It needs to be observed that the utility of which the economist speaks is not always the utility recognized by the moral philosopher or the physiologist. By that term the economist signifies only that an article answers a felt human want; that men have a use for it.

The appetite from which that sense of want arises may be vicious, the object itself may be prejudicial, even pernicious. Intoxicating liquors are, in their main uses, injurious to body and to mind; but so long as men want them, they have utility, in the economic sense. So long as men want them and can only get them by giving something for them, they have also value. Nay, the prussic acid which a desponding wretch buys of the druggist has its value as truly as the medicine which a father buys to save his child's life, and has its utility, in the economic sense, as well.

118. Is Value a Momentary Phenomenon?—We say, value is power-in-exchange. Some writers, using this definition, have proceeded to argue that value is a momentary phenomenon, beginning and closing with the act of exchange, and that an article has value only when it is exchanged; only while it is exchanging.

Is not this to confound our knowledge of a thing with the thing itself? A man owning an article can not know precisely what it is worth until he comes to exchange it. But it may all the time be beyond the possibility of doubt that the article has purchasing power; it would bring something in an exchange.

One owns a house in New York. He can not know at any given time, without resort to an actual exchange, what its value is, since value is power-in-exchange, and to an exchange, as to a quarrel, there must be two parties. The owner's personal estimate does not fix the value, which may prove much below that estimate. But while the owner may not know what is its power-in-exchange, there may be no room for doubt that it has such power. If it would not sell for $30,000, his estimate, it would bring $10,000 in any conceivable state of the market; but if it only brought $5,000, or $5, it would have value.

A farmer in Illinois has 1,000 bushels of wheat, and sells 500 bushels at $1.50. He knows that the remaining 500 bushels have value; but, just what that value is, he can not know. That the wheat would go off at some price, is beyond question; but it might take a considerable reduction, say to $1.45 or $1.40 to carry it off; or, on the other hand, a change in the market might put the price up to $1.55.

There are, indeed, circumstances where a man may not be able to know that an article in his possession has value unless he actually finds a purchaser for it. These are cases where the value of an article is, at the best, low; or where the uses of an article are few, and the demand for it spasmodic and intermittent. But to say that value is a momentary phenomenon, only emerging in the presence of a purchaser, and remaining only during the consummation of a bargain, seems much like saying that a body has weight only while some one is lifting it.

119. What is the Relation of Labor to Value?—We have said that value is the power which an article confers upon its possessor, irrespective of legal authority or personal sentiments, to command in exchange for itself the labor, or the products of the labor, of others.

Does that power arise solely and necessarily from the fact that labor has been bestowed upon the production of that article? No. It is true that men do not commonly give labor for that which has not cost labor; and that, on the whole, and in the long run, the respective values of a number of articles will, at least in the same community,* be nearly according to the amounts of labor that have been expended upon them, severally. But it is not because an article has cost labor that it possesses value. That is because it can not now be obtained without labor. In any given instance it is not necessary that a thing, to have value, should itself have cost labor in any degree; while it is not at all uncommon to find an article having a value equal to that of another article which cost twice as much labor as itself.

120. Prof. Senior's Statement.—Prof. Senior remarks: "Any other cause limiting supply, is just as efficient a cause of value in an article, as the necessity of labor to its production. And, in fact, if all the commodities used by man were supplied by nature without any intervention whatever of human labor, but were supplied in precisely the same quantities as they now are, there is no reason to suppose that they would either cease to be valuable, or would exchange in any other than their present proportions."

Prof. Senior elsewhere inquires: "Suppose meteoric iron were the only form in which that metal were produced, would not the iron supplied from heaven be far more valuable than any existing metal?"

121. Here is an autograph of John Milton. The lines may have been written to a friend, or from a mere freak of fancy, or to occupy an idle moment. Labor, in the economic sense, there was none. Yet the autograph may be worth $20; that is, may command for its possessor the labor of a skilled work-

* The significance of this qualification will be seen when we come to speak of International Exchanges, in the following chapter.

man for ten days, of ten working hours each. Here is a high degree of value (that is, command of the labor of others) where yet no labor has been. The explanation is found in the fact that Milton is dead, and his remaining autographs are few, while many people want them, and want them very much.

This is an instance of what may be called "monopoly-value," or as some prefer to call it, scarcity-value. The value here is altogether irrespective of the amount of labor expended upon the production of the article, simply because the article can not be reproduced, or the stock of it replaced by labor.

122. Cost of Production, or of Reproduction.—Again, take the case of an article which, by reason of the discovery of new fields of the raw material, or of some mechanical invention, can now be produced with the expenditure of half as much labor as formerly. Will the value of the stock of such goods on hand be influenced by the original cost of producing them? Not at all. They will exchange for other products on the same terms as the goods brought into the market under the new conditions.

In the same way, if the amount of labor required for the production of this kind of goods should suddenly increase, from the diminution of the supply of materials, or other cause, the stock on hand would acquire a higher value, corresponding to the cost of bringing in new goods of the same quality.

Hence, in respect to all goods which can be produced, or the supply of which can be replaced, within the time during which those who want them are willing to wait for them, we say that *value is determined not so much by the cost of production as by the cost of reproduction.* They are exchanged for the products of others, not necessarily in proportion to the amount of labor they actually required, but, rather, according to the amount of labor which would now replace the stock.

123. Time an Element.—I said, "within the time during which those who want them are willing to wait for them." The fact that goods can not be reproduced, or the stock of them renewed, without a certain delay, may, for a time, confer a monopoly-value on the existing stock. Thus, if the supply of food in a city had nearly failed, the fact that an abundance were certain to arrive in two weeks would have little or no effect on the value of the scanty store remaining. Men can not wait two weeks for food. They must have it at once. In their urgent necessity, they will exchange their labor, or the products of their labor, for continually smaller quantities of meat and bread, up to the very moment that the ships which bear the new supplies drop anchor in the harbor.

124. It is not Always the Cost of Reproduction.—But while, as between the cost of production and the cost of reproduction, it is the latter, and not the former, which determines the power an article shall have in exchange ; it is not true that value is always determined by cost of reproduction. It may be, in regard to any given commodity, at any given time, that the cost of reproducing it would be greater, even far greater, than the price at which it sells. How can this be? I answer that this might occur through a diminution in the occasions for the use of that article.

Two generations ago, every decent family possessed a spinning-wheel, and spinning-wheels then bore a price fairly proportioned, we may suppose, to the cost of their production with the tools and materials then available. A little later, when it ceased to be customary to wear homespun, spinning-wheels may be said to have had no value at all. They were banished to attics, or turned into playthings for children, and quickly smashed to pieces. To-day, a fashion has come in, by which the spinning-wheel becomes the companion of the dado, æsthetic furniture, and Queen Anne windows ; and a well-preserved and authentic specimen is worth more than the sum at which a good reproduction could be made and sold.

125. Demand and Supply.—If neither cost of production nor cost of reproduction determines the power which an article shall have in exchange, is there any principle of universal application on which value rests? I reply, yes: Value depends always and wholly on the relation between demand and supply.

These terms require to be defined. It will not answer to trust to the ideas which the words of themselves call up in the mind of the reader. Demand and supply alike have reference (1) to a certain article, and (2) to a certain price. In the economic sense, demand means the quantity of a given article which would be taken at a given price. Supply means the quantity of that article which could be had at that price.

Neither of these two elements of demand and supply must be omitted. From the neglect of one of them by many economists great confusion has arisen. Nearly all writers have seen that demand must have reference to a certain article, be it wheat, or potatoes, or iron, or wool, or something else in particular; that there is no such a thing as a demand indiscriminately for meat, potatoes, iron, wool, and all other articles in the market. In the same way it is seen that the word supply has no significance unless some one article is in view. It has not, however, been so clearly apprehended and strongly held in mind, that demand and supply both have reference to a certain price.

126. Desire is not Demand.—It has been said that demand means the quantity of any stated article which would be taken at a stated price. Demand can possibly come only from those who could give the price. So we see that desire is not demand. As Mr. Thornton says, there is no demand, economically speaking, in the hungry eyes of a penniless boy, looking at tarts through a pastry-cook's window. Without pennies, an unlimited longing and capacity for their consumption would not enable that boy to contribute aught to the demand for tarts.

127. Reduction of Supply.—Let us illustrate the application of the terms demand and supply in economics.

We will take the case of an island far out at sea, inhabited by a population mainly engaged in fishing and agriculture, having, on one side, a beach which is strewn with vast deposits of seaweed, which has been found to be a very good dressing, or manure, for the cultivated fields of the island. A hundred of the islanders are accustomed to get out the seaweed, in intervals of fishing or of cultivating their own little properties, selling it to the farmers inland.

We may suppose that this manure is found to increase the yield of the lands to which it is applied to such an extent that there are a thousand farmers who will each give ten bushels of wheat, this year, for five loads of seaweed. There is, then, a demand for five thousand loads at the price of two bushels of wheat per load. Now the supply—that is, the amount offered, or ready to be offered, at this price—may be greater or less than five thousand loads. It may be that the catch of fish along the shore is so abundant this season that all those who are accustomed to get out the seaweed find they can obtain more by fishing. There may, then, be no supply whatever, at this price. And it may happen that there will be no demand for seaweed at any higher price. The farmers may be agreed in believing that, what with the labor of applying the manure, and what with the necessity for paying for it months before the harvest, seaweed is not worth to any man more than two bushels of wheat. In this case, none of this article will be gathered, and the supply will be *nil.*

2d. It may happen that, in spite of the superior attractions of fishing, this season, a certain number of those who habitually gather the seaweed may continue to do so, some because of the force of habit; some because they know that the persons whom they have been accustomed to supply will look to them for it; some because their boats and nets are out of repair; some because of sickness in their families, indisposing them to go far from home. So that it may result that a thousand loads will be gathered. This may all be sold at two bushels of wheat per load.

Those who buy may be those who have usually bought of the persons who now have to sell, and this may be the sole or the determining reason why the seaweed is sold to them, and not to others; or they may be those whose farms lie nearest to the shore, and hence are first reached by the carts laden with the manure; or they may be those who "spoke first" for seaweed, early in the season. Any one of a number of reasons may control the selection of the persons who shall receive the thousand loads, out of the larger number who formerly purchased five thousand loads. And this, it will be observed, occurs without raising the price of seaweed, although the amount gathered has been greatly reduced.

3d. Again, it may happen that among the former purchasers of the seaweed will be found a considerable number of farmers, wanting in the aggregate 2500 loads, who esteem that article as worth more to them, per load, than two bushels of wheat; and, finding that it can not be had for the usual price, these may begin to offer, first, a quarter and, then, a half bushel more, in order to secure each the amount required by his own land.

Who, out of the former class of purchasers, shall be so disposed, may be determined by any one, or more, of several causes. It may be wont, it may be fancy, it may be obstinacy, or, it may be that their lands are of a nature peculiarly to need such dressing, and to respond with more than ordinary liberality to this expenditure in their behalf. This demand for seaweed may be found strong and persistent enough to fix the price at two and a half bushels of wheat, per load; and at this price enough of the fishermen may be induced to give up their fishing ventures to procure the required amount of 2500 loads.

128. Increased Supply.—We have given three cases where a reduction in the supply of seaweed brings up the question whether the demand shall prove sufficient to raise the price. Let us take successively a few cases of an increase of the supply at the previously prevailing price. An unusually heavy storm bringing the seaweed in large masses far up on the shore, or the invention of some new tool for getting it out, may enable each man engaged in this business to bring to market, with the same labor, a much greater amount; or a bad season for fishing may cause a larger number of persons to seek to get a livelihood in this way. Ten thousand loads are now produced, or are ready to be produced, at two bushels of wheat per load. This, then, is the supply; and it is to be observed that this is the supply equally whether the ten thousand loads are actually dug or not, if only those who are engaged in this business are ready to bring to market that amount at that price. In this situation one of several things may happen.

1st. The increase of supply may coincide with an increase

of demand, due to the breaking up of new lands for tillage, or to the failure of some other species of soil-dressing previously used by many farmers, or to a wider popular knowledge of the advantage of using the seaweed. This increase of demand may be just such as to take off the entire ten thousand loads, at the customary price.

2d. That result is, however, unlikely. Even if an increase of demand should coincide with such a large and sudden increase of supply, it would be strange if the coincidence were so complete as to leave the price just where it was. If we take the more reasonable supposition that there is either no increase of demand, or an increase less than the increase of supply, shall we have, under the conditions existing, a new price resulting? In strict theory this is not necessary. It is conceivable that, while the producers of this article stood ready to deliver ten thousand loads at two bushels of wheat a load, their interests, feelings, and habits, with respect to labor and subsistence, might be so balanced, that, rather than take less than the customary price, they would allow the production to fall to five thousand loads.

3d. But this, again, is not probable. Although, as we shall see later (par. 145), there is great power in custom to fix prices, so much so that articles often keep the same price for years, in spite of considerable alterations in the conditions of production, it is not to be expected that so great a change as we have supposed to occur, would fail to establish a new price. The producers of seaweed being prepared to furnish ten thousand loads, and the purchasers being accustomed to take only five thousand, it is probable that the desire of individual producers to keep themselves fully employed at the business would induce Competition among the sellers of this article.

129. What is Competition?—This is the most important word in the theory of value. I have now used it for the first time, though it might have been introduced with equal appropriateness, a moment ago, in describing the change of price from two to two and a half bushels per load.

Competition signifies the operation of individual self-interest, among the buyers and the sellers of any article in any market. It implies that each man is acting for himself solely, by himself solely, in exchange, to get the most he can from others, and to give the least he must himself.

1. The idea of competition is opposed to combination. Wherever, and in whatever degree, buyers or sellers act in concert, whether by insisting upon a certain price, or by regulating the amount to be bought or sold, there competition is, in so far, defeated. In competition every man is supposed to be active and alert to slip in ahead of every other man and sell his own product first, and sell it at a higher price if possible. Men in this state act as freely and as independently as the minute particles of some fine dry powder absolutely destitute of cohesion. If any two particles in the economic mass stick together, so that one must move when, and as, and because, the other does, competition is in so far defeated.

(2) Competition is also opposed to custom. If in any degree one buys or sells at a certain price, if he buys or sells in a certain place, if he buys or sells of or to a certain person, because he has done so in the past, he obeys the rule of custom. In competition men are assumed in every transaction to seek and find their best market, that is, the place to buy or to sell, in which, at the time, and under the circumstances existing, they can get most for what they have to sell and will give least for what they wish to buy.

(3) Competition is opposed to sentiment. Whenever any economic agent does or forbears any thing under the influence of any sentiment other than the desire of giving the least and gaining the most he can in exchange, be that sentiment patriotism, or gratitude, or charity, or vanity, leading him to do any otherwise than as self interest would prompt, in that case, also, the rule of competition is departed from. Another rule is for the time substituted.

130. The Action of Competition.—Such is competition in the economic sense. Now let us return to our island. We have said that, with the producers of seaweed ready to get out and deliver ten thousand loads, while formerly but five thousand were used, it was not likely that a demand for the additional amount would arise to carry off the entire amount, at the customary price of two bushels of wheat a load ; and that, consequently, competition would probably set in among the sellers of this article. Since there are not buyers enough to take off the whole supply, each producer will try to sell all his own stock, no matter who else does not ; and since there is reason to apprehend that the price will sink below two bushels, he will try to sell as near that figure as possible, and, hence, he will sell as soon as he can find a purchaser.

Through this force the price will begin to decline. It may be by slow degrees ; it may fall tumultuously. At two bushels of wheat, a load, demand and supply are unequal—ten thousand loads are offered * : only five thousand are ready to be taken. At one bushel and three pecks, the supply will perhaps sink to nine thousand loads, since some of the more adventurous among the producers, the more daring and skillful fishermen among them, or those having the best gardens and fields around their cottages, may decide that they can do better for themselves. Meanwhile, we may suppose the demand to rise to six thousand loads, so numerous are the farmers who think that, at that price, it will pay them to use the dressing freely on their lands. At a bushel and a half, demand and supply still more nearly approach each other. At the new price, the quantity offered—the supply—rapidly falls off. Meanwhile the demand has increased, since, at a bushel and a half for a load of manure, the net produce of the fields, that is, the amount of wheat remaining in the hands of the farmer after paying for the manure, may be appreciably enhanced. Supply and demand may now stand, respectively, at eight and at seven thousand loads.

Supply and demand remaining still sundered, it is necessary that there should be a further movement of price to

* We have before stated that the supply of any article is not necessarily confined to the stock in markets or warehouses, but embraces all that producers stand ready to bring forward at the price named, within the period over which the demand extends. In the present illustration, we are assuming the producers to be getting out the seaweed from day to day.

bring them together. Whether that step shall be a short one, or a long one; whether supply and demand shall be equalized at a price much, or but little, below a bushel and a half, depends on two things, first, the utility to the farmers of the soil-dressing, when in excess of seven thousand loads, which we may call its Final Utility; and, secondly, the ability of the producers to do something profitable besides digging and hauling seaweed.

131. Final Utility.—This term has been used, in the foregoing illustration, with reference to the entire supply of seaweed in excess of seven thousand loads, be that excess one hundred, or nine hundred loads. Strictly speaking, however, the term should have reference only to the last appreciable quantity which the purchaser is ready to take and which a producer is ready to supply.

The following is Prof. Jevons' illustration of the difference between the total utility of any commodity, and the utility belonging to a particular portion of it.

"A pound of bread, per day, supplied to a person, saves him from starvation, and has the highest conceivable utility. A second pound, per day, has, also, no slight utility; it keeps him in a state of comparative plenty, though it be not altogether indispensable. A third pound would begin to be superfluous. It is clear, then, that utility is not proportional to commodity. The very same articles vary in utility, according as we already possess more or less of them."

This descending scale of utility may be applied to successive quantities of seaweed, for the dressing of wheat lands. A farmer having a certain breadth of arable lands might profitably give two and a half bushels per load for the first ten loads, with which to dress certain of his fields. If no one stood ready to supply more of the seaweed, at a lower price, two and a half bushels would be determined as the price of the article. Were he to buy five other loads, he might have to apply them to other fields, the return from which would not justify the payment of more than two and a quarter bushels, a load. Now, it might be that a producer stood ready to deliver the additional quantity at that, but at no lower, price : if so, two and a quarter bushels would measure the final utility of the manure, and this will be its price.

Were the farmer to buy three more loads, he might have to apply them to still other fields, from which the enhanced return would justify the payment of two bushels a load, but no more. As, however, it takes two to make a bargain, his readiness to buy at this price would not make this the price of seaweed. It is only when a producer is found ready to deliver the commodity at the price, that a new price is determined. It might even happen that the farmer would be willing to take two more loads, if he could get them for a bushel and a half, a load, and that a producer would appear, willing to deliver the article at that price.

Now, according to the course of our illustration, the farmer has bought twenty loads ; but the utility of the several parts of that aggregate amount has varied widely ; the utility of the first part was very great ; the utility of the last part comparatively small.

132. But One Price for a Commodity.—We have thus far assumed, for the purpose of illustrating the declining utility of successive portions of a commodity, that the farmer purchased the ten, the five, the three, and the two loads of seaweed at different times, and at prices corresponding to the gain in the wheat crop resulting to him from the application of the manure.

But suppose that the farmer had purchased the twenty loads at the same time, it is evident he would have paid one price for the whole. What would have been that price? Would it have been the highest price paid for any portion? Clearly not, since we have seen he could only afford to put the dressing upon certain of his fields, on condition of getting it at a much lower price. Would it have been at a price, the mean between the highest and the lowest? Just as little ; for we have seen that producers stood ready to sell at one and a half bushels per load, which would not have been the case had the demand been sufficient to take off the supply at a higher rate.

If, in an open market, under full competition, any portion

of a given commodity is to be sold at a certain price, then will all the portions of that commodity, sold at the same time, be sold at that price, whatever the degree of utility which may accompany each such portion. If I buy a quantity of food for my own consumption, I do not pay for that part which would suffice to keep me alive, a price such as I would pay, were it necessary, to be saved from starving ; for another part of the food, a price corresponding to the discomfort and dissatisfaction I should feel in being insufficiently nourished ; and, for a third part a price corresponding to the pleasure of ample and generous sustenance. I pay oné price for the whole, the same for every equal part. That price measures the final utility of the food to me : that is, the utility of the portion at which I cease to buy, the portion beyond which I would as soon keep the price in my pocket as have more of the food.

Prof. Jevons states the case thus : "When a commodity is perfectly uniform or homogeneous in quality, all portions may be indifferently used in place of equal portions ; hence, in the same market, and at the same moment, all portions must be exchanged at the same ratio. There can be no reason why a person should treat exactly similar things differently, and the slightest excess in what is demanded for one over the other, will cause him to take the latter instead of the former. In nicely balanced exchanges it is a very minute scruple which will turn the scale and govern the choice. A minute difference of quality in a commodity may thus give rise to preference, and cause the ratio of exchange to differ. But when no difference exists at all, or when no difference is shown to exist, there can be no ground for preference, whatever."

133. What Constitutes an Economic Difference?—In the foregoing paragraph, Prof. Jevons speaks of commodities between which no difference exists. Of course there are no two articles in the universe precisely identical. What Prof. Jevons means is that there may exist no difference, as viewed by the would-be purchaser, with reference to some use to which the two commodities may be put, which use two commodities, apparently varying in many respects, may indifferently serve.

And it is to be noted that the existence or non-existence of an economic difference, will depend on the quality of the individual exchanger, on the purpose he has in view, on the scale of his transactions, and on other causes. Thus, a large dealer in poultry may buy five hundred pairs of chickens, in gross, only satisfying himself by a rapid examination that none fall below a certain standard as to size and condition. His customers, however, will inspect the individual fowls, with the greatest carefulness, and will perhaps be determined in their choice by considerations the most minute, and, possibly, whimsical. In the same way a wholesale lumber merchant may buy, in gross, a large amount of stock at a uniform price, and a half dozen of his customers may the next day go through his yards, each taking out, by preference, a certain portion as peculiarly adapted to some job of work he has on hand.

The fact that several commodities have a generic name in common does not constitute them the same articles for the purposes of exchange. Thus, corn is not sold in the Chicago market as corn, but as corn No. 1, or corn No. 2. Spring and Winter wheat never bring the same price ; they are not one kind of commodity, but two, and a reason for a preference between them always exists.

The proposition we are considering further requires to be modified with regard to the obstacles to exchange, the ignorance or indifference of exchangers, etc. The consideration of these causes, as qualifying the principle that there can be but one price for any commodity, in the same market, at the same time, will be more conveniently postponed to the title (par. 149) The Friction of Retail Trade.

134. What is a Market?—Many definitions have been given to the word, market. As I apprehend it, the term, in political economy, should have reference, first, to a species of commodity ; secondly, to a group of exchangers.

In this view, there is no market which is a market indistinguishably for all or for several commodities, as for tea, iron, cotton and wheat ; but there is a market for each commodity, by turns, as a market for tea, in which tea is bought and sold ;

a market for iron, in which iron is bought and sold. Thus, there are as many markets as there are separate commodities.

Secondly, a market embraces all those who contribute to the supply of or the demand for a given commodity in any place. Hence, all those who are ready to buy of or sell to each other belong to the same market, no matter where they live.

I say, who are ready to buy of or sell to each other. It does not follow from this that all who in the same place are buying and selling the same article belong to the same market. Thus, suppose there are in New York five importers of tea, fifteen wholesale dealers in that article, a hundred retailers, and a half million consumers. All these do not belong to the same market. The importers of tea and the wholesale dealers constitute one tea market, the wholesale dealers and the retailers constitute another tea market; the retailers and the domestic purchasers constitute still another tea market. There are as many markets as there are groups of exchangers. In the case supposed, there are three tea markets; each has its own group of buyers and sellers; and in each of the three, at any time, tea is sold at a price different from that at which it is sold in any of the others. Thus, the price for precisely the same sort of tea, in the market made up of importers and wholesale dealers, may be $1.00; in the market made up of wholesale dealers and retailers, $1.10, and in the market made up of retailers and domestic purchasers, $1.25.

Hence we see that, without such a definition of the word market, it would not do to say that there can at any time in any market be but one price for a given commodity. There is never a day, in any great mart, when tea, iron, wool, wheat, or what not, is not selling at several different prices, it may be in the same street.

135. But while within a great mart there may, thus, be many markets, any one of these markets may extend far beyond the limits of that mart. To pursue the illustration already offered, the five New York importers of tea may sell not to the fifteen wholesale dealers of that city only, but to twenty other wholesale dealers in Brooklyn, Jersey City, Newark and other places within a radius of twenty or of fifty miles. A market is thus constituted of the five importers and these thirty-five wholesale dealers. Every one of the latter belongs as distinctly to that market as that one who lives nearest the City Hall, for he contributes as truly to the demand for tea in that market. Again, this body of wholesale dealers, thus re-enforced, may sell not to a hundred but to a thousand retailers scattered throughout all that region. This group of exchangers makes up the market, and not the fifteen wholesale dealers and the one hundred retailers of the city of New York only. These one thousand retailers, again, sell, not to half a million, but to a million and a half of consumers of tea.

All persons whose demand for, or whose supply of, a commodity goes to make up the aggregate demand for or supply of that commodity, in any given place, and hence to affect the price of that commodity in that place, belong to the same market.

136. But it may be said: this would make the whole world belong to the same market, and would, hence, take all significance out of the word. By no means. In the market which is made up of the five importers of tea, all perhaps having warehouses on one wharf in New York, and the thirty-five wholesale dealers of the surrounding region whom they supply, the price of tea will not, probably, be appreciably different from that which is paid in the market made up of the four Boston importers of tea and the twenty-five wholesale dealers who buy of them. If, for instance, the New York price were to be lower than the Boston price, the New York importers would begin to offer their stock in Boston, to get the advantage of the higher price there prevailing, and would hence contribute to the supply of tea there, and hence would come, so far forth, and for the time, to belong to that market.

But, in the market constituted of the wholesale dealers and the retailers of tea in and around New York, the price of tea may be one or two cents lower than in the corresponding market around Boston, without any of the New York wholesale dealers sending their stocks to New England, or any of the New England retailers coming to New York to take advantage of the lower price.

In the market constituted of the retailers and the domestic purchasers of tea, far wider differences may exist. The price of the same quality of tea might be, and might long remain, five or ten cents higher in the grocery stores of Newark than in those of Worcester or Nashua, without a single New England grocer going to Newark to retail his tea, or a single Newark householder going to Worcester or Nashua to lay in his year's supply.

I repeat my proposition : all those persons who contribute to the general demand for any commodity, as felt in any place, or to the supply of that commodity there available for purchase, and who, hence, serve, as buyers or as sellers, to affect the price of that commodity in that place belong to the same market.

137. Normal Price.—If there were a good market for any given commodity, *i. e.*, if competition were perfect ; (1) if there were no large stock of that commodity, but it could be produced freely and equably throughout the year, as wanted ; (2) if the demand for it were uniform and strong, about the same quantity being required for use in every equal period of time ; (3) if no large "plant," or machinery, or great amount of capital in other forms, were required for its production ; (4) if the producers of that commodity had an easy resort, or economic escape, to occupations in which other commodities were produced, and if, in turn, producers in other occupations could readily and successfully take up the production of the commodity in question, then the price of that commodity would, at any time, be close to the cost of production. *By cost of production we are to understand, not the average cost of the whole supply, but the cost of that part which is produced at the greatest disadvantage.*

That price would express the Final Utility of the commodity in question, that is, the utility of the portion which, at the price, it was just worth the consumer's while to purchase. That price would also express the sum of the efforts and abstinences of those producers who brought forth this commodity under the least favorable conditions, of all who contributed to the supply. Inasmuch as this price is to be paid alike by all purchasers of this commodity, it follows that those who have produced it under more favorable conditions* will obtain a remuneration which will represent more than the sum of their individual efforts and abstinences.

A price which corresponds closely to the cost of production may be called Normal Price.

138. Market Price.—Inasmuch as the conditions recited in the foregoing paragraph are never fully realized, there is for every commodity, in every market, a Market Price which differs more or less widely from the normal price.

This market price always measures the Final Utility of the commodity, that is, the utility of it to the last purchaser to whom it is just worth while to buy of it, at that price. Otherwise, that person would either not buy, which, by leaving a portion of the supply untaken, would determine a new and lower price, at which he or some one else would buy; or, he or some one else would buy more of it, which, by adding to the demand, would determine a new and higher price.

But while market price must always measure the utility of the commodity to the last purchaser, that is, the person to whom it is just worth while to buy at that price, market price does not always measure the efforts and abstinences of the last producer, that is, the person producing under the greatest disadvantage: to whom, therefore, it is only just worth while to produce at that price. It is in this latter respect that market price differs from normal price.

139. Relation of Market Price to Normal Price.—The causes which make market price differ from normal price are various. The illustration of them might be extended indefinitely. They may be grouped as follows:

I. The existence of a stock. For the purpose of exhibiting in its simplest form the operation of supply and demand,

---

*When we reach the department of Distribution, Part IV, we shall give the generic name of Rent to this excess of price over cost of production.

I took an article of which, it was assumed, no considerable stock existed at any time. The seaweed was supposed to lie in vast deposits on the shore, and to be got out (produced) as required. This is a condition which tends to keep market price close to normal price. In the case of most commodities, however, a considerable stock always exists : a fact which profoundly influences market price.

The existence of a stock is determined by various causes. In order that there may be grain to form the food of the long winter and early spring, seed must have been sown and the growing crop cultivated months previous. In order that there shall be a supply of wool in the market, sheep must have been bred years before. Many commodities make no such requirement. In order that there may be grain, the processes of production must have been begun months back ; but, given grain, it is only necessary, in order to have bread, that the miller should have a day's notice, and the baker time to heat his oven. Hence, with an immense stock of grain, amounting to thousands of millions of bushels, there may be but a small stock of flour, of which only a minute fraction will, at any time, be in the form of bread.

140. Distinction between Stock and the Supply.— The stock of any article in existence, at any time, must not be confounded with the supply of that article, considered as a commodity in the market.

By the word supply, we express the quantity of a commodity offered at any given price. At one price the supply may be but a small fraction of the stock. At successively higher prices, larger and larger portions of the stock would be offered, that is, would come to constitute the supply — until a certain price would take off the entire stock.

Indeed, the supply may even become greater than the stock, under a highly speculative organization of trade. Thus, in the grain or cotton market, or in the market for railway shares or government bonds, brokers daily offer to sell and contract to deliver vast amounts of the several commodities in which they deal, of which, perhaps, they possess little or none at all.

Sometimes it happens that those who are offering such commodities are entrapped* by a combination of purchasers into contracts to deliver, on a certain day, more than the entire quantity within reach, or even in existence. In such a case, the supply is still the amount offered at the price. This it is, and not the stock, which, taken in connection with the demand for the commodity, determines the price.

141. The necessity in some cases, the usage in others, of meeting the demand from a stock, and not out of daily production, causes market price to diverge from normal price, through excess or deficiency of production.

In order that there may be wheat, three millions of persons, more or fewer, in the United States, plant the grain many months previous to the anticipated consumption of the wheat by the miller and the baker. These persons break up the land and sow the seed without mutual understanding as to the extent of their operations. Each is governed by a notion, more or less vague, as to the probable demand for wheat. It is not at all a matter of certainty that the mistakes in calculation of one farmer will offset those of another. On the contrary, there is a strong tendency in the errors of producers to accumulate all on one or on the other side of the line of equable production.

If the price of wheat, owing to a deficient supply, has been high, almost all producers will be found, the next year, largely planting wheat. This is likely to produce a surplus which will perhaps bring down the price below the average, whereupon farmers, with almost as much unanimity as in the former case, will, the next year, diminish their operations in this direction. Those who are sagacious enough to look about them and say: Others are planting wheat freely, therefore, I will plant something besides wheat, are exceptional. In productive industry it is the rule that men go in droves; act under common impulses, with the result of causing excess and deficiency to alternate with great rapidity and often great violence. And this holds good, not alone of persons in the

---

* This is called a "corner."

lower departments of production. It is almost equally true of merchants and manufacturers and bankers. The select few who have the coolness and the sense to buy when others are most eager to sell, and to sell when others are most eager to buy, reap rich harvests of gain.

142. Substitution of one Commodity for Another in Use.—The influence upon price of an excess or deficiency in the stock of a commodity may be greatly diminished through the tendency to substitute one article for another in use. Thus, the cereals are, to a great extent, substituted for each other in use; one kind of meat for another,* and even bread for meat, or meat for bread, in the case of a marked deficiency of one or the other. If the crop of wheat be short, maize, barley, rye, buckwheat and oats are increasingly made use of as food; with a short crop of all the grains, resort is had to the cheaper kinds of animal food. The result of such substitution is to raise the price of the substituted article, and to prevent the price of the article for which it is substituted from rising as high as it otherwise would. The two commodities are thus, for the time, and in a degree, joined together in price. A mutual dependency is established between them.

143. Liability to Deterioration.—The influence upon market price of an excess in the stock of any commodity is greatly controlled by its liability, or non-liability, to deterioration. In the case of some commodities, the variations in price due to this liability are such as to make it appear that price has cut itself wholly clear from cost of production, or cost of reproduction. A commodity exceptionally subject to this condition may lose ten, thirty, fifty, or seventy per cent. of its price in a few days, or even in a few hours. Thus, in fish markets, the price of a fish might have been a shilling when the market opened at 5 o'clock in the morning, eightpence at 10 o'clock, sixpence by noon, while at three or four

* "We must, in fact, treat beef and mutton as one commodity of two different strengths, just as gold at eighteen carats and twenty carats is hardly considered as two, but as one commodity, of which twenty parts of one are equivalent to eighteen of the other."—Jevons—"The Equivalence of Commodities."

o'clock in the afternoon one could have it on his own terms. In the same way, strawberries are often sold on Saturday night at one-half or one-third the price of the morning.

The necessity of storage, in the case of a postponed sale, has often the same influence on the price of a commodity as liability to deterioration. The dealer, not having facilities for storing his stock, may be disposed to let it go at a very low price.

144. II.—Organization of Industry and Existence of Plant.—A second cause which makes market price differ from normal price is found in the organization of industry and the existence of machinery and "plant."* It was to get rid of this cause that, in our extended illustration of the influence of supply and demand upon price, we took a simple "extractive" industry, the gathering of seaweed along the shore, which could not be supposed to involve the use of numerous or expensive instruments, or the exercise of much skill, and that we assumed the persons so engaged to be in a position readily to turn themselves to tillage or the fisheries, in case of a falling off in the demand for seaweed.

145. III.—Customary Price.—Another cause which makes market differ from normal price, is the force of custom. We owe the existence of a customary price, in some things, to the power of public opinion, which determines that there shall be a stated, well-known price for certain services and certain commodities; and, in other things, to habit or the mental inertia of purchasers. Thus, in the former case, public opinion would not tolerate varying and uncertain prices of admission to places of public amusement, varying and uncertain tolls over bridges or fares on public conveyances, varying and uncertain fees for the performance of necessary services, such as those connected with physical comfort, the preservation of life, or the burial of the dead. It is seen and felt that to leave the buyer to haggle and bargain at the door of a theater over the price of admission; on the brink of a river as to the sum

* "Prices are liable to great fluctuations in trades in which there is a great use of fixed capital."—Marshall—"Economics of Industry."

to be paid for a cast across the stream; in the sick room, about the fee for a prescription or the medicine that is to save life or relieve pain, would be indecent, intolerable.

Hence, public opinion prevails to establish a price on all such occasions, which is alike irrespective of the actual service rendered in the individual instance, and of the cost of rendering that service. The rule of final utility is here suspended or altogether abolished. The traveler might be willing to give a large sum, rather than pass the night in a storm, without shelter, on the bank of a river, but he gets a cast across for the customary price. The father would give all his fortune, were it needed, for the prescription to save his child's life, or the medicine which the prescription calls for; but, instead, under the rule of customary price, he pays the physician two dollars, or a guinea, as the case may be, and, at the apothecary's, pays for the medicine by the ounce, in silver, though he would pay for it, drop for drop, in his own blood, could it not be had otherwise.

Where public opinion can not be trusted to establish a customary price, in cases like the above, the law generally enters and fixes the rates at which commodities and services shall be sold. Of course, the prices paid must be sufficient to make it worth while to keep up the service, whether of the apothecary, the physician, the ferryman, or the actor or opera singer; but the price to be paid is made independent of the wealth or poverty, the knowledge or ignorance, the little or the great need, of the individuals purchasing.

146. Influence of Habit on Price.—Far beyond the range of customary price, in the limited class of cases above referred to, is the effect of habit and mental inertia, in restraining, or wholly repressing, the movements of price. In the former class of cases, the seller consciously submits to a restraint upon his freedom of action imposed from without, viz., by public opinion or law. In the far wider field now in contemplation, buyers and sellers are left free, so far as outside influence is concerned, but are constrained, in a higher or lower degree, by the laws of their mental constitution. No human being ever escapes from the force of habit. It is always easier to do what we have done before than to do what we have never done; to do what we have done twice than what we have done but once; to do what we have done often than what we have done seldom.

The degrees in which men are thus bound by habit differ widely. A capability of taking the initiative in action, mental courage and activity, freedom from fear and superstition, a readiness to meet new conditions and perhaps even a pleasure in encountering risks and odds, are among the fruits of culture; they constitute an inheritance in families; they even become a characteristic of nations and races.

The effects of habit upon prices are important. Habit always in some degree, often in a great degree, resists the economic tendency to a new price. The effect is seen at its maximum in wages, the price of labor. A day's wages often remain the same through years. So strong is this tendency that wages sometimes remain unaffected by the presence of a number of unemployed laborers. Instead of wages falling until all the laborers are brought into service at the reduced rates, employers continue to pay the old rates to a smaller number of workmen.

Over the price of goods habit exerts an influence not less real, though not equally powerful. It often suffices to keep price stable against an economic reason for movement, and even when movement takes place, it begins later and ceases earlier, by reason of this constant resistance.

147. The Moral and Intellectual Elements of Demand and Supply.—Our definitions of demand and supply, as respectively the quantity of any given article which purchasers stand ready to take at a certain price, and the quantity which producers or holders stand ready to deliver at the same price, clearly recognize a moral and an intellectual element alike in demand and in supply. "Stand ready" to take or to deliver. Any thing which affects that readiness, is, then, an element of demand or of supply. Supply is not a stock (Par. 140), a definite quantity, which must be sold, whether or no. It may be that out of a large stock, holders stand ready to deliver but a small quantity at the price offered.

The reason for withholding the stock may be found in the physical conditions attending the reproduction of the article, *e. g.*, a scarcity of the material out of which it is made, or the reason may be found in an intellectual apprehension, just or mistaken, of the state of the market, or the probabilities of the immediate future ; or, waving this consideration, the reason for a larger or a smaller quantity being offered or taken at a certain price may be moral, that is, may be found in the greater or less tenacity of purpose, or the greater or less courage to undertake risks and sustain arduous and doubtful enterprises.

In all variations between normal and market price, moral and intellectual elements are important factors. It often happens that the producers or holders of an article, anticipating a rise of price, on some account which may prove to be wholly fictitious, will keep back the entire stock, only to sell it, a little later, at a price far below that which they could have obtained for it while the false apprehension lasted.

More or less, false apprehensions enter to affect the demand for and the supply of every article in every condition of the market ; but the influence of this cause may be in one period ten times or a hundred times as great as in other periods. The contrast between a placid noonday and a "hurricane eclipse of the sun," is hardly more marked than the contrast between a peaceful, sluggish market and one excited by mysterious rumors, emanating no one knows where, or wrought to frenzy by false reports manufactured by the parties to some great jobbing interest.

148. Retail Contrasted with Wholesale Trade.—The foregoing holds good even of the wholesale markets, where the parties who buy and sell commodities are picked and skilled men, long familiar with the conditions of the articles in which they deal, with large opportunities, whether by price-currents, newspaper, post or telegraph, or by special and secret inquiry, for ascertaining all the facts bearing on the question, at what price they should buy or sell.

In retail trade, the moral and intellectual elements of demand and supply play a much more important part. On one side is the merchant, who by frequent resort to the wholesale dealer is kept advised of the conditions of the market. On the other side is the "customer," a creature of custom, as the term implies; often ignorant in the widest sense of the word, unintelligent and untrained; always and necessarily ignorant in the special sense of being unacquainted with the conditions which should determine price, not knowing what a commodity ought to cost, and, in the case of many classes of commodities, unable to judge of the quality of the goods offered, perhaps at the mercy of the dealer in the matter of the measure or weight.

The merchant, again, is the possessor of capital, and can wait to dispose of his goods at the best time. The customer, on the other hand, is generally in urgent need of commodities for immediate use, and frequently poor, so that he must buy in small quantities; perhaps even, in debt, so that he feels under a strong constraint to trade only with his creditor, who thus holds him at a double disadvantage, for how can he quarrel, as to quality, measure, or price, with the man whom he is not able to pay for goods already had and consumed?

149. The Friction of Retail Trade.—From the ignorance and inertness of the "customer" arises what may be called the Friction of Retail Trade. "Retail price," says Mr. Mill, "the price paid by the actual consumer, seems to feel slowly and imperfectly the effect of competition, and where competition does exist, it often, instead of lowering prices, merely divides the gain among a greater number of dealers. It is only in the great centers of business that retail transactions have been chiefly or even much determined by competition. Elsewhere it rather acts, when it acts at all, as an occasional disturbing influence. The habitual regulator is custom, modified from time to time, by notions existing in the minds of purchasers and sellers, of some kind of equity or justice."

And referring to this manifest inability of the customer in retail trade to look out for himself, in a struggle with the expert dealer, Prof. Cairnes says: "Between persons so qualified the game of exchange, if the rules be rigorously enforced, is not a fair one; and it has consequently been recognized universally in England, and very extensively among the better class of retail dealers in Continental countries, as a principle of commercial morality, that the dealer should not demand from his customer a higher price for his commodity than the lowest he is prepared to take. Retail buying and selling is thus made to rest upon a moral rather than an economical basis, and, there can be no doubt, for the advantage of all concerned."

150. Economic Forces Never Cease to Operate.—I am disposed to think that these eminent economists overrate the disability under which the customer suffers in retail trade; and, secondly, that the inference they draw from the undoubted fact of the general prevalence of a customary price, viz., that this shows that competition is not the regulator of such trade, is not fully justified. To take an analogous case, let one look around him, in any highly organized community, and he will see very little display of force in compelling proper things to be done, or in repressing acts injurious to society. He will see on every side men doing just and decent and even courteous and kindly things, respecting the rights of others and making use inoffensively of their own powers and privileges, just as if all this were natural and pleasant to them, as, indeed it has, to a great degree, become. These actions appear to be spontaneous and instinctive; and one thus looking around on the orderly and civil procedure of daily life, whether in social intercourse or in business, might think that force was not, in any proper sense, the regulator of that community; he might conclude that good will towards others, self-respect and public spirit were universal. Yet if that power which in every civilized state is always at hand, however veiled or disguised, to protect person and property, to repress lawlessness and to punish crime, were once withdrawn, society would speedily be transformed, and the occurrence of every form of rapine and violence would instruct the observer that, behind the fairest show of order, right dealing and courtesy, stands the armed force of the community.

So, while within certain limits, competition seems to disappear wholly from retail trade, and custom and respect for the rights of the purchaser enter to banish "higgling" from the market and to impose the one-price system, and thus retail buying and selling, as Prof. Cairnes says, comes to rest upon a moral basis, yet the economic forces always lie beneath, as the bed-rock below which the effects of moral forces can not go. Let the cost of an article rise above the customary price, and merchants will make an advance upon that price, in spite of custom. Let merchants demand an utterly exorbitant price, and competition will spring up, even among the least intelligent and least enterprising buyers.

CHAPTER II.

THE THEORY OF INTERNATIONAL EXCHANGES.

151. We stated, in paragraph 119, that, on the whole and in the long run, the respective values of a number of articles will be nearly according to the amounts of labor that have been expended upon them, severally. That this will be true throughout any small community is seen in the consideration that, if certain articles failed to have as much, or nearly as much, value for the unit of labor as other articles produced in that community, some of the laborers who had been engaged in the production of the articles thus disparaged in exchange, would set themselves to making some other article or articles more highly appreciated. Either this would, at some stage, raise the value of the disparaged articles, through reducing the supply of them ; or, if the community cared so little for those articles as not to be willing to pay a higher price for them, production in those lines would ultimately cease.

Subject to important exceptions—such as will be indicated in paragraphs 339-342—the respective values of articles will be regulated in the way that has been indicated, within any small community. Is any modification of this conclusion required, as exchange is conceived to be carried on between distant communities, constituting, perhaps, distinct nations ?

152. We shall reach the essence of the matter if we assume the trading world to be confined to half a dozen islands, which interchange their products freely, but between which no movement of labor or capital ever takes place. One of these might have a tropical climate and rich soil, producing in abundance tea and coffee, tobacco, sugar and molasses, silks, spices and dye-stuffs. The population of this island we will assume to be in excess, the point of diminishing returns (par. 51) having long since been passed. Island No. 2 is like island No. 1, except that the point of diminishing returns has not yet been reached. Island No. 3 lies in some northern sea, producing hemp, wool, flax, and the cereal grains. Island No. 4 is the land of oil and wine. Island No. 5 is filled with extensive mines of coal and the useful metals. Island No. 6 has a poor soil, a bleak climate, and a scanty population, whose production comprises only ice, lumber, fish and furs.

What, now, will be "the exchanging proportions" or terms of exchange, between these islands, at any given date? Will it still be true that the values of their respective products will be nearly according to the amounts of labor (omitting capital, for the time, from consideration) which have been involved in their production, severally? I answer, that, at any date which we may take for the purpose of our illustration, this would not necessarily be so. Assuming the strength, skill, intelligence and energy of all the laborers in all the islands to be equal, a given amount of labor in one island might command the product of two days' labor in another island, while commanding the products of only half a day's labor in still another. This supposition is not an unreasonable one. Differences as great exist to-day among the countries of the world, even after making the allowances necessary to bring the several laboring populations to an equality in the respects of strength, skill, intelligence and energy.

153. What, then, would govern the exchanging proportions subsisting between the several islands? I answer that the only explanation which anywhere, at any time, can be offered for existing ratios of exchange, is found in the relation between supply and demand. Within each of the several islands taken for the purpose of our illustration, values would approximately be regulated by labor, according to the principle first stated. But, as between themselves, each of these islands would constitute a unit, whose terms of exchange with all the other islands would be determined by the Equation of International Demand, to use the phrase of Mr. J. S. Mill. What is meant by this formidable phrase? This: that values, in exchanges between these islands, will be governed by the demand of each island for the productions of all the other islands, as against the demand of all the other islands for those commodities which itself produces. In the case supposed, the play of economic forces may result in giving to a day's labor in one island a very great purchasing power in comparison with a day's labor in any other island, and a vastly greater purchasing power in comparison with a day's labor in some one other island.

Thus, we might suppose the taste for olive oil and wine to be, at the date we have taken for the purpose of this illustration, not widely spread among the other islands. In some, the uses of olive oil might not be known at all. In that case, there would be but little demand for the productions of island No. 4, as a whole. As between the producers of olive oil and the producers of wine, the force of competition would operate steadily to bring about the result that a day's labor in a vineyard would yield as much purchasing power as a day's labor in an olive grove. But, while the producers of olive oil and the producers of wine would thus be brought upon an equality as regards each other, both classes of producers would be at a disadvantage in comparison with producers in the other islands, generally. We might say, with the producers of any other island; or we might suppose that, the mechanic arts being still in a backward state, island No. 5 would experience a still smaller demand, relative to its laboring population; and the inhabitants of that island might be obliged to continue getting out iron ore, smelting it in their furnaces, working it up in their forges, only to sell the products of a very long day's labor for the products of nine hours' labor in island No. 6; ten hours' labor in island No. 4; six hours' labor in island No. 3; five hours' labor in island No. 1; three hours' labor in island No. 2.

We have said, five hours' labor in island No. 1, and three hours' labor in island No. 2. How is this? The productions of these two islands are the same; their soil and climate we have assumed to be the same. Truly; yet the fact that in one of these islands the stage of diminishing returns has been reached and passed necessitates, as we have seen, a lower per-capita production: a difference which might not be exaggerated in the ratio of three to five.

If, now, we assume a sudden development of the mechanic arts and a rapid and extensive use of iron in tools and machinery, island No. 5, from being at the foot of the scale, as regards the purchasing power of a day's labor, might rise almost instantaneously to the top. A day's labor there might come to command the products of a day's labor in an island previously the most favored; might soon come to command the products of two or three days' labor almost anywhere else. What island No. 5 has to sell has now become of supreme importance. The sugar planters of Nos. 1 and 2, the wheat growers of No. 3, the lumber operators and ice cutters of No. 6, find that they can greatly increase their production with implements and machines made of iron. The iron-workers, therefore, realize rich gains, and fare sumptuously upon the products of all the other groups of laborers.

Now, upon the assumption that labor and capital do not flow from one island to another, but only products are imported or exported, each island would be left indefinitely to its own economic lot, be that a hard one or a fortunate one, according to the demands from all the other islands for its characteristic products.

154. In the case of these separate communities, does the failure of values to correspond to amounts of labor, depend upon the question of nationality? I answer, no: the failure of correspondence between value and labor would occur just as fully between two islands which were subject to the same government, as between one of these islands and still another island under a different flag. The condition we have noted is due entirely to the fact assumed at the beginning, *viz.:* that labor and capital do not pass from one of these trading communities to another. It has nothing to do with nationality. Among different communities, be these large or small, distant or near, there will be an incessant tendency, due to changes of population, to changes in the arts, to changes in commercial demand, to the varying character of the seasons, and to a score of other causes, to disturb the relation between labor and value. Except as these causes may offset each other, the one force which should restore the equilibrium that has been disturbed, is to be found in the movement of labor or of capital, or of both, from the communities where the unit of labor or of capital receives the smaller return to the communities where it receives the larger return. If that movement does not, in fact, take place, the differences noted may continue and may even increase from age to age.

If, then, the failure of values to correspond to amounts of labor expended, has nothing to do with the fact of nationality, why should the economists, generally, have written of International Values, of International Trade, of the Equation of International Demand? I answer, because nations seemed to them to furnish the most convenient units for illustrating the operation of the forces concerned. It is true, it was true even when Ricardo developed this theory, in the early part of the century, that there are definite portions of the same nation between which the movement of labor and capital takes place as slowly and tardily as, often, between two separate nations. It is even true that there are groups of nations perhaps widely sundered geographically, between which this movement takes place far more readily than between contiguous sections of the same country.

Still, it is true now, and was true in a much higher degree when Ricardo wrote, that obstructions, physical, intellectual and moral, to the movements of labor and capital, tend to gather themselves along the boundary lines of nationality. This arises from differences of speech, of race, and perhaps, also, of religion, from prejudices against aliens, perhaps, also, laws putting them at a disadvantage; from reluctance at self-expatriation, from physical obstacles of a marked character, which often, though not always, serve to divide nations from each other. Between any two given nations all the causes above noted may enter to raise to a maximum the resistance to migration. Between other two nations, only a part of these causes may operate, and may operate with greatly diminished force.

It was the foregoing considerations which induced the economists to take nations as the units for illustrating the economic effects of a cessation of the movement of labor and capital between separate communities. It has led, however, to misconception at two points: first, by creating the impression that because nations were taken as units in this discussion, nationality was the real reason for the phenomena observed; secondly, by diverting attention from the effects of a cessation of such movements within the limits of nationality. It would be safe to say that there are nations divided into a half-score of sections, between the two most friendly and fully contiguous of which the movements of labor and capital are scantier and slower than between certain two other nations, though separated by thousands of miles.

Wherever the movement of labor and capital ceases, there all the effects which are, by the economists, attributed to national differences, become fully realized. In just so far as those movements are reduced or retarded, the natural operation of competition, in restoring the normal relation of value to labor, is deferred or defeated. Even where movements of labor and capital actually take place, they may be so tardy and difficult that local causes may go on producing inequalities between the purchasing power of labor in neighboring communities, much faster than competition can efface them.

155. It follows from what has been said, that, in the exchanges of two considerable communities, be the same distinct countries or isolated portions of the same country, from one to the other of which movements of labor or capital do not take place or take place so tardily and painfully that they fail to keep up with the tendencies to divergence indicated in the preceding paragraph, it follows, I say, that in the exchanges between two such communities, articles may be imported into one of these communities, notwithstanding the fact that it could there be produced at a lower cost than in the community from which it was exported ; and this state of things may, under the conditions recited, continue indefinitely.

This would scarcely happen between small contiguous communities. If in one of such communities, A., a certain kind of goods could be produced at lower cost than in communities B., C. and D., all the labor and capital, employed, within that group, in the production of that article, would pass over into A.; and the entire production of that article for that group would soon take place in that single community. As a result of this play of economic forces, no one of these communities would long import from any other any kind of goods which it could possibly itself produce at a lower cost.

Between communities or countries, however, experiencing no movements of labor or capital, exchanges of goods may, as we said, continue indefinitely to take place, notwithstanding the fact that the importing countries could, if they would, themselves produce many of the articles at a lower, perhaps a much lower cost than that at which they are actually produced in the countries from which they are brought. Thus, to return to our six trading islands, we might suppose that the demand for olive oil and wine had become so great that the inhabitants of island No. 4 could, by one day's labor in their vineyards or groves, command the products of two days' labor in island No. 1. If this were so, it might clearly be for their interest to continue producing olive oil and wine only, even though their soil and climate were such as to enable them to produce sugar or coffee or tea or spices at two-thirds the cost of which they were actually produced in island No. 1. By applying all their labor force and capital force to that for which they had the most marked qualification, they would, in the result, obtain more of any and all products which they might desire, than if they were to give up a certain portion of their labor power and capital power to the production of articles in respect to which their natural advantage would be less than in raising oil and wine, though it might be greater than that enjoyed by the actual producers of the articles in question.

156. That such would be the normal operation of the principle of self-interest will readily appear if we take the case of a skilled mechanic, say a blacksmith, in an agricultural community. The smith may have been brought up on a farm, and he may, conceivably, be so strong, so quick in his motions, so handy with tools, that he could, to-day, do one-fourth more of farm work than any one in the neighborhood. Since then, he can do farm work better than the farm hands, will he leave his forge? That will depend on the "Equation of Demand." If there be several blacksmiths in the community, so that the demand for the work of each blacksmith is small, and if the other blacksmiths are as well able to work at the forge as himself, but are not, like himself, able to turn advantageously to farming, his economic interest may impel him to agriculture. If, on the other hand, he is the only blacksmith in the community, the demand for his work will certainly be great, perhaps so great as to enable one day's labor on his part to command two ordinary days' labor on the farm. In this case it would be the height of folly for him to leave his forge, since there he can acquire a value represented by 2, while on the farm the value of his product will be represented by only $1\frac{1}{4}$.

The reason of the case will appear still plainer if we contemplate a country physician, who, having been brought up on a farm, and being accustomed to cultivate a small tract, for his health and pleasure, in the intervals of practice, might easily be as good an agriculturist as many of his neighbors. The question is, shall he buy farm products or raise them himself? I answer: so far as health and pleasure, in the intervals of practice, allow, he will do well to cultivate the land; but as a matter of business he can not afford to sacrifice the smallest part of his professional work for the sake of raising vegetables instead of buying them. As a physician, he can easily command three or four days' labor, for one of his own. Even were he the best farm hand in the county, he would be throwing away a great economic advantage, were he to attempt to raise from the soil all that which he desired to consume.

157. Now, what we have seen the blacksmith and the country physician doing, nations and smaller communities are continually doing, under the operation of the principle of self-interest. Many a country imports, generation after generation, commodities *a., b. and c.*, which it could produce more cheaply than those who made them. The reason is, that there are other branches of industry, *x., y. and z.*, in which it has a still higher relative advantage. So far as movements of labor and capital take place, there will be a constant tendency for laborers and capitalists to come to the more favored country, and here set up industries, *a., b. and c.* But this will, at the best, go on slowly; and it may be altogether defeated by the discovery that commodities, *m., n. and o.*, can be produced in the country in question, not, indeed, so advantageously as *x., y. and z.*, but far more advantageously than *a., b. and c.* Consequently, all the additional labor and capital coming into this country, in this generation and perhaps in the next, may be directed toward building up industries *m., n. and o.;* and commodities *a., b. and c.* may continue to be imported.

158. Such being the conditions under which trade takes place between countries, from one to the other of which movements of labor and capital do not occur, or occur so tardily as not to overtake the tendencies to local disturbance which have been dwelt upon, we have to note two things in closing this chapter.

First, in any country, the value of an imported article does not tend to be determined by what would be the cost of production of that article in that country. It does not even tend to be determined by its cost in the country in which it was actually produced. The normal value of such an article, in such a place, depends on *the cost of production of the article which is exported to pay for it*, transportation being taken into account.

Second, while it is for the interest of a country enjoying great economic advantages, to apply its labor power and capital power to certain lines of production, only, looking to purchase from others many classes of commodities which it could produce as well as or even better than they, such a course is also for the economic interest of the countries with which it trades, since they are thereby enabled to obtain the products of the former country, at a lower, probably much lower, cost than that at which they could hope themselves to produce these, or to obtain them from any other quarter.

CHAPTER III.

MONEY AND ITS VALUE.

159. Exchange Arises out of the Division of Labor.—Men become the producers of that which they expect to consume but in part, if at all. Their choice as to what they shall produce, ceases to be determined by considerations affecting their personal wants, and comes to be determined mainly, if not wholly, by considerations affecting their abilities and aptitudes. They no longer produce that which they desire to eat, drink or wear. They produce that one among many things known to the market which they can produce to the best advantage, let who will, in time, eat, drink or wear it. Their own wants they look to see, in turn, satisfied by the labor of others.

To the market all producers bring their several products, or such part thereof as they do not care individually to consume. From the market each late producer, now become a consumer, carries away that which he is to eat, drink, or wear, or otherwise enjoy. In the market is done that which we call exchange.

The economic function of exchange is to bring producers and consumers together, and thus allow the division of labor to be carried as far as it will increase production. The division of labor has no economic virtue except so far as it increases production. When that point has been reached, a further subdivision of occupations and employments would be useless, or of merely curious interest. Exchange, in turn, has no virtue except as it allows the division of labor to be carried out. Its sole function, economically, is to enable each species of wealth, each article known to the market, to be produced in the place and by the person where and by whom it can be produced to the greatest advantage.

160. The Economic Function of Money.—In its function of bringing producers and consumers together, exchange discovers the need of the great agent of which we are about to speak—Money. Just as the occasion for exchange arises out of the fact of the division of labor, and as the economic efficiency of exchange is limited to that occasion, so the need of money arises solely out of the fact of exchange, and the economic efficiency of money is limited strictly to the occasion for exchange. The interests of a community require as much exchanging as will secure that division of labor which will achieve the highest productiveness of land, labor and capital; and they require no more exchanging than this. They require as much money as will enable that amount of exchanging to be effected with the least effort and with the greatest assurance of a transfer of real equivalents; and they require no more money than this. No economic efficiency other than or beyond that indicated, can justly be attributed to money.

But how does money facilitate those exchanges which it is for the interest of society to have effected? Just what is the function of money?

161. Double Coincidence in Barter.—Money facilitates exchanges by dispensing with that double coincidence, of wants and of possessions, which barter, *i., e.* exchange without the use of money, involves. We have seen that, so far as the division of labor is carried out, men cease to produce all or even the greater part of what they wish to consume. Producing that which they can produce to the best advantage, they look to others for those particular articles which are required for the supply of their individual wants. The producer and the would-be consumer of each article, therefore, must get together, somehow, or else the wants of the community will remain unsatisfied.

But that each producer for himself should find some person

who has what he wants and at the same time wants what he has, would involve very roundabout exchanges, occupying a great deal of time, and occasioning much delay and frequent disappointments. The bootmaker who wanted a hat for his own use might find many persons who would be glad to get pairs of boots, but had no hats to give in exchange, and several persons who had hats, indeed, to sell, but were already supplied with boots, before he found one person who both had hats and lacked boots. And, moreover, when that person were found, a further difficulty would probably arise from the failure of an exact equivalency between the two articles to be exchanged. A pair of boots might be worth more than a hat; perhaps three pairs of boots might be worth four hats. Yet the bootmaker wants but one hat; the hatter wants but one pair of boots. Things would soon get into a fearful muddle, this way.

But if, by general consent, formal or implied, the producers of the community should hit upon one article which they would all agree to take in exchange for whatever they wished to sell, a vast saving of time and labor, of annoyance and disappointment, would be effected, especially if the article so taken should be one, say, wheat, susceptible of minute division, without loss of utility.

162. Money, the Medium of Exchange.—What shall we call the function which the wheat would in this case perform? Clearly it is something altogether beyond and in addition to its ordinary natural function, as wheat, which is simply to be made into flour, to be, in turn, made into bread. In the use proposed, the wheat would serve another purpose. What shall we call that purpose?

The function performed by the wheat, in the instance given, is that of a Medium of Exchange. The significance of the word medium, in this connection, is found in the fact that the wheat becomes an intermediate thing in the commerce between the producers and the consumers of any and of every article. The wheat is no longer an end, as when used for food, but a means to an end, which end may be boots, or hats, or groceries, or what not. The person who takes wheat for what he has produced may already have more wheat than he could eat in a year. He does not take it with a view to eating it, but because with it he can obtain, in kinds and quantities and at times to suit his wants and convenience, whatever he may wish to eat, drink, or wear, or to warm or house himself withal.

Now, the function which has been described is the Money function. Money is the medium of exchange. Whatever performs this function, does this work, is money, no matter what it is made of, and no matter how it came to be a medium at first, or why it continues to be such. So long as, in any community, there is an article which all producers take freely and as a matter of course, in exchange for whatever they have to sell, instead of looking about, at the time, for the particular things they themselves wish to consume, that article is money, be it white, yellow, or black, hard or soft, animal, vegetable, or mineral. There is no other test of money than this. That which does the money-work is the money-thing. It may do this well; it may do this ill. It may be good money; it may be bad money—but it is money all the same.

163. Universal Acceptability of Money. — We said, all producers, since it is not enough that an article is extensively used in exchange, to constitute it money. Bank checks are used in numerous and important transactions of exchange, yet are not money. It is essential to money that its acceptability should be so nearly universal that practically every person in the community who has any product or service to dispose of will freely, gladly, and of preference, take this thing, money, instead of the particular products or services which he may individually require from others, being well assured that with money he will unfailingly obtain whatever he shall desire, in form and amount and at times to suit his wants.

When any article, no matter what its substance or form, acquires this degree of acceptability, no matter how obtained or how retained, so that each person, in his place in the industrial order, without the expectation of consuming this article, and without reference to the character or credit of the person offering it, takes it freely from any man whenever he has anything to sell, because he knows that any other man will freely take it from him whenever he may wish in his turn to buy, that article becomes money, and remains money while that condition continues. To serve as the medium of exchange is the money-function, and whatever does this is money.

164. Money and Civilization.—It is evident that the introduction of money, even in a primitive state, vastly facilitates exchanges, and renders it easy to carry out the division of labor. It is further evident that the use of money is a condition precedent to an advanced state of industrial society. The division of labor could not without it be carried so far as is involved in complicated manufactures and extended commerce.

"It has been wisely said," remarks M. Chevalier, "that no machine economizes labor like money, and its adoption has been likened to the discovery of letters."

The allusion is probably to the noble sentence of Gibbon: "The value of money has been settled by general consent to express our wants and our property, as letters were invented to express our ideas; and both these institutions, by giving a more active energy to the powers and passions of human nature, have contributed to multiply the objects they were designed to express."

165. Historical Forms of Money.—We have said that any article which acquires a certain degree of acceptability throughout the community, would thereby become money, whatever its material or form. Yet material and even form may have much to do with securing to any given article, at any given time, the requisite degree of acceptability. The industrial habits and the tastes of a people and their social conditions may make that money which among another people would be an impossible money. Rock salt long served the Abyssinians as money; rice, the dwellers on the Coromandel shore; cacoa, the aboriginal Mexicans; olive oil, the inhabitants of the Ionian islands; wampum, the early New Englanders; tobacco, the early Virginians and Marylanders; tea, compressed into small cakes, the Russians; dates, the savages of the African oases; beaver and seal skins, the peoples of many northern lands. Cattle and sheep were employed as money, alike by the early Greeks, by the Romans who conquered the Greeks, and by the Teutons who conquered the Romans.

166. The Metals as Money.—But, of all substances, the metals have enjoyed the widest use as money, from a remote period. Iron, lead, tin and copper, one or another, have been thus employed in nearly every country whose history is known.

From its numerous and important uses in the domestic arts, in the chase, and in warfare, the first-named metal was the subject of such wide and constant demand as to make its further use as the general medium of exchange, *i. e.*, as money, very simple and natural. The art of mining being in early times very crude, small quantities of iron represented a large amount of labor, and thus contained a high purchasing power. Moreover, in comparison with wheat, cattle, and many other primitive forms of money, iron cost little or nothing to keep and was but little subject to waste, while a given mass could easily be divided into pieces of any required dimensions, which could again be reunited, by fusion, or by welding when heated. The money of Lacedæmon was of iron; the Swedes used money of this metal during and after the exhausting wars of Charles XII.; and iron is still reported to be so used by the inhabitants of Senegambia.

Lead was extensively employed as money by the early Romans and the early English, and is still used in the same way by the Burmese. Tin was used by the Mexicans as money; was long so employed in Sweden, in long, flat blocks; and is even now a medium of exchange among the Chinese and Malays and in Prince of Wales Island.

But more than iron, tin or lead, has copper, in the later centuries, been used as money. Having, from its cost of production, a high value for its bulk, it came to supersede iron in this use, when the latter metal became too cheap to form a convenient money. During the silver famine of the middle ages, copper returned to be the chief money of circulation in Europe. And though, after the revival of silver production through the discovery of Mexico and Peru, it fell out of use as a principal money of wealthy and prosperous countries, it has remained a considerable element in the monetary circulation of the world, even to this day.

Platinum was for a brief period, between 1828 and 1845, used as money in Russia, where that metal is produced; but the great difficulty of rendering platinum, now from ingots into coin, and again from coin into ingots, prevented the success of this experiment, notwithstanding that platinum is justly regarded as one of the noblest of the metals.

167. The Precious Metals.—All the other metals, however, pale before the light of two transcendent substances, the Precious Metals, so-called, silver and gold. Having numerous important uses in the industrial arts; possessing the highest adaptation for the purposes of ornament and decoration, these metals have always and everywhere exerted, beyond all other objects of human desire, a strange, a mysterious fascination upon the minds of men.

168. Coinage.—Under the title, coinage, we may take account of all methods of determining, for easy popular recognition, the quantity and quality of individual portions of that which is used as money. It is in their adaptations to the art of the coiner that the metals, and especially the precious metals, exhibit their most marked qualifications for use as money. With some kinds of money, indeed, no such mode of determination is required, the divisions being natural, as in the case of the red feathers and shells used as money, or of cattle and sheep, which only need to be counted.

With other, and indeed, most, forms of money, it is necessary to give a customary shape to the pieces to be so used. The Abyssinians, who used rock salt as money, cut it into bricks of uniform dimensions, so that each person taking a brick in exchange might know how much salt he was receiving. Here, the problem was merely mechanical; no chemical tests were required. The salt being of reasonably uniform quality, the receiver was only interested to know its quantity.

With money of gold and silver, and even of copper or iron, however, both the quantity and the quality of each piece offered may be brought into question, unless some means be adopted by which the piece shall be made to exhibit unmistakably the amount of pure metal it contains. The problem is thus both a mechanical and a chemical one, and is solved by what we call, in the limited sense, Coinage. The metal is melted, and in that state is brought to the required degree of purity, or "fineness." It is then cast into ingots, and by successive mechanical processes, with machinery of great delicacy and power, drawn out to the required thickness, cut into planchets, "milled" around the edges, and stamped on both sides* with devices expressive both of the sovereignty of the nation under whose authority the coins are struck, and of the quality and quantity of the metal contained.

Coinage has generally been regarded as an act of sovereignty, and the counterfeiting of the coin has been widely punished as treason. In England, the King's sovereignty only extended to the coinage of gold and silver, the private coinage of copper not having been prohibited until the present century. So important is the money-function, so strong is the tendency to abuse the privilege of coining, so helpless are the mass of the community, especially the poor and economically weak, under a corrupted coinage, that, even in popular governments, where prerogative is not known, the private minting of money is punished by grave penalties. That coins shall fully perform their office as money, they must be taken readily, without suspicion, or at most, after a brief inspection such as even the ignorant and inexpert can give.

169. What Determines the Value of Money?—It is only the present inquiry which brings the topic of money into the department of exchange. Otherwise, money belongs to the department of production, as clearly as does any other agency

* At first, coins were impressed on one side, as is now the "gall," the only native coin of Cochin China. This allowed the metal to be shaved from the smooth side of the coin. Afterwards characters were stamped on both sides, but the area of the coin was not fully defined, allowing the edges to be clipped, as is largely the case with the Tomans of Persia. Later improvements surrounded the coin with a well-defined rim, while the edges were milled to still further protect the integrity of the piece.

of trade or transportation, cattle, carts, railways or banks The mining of the precious metals is governed by the laws which regulate the production of other kinds of wealth. The minting of gold and silver is equally a branch of production. Assayers, refiners and coiners are as much producers of wealth as the laborers employed in a pig-iron furnace.

But under the title, Exchange, we may properly inquire why any one article, produced as we find it to be produced, under existing conditions, exchanges for so much of any other article, and not for more or for less. Pre-eminently in respect to iron or copper, silver or gold, when cut into planchets and stamped as coin, do we need to raise this question and discuss it in all simplicity and severity of reasoning, because the subject has been allowed to become involved in a thousand difficulties, from the lack of clear definitions and from the failure rigorously to exclude every thing alien or adventitious. The discussion of the laws of money has engendered so much passion and prejudice as to make it hard to secure a respectful attention, or even a rational attitude of mind towards any statement of monetary doctrine which differs in the minutest particular from that of the hearer. Men who are candid and even liberal in politics and religion become furiously or stupidly fanatical as soon as their views on money are controverted. When Sir Walter Scott made a surly critic say to the author of certain Letters on the Currency, "In your ill-advised tract you have shown yourself as irritable as Balaam and as obstinate as his ass," he evidently intended to characterize the whole race of writers on this theme.

The value of money, like the value of any thing else, is purely a question of demand and supply. The cost of producing money is only important as affecting the supply. Limit the supply,* and it does not matter whether there be any cost of production or not. The advantage of taking that for use as money which has an appreciable, definite, and, as far as may be, constant cost of production, is found in the fact that the

*I have already quoted (par. 120) the remark of Prof. Senior that "any other cause limiting supply is just as efficient a cause of value in an article, as the necessity of labor to its production."

supply of such money will be limited by natural causes, instead of being left to law, convention or accident.

170. What is the Demand for Money?—The demand for money is the occasion for the use of money in effecting exchanges. In other words, it is the amount of money-work to be done.

This is not determined by the gross volume of the wealth of the community, since all that wealth is not to be, in fact, exchanged. For a similar reason, it is not determined by the amount of the annual production of the community.

It is not determined even by the volume of products to be exchanged, inasmuch as some classes of these may require to be exchanged several times, and some but once. Moreover, in spite of the difficulties of barter, many products are, through a fortunate coincidence of wants and of possessions, especially in agricultural communities, exchanged against each other. More important still, the modern organization of commerce, especially through the agency of banks, provides for the creation, and subsequent cancellation, of indebtedness* on account of products given and taken in exchange, to an extent which vastly diminishes the actual use of money in effecting transfers.

171. The Money-Demand a Reality.—Not the less, is the demand for money a reality. Banks and clearing-houses, checks and book credits reduce the occasion for the use of money, but they do not supersede its use altogether, nor are there any signs that they will do so in any future, near or remote. In every community, though in some more than others, goods are offered for money. Men seek money, having in their hands wherewithal to pay for it. Some of them must have money, whatever it cost. With others any appreciable increase in the difficulty of getting money, or any appreciable doubt as to the "goodness" of that which is circulating in the community, does away with the disposition to obtain it, drives them to barter, and thus destroys a portion of the demand for money.

Some part of the exchangers of every community may be

* This function of banks will be spoken of, more at length, under that title in Part VI.

regarded as always on the verge of barter. They could exchange their products for the products of others which they wish to consume, without unreasonable trouble. Others, again, would exchange their products for money in the face of very great difficulties and embarrassments ; yet for each of these is a point at which difficulties and embarrassments will give rise to an effort, which will thereafter increase rapidly in force, to resort to barter or to credit, as the means of escaping the use of money. Should the matter proceed far enough, production will even be limited or modified to meet the exigency.

172. Effect of Discredit on the Money-Demand.—Thus, if the money of a country be openly discredited, as in France prior to and during the Hundred Years' War, and, again, during the Revolution ; in England, under Henry VIII. and the Protector Somerset ; in the United States, during the circulation of the so-called Continental currency ; and in Italy, through many dreary periods of her history, men will not only resort increasingly to barter or to credit, but such discredit of the coin or other circulating medium may become a force which will operate powerfully to modify and even to limit production. Men will produce fewer things and those different from what they would have done under conditions more favorable to the division of labor and the consequent exchange of products.

This, however, can never be carried so far as totally to dispense with the use of money. In any society above the barbarous state, something must be used, to some extent, as money, so long as production goes on at all.

We see, thus, that the demand for money has no definite relation to the total wealth, or the annual product of a community, or even to the volume of products to be exchanged. The demand for money varies with the amount of money-work to be done, which, in turn, varies with the industrial organization of communities, with seasons, and with circumstances innumerable. Not the less, however, as we said, is the demand for money a real thing. Goods are offered for money ; and, with a given supply, the more goods are so offered, the higher will be the value of money—that is, prices will fall. The fewer goods are offered, the lower will be the value of money—that is, prices will rise.

173. Value and Price.—It will have been noticed that, in the foregoing paragraph, I have used the word price as signifying the money-value of goods. As we stated in a previous chapter, value is the generic term which expresses power-in-exchange. Price is power-in-exchange-for-some-one-article. Where money is used, price commonly expresses power-in exchange-for-money. Where nothing to the contrary is intimated, the price of an article is understood to be the value of that article in terms of money—the amount of money it will command in exchange.

174. What is the Supply of Money?—If such is the demand for money, what is the supply? It is the money-force available to do the money-work required to be done, in the given community, at the given time. The money-force, or the supply of money, is not measured by what is usually called the amount of money, that is, the number of gold dollars or bits of paper used as money, but is composed of two factors—the amount of money and the rapidity of circulation. "The nimble sixpence does the work of the slow shilling." There may be as much money-force in 1000 dollars, each of which passes from hand to hand four times a week, as in 4000 dollars which change owners but once from Monday morning to Saturday night. The rapidity of circulation varies widely among different communities, according to the density of settlement, the prevailing occupations of the people, the facilities for the transportation of freight and passengers. And the rapidity of circulation not only varies according to such general conditions, but it varies from day to day, with the state of trade and the temper of the public mind.

175. The Money Supply a Reality.—But while the money-supply varies thus incessantly, it is none the less a real thing; so real that, at any given time a decrease of the supply of money will enhance its value—that is, will lower prices; and an increase of that supply will reduce its value—that is, will raise prices.

We have spoken of reducing the value of money as equivalent to raising prices; and of enhancing the value of money as equivalent to lowering prices. This is manifest enough to anyone who thinks of the matter; but the student of political economy needs to become so familiar with this equivalency that he will not have to think consciously about it; but the one mode of expression will always and instantly suggest its equivalent. To enhance the value of money is, of course, to give a larger purchasing power to each integral part of the circulating money—that is, to each piece or coin, and to any given number of pieces or coins. But if money purchases more of other things, other things, conversely, purchase less of money—that is, bear lower prices.

On the other hand, to say that the value of money is lowered, is to say that money purchases less of other things; but if money purchases less of other things, other things, conversely, purchase more of money—that is, bear higher prices.

176. International Distribution of Money.—We have seen that it is impossible to say what, at any time, in any community, is the demand for money, or the supply of money. We have now to see that, with money having a natural cost of production, no one has any need to know, either how much money there is, or how much is needed, inasmuch as the demand for money will, under such a system, easily and surely, because automatically, bring in the due supply required to enable all the exchanges of the community to be transacted with the minimum of effort and delay, and with the highest assurance of the exchange of real equivalents.

The territorial distribution of money is effected through the agency of Price.

Let us suppose that, of two trading countries having the same kind of money, the amount in each, *i. e.*, the number of pieces or coins, is such that, the rate of circulation being what it is, and the demand for money what it is, the scale of prices in the two countries precisely corresponds, cost of transportation of goods being, for the purposes of the illustration, left out of account. Now let us suppose that, all other elements of the case remaining unchanged, the amount of money in one of these countries, A, is suddenly and largely increased, say, by the discovery of treasure or by the opening of new mines. The supply of money having thus been increased, the value of money, as we have seen, must decline, that is, prices must rise. A given amount of money will purchase less of other things than before, which is equivalent to saying that other things will purchase more of money.

Now, if goods will purchase more money in that country, the owners of goods in the other trading country, B, will at once feel themselves impelled by self-interest to send their stock thither, to secure the benefit of the higher prices. Having exchanged goods for money in A, they will bring the money back to their own country, B. Why not invest the money in the country where they sold the goods? Because, by the conditions assumed, though A is, as they have found, an excellent market to sell in, since prices are high, it is, from that very fact, a bad market to buy in.

177. And while all owners of goods in B are hurrying to get their goods to A, in order to take advantage of the higher prices prevailing there, every holder of money in A is equally impelled to get his money as soon as possible to B, in order to take advantage of the lower prices there. Where all parties are so fully agreed, the thing is likely to be done quickly. Money flows from A to B until the equilibrium which was disturbed has been restored, that is, until the general scale of prices is the same in both countries. After this, the two countries will continue to trade as before; but each will keep its own money. A will pay for the cotton, rice and sugar of B with its own wheat, lumber, coal and ice.

178. The Money Movement Automatic.—It will be observed that the movement of money which has been described was not due to any one discovering that A had more money than it needed, or than its proportional share. No statistician or banker announced this result after computing the demand for money and the supply of money in that country. The exchanges which restored the equilibrium of prices were due wholly to the action of individuals, moved by a view of their own interest. Not one of them cared, perhaps not one of them knew, whether money was in excess in A, or not, but each, finding that by sending goods from B to A, or money from A to B, he could secure a profit, contributed to the result.

We have seen, in speaking of retail exchanges (par. 149), that a great amount of resistance is experienced in the operation of what are called "the laws of trade," and we shall have occasion to note, when we come to speak of wages, that the laborer's inertia, ignorance and poverty defer greatly, and even sometimes defeat altogether, the movements from place to place, or from occupation to occupation, which is required to secure his interests.

While the actual freedom and fullness of movement can, in no department of economic activity, reach the theoretical maximum, the result is more nearly obtained in the department under consideration than in any other. The persons who ship goods or money, in consequence of excess or deficiency in the money supply, being merchants of large experience and ample means, kept fully advised of the state of the markets by weekly letters and price-currents, and in later years, by information received daily, and now, even by hourly reports, through land telegraphs and ocean cables, the actual here closely approximates the theoretical readiness and completeness of movement. At the same time, it is easy to exaggerate even that readiness and completeness.

179. Picking or Selecting the Coin.—We have seen that any local excess of money, as between one country and another, immediately sets in motion forces which tend to restore the equilibrium. The local excess of money also promotes the use of the precious metals in the industrial and decorative arts. This application of the metals, always considerable, may be readily increased through a reduction in their value. As less and less of other things, wheat, iron or cotton, or of labor which produces all these things, will purchase a given amount of gold and silver, more gold and silver go to the melting pot.

In the case of exportation, or the melting of coined money, due to local excess, what determines the selection of the coins to be exported or melted? Is it purely a matter of chance, or is it controlled by the comparative proximity of coins to the place of exportation or the seat of the manufacture of jewelry, or of dental goods, or of photographers' supplies; or does some distinct economic force enter to decide that certain coins shall go and others stay? Let us inquire.

180. Irregularities in the Coin.—In the process of coining, it is inevitable, notwithstanding the truly admirable science and skill applied to this art, that differences should exist between coins. The mints of some countries do their work much more exactly than others; * but the best mints can not turn out pieces absolutely uniform in fineness and weight. A certain range of variation must be allowed, and this is generally formulated by law, and is known as the "tolerance" of the mint.

Even were all coins issued of exact uniformity, the wide difference in usage would soon make an appreciable difference in their weight. Some go early into hordes or deposits; others are worn down by almost continuous circulation; others still are dealt with illegitimately by clipping, punching, and "sweatting," till a considerable portion of their substance disappears.†

---

* Three gold coins, the Russian Imperials, the French Napoleons, and the American Eagles, are bought by the Bank of England without remelting. The United States Mint turns out the finest gold coin of the world; the Russian Mint the next best. The mint of France was, fifty years ago, charged with grave errors, all on one side, viz., in favor of the minters; but that mint is now of high authority. The mint of Great Britain has until recently been badly managed and has done poor work, in comparison with the others named, not out of any dishonest intention, or lack of mechanical skill, but from adherence to old fashions and antiquated machinery. Mr. Ernest Seyd and Prof. Jevons concurred some years ago in a very unfavorable criticism of the establishment on Tower Hill. More recently there has been improvement.

† Prof. Jevons estimated the proportion of "light" sovereigns in England, that is, of sovereigns reduced below the legal standard for circulation, to be 30 per cent., the proportion in some agricultural districts ris ing to 44 per cent.

If, now, with a body of coin of unequal value, a demand for the money-metal arises, for export or for use in the arts, the process of picking or selecting coin will at once begin. All merchants and bankers dealing largely in coin will lay by those of full or nearly full weight, and throw the lighter specimens back into circulation.

This process of picking or selecting coin, begins early in the history of such a demand as has been indicated, and proceeds steadily as long as that demand lasts. The operation costs practically nothing, and the profit, where great numbers of coins are daily handled, is large and certain. Clerks and cashiers become so expert that they can tell light coins by the touch, while, if doubt exists, a pair of adjusted scales will in an instant decide the question.

181. Gresham's Law.—The observation of this process of picking or selecting coin has led to the statement of the economic theorem, known as Gresham's Law,* viz., that "bad money always drives out good money."

Thus baldly stated, as in most treatises it is, the theorem is false. That effect will not be produced unless the body of money thus composed of heavy and of light coins, is itself in excess of the needs of the community, as determined by the law of the territorial distribution of money, which has been stated. In a country in which money is, according to this standard, deficient, a light coin may have, by reason of that deficiency, a higher purchasing power than a heavy coin in a country in which money is in excess.†

182. The Value Denominator, usually called the Measure

---

* From Sir Thomas Gresham, founder of the Royal Exchange of London. Died 1579.

† Mr. Ricardo clearly expressed this necessary qualification of Gresham's Theorem, but, in doing so, has been followed by few writers. It is, he says, "a mistaken theory to suppose that guineas of 5 dwt. 8 grains, can not circulate with guineas of 5 dwt., or less. As they might be in such limited quantities that both the one and the other might actually pass in currency for a value equal to 5 dwt. 10 grains, there would be no temptation to withdraw either from circulation; there would be a real profit in retaining them."

of Value.—Thus far we have spoken of but one function of money, that of the Medium of Exchange, and we have written as if there were but one. This has been for the purpose of fixing the reader's attention strongly on the work of money, as the medium of exchange.

In addition to this function of money, however, nearly all economists are agreed in recognizing another independent and co-ordinate function of money, viz., as a "Measure of Value." "A second difficulty," says Professor Jevons, "arises in barter. *At what rate* is any exchange to be made? If a certain quantity of beef be given for a certain quantity of corn, and, in a like manner corn be exchanged for cheese, and cheese for eggs, and eggs for flax, and so on, still the question will arise —how much beef for how much flax, or how much of any one commodity for a given quantity of another? In a state of barter, *the price current list* would be a most complicated document, for each commodity would have to be quoted in terms of every other commodity, or else complicated rule-of-three sums would be necessary. Between 100 articles there must exist no less than 4950 possible ratios of exchange. All such trouble is avoided if any one commodity be chosen, and its ratio of exchange with each commodity be quoted. Knowing how much corn is to be bought for a pound of silver, and, also, how much flax for the same quantity of silver, we learn without further trouble how much corn exchanges for so much flax. *The chosen commodity becomes a common denominator or common measure of value*, in terms of which we estimate the value of all other goods, so that their values become capable of the most easy comparison."

183.—An Incidental and Subordinate Function.—Admitting the importance of having a value-denominator, in which the prices of all articles shall be expressed, we can not admit that this constitutes a separate and independent function of money, since it is evident that gold or silver, or any other article, can only serve as a value-denominator by and through being used as the medium of exchange.* It is only because

* Hence we see the error of Prof. Bowen's statement: "We can do without money as a medium of exchange, and can even barter commod-

silver, for instance, is, in fact successively exchanged against all the articles in the market that the respective values of these articles, in terms of silver, become known, and that it, hence, becomes possible to make up the price-current with 100 specifications, *e. g.*, and not with 4950. Instead of this being an independent and co-ordinate function of money, therefore, it is merely an advantage resulting from the use of money as the medium of exchange. It is, at most, an incidental and subordinate function. The better statement, still, would be that money serves as

I. The Medium of Exchange:

(a) Dispensing with the double coincidence required in barter.

(b) Furnishing a value-denominator.

184.—II. The Standard of Deferred Payments, usually Called the Standard of Value.—We have seen that it is of the essence of a sale for money, that the producer, or whoever at the time stands in the place of the producer, parts with his product, receiving therefor something which he does not expect personally to consume. His reason for receiving this article in exchange for his product is that with it he expects to obtain, in time and place and amount most suitable to his convenience, that which he shall desire to consume. In other words, he, by the act of exchange, defers his own consumption of the equivalent of his product, taking a piece or pieces of money, as a sort of certificate or pledge that he shall receive such an equivalent whenever he gets ready to enjoy it. It was in this view of money that Adam Smith said: "A guinea may be considered as a bill for a certain quantity of necessaries or conveniences upon all the tradesmen of the neighborhood." *

---

ities for other commodities without the use of any medium. But we can not do without money as a common standard or measure of value." Were we to do without money in the former capacity, we should perforce have to do without it in the latter, inasmuch as it is only by being actually used as a medium of exchange, that the power of money to purchase each commodity by turns became known.

* Prof. Senior calls money "Abstract Wealth."

It will appear that, looking toward the satisfaction of the producer's wants, a sale for money is only half a transaction. He sells his product for money, and must, in turn, sell, so to speak, his money for the product of others, such as he may desire personally to consume. To do this, however, though a two-fold transaction, requires far less of time and labor, and involves far less liability to ultimate disappointment, than the attempt to secure the "double coincidence of wants and of possessions," spoken of in par. 161.

185. Money a Pledge of Future Enjoyment.—But while, in the very act of a sale for money, the producer defers his acquisition of the products of others, the question, when that acquisition shall be realized, remains for himself alone to answer. He has the money, and whenever he chooses to step into a shop and lay it down upon the counter, he may take his equivalent then and there, whether in meat or flour or groceries or clothes or tools for his trade.

186. Sales on Credit.—We are now to contemplate transactions of a different character, which give rise to a new function of money, viz., exchanges where the equivalent is not, at the time, received by the seller of goods; but where future payment is promised. These transactions are known as Sales on Credit, because the willingness of the producer to part with his goods, without at the time receiving an equivalent, depends upon the credit of the purchaser, or the degree of confidence attaching to his word or his bond. In such a case, the purchaser's character for honesty, his responsibility, as measured by the amount of his possessions, and the efficiency of the law in enforcing payments, all must be taken into account.

187. The vast extension of credit-sales under the modern organization of trade, makes a new and very important requirement upon that article which is to be used as money, viz., that, in addition to being conveniently portable, not liable to deterioration or accidental injury, easily subdivided, etc., it shall be reasonably stable in value. Where a man takes money in his hand as the equivalent of the product sold, which we call a sale for cash, he has no anxiety on this account. He may exchange his money for goods the same day. If not, it is because he does not choose to do so. The matter rests with him. But if a man is to forbear payment for a considerable time, it becomes of great importance that he should know what that which he is to receive at a distant date will be worth to him when he gets it. On the day of the sale, the money which is stipulated is worth the goods; otherwise, the sale would not have taken place. On the day of payment, the money may be conceivably worth twice the goods, or only half the goods. The risk of some undeserved loss, the chances of some unearned gain, are inherent in the nature of sales on credit. Whether that risk of loss or chance of gain shall be great or small, will depend on the degree of stability which attaches to the value of the article used in that community, during that period, as money.

It is evident that articles which might be equally well fitted for use as money in sales for cash, that is, which might be otherwise equally well fitted to serve as the medium of exchange, may be very differently qualified to serve as what we call the Standard of Deferred Payments.

188. The Grains and the Metals.—Thus, if we compare the grains and the metals, we note that the former are quickly consumed, the greater part in the first year, all within the second year; while the latter last, even in active use, many years. The average "life" of iron may perhaps be stated at fifteen to twenty years; the life of copper is much longer, and that of gold and silver covers several human generations.

From these facts it results that, if the production of any grain, *e. g.*, corn or wheat, falls off considerably, in any year, through excess or deficiency of moisture or heat, the value of that grain will rise rapidly, it may be to an inordinate height. The production of gold or silver, and, in a lower degree, of copper or iron, might be sensibly diminished for years without greatly affecting the quantity and, by consequence, the value of the existing stock.

Now, if wheat were to be used as money, it would not infrequently happen that, in the irregular alternation of good and bad harvests, a producer selling his goods on one or two years' credit, would, when the payment came to be made, receive one-half as much more, or even twice as much in value, as he would have received had the payment been made at the time of the sale; or he might receive only two-thirds or even only one-half what his goods were then worth. Nor could the injuries which the producer might suffer by receiving less than the value of the goods he parted with, be trusted to be compensated by the unearned gains he might make at other times. So irregular and unaccountable is the occurrence of bad seasons, that one man might have nearly all bad luck and another nearly all good luck. The former might be ruined, bankrupted, and driven out of his shop or farm, before the tide turned in his favor. As many as seven successive bad seasons have been known in England. On the other hand, the metals are not subject to frequent value variations of great extent, though liable to incessant oscillations of moderate range. Gold and silver, especially, on account of their high degree of durability, are almost exempt from the influence of the production of a single year.

189. Fluctuations in the Value of the Precious Metals.— But while the precious metals are thus almost a perfect "standard of deferred payments," from one year to another, they are yet subject to great periodic variations from generation to generation and from century to century. The production of the precious metals is of the most spasmodic character. At times, a flood of gold, or of silver, or of both, has poured from newly-opened mines, as after the discovery of the mines of Potosi in 1545, and of the mines of California almost coincidently with those of Australia, in 1849-51; at times, on the other hand, mining industry has almost wholly ceased, either from the exhaustion of known deposits, or as the result of war or civil disturbance. Such a cessation of mining industry followed the invasion of the Roman Empire by the Teutonic tribes. The series of revolutions and insurrections in the Spanish American States, beginning in 1809, destroyed the mining machinery, scattered the mining populations, and closed the mines of regions which had previously been among the most prolific sources of the world's supply of metallic money. In agriculture, however, while incessant fluctuations in the supply of the grains, even those most largely and widely planted, result from the mutability of the climate, the changes from generation to generation, and from century to century, are not so far reaching.

The vast breadth of arable land of reasonably uniform quality; the simplicity of the processes of agriculture, and the wide diffusion of the art of tillage; the comparative immunity of the soil amid ravages which greatly impair, perhaps permanently cripple, manufacturing, and in an even greater degree, mining industry; the limited applicability of the principle of the division of labor to agriculture and the relative inefficiency of machinery in its operations: these causes combine to render bread-corn, in truth, what Francis Horner pronounced it to be, "the real and paramount standard of all values."

190. Corn Rents.—The superior stability of value of the cereals, through long periods of time, has led to the suggestion that, in the case of contracts extending over considerable terms of years, grain should be adopted as the standard for determining the obligations of the debtor, the rights of the creditor. To a limited extent this has been done; but the tendency to express the consideration of all sales in terms of that which is the current money of daily use in the community is so strong that few persons, even of those who are acting as trustees, take the trouble thus to guard the interests they represent. The manifest convenience of having that for the standard of deferred payments which is also the medium of current exchanges, the indolence and want of initiative in the mass of mankind, perhaps, also, a superstitious regard for the precious metals, combine to withstand the reasons which urge the expression of rents, interest and annuities in terms of some leading grain, in the case of long leases, permanent loans and fixed charges upon land.

191. Multiple or Tabular Standard.—It has even been proposed to go further, in the effort to avoid those undeserved losses which result to debtors or to creditors, from changes which take place in the value of even the precious metals through long periods of time. The scheme for a multiple standard or tabular standard, to form which a great number of articles should be joined together, in order that their individual value-variations may offset each other, was, early in the century, suggested by writers in England and Germany, and has more recently been advocated by Prof. Jevons of the former, and by Prof. Roscher of the latter country. This proposed scheme will be briefly discussed in Part VI.

CHAPTER IV.

MONEY AND ITS VALUE—CONTINUED—DEBASED COIN: SEIGNIORAGE.

192. Debased Coin.—We now approach a question which should be decided entirely upon the principles regulating the value of money already laid down, yet which is the subject of so much misconception, which has been so covered-over with false reasoning and which is so sure to arouse prejudice and passion, that it is needful for the teacher to accompany the student over the ground, and, if possible, save him from the pitfalls and quagmires into which trained logicians and practiced writers have fallen. Prof. Jevons has remarked that a kind of intellectual vertigo attacks all who treat this fatal theme of money; and we have now reached the point where most people lose their heads. The beginner ought not to be left to find his way here alone, even if he has already been provided with the chart and compass to guide his steps.

193. Seigniorage.—The most safe and convenient entrance to this land of gins, and snares, and griefs, is through seigniorage. That term has long been applied to the amount of metal abstracted by government, or the lord, the seignior, before coinage. Seigniorage may be of two kinds, or rather two degrees.

1. When the cost, either actual or approximate, of coinage is taken out, and thus the state or the lord is reimbursed for the expense.

2. When more metal than is necessary to repay the expense of coinage is abstracted; and thus the state or the lord makes a profit by the coinage.

194. Cost of Coinage.—Let us consider the first. Shall the value of the coin be computed according to the market value of the contained metal, viewed as so much bullion, or shall the cost of the mintage be added to the value of the metal? For instance, if the expense of making the coin called a dollar be one cent, shall the coin contain a hundred cents' worth of gold or silver, or shall it contain only ninety-nine cents' worth, and the cost of the coinage be added to make up the dollar?

On this point the opinions of economists and the practice of governments differ. Although the question involved is not wholly economic in its nature, but is in part matter of political and fiscal expediency, we will here briefly state the arguments on the one side and the other.

On the one hand, it is said that gold and silver, being wanted in the form of coins, are, for that reason, worth more in coin than in bullion. Serving an additional use as coined money, they are the subjects of a demand over and above what exists for uncoined bullion, a larger demand justifying a higher price.

It is urged that there is no more reason why gold in coin should not be valued higher than gold in bars, than there is why gold in bars should not be valued higher than gold imbedded in quartz. Note the treatment of the other metals, it is said: Iron is sold in the form of plates, rivets, rods, and chains, at more than the price of iron in the pig. In the same way, if gold in coin costs more, and is more useful than in ingots, those who want it in the form of coin, and not the whole community, should pay for the coinage.

Moreover, it is urged, if such a charge be not made, a vast amount of metal will alternately be coined and melted down, recoined, and again melted. A seigniorage charge will put a premium upon the exportation or melting of coin so that bullion will be taken instead.

195. Gratuitous Coinage.—It was in this view that Dudley North called gratuitous coinage * "a perpetual motion found out, whereby to melt and coin, without ceasing, and so feed goldsmiths and coiners at the public charge."

In the face of these considerations, however, some of the greatest commercial nations, England foremost among them, have maintained gratuitous coinage. Nor is this course wholly without economic justification.

It is said that, while the expense of equipping, officering, and operating a mint is large, the difference in expense caused by minting more or fewer coins, is very small. For this, it is argued, the country establishing gratuitous coinage is compensated by the instantaneousness with which the export of gold follows the slightest accumulation in excess of the wants of trade.

196. Seigniorage in Excess of Cost of Coinage.—So much for seigniorage which only covers the cost of coinage.† We

---

* The distinction between gratuitous coinage and free coinage, is not sufficiently observed. Where no seigniorage charge is made, but the coin contains the full amount of bullion which corresponds to its mint value, *i. e.*, when the dollar contains one hundred cents' worth of metal, that is gratuitous coinage. Free coinage exists, where any owner of bullion has the right to have it coined on the same terms as the government, or as any other citizen, whether with or without a seigniorage charge. Thus free coinage exists in England in regard to gold. Any subject can bring gold, in any amount, to the mint and have it made into gold coin; but free coinage does not exist with respect to silver, that metal being coined only in such amounts as the Government, through the Bank, deems necessary for supplying the people of the Kingdom with "change."

In the United States free coinage exists also in regard to gold; but the coinage of silver is restricted. By the law of 1878, the Secretary of the Treasury must coin two millions of silver dollars a month, and may coin four millions, but no more. The coinage of half and quarter dollars, and of smaller pieces of silver, is governed by the same principle as in England. During the continuance of the bi-metallic system (Part VI) in the states of the "Latin Union" (France, Italy, Belgium, and Switzerland), free coinage existed in regard to both metals. The coinage of silver is now restricted in those countries.

† M. Chevalier has proposed to apply the term *Brassage* to the charge for the actual cost of coinage.

have now to speak of mint charges which exceed that cost, and become a source of revenue to the state. In the old days of high prerogative, kings frequently made their sole right of coinage a means of profit. In England, during the reign of Edward IV., the seigniorage on gold was above 13 per cent.; during the reign of Henry VII., it once rose to 16 per cent. These, however, were exceptional instances in England. In France, in Italy, and in most of the countries of continental Europe, before the great revival of modern commerce, debasement of the coin was a favorite resort of weak or profligate monarchs. Both in quantity and quality, in weight and in fineness, the circulating money was pinched and robbed, until the actual amount of pure metal bore sometimes a ludicrously small ratio to the original fine contents of the coin. The English "pound" was once a pound-weight of silver. The pound of standard silver is now coined into 66, instead of 20 shillings. The "pound scots," of which we read, had but $\frac{1}{36}$ of its original weight. The florin and the Spanish maravedi were once pieces of gold. The former is now a piece of silver; the latter a piece of copper.

197. What is the Effect of Seigniorage on the Purchasing Power of Coin?—On this subject I follow Mr. Ricardo without deviation, believing that he was the economist who most fully and justly apprehended the relations of money to price; and that departure from the principles laid down by that great thinker leads to confusion, misconception and needless controversy.

Let us suppose that a certain country requires for the purposes of domestic trade 1,000,000 pieces, each containing 100 grains of fine gold. This would involve the use of 100,000,000 grains of gold as money; and a certain average level of prices would result from the relation between this amount (its rate of circulation being assumed constant, for the purposes of the following illustration), and the demand for money arising from the exchanges actually requiring to be effected by the use of money.

Now, suppose the principle of seigniorage to be introduced, the sovereign, out of every hundred grains brought to the mint, taking one to repay the actual cost of coinage, putting into circulation 1,000,000 pieces of 99 grains each, and placing 1,000,000 grains in his storehouse as treasure, or causing it to be manufactured into plate or ornament. There are now only 99,000,000 grains of gold in circulation, but the same number of pieces, each of the same "mint-value," *i. e.*, 100 grains.

Will each piece now purchase as much of other commodities as before, or less?

I answer, as much. There is the same demand for pieces for the purposes of exchange; there is the same supply; the same prices must result.

But suppose the sovereign proceeds further, and takes, not one grain, but ten, from every hundred, issuing 1,000,000 pieces of only 90 grains each. Will the purchasing power of each piece be affected? Not in the least. There is the same demand for pieces, the same supply. People still want pieces of money; can only get them by giving commodities for them; have as many commodities and no fewer to give; and there are just as many pieces and no more to be obtained in this way.

198. Excessive Issues.—But let us take a step in a different direction. Let us suppose that the sovereign, instead of placing in his treasury the 10,000,000 grains which he took under his right of seigniorage, coins this gold also into pieces of 90 grains each, and pays them out for personal or public expenses. What will be the result? Depreciation will at once begin. The 90,000,000 grains, when coined into the same number of pieces of the same official (mint) denomination as the 100,000,000 had been, retained the same purchasing power; but when the 100,000,000 are coined into a larger number of pieces, the purchasing power of each piece at once falls.

199. Ricardo's Statement.—"While the state alone coins," says Mr. Ricardo, "there can be no limit to this charge of seigniorage; for, by limiting the quantity of coin, it can be raised to any conceivable value."

"On the same principle," he remarks, "viz., by a limitation

of quantity, a debased coin would circulate at the value it should bear if it were of legal weight and fineness, and not at the value of the quantity of metal it actually contained."

"In the history of the British coinage," he continues, "we find, accordingly, that the currency was never depreciated in the same proportion that it was debased, the reason for which was that it was never increased in quantity, in proportion to its diminished intrinsic value."

Mr. Ricardo did not flinch from the assumption of a seigniorage of 50 per cent. "There can," he asserted, "exist no depreciation of money, but from excess. However debased a coinage may become, it will preserve its mint value; that is to say, it will pass in circulation for the intrinsic value of the bullion which it ought to contain, provided it be not in too great abundance."

This doctrine, which has proved "a hard saying" to many economists, a stumbling-block and a rock of offense to many readers, is, it will be observed, merely the rigorous, courageous application of the principle that the value of money is determined solely by the relation between demand and supply. I believe it to be the true doctrine of monetary circulation.

It is not to be thought that Mr. Ricardo advocated a seigniorage in excess of the cost of coinage. "The limits beyond which a seigniorage can not be advantageously extended," he says, "are the actual expenses incurred in manufacturing the coin." The objections to a debased coinage are two: First, inasmuch as the mint value of such coins is above the value of the bullion they contain, the excess of such coins in circulation may proceed to a high degree, producing mischievous effects upon trade and industry, before exportation begins, since, for use in foreign lands, the coins have value only according to the amount of pure metal in them. Secondly, the practice of reducing the amount of bullion in the coins is deemed to be a dangerous one, because there is no point at which we can be sure it will stop. Every fiscal exigency of the government will suggest fresh attacks upon the integrity of the coin.

These objections, the first of which alone is based upon economic principles, are precisely those which we shall see (pars. 441-445)offered to the issue of inconvertible paper money.

200. The Omitted Proviso to Ricardo's Statement.—There is one proviso which should be attached to any statement of Mr. Ricardo's theorem regarding the value of debased coin. That Mr. Ricardo failed himself thus to qualify his proposition "that, however debased a coinage may become, it will preserve its mint value," has caused much misapprehension of his views. The required proviso has already been intimated (par. 172), when we were speaking of causes which may diminish the demand for money.

If debasement of the coin be carried so far and carried on so long that a popular reluctance to receive the money pieces be generated, sufficient to cause men to modify or limit their production in order to avoid exchanges, or to cause them to encounter the inconveniences of barter rather than handle the distrusted coin, then depreciation may result. That is, the supply of money will become excessive through the blow inflicted upon the demand for money. But this can happen on no other condition; and a popular reluctance to receive coins is not a necessary consequence of debasement. Why do men take money at all? We said, in first describing the money function, that it is not because they have, at the time, any personal use for the gold or silver or iron or leather, or paper, or wood, of which it may be composed; but it is taken as a means of obtaining, in due time and place, that which they do desire to consume. Men take money because they believe others will, in turn, take it from them. If a man be only assured of this, he has no reason to care, in fact he does not care, what the money is made of, what the coin contains.

201. Depreciation not a Necessary Result of Debasement.—Let us suppose the coin of a country, without being increased in amount, to be debased three per cent., and the fact to become known. The habit of accepting the coin is strong; the acquired momentum of the circulating mass is great; men must (1) either take the coins in exchange for their products, or (2) they must cease to produce; or (3) they must change their industry and produce that which does not need to be exchanged, *i. e.*, that which they will themselves consume ; or (4) they must resort to barter. Now, any one of the latter courses involves an initial loss, greater, doubtless, much greater, than any possible loss in receiving coin debased three per cent. For this reason men continue to receive the coin, or, more properly, they continue to receive it without reasoning at all about the matter, having been accustomed to take it freely. If any man, more thoughtful than his fellows, hesitates to accept the money pieces, his doubts vanish on beholding all around him receiving it without demur. That is all he needs. If others will take the coins from him, his own occasions will, in turn, be answered. He does not want to eat the coins, or to make them into jewelry, but to use them in buying the necessaries of life. If they will do that, they are good enough for him. And so a full and free acceptance of a debased coinage might be established, in spite of a momentary feeling of reluctance, or even without such a feeling arising at all. Just this condition of things has existed, in many a country, many a time.

Suppose that, after the community has become accustomed to a seigniorage of three per cent., some exigency of government, or the greed of the prince, should lead to a further equal debasement of the coin, making a total of six per cent. In that event, either the habit of accepting the coin of the realm would maintain the circulation of the debased money, or, if that circulation were to be challenged by popular objection, then the question would be presented to every man, as before, whether he would take this debased coin, or cease producing, in whole or in part, or change his industry so as to produce articles which would not require to be exchanged, or, lastly, resort to barter. It might easily happen that to do any one of the things last spoken of would cost any producer more than the possible loss by accepting coin debased three per cent. further; and, so, a full and free circulation of the debased coin might be maintained.

202. And it is to be borne in mind that this coin circulates at its mint-value, not at a discount of six per cent., or of any other rate. There is no reason why the coin should be subjected to a discount. Assuming, as we have done, that the habits of the people in regard to production and trade have not been, as yet, changed by the debasement of the coinage, there are just as many goods to be exchanged as before. Just as many money-pieces are, therefore, needed, while no more money-pieces are to be had, since we have all along made the condition that the metal abstracted by the government should not be put into new coins.

203. Depreciation Results from Excessive Issues. — But now let us suppose that, when the debasement has proceeded to the extent of ten per cent., government takes the gold and silver it has abstracted, and issues it in the form of new coin debased like the other. Immediately depreciation will set in. The value of money, like the value of any thing else, is determined by the relation between demand and supply. The goods to be exchanged for money pieces remaining the same in amount, and the number of pieces having been increased, the purchasing power of each piece falls.

So far the effect is the same as in the case of an excess of full-metal coin ; but, as depreciation proceeds, the essential difference between the two kinds of money appears. With an excess of full-metal coin, exportation begins at once. The country becomes a good market to sell in, a bad market to buy in, both for the same reason, viz., prices are higher there ; and the course of exchange will speedily bring in the remedy. With debased coin, however, no outlet is afforded until the depreciation reaches the point when the 90 grains of fine metal in the coin will bring more abroad, melted down, than the coin (though of the mint-value of 100 grains) will bring at home. Within this limit, depreciation may proceed without remedy.

204. Inflation.—A permanent excess of the circulating money of a country, over that country's distributive share of the money of the commercial world, is called inflation. Its influence on industry and trade, and on the distribution of wealth, will be discussed hereafter.

CHAPTER V.

INCONVERTIBLE PAPER MONEY.

205. In monetary science, the true entrance to paper money is through seigniorage. If we have rightly apprehended the relations of seigniorage to the circulation of coin, and to prices, we need have no difficulty in dealing with any question arising under the present title.

"The whole charge for paper money may be considered as seigniorage." This remark of Mr. Ricardo is true and very significant. We have seen that the State may withhold from the coin one per cent. of the pure metal, to cover the cost of coinage; that it may withold ten per cent., as a means of securing revenue for the treasury; that the State may go further and, by successive invasions of the coin, take out two-thirds of the money metal, as in the case of the English pound sterling, or all but three per cent., as in the case of the pound Scots; that it may even go further still and substitute copper for gold, as in the case of the Spanish maravedi.

Now let the last step be taken in the same direction, and, instead of pieces of metal, let the public treasury issue pieces of paper bearing the names of the superseded coins, and we shall have a body of money governed by precisely the same principles, alike as to circulation and as to the resulting prices of commodities, as a debased coinage. Paper money is money upon which the seigniorage charge is one hundred per cent.

206. Historical Instances of Inconvertible Paper Money.—The invention of paper money, like many another great discovery, is traced to the orient. When Marco Polo visited China in the twelfth century, he found in circulation a money consisting of pieces cut from the inner bark of the mulberry tree. These were issued "with as much solemnity and authority as if they were of pure gold and silver." A century later, one of the rulers of Persia introduced paper money in direct imitation of the Chinese, the imitation extending even to devices and names; but the experiment here was less fortunate than the Chinese experiment, since, after two or three days of enforced circulation, the markets were closed, the people rose, the officials were massacred, and the money disappeared. A century later, we hear of paper money in Japan.

It took the duller-witted races of Europe some centuries more to comprehend the mysteries of paper money; and meanwhile princes had to content themselves, when hard-up, with operating upon the coin, swearing their coiners not to divulge the secrets of the mint, and juggling their people just as far as the omnipresent scales and acids of the banker would permit. But when paper money became once fairly introduced into Europe, it was, like some of those other inventions and discoveries referred to, rapidly improved in its details and extended in its applications.

An eminent writer on finance, M. Wolowski, claims for his native country of Poland the proud distinction, as he regards it, of having been the only nation in Europe which has given no example of the issue of paper money; but it is to be remembered that Poland lost her independence a long while ago. Had she survived to the present time, it is not unfair to believe she would have her paper money history equally with the gigantic neighbors who crushed out her national life.

Of the present States of Europe, all which border on the Mediterranean, excepting France and Italy, have inconvertible paper money, issued by government. Russia, though both a northern and a southern State, casts in its lot with the Mediterranean nations in this respect. The northern tier of countries, Great Britain, France, Belgium, Holland, Germany, and Scandinavia, have paper money, indeed, but of that class which we shall describe, under a subsequent title, as Bank Money.

207. Characteristics of Inconvertible Paper Money.— The kind of money of which we are writing may either be issued originally by the State, as in the case of the present paper money of most of the southern States of Europe already mentioned; as in the case of the "assignats" and "mandats" of the French revolutionary epoch; as in the the case of the "Continental currency" of the American revolution, and of the "Greenbacks" and "Confederate notes" of the war of secession ; or, secondly, it may result from the degeneration of bank money, originally issued with the character of convertibility, but, by some exigency of government or stress of commercial misfortune, losing that character, and protected in its inconvertibility by law, as in the case of the English Bank money of the "Restriction" (1797—1821), as in the case of the notes of the Bank of France during the revolution of 1848, and, again, during and after the war of 1870-71, and as in numerous other cases of minor importance.

Generally speaking, forced circulation is an attribute of this sort of money, though that character may be disguised, especially in the case of degenerated bank money, by one artifice or another. For instance, the money may not be made legal tender, but all remedy at law may be taken away from creditors who refuse to receive it.

Paper may be declared to be redeemable in coin ; that promise may even be borne upon the face of the paper ; but if provision be not made so that, in fact, every holder of a note can obtain coined money therefor at will, the paper is inconvertible. If any conditions to redemption are interposed, it is none the less inconvertible than if redemption were not even promised.

The pledge of public lands or stocks for ultimate payment, makes no difference, in this respect. No paper money is convertible, the full, immediate and unconditional redemption of which is not, at all times, within the choice of the holder.

208. Is this Properly Called Money?—American economists have generally agreed to deny the title, money, to such issues. Indeed it is as much as one's reputation for economic orthodoxy is worth, to concede that inconvertible paper may become money.

If we seek a reason for this attitude of the economists, we find that it is because they deprecate the use of such a "circulating medium," deeming it mischievous, pernicious, destructive of industrial and social well-being. But, as I have ventured elsewhere to remark, it would be as reasonable to deny that whisky is drink, because we deprecate its use as drink, as to deny that inconvertible notes are money because we deprecate their use as money.

The economists have dealt with the subject as if the question were necessarily this, money or not money? money being assumed to be, not only a good thing in general, but always beneficial, in all relations and under all circumstances. And, inasmuch as they think they have shown (in which I fully agree with them), that the use of inconvertible paper produces very injurious effects, they deny that it is entitled to be called money.

According to the views presented in this treatise, the sole test of money is the performance of the money function. As has been said, that which does the money-work is the money-thing. If it does this work well, it is good money; if it does this work ill, it is bad money.

209. May Paper Money Serve as the Common Medium of Exchange?—About this there can, I conceive, be no doubt whatever. Take the United States "Greenbacks" of 1862 to 1879. Did producers accept them readily in full payment for goods? Yes, with the utmost readiness. Did men resort to barter to avoid the use of this medium of exchange? No. Did men refuse to produce, or contract their production, or modify it, lest they should have to receive those circulating notes in payment? Again, no.

There never had been a period in our history when the division of labor was carried further; when the differentiation of industry and the diversification of production went on more rapidly. This is the sure test of the performance of the money function. The differentiation of industry and the diversification of production involve increasingly the use of money. Whenever production is being enlarged and diversified, there, without any question, something is acting successfully as the medium of exchange.

Observe that it is not now a question of prices, of how many dollars in greenbacks were required in 1864 or 1874 to buy what ten dollars in gold would have purchased in 1860, or would purchase at the present time. That, as we have seen, is a matter of the volume and rapidity of circulation. The question now, is simply as to the freedom and fullness of circulation.

It is not asserted that such paper is always and everywhere money. It becomes money when it begins to do the money-work; it remains money as long as it continues to do that work; it falls out of the category of money when it ceases to do that work. After the American Congress had issued the "Continental" money in such quantity that even the treasury ceased to keep a record of the issues, and the value had sunk to 200:1 of silver, there is no question that, for a short period before the notes finally disappeared and silver came back, the notes ceased to be money. Men would not take them; modified their production, or curtailed it to avoid the necessity of taking the discredited paper; resorted increasingly to barter, in spite of all its inconveniences. The same fate befell the French "mandats" after the revolutionary authorities had issued "assignats" to an amount popularly stated at forty-five thousand millions of francs. The Confederate notes ceased to be money upon the collapse of the government that issued them.

210. May Paper Money serve as the Value Denominator?—It is at this point that the economists appear to me most deeply in error, insisting, as they do, that here is something which metal money does, but paper money can not do.

It was said, in the last chapter, that money, in performing the function now in question, is commonly spoken of as the "Measure of Value." Now, what money does in this connection is no more than to serve as the common denominator of values, as described by Prof. Jevons, in par. 182. It was shown in the pages immediately following, that this function is not a separate and independent function of money, but a purely incidental and subordinate function; that not only is any thing which is competent to serve as the general medium of exchange, adequate also to serve as the common denomintor of values; but that any thing which does, in fact, serve as the medium of exchange, must, in the very act and part of doing so, create the price-current, which is what is sought under this title.*

* The idea that values are "measured" by money, has a great deal of tenacity. A somewhat more extended discussion of this question will be found in my work on Money, Chap. XIV.

If corn, beef, wool, potatoes, coal, and all other articles in the market are daily exchanged for that one article—money—no matter of what it consists, or why it became money, we have, as the direct result of those transactions, the means of comparing the values of corn, beef, wool, and all other articles: that is, we have our price-current. If all those articles are exchanged against pieces of paper, we obtain their exchanging proportions just as really, just as accurately, readily and intelligibly, as when they are exchanged against pieces of gold, silver or copper. If one article brings three pieces of paper, another ten, another eight, we learn the comparative value of those articles as quickly and easily as if the first brought three pieces of silver, the second ten, and the third eight.

211. May Paper Money Serve as the Standard of Deferred Payments?—We have seen that paper money may become the general medium of exchange, being taken as freely and eagerly as money of silver or gold. We have also seen that whatever serves as the general medium of exchange does, by that very fact, serve, also, as the common denominator of values, furnishing the price-current from which are determined the exchanging proportions of all commodities in the market.

That paper money may serve as the standard of deferred payments goes without saying. As was stated under a previous title, forced circulation is generally an attribute of this sort of money, and where that is the case, such money becomes, by definition, the standard of deferred payments. By it the obligation of the debtor, the claim of the creditor, is measured, as of course. Even where paper money is not made legal tender, it is almost, if not quite, as likely to become the standard of deferred payments as a money of silver or gold. The tendency to express the consideration of all sales in terms of that which is the current money of daily use, is so strong that few persons, even of those who are acting as trustees, will take the trouble to make leases, rents, annuities or interest upon loans payable in any thing but the ordinary circulating medium of the time.

The notes of the Bank of England were not legal tender, in the ordinary sense, during the period of the "Restriction"; yet, though they ceased to be convertible in 1797, the first instance, so far as I am aware, of a refusal to accept such notes in payment of debts, was that of Lord King, in 1811; and this refusal took place, as Lord King claimed, not from any selfish motive, but purely in order that, by strongly attracting public attention to the unfortunate monetary condition of the kingdom, he might promote the resumption of specie payments.

During the circulation of the legal tender greenbacks in the United States, every person who wished to make contracts for future payments in terms of gold or silver, was at liberty to do so; yet it is notorious that few took advantage of their legal right in this respect. That which had become, no matter how, the current money of daily use became, for that reason alone, the almost universal standard of deferred payments.

It is another question whether paper money performs this function with justice to debtor and creditor, or with advantage to the general community. That question we shall meet further on.

212. What Determines the Value of Paper Money?— What determines the value of any kind of money? What determines the value of any thing? Demand and supply. The demand for money is, as we saw (par. 170), the amount of money-work to be done, the amount of exchanging requiring to be effected through the use of money. The supply of money is the money-force available to do the money-work. It is compounded of the volume of the circulating money and the rate of circulation. Supposing the occasion for the use of money—the demand—to remain the same, and the rate of the circulation of paper to be the same as that of metal, the value of a body of paper money would be the same as that of a body of money consisting of as many pieces of metal as there were pieces of paper, the pieces being of the same "denominations," whether stamped with the mint-press or the printing-press.

We said: "Supposing the rate of circulation of paper to be the same as that of metal." I am aware of no reason for supposing that any difference in the rate of circulation of metal money, on the one hand, and of paper money on the other, would exist, if all other conditions were alike, of sufficient importance to be taken into account. The paper would, of course, be handled somewhat more easily, would be remitted by mail or parcel-delivery somewhat more readily and safely, and thus a thousand dollars, so-called, in paper would do somewhat more money-work than a thousand dollars in metal. The difference in that respect would, however, not be important.

We may accordingly drop this proviso. We also said: "Supposing the occasion for the use of money—the demand—to remain the same." Will the demand for money be affected by the substitution of paper for metal? The popular opinion undoubtedly is that the mere fact of the emission of inconvertible paper produces discredit, so that such money, irrespective of any excess, at once becomes distrusted and avoided.

213. Depreciation not a necessary consequence of Inconvertibility.—The opinion above stated is unfounded. We saw (par. 201) that depreciation is not a necessary result of debasement of the coin. Not only will the same line of reasoning establish the proposition that depreciation is not a necessary result of the issue of inconvertible paper; but historical instances not a few exist of such paper money maintaining itself for a time in circulation without discredit and without depreciation. It is undoubtedly true, as Prof. Bonamy Price asserts, that "experience has proved that it need not of necessity suffer any depreciation of value."*

* On a point so vital it may be well to add authority to reason, especially as current American literature misrepresents the real purport of economic opinion on this subject.

Mr. Thomas Tooke, the most eminent economic statistician of the world, explicitly and repeatedly states that depreciation is not a necessary consequence of inconvertibility.

Mr. James Wilson, founder of the London *Economist*, and a states-

214. Inconvertible Paper always issued as Cheap Money. —The moving cause in the issue of inconvertible paper money has been its cheapness, as compared with the metal money which it has replaced. Whatever excellencies may have been reflectively discovered in such money after it had come into circulation, I am not aware that the institution of such money has been due, in an individual instance, to any other virtual reason than that which has been expressed.

We saw that the sovereign first pinched the coin, say, one per cent., under the name of seigniorage, to meet the cost of coinage, and then, finding the opportunity too tempting, took out it might be five, it might be fifteen per cent., or even more, for his own benefit. The issue of paper money, is in effect, the exaction of a seigniorage of one hundred per cent. At times, that exaction has been made in cold blood, at the dictate of avarice; at times, and indeed, more often, the exaction has appeared to be justified, if not sanctified* by some great exigency of national life.

---

man and financier of wide experience, declares that if the amount of inconvertible paper be properly regulated, "there is no reason whatever why such notes should suffer depreciation."

M. Courcelle-Seneuil, a French writer on Finance, whose views are entitled to much consideration, expresses the opinion that if the emissions of paper money be moderate, they may have the same value as metallic money.

I have made use of three names of the first rank in the economics of finance. Let me now quote, at greater length, the most illustrious writer known to monetary science.

"The whole charge for paper money," says Mr. Ricardo, "may be considered as seigniorage. Though it has no intrinsic value, yet by limiting its quantity, its value in exchange is as great as an equal denomination of coin, or of bullion in that coin. It is not necessary that paper money should be payable in specie to secure its value; it is only necessary that its quantity should be regulated according to the value of the metal which is declared to be the standard."

* Hence the phrase the "the blood-stained Greenback." Lest I should be misunderstood, let me say that it is my firm belief that the issue of inconvertible paper money is never a sound measure of finance, no matter what the stress of the national exigency may be. I believe it to be as surely a mistaken policy as the resort of an athlete to the brandy bottle. It means mischief always. If there is ever a time when a nation needs

215. Without any such stress of fiscal necessities as those caused by war, paper money has been frequently issued by governments as a fiscal resource, to enable public works to be created, to meet an unexpected deficiency of revenue, or even, as in the case of some of the early American colonies, to set bounties on manufactures or the fisheries. There is always a great temptation, to statesmen and to people alike, in times of emergency, in the knowledge that it is possible to replace a money of high cost by a money of low cost, of cost, indeed, so small that it may be called no cost.

216. Is it really Cheap Money?—That depends on whether it be good money or not. The money function is so important, so vital, in the industrial system, that there can be no true economy in any money but the very best. If the first cost of money can be saved, in whole or in part, without loss of efficiency or safety, that course is unmistakably dictated by the same law of the human mind which impels the individual to go to his object by the shortest path, or to buy in the cheapest market. To use a money which has to be dug out of the depths of the earth, drilled and blasted out of rock, perhaps at the depth of two thousand feet where water almost boils from internal fires, when a money in every way as good could be made from paper-pulp and printed with a steam press, would be the extreme of wastefulness. On the other hand, to use any but the best money, that which will perform the money function in the most perfect manner, would be economy

---

its full collected vigor, with a steady pulse, a calm outlook, a firm hand, a brain undisturbed by the fumes of this alcohol of commerce—paper money—it is when called to do battle for its life with superior force. It is to my mind the highest proof of the supreme intellectual greatness of Napoleon, that, during twenty years of continuous war, he never was driven to this desperate and delusive resort. I hold any man to be something less than a statesman, in the full sense of that word, who, under any stress of fiscal exigency, supports or submits to a measure for the issue of paper money not convertible, at the instant, on demand, without conditions, into coined money. The political arguments by which such measures are always supported, on the outbreak of war, seem to me the veriest trash, due half to ignorance, and half to cowardice.

of the same sort and degree as putting rotten timbers into a bridge because they were cheaper than sound timbers.

217. Is it, then, Good Money?—I know of nothing in the history of inconvertible paper money to indicate that such money, when issued of a denominative value not to exceed the mint-value of the coin which would have circulated in the community under the law for the territorial distribution of money which has been stated (pars. 176–80), may not serve as the general medium of exchange, so far as the internal* trade of a country is concerned, in every way as satisfactorily as the coin itself. Indeed, if any preference exists, it will be in favor of the paper money, as more convenient to handle, more readily transported, more successfully concealed.

Moreover, it has, I think, been sufficiently shown that whatever acts as the general medium of exchange, in the very act of doing this performs the function of a common denominator of values, furnishing a price-current in which the values of all commodities are expressed in terms of that one article.

But as regards the function of a standard for deferred payments, a wide difference may exist between two articles which might, with equal convenience, be used as the medium of exchange. It might happen that an article having a decided preference in the latter function would be found far inferior in the former function; might even be miserably deficient in the requisites of a standard of deferred payments. Let us, then, inquire further respecting inconvertible paper money, on this score.

218. Inconvertible Paper Money as the Standard of Deferred Payments.—In the fact that this money has no natural cost of production, lies the possibility, not merely of gross injustice as between individuals and classes of the community (which is not an economic consideration), but also of grave industrial evils, and even disasters of the most appalling character. Mr. Ricardo has rightly said that, by limiting the supply, any degree of value can be given to the money of a country, be it of gold and silver or of paper; but in the case

---

* The relations of inconvertible paper money to foreign trade and international exchanges will be spoken of in paragraph 220.

of the last no limitation of the supply is set by natural forces. Paper money has no cost of production. The expense of printing a dollar bill is so small, that, for purposes of economic reasoning, it may be disregarded altogether, while the expense of printing a ten-dollar bill or a hundred-dollar bill or a thousand dollar bill is no greater. The limitation of supply in the case of such money, therefore, must be left to law, convention, or accident.

We have seen that it would require many years of highly stimulated production to affect appreciably the world's stock of the precious metals, and, by consequence, the value of those metals. The cereal grains, indeed, being consumed in one or two years after their production, may be increased in quantity more rapidly, say, twenty or thirty per cent. in a year, as the result of exceptionally abundant harvests; yet even here human volition only controls the elements of production to a limited extent; and increase on such a scale could not be carried forward more than two or three years at the furthest. In the case of paper money, however, the stock may be increased, at the will of the issuer, to any extent, within the briefest period. The quantity may be trebled, decupled, centupled, by the operations of the printing-press.

219. Domestic Effects of Inflation.—The value of money depending, as has been shown, upon the relation of supply to demand, an increase of issues implies a loss of value in each given quantity of money. This involves a corresponding loss to all creditors, and a corresponding gain to all debtors. That result, being brought about by legislation or by the act of the prince, is properly termed confiscation. So far as it concerns only the existing body of debts, the question of confiscation is of interest only from the point of view of political equity. But such a measure also becomes a highly destructive force within the field of present and future industry, dealing a grievous blow at the instincts of frugality in the individual, and at the organization of the industrial body for the purposes of production and exchange.

Such a blow once dealt might in time be recovered from; but if new fiscal exigencies of the government, or the political pressure of the debtor class draw out other issues of inconvertible paper, not only will the value of the money continue to sink, through excess of supply, but another cause will begin to work in the same direction. The money demand will receive a shock such as has been described in par. 200, which may operate slowly and continuously, or may produce a sudden collapse of the circulation, the treasury crowding out the paper upon a reluctant and indignant people, who will none of it; who, through experience of grave losses in the past, shun it as they would the plague, contracting their industry, or changing its form at whatever sacrifice, or resorting to barter in spite of all its inconveniences, to avoid the use of the detested money. This was the fate, at the last, of the American "Continental Currency," and of the "Assignats" and "Mandats" of the French revolution.

Such are the possibilities attending the issue of paper money by the government. It may be asked what are the probabilities of the case? As we have here reached the limit of strictly economic inquiry, I prefer to postpone our answer to this question to Part VI., where, under the title "Political Money," the subject will be briefly treated in its political and historical aspects.

220. Inconvertible Paper Money and Foreign Exchanges.—But before we leave the topic of inconvertible paper money, we have to view another phase, *viz.*, its relation to International Exchanges. Thus far, we have spoken of the issue of paper money by government, only in its effects upon domestic trade and production. We are now to consider its influence upon the commercial relations of the issuing country with foreign countries.

By the mere fact of the adoption of this kind of money, a country loses all the advantages of an automatic regulation of the money supply through the normal movements of trade. Paper money finds no outlet in international commerce. It can not be exported and retain its value. Hence its regulation becomes purely mechanical. Having no natural cost of production, it will not, if in excess in any country, flow away in obedience to the law which governs the distribution of a money having acceptance abroad equally as at home. If issued in excess, it can only be removed by being pumped out by the same force which originally issued it.

Even where the excess of such paper money, over what would have been that country's distributive share of the world's money, be not enough to produce grave disturbances of domestic industry, the effect on foreign trade will yet be momentous. The immediate result of any excess must be to establish a premium upon that metallic money in which alone foreign balances can be paid.

To one who is not familiar with the largest operations of commerce this may seem a small matter; yet, if we may trust those who are best qualified to decide such questions, the money of a commercial state can not depart, by the narrowest interval, from the money in which international balances are discharged, without creating obstructions, exciting apprehensions and even occasioning losses, to which modern trade, with its highly developed and acutely sensitive organization, will not submit, or will do so only upon the payment of heavy fines by the offending community.

During the German war, and for some years after, *viz.*, from 1871-1877, the notes of the bank of France were inconvertible; yet such was the sagacity and prudence of the directors of that institution that at no time was there any considerable discount on that money, the premium on gold being often but a small fraction of one per cent. Yet, slight as was the disturbance of the domestic circulation, Mr. Bagehot, in his standard work, Lombard Street, written during the period of suspension, attributes to it the most momentous consequences.

"The note of the bank of France," he says, "has not, indeed, been depreciated enough to disorder ordinary transactions. But any depreciation, however small, *even the liability to depreciation, without its reality*, is enough to disorder exchange transactions. They are calculated to such an extremity of fineness, that the change of a decimal may be fatal, may turn a profit into loss. Accordingly London has become the sole great settling-house of exchange transactions in Europe, instead of being, as formerly, one of two."

CHAPTER VI.

BANK MONEY.

221. The Characteristics of Bank Money.—To secure the superior convenience of paper money, and, in a degree, also, its cheapness, as contrasted with money of metal, while retaining the comparative stability of value which characterizes the latter, and to keep the local circulation in such close communication with the general circulation of commerce as to insure the automatic regulation of the money supply, bank money has been invented.

The essential characteristic of such money is that the paper is instantly convertible, on the demand of the holder, into coined money. Whenever, by the unrebuked and unpunished lapse of the banks issuing paper money, as so frequently in the early history of the United States, or by the action of government upon its own initiative and for its own purposes, the money so issued fails to be convertible to the full extent indicated, it becomes inconvertible paper money. Nothing entitles paper to be called bank money except full, instant, unconditional redemption in coin. There is no stopping-place between this condition and inconvertibility.

Generally speaking, this sort of money is issued by institutions which, whether under State patronage or not, are so far disconnected from the government that their officers and agents can be sued in courts, and their assets and effects be attached for the recovery of the amount promised by the bank notes to be paid on demand. In this matter of connection with the State, however, there is found among banks, in one country or another, every degree from least to largest. In some instances the true character of bank money has been preserved in the case of institutions having what would appear a dangerously close connection with government.

222. The Origin of Bank Money.—Bank money in its modern form was first issued in Sweden, in 1658. The Bank of Scotland issued £1 notes as early as 1704, while the Bank of England did not issue notes below £20 prior to 1759. The issue of bank money, proper, did not begin in America until after the revolution, although nearly every colony had been, at one period or another, deluged with inconvertible paper money. The great bank money countries of to-day are the United States and the States of Northwestern Europe.

223. The Coin Basis of Bank Money.—We have said that, in addition to the superior convenience of bank money over coin, the motive for issue is found in its comparative cheapness. Banking experience has shown that a much larger denominative amount of notes can be kept in circulation than is held of specie for redemption.

On all this excess, the issuer of the notes derives a profit which is measured by the rate of interest on his loans, after deduction is made of the expense of maintaining the service. The metal thus displaced from circulation is exported, or melted down for use in the arts.

The advantage to the community of this saving in the cost of the money used in effecting exchanges, is thus conceived by Adam Smith.

"The gold and silver money which circulates in any country may very properly be compared to a highway, which, while it circulates and carries to market all the grain and corn of the country, produces itself not a single pile of either. The judicious operations of banking, by providing, if I may be allowed so violent a metaphor, a sort of wagon-way through the air, enables the country to convert, as it were, a great part of its highways into good pastures and corn-fields, and thereby to increase very considerably the annual produce of its land and labor."

The amount of saving effected by bank money varies, in the first instance, according to the proportion of coin, or "specie," as it is commonly called, reserved to meet demands for the redemption of the notes: to serve, that is, as the basis of the circulation.

That proportion is different in different countries, and often in different banks in the same country. The most common legal minimum reserve is one-third. In Leipsic, before the unification of Germany, the specie reserve was two-thirds, while in Bavaria it was but one-fourth.

Before tbe war of secession, the banks of the United States held an absurdly small amount of specie, the proportion in some States falling to ten, five, or even three per cent. But the so-called bank money of many of the States of the American Union, during certain periods in the early history of the nation, was really nothing but inconvertible money, hardly the pretense of redemption being maintained.*

224. The Banking Principle.—The view of the operations of bank money which is held by the great majority of writers of repute, in nearly all countries, is that, when really convertible into coin on demand; with all reasonable facilities existing for redemption, and with redemption actually taking place from time to time; with a public opinion which does not allow to be questioned the right of any man anywhere, for any reason or for no reason, to require coin, for any and all notes he may hold; and with exemplary penalties,† pro-

---

* Mr. Condy Raguet thus describes the action of American banks during this period, when in a state of suspension:

"Banks, when they default in their payments, not only never ask the indulgence of their creditors, for any specified extension of time, but they do not even think themselves under obligation to pay interest to the creditors for the funds they forcibly detain from them; nay, they frequently, in the midst of their insolvency, declare dividends of the very profits which actually belong to their creditors."

Of an earlier period Mr. Gallatin has written: "It was the catastrophe of the year 1814 which first disclosed not only the insecurity of the American banking system, as then existing, but also that, when a paper currency, driving away and superseding the use of gold and silver, has insinuated itself through every channel of circulation, and become the only medium of exchange, *every individual finds himself, in fact, compelled to receive such currency, even when depreciated more than twenty per cent., in the same manner as if it had been a legal tender.*"

†"By convertibility of the paper," says Mr. Tooke, "according to the ordinary signification of the term when applied to bank notes in this country (England), is meant that a holder of a promissory note—payable on demand—may require payment in coin of a certain weight and fineness, and in the event of refusal or demur, such payment is enforced by law against the issuer, to the utmost extent of his property. *The issuer,*

vided by law and enforced by the courts, for the first failure or the slightest delay on the part of banks to make good their promises, such money acts in all respects precisely as would a body of money composed wholly of coin. It is held to be fully subject to the law (par. 176) which governs the territorial distribution of money consisting of the precious metals only; and to have every economic virtue which belongs to such money, with the added advantage of greater cheapness and greater convenience in use.

"We are willing," says Mr. Tooke, the leader of the school of economists known as the advocates of the "Banking Principle," whose theory I have stated, "we are willing to consider a metallic currency as the type of that to which a mixed circulation of coin and paper ought to conform. But, further, we contend that it has so conformed, and must so conform, while the paper is strictly convertible."

The same opinion is expressed, with great emphasis, by Mr. Fullarton and Mr. James Wilson, and by M. Courcelle-Seneuil.

225. The Currency Principle.—The view of bank money which has been stated in the foregoing paragraph, is that which is held by a majority of writers of reputation. The opposite opinion was maintained by a school of economists in England, comprising the advocates of the so-called "Currency Principle," the leader of the school being Lord Overstone.

In the view of this school, something more than sound banking is needed to give a country good bank-money. If numerous, competing banks are left free to issue notes in such quantity and of such denominations as their own interests may dictate, with such specie reserves as their own prudence alone may suggest, there will always be the probability and often an extreme danger of over-issue, a body of bank-money so composed not being wholly amenable to the law of

---

whether a private or joint-stock banker, is considered to have failed. The circulation of his notes is at an end, and he is subject to the process usual in cases of insolvency."—["History of Prices."] Compare this with the state of things disclosed by Mr. Raguet, in the foot-note last preceding.

distribution which governs metal money, but possessing the capability of temporary and local inflation.

This opinion was ably maintained by Lord Overstone, Mr. Norman and Colonel Torrens, against the views of the Bank of England, and after a long struggle, the economists of this school triumphed in the enactment of the Bank Act of 1844* which still governs the note-circulation of England, though the principle on which it was framed is now challenged by many of the best financiers and economists.

In the United States, owing doubtless to gross abuses of the right of bank-note issue, such as have been adverted to in a note on a preceding page, the views of the English currency school obtained an acceptance among professional economists and writers on finance even wider and more complete than in England, although in but few states did this lead to legislation in any degree comparable, in scope or stringency of operation, to the English act of 1844. The leading writers on this question in the United States, were Messrs. William M. Gouge, Condy Raguet and Amasa Walker.

226. The Currency Principle vs. the Banking Principle.—The question whether a body of money composed partly of coin and partly of bank notes fully convertible into coin, acts in all respects as would a body of money composed wholly of coin, or, on the other hand, has the capability of being issued in local excess and so maintained for a long enough time to affect local prices, and thus initiate abnormal movements of

---

* The principal features of the act of 1844, as affecting the circulation, are as follows: 1st. The Bank of England is allowed to issue notes, in a constant sum of £15,000,000, without any specie basis. For all notes above this, it must have, pound for pound, a specie reserve, of which one-fifth may be silver. [This last in consideration of the commercial and political relations of England with India, which has silver money.]

2nd. The issue department and the banking department of the Bank are completely divorced, becoming as separate as the Customs and the Internal Revenue bureaus of our own government.

3rd. No London bank can issue notes, nor can any bank chartered since 1844; while the issues of the English banks then existing are limited to their ordinary outstanding circulation prior to that date.

trade and production, I regard as the one open question in the theory of money. Brought up in the school which held the latter view, my own reading and reflection have confirmed me in the belief that there resides in bank money, even under the most stringent provisions for convertibility, the capability of local and temporary inflation. The arguments on the two sides of the question are so evenly balanced, and the statistical evidence is so ambiguous, that differences of opinion are likely long to exist between men of intelligence and candor. I freely confess that the preponderance of authoritative opinion is against the view I hold.

CHAPTER VII.

THE REACTION OF EXCHANGE UPON PRODUCTION.

227. Evil Possibilities involved in the Division of Labor. —We have seen that the division of labor is an essential condition of large and varied production. But the division of labor, when carried far, involves possibilities of loss and disaster. These become more and more serious as production becomes more and more extended and complicated, until, in the most highly organized industrial state, we have to explain the failure of a community to realize its full productive capability, mainly by reference to industrial misadventures and even, at times, a partial paralysis of the productive powers of the community, originating in this very source.

The cause of the trouble adverted to is found in misunderstandings between producers and consumers, whom it is the nature of the division of labor to set apart, and, in an advanced industrial state, widely apart, often by half the circumference of the globe.

It is evident that, were there no division of labor into separate occupations, the relation between production and consumption would be a simple one. Production would, within the capabilities of the several agents concerned, *viz.*, land, labor, and capital, only be limited by the effective desire of the several individuals of the community to consume wealth. Each man would work by himself, for himself, producing those things, and those only, which he wished personally to eat, drink or wear, or house or warm himself withal. There would here be no question of a market, for every man would be his own customer.

From this point, we may mark off three stages of industrial development.

228. The First Stage.—The first is where distinction of trades is introduced, and men no longer consume all, or perhaps any part, of the articles they have produced ; yet where consumers live near the producer, and are personally known to him. In this condition, production, except in agriculture, generally waits for an order from the consumer. If goods are produced in advance of an order, the kinds are few, the forms are simple, the styles standard. There is, moreover, the reasonable expectation that some certain person, or some one out of a certain group of persons, will surely and soon need the goods, and will become the consumer. Here, we see, is not much liability to a misunderstanding between producer and consumer.

229. The Second Stage.—The second stage is where the element of personal acquaintance between producer and consumer disappears. Production no longer waits for orders, but anticipates demand. Goods are produced for a general market, and upon a calculation of the quantity probably to be required. The individual producer has no longer his own circle of customers ; but competes with other producers for the largest possible share of the patronage of a wide circle of consumers. Yet it is still true that production is carried on by artisans working singly or in small groups. Tools and implements are simple and inexpensive ; there is little of "plant" or fixed capital. Fashions are few and styles remain standard through long periods of time. Here, manifestly, the opportunity for misunderstandings between producer and consumer exists in a higher degree than under the former conditions described. Yet even here production may still go on with tolerable uniformity: all hands working steadily through all the seasons of the year, with a reasonable assurance that all goods which are well made, will find a market at fairly remunerative prices.

230. The Third Stage.—The third stage is reached, when increasing facilities of communication make the world one trading community. Then production becomes highly diversified, and the specialization and localization of trades proceed so far that one country, or perhaps one group of towns, produces the greater part of all the goods of a certain sort which are consumed throughout the world. Then luxury and refinement of living are carried to the maximum, so that not only are classes of goods multiplied almost indefinitely, but fashions and modes enter till standard styles almost disappear, each season bringing minute modifications of demand which are not to be satisfied except by an exact compliance, even the colors and shades of one year becoming intolerable the next.

It will appear that conditions like the foregoing increase enormously the liability of misunderstanding between producers and consumers. The possibilities of error in supplying the markets, no longer of a village, but of the world, become tremendous.

231. The Appearance of the Entrepreneur.—But it must further be added, that powerful and complicated machinery is now introduced, and costly structures and "plant" are required. Great numbers of operatives, of both sexes and all ages and of every degree of strength and skill, have to be gathered under one roof, each knowing only his or her own part; all requiring to be instructed and equipped, organized, energized, and directed by the intelligence and will of one man. In other words, we have reached the entrepreneur stage (pars. 106–9) of industrial development.

The introduction of the principle of mastership into industry makes a great gain of productive power; but this gain is not secured without an appreciable loss. The entrepreneur (to anticipate, for a moment, a topic in Distribution), finds his motive for organizing and conducting the great enterprises of modern industry in the profits (pars. 302, 429) which he hopes individually to realize. His entire personal interest is found here. It is, perhaps, to secure a net profit of twenty thousand dollars, that he leases land and buildings, and borrows capital, and hires the labor requisite to achieve an annual product of half a million of dollars. If, then, the conditions of trade and industry are such as to destroy for the time his profit ; much more if they are such as to threaten a loss which will impair the integrity of the capital, his interest in production is greatly diminished, if not destroyed. He will either cease producing entirely, or, which is more likely, will contract the scope of his operations. Were he to produce $500,000 worth, as heretofore, a small fraction of his stock unsold might sweep away his own gains for the year, or leave a deficit ; whereas, were he to produce but $400,000 or $350,000 worth, he would probably dispose of his stock at prices high enough to make himself good and perhaps leave a small margin of profit, while holding his laboring force and his customers together.

232. Fluctuations in Production:—Such being the conditions under which production takes place, under the modern organization of industry, we note that there is in the nature of the case a continuous loss through the failure of the producing body to meet, promptly and precisely, the demands of the body of consumers. Wherever, from any cause, there is a failure correctly to anticipate those demands and supply them perfectly, in time, in degree, in form, loss of value results. That there should be such failure in part, is inevitable.

But the loss which we had chiefly in view in beginning this chapter, and with reference to which we have written this long introduction, is not the steady, continuous loss of value due to the inability of those who direct production to comprehend, fully and seasonably, the varying demands of distant markets. It is the occasional loss resulting from the frequent and often furious fluctuations which are involved in the modern organization of trade and industry.

From that organization the alternation of highly stimulated and of deeply depressed production appears to be inseparable. The course of trade and industry through the cycle which the conditions of modern life seem to have established, is so well described by Prof. Alfred Marshall that I can not forbear to give it in full:

"The beginning of a period of rising credit is often a series of good harvests. Less having to be spent in food, there is a better demand for other commodities. Producers find that the demand for their goods is increasing, they expect to sell at a profit, and are willing to pay good prices for the prompt delivery of what they want. Employers compete with one another for labor; wages rise; and the employed in spending their wages increase the demand for all kinds of commodities. New public and private companies are started, to take advantage of the promising openings which show themselves among the general activity. Thus the desire to buy and the willingness to pay increased prices grow together; credit is jubilant and readily accepts paper promises to pay. Prices, wages and profits go on rising; there is a general rise in the incomes of those engaged in trade; they spend freely, increase the demand for goods, and raise prices still higher. Many speculators, seeing the rise, and thinking it will continue, buy goods with the expectation of selling them at a profit. At such a time a man who has only a few hundred pounds can often borrow from bankers and others the means of buying many thousand pounds' worth of goods; and every one who thus enters into the market as a buyer, adds to the upward tendency of prices, whether he buys with his own or with borrowed money.

"This movement goes on for sometime, till at last an enormous amount of trading is being carried on by credit and with borrowed money. Old firms are borrowing, in order to extend their business; new firms are borrowing in order to start their business; and speculators are borrowing, in order to buy and hold goods. Trade is in a dangerous condition. Those whose business it is to lend money are among the first to read the signs of the times; and they begin to think about contracting their loans. But they can not do this without much disturbing trade. If they had been more chary of lending at an earlier stage, they would simply have prevented some new business from being undertaken; but when it is once undertaken, it can not be abandoned without a loss of much of the capital that has been invested in it. Trading companies of all kinds have borrowed vast sums with which they have begun to build railways and docks and ironworks and factories; prices being high they do not get much building done for their outlay; and though they are not yet ready to reap profits on their investment, they have to come again into the market to borrow more capital. The lenders of capital already wish to contract their loans; and the demand for more loans raises the rate of interest very high. Distrust increases; those who have lent become eager to secure themselves and refuse to renew their loans on easy or even on any terms. Some speculators have to sell goods in order to pay their debts; and by so doing they check the rise of prices. This check makes all other speculators anxious, and many rush in to sell. For a speculator who has borrowed money at interest to buy goods may be ruined if he holds them a long time even while their price remains stationary; he is almost sure to be ruined if he holds them while their price falls. When a large speculator fails, his failure generally causes that of others who have lent their credit to him; and their failure again that of others. Many of those who fail may be really 'sound,' that is, their assets may exceed their debts. But though a man is sound, some untoward event, such as the failure of others who are known to be indebted to him, may make his creditors suspect him. They may be able to demand immediate payment from him, while he can not collect quickly what is owing to him; and the market being disturbed he is distrusted; he can not borrow, and he fails. As credit by growing makes itself grow, so when distrust has taken the place of confidence, failure and panic breed panic and failure. The commercial storm leaves its path strewn with ruin. When it is over, there is a calm, but a dull, heavy calm. Those who have saved themselves are in no mood to venture again; companies whose success is doubtful are wound up; new companies can not be formed. Coal, iron and the other materials for making fixed capital fall in price as rapidly as they rose. Iron works and ships are for sale, but there are no buyers at any moderate price.

"Thus the state of trade, to use the famous words of Lord Overstone, 'revolves apparently in an established cycle. First we find it in a state of quiescence—next improvement, growing confidence, prosperity, excitement, overtrading, convulsion, pressure, stagnation, distress, ending again in quiescence.'"

233. Periodicity of Panics.—So frequently have trade and industry made this weary round, that the writers on finance have undertaken to establish the law of the periodicity of panics and hard times. The term of ten years is that most often fixed upon for the completion of the cycle. There is at least a very curious series of coincidences to give some substance to this hypothesis.

But whether there are, indeed, forces operating which bring about commercial convulsions and industrial distress at regular intervals, or not, it seems clear that, under the conditions depicted in the first part of this chapter, it is inevitable that the producing and exchanging body should alternate frequently and even violently between a state of depression and partially suspended activity, and a state of highly animated, excited, almost convulsive exertion, in which the agencies alike of production and of exchange are strained to their utmost to meet demands which are stimulated to the highest extravagance by a universal passion of speculation.

234. Loss of Productive Force.—It is evident that this is not an order of things under which the largest production of wealth takes place. The two extremes do not offset each other, with the same result as if production had been proceeding calmly and equably through the entire period. On the contrary, each extreme involves great and permanent loss of productive force. There is much misdirection of energy, much waste of material, much vital injury to labor power and capital power, in the haste and strain and fever of highly stimulated effort.

On the other hand, the long, dull spell of inactivity that succeeds is not given wholly to recuperation of exhausted energies, renewal of stocks of materials, repair of machinery and plant. It is not a waste of time, merely, involving a proportional loss of productive power : that inactivity becomes itself a cause of mischief. It induces in the working classes a lethargy, a despondency, a recklessness, which are forces productive of evil. It generates habits of lounging and of drinking, perhaps of tramping, which may not be shaken off even with renewed employment.

235. "Hard Times." — Nothing needs to be added, of clearness or of force, to Prof. Marshall's statement of the course which trade and industry run from the time they first cross the line of reviving prosperity to the moment they plunge into the abyss of broken credit, falling markets, commercial panic, failing banks, and general distress. But there is one industrial phenomenon of great significance in respect to our question, why the actual production of a community comes so far short of its productive capability? which economists have not been accustomed to explain : this is, the long continuance of the periods of industrial depression and of restricted production.

It will readily appear that, after running such a rig as has been described, the agencies of trade and industry will require time to refit. The track must be cleared of the wreck. The places left vacant by the casualties of the great crash must be filled by new men. But the actual time covered by the period of depression is sometimes much longer than can be accounted for by the mere loss and destruction of a panic. "Hard Times" are protracted long after the capital power and the labor power of the community are in condition to resume their interrupted functions.

For several years after the panic of 1873, in the United States, industry did not reach its former proportions. During that period vast amounts of labor power and capital power remained unproductive. Tens of thousands, if not hundreds of thousands, of laborers were unemployed ; an even greater number were employed only on half or three-quarters time. Hundreds of furnaces were out of blast ; thousands of water-wheels ceased to turn ; thousands of engines stood still. Yet, during this time, these workmen had occasion to consume food and clothing for themselves and their families ; needed to work to earn the means, and were honestly willing, yea, heartily desirous to work. All this time the owners of capital were ready to secure a return for their investments, if they could find opportunity ; the conductors of business were eager to win a profit by employing their abilities and experience in productive industry. Why, then, was it, when all were willing to work and needed to work, that they did not work? What was the force that kept these laboring men, these water-wheels and engines, these capable conductors of business, idle so long ?

236. Diversified Production.—We have seen that, as society makes progress toward a minuter organization of industry, productive capability is enhanced, but that, coincidently, at each stage, the opportunities for misunderstanding between the body of producers and the body of consumers are greatly multiplied, while labor power and capital power fall more under the control of men of exceptional abilities, with whom comes to rest all initiative in production.

Now, if we examine the list of articles sold in the market, in a modern community, we shall find some of them supplying wants which are constant and vital. We shall find others which minister to the most delicate tastes or gratify only the merest casual fancies. In a country like England, France, or the United States, tens of thousands of laborers are employed in producing articles of the most trivial character: fireworks, toys, bonbons, fripperies of dress, while hundreds of thousands more are employed in producing articles deprivation of which would not induce cold or hunger, or impair health, or be incompatible with public decency or personal self-respect.

237. Propagation of Economic Shocks.—Let us suppose, as the result of a period of prosperity, the variety of products to have been carried to a very high point, when a disaster, primarily affecting either industry or trade, it matters not, befalls a community. It may be a great fire, or a great flood, or an epidemic of yellow fever, or the destruction of some leading crop. No matter where it comes from, or where it first strikes, the immediate effect is to diminish the productive power of the community, as a whole. At once the consumption of those articles which are least essential to comfort and decency is checked. If we suppose the thousands of articles known to the market to form twenty-six groups, A to Z, their utility to the consumer regularly declining from the top of the list to the bottom, we may assume that the first effect of the calamity will be to reduce the consumption of articles forming groups X, Y and Z. No matter, as we said, where the blow first falls, the laborers affected produce for the time less, and must limit their own consumption accordingly, which they do by restricting their use of articles below W.

The labor and capital employed in groups X, Y and Z, can not easily or soon be transferred to other groups. The laborers, especially, find that the present is no time to seek employment in other avocations. They must stay where they are, and do the best they can there. Hence they find themselves employed on part time, and at reduced wages. The sums they formerly earned were expended in purchasing articles all the way from A to Z. In their sudden poverty they are obliged to cut off their own consumption of all articles except those which are necessary to comfort and decency, say from A to M, inclusive.

But this action of producers X, Y and Z involves a diminished demand for products, N to W. Each group of producers, at this end of the line, are obliged to curtail still further their consumption of articles X, Y and Z, while producers from S to W begin to restrict their use of articles below T. This action, however, becomes at once the cause of new effects. The unfortunate representatives of X, Y and Z are now obliged wholly to deny themselves all products from H downwards; producers T to W, in turn have to give up indulgence in products below N; producers N to S, in consequence, no longer purchase products below R.

The shock next reaches groups I to M, who have to diminish their consumption, to correspond to the reduced demand for their own products; X, Y and Z are now glad to get enough of A, B, C and D to barely subsist upon; while S, T, D, U, V and W carry their retrenchment upwards, till they stop at

M. And so the movement goes forward until the favored producers A to D—favored, in that the articles they produce are of vital importance—experience some diminution of demand, and, producing less in consequence, have less to give in exchange for the products of others. So a stone, thrown into a lake, sets in motion a wave which extends outwards in all directions till it reaches the bank, even in the most retired nook along the shore.

238. Aggravation of Economic Shocks. — It is evident that, were the community perfectly intelligent and self-possessed, the ultimate result of this play of forces would be the distribution of the whole initial shock over the entire producing body. No addition would be made to the shock as the movement proceeded, and the effect upon each successive group of producers reached would be less and less. Those producing articles the most essential to life, health and social decency would suffer to hardly an appreciable extent, as the wave set in motion by the rock thrown into the lake becomes the merest ripple against the shore.

This is all that is necessarily involved in the propagation, through economic media of perfect elasticity, of an original blow like that assumed. In fact, industrial injuries are at times distributed in this way throughout the producing body, without panic, without apprehension, even without observation.

Let, however, the shock be sharp and severe, and communicated in some startling form, and let it occur when the public mind is in an apprehensive mood, or when the commercial body is unstrung by political or social disturbances, and we may see the impulse propagated with increasing force, from subject to subject, till the movement acquires fearful violence.

239. The Industrial Panic.—The commercial panic we are all familiar with, by experience or report. We know how some slight cause, acting on the fears and imaginations of men, will overthrow the financial structure of a nation in a few weeks, perhaps days, prostrating the proudest houses, and spreading ruin far around. There is nothing that can stand against panic. One man's fear makes another man afraid. One man's fall brings down another, who, but for that, might have stood firm ; and thus the mischief proceeds, from bad to worse. So much for the trading body.

The progressive aggravation and acceleration of the forces of mischief throughout the producing body takes place not less surely, though it is here less ostensive.

A manufacturer feels the demand for his goods fall off somewhat. In ordinary times he would receive the fact as an intimation to reduce his production, but only to a corresponding extent. Indeed, in good times he would receive that intimation in a somewhat skeptical spirit. He would not be disposed to believe that any serious check was to be experienced. He would look to see trade start up again, and, in this mood, would reduce his production somewhat less than correspondingly. To that extent, he would speculate : that is, would anticipate events and discount the future. For the moment, then, he would transmit the shock, not aggravated but mitigated.

But let the shock be at first severe, and let it come upon the public mind in a suspicious mood, and the matter will take another turn. The merchant feels the demand for his goods fall off abruptly. He fears there is more to come. He is determined not to be caught with a large stock on his hands, and, in his orders to the manufacturer, he exaggerates the natural and proper effect of the change in the market. The manufacturer, on his part, knows nothing directly of the actual falling off in demand. He only learns it as it comes to him heightened by the apprehensions of the merchant. In his turn, he exaggerates the evil and reduces his production more than proportionally. His anxiety now is, not to make a profit, but to avoid loss. He knows he will be safe if he runs his mill on half or three-quarters time.

And it is here that the cause indicated in par. 231 begins to operate with great and destructive force. The entrepreneur's personal concern in production being derived wholly from his contemplated profit, which may be but a small percentage of the value of the goods produced, his individual interests may, for the time, become divorced from those of his laborers or of the general community. In his anxiety to save himself, he may act with as much needless cruelty as men do when panic-stricken in a fire or a wreck.

240. But the action of manufacturer Z, whether wisely or unwisely taken, becomes, as we have seen, an element in the conditions of production for all the lower letters of the alphabet. As he pays less wages, his workmen have less to spend for the products of other branches of industry. The merchants in these lines, feeling the falling off in demand, exaggerate it in their orders to manufacturers, especially manufacturers X and Y. These, in turn, apprehensive of worse to come, curtail their operations more than correspondingly, and so the movement proceeds, with increasing violence.

And, let us repeat, however unnecessary Z's action in reducing his production below a certain point, yet, if he actually does so, that action makes a corresponding reduction in X and Y's operations a necessity of their situation : just as truly so as if Z had a good reason for what he did. And if, in turn, X and Y become alarmed, and overdo the thing, that of itself constitutes an obligation upon manufacturers higher in the alphabet to cut down work and wages.

241. How Far may this be Carried ?—Two questions arise upon this view of the power of apprehension and suspicion to aggravate the force of any industrial or financial shock. The first : how far may it be carried ? the second, how long may it last ?

May the movement to check production proceed until all industry is locked fast in "a vicious circle" : no one producing, because others will not consume, while no one is able to consume the products of others because he himself produces nothing with which to buy them ?

I answer, no. The staple industries, especially those yielding the necessaries of life, will never be suspended. The demand for their products is so constant and certain that panic has little power over them. Groups A to D will, therefore, continue to produce nearly as much as before ; not, indeed, quite so much, because there will be individuals, thrown out by the revolution at the foot of the alphabet, who are unable to find a new place where they can produce enough to purchase even the barest subsistence. Groups E to H, or K, moreover, having to do with articles essential to comfort and social decency, will withstand the shock communicated to them sufficiently to maintain a production not very far below that of good times.

Now, so long as A to D produce liberally, and E to H or K, still produce considerably, all persons employed within those groups will have the means of purchasing the products of groups further down the list ; and so industry will be kept alive, though but just alive, in those groups which produce articles not essential to life, or health, or decency.

242. How Long may such a Condition Last?—I answer: in theory, it may last indefinitely. Practically, it is liable to be terminated, after a longer or shorter period of suspense, by reviving courage and enterprise on the part of men of affairs, or through the stimulus to production administered from some quarter. It may be so slowly as to be almost imperceptible ; it may be so rapidly as to outrun calculation, that the expansion takes place. This will depend much on the natural temper of the community ; much on the immediate cause provoking renewed enterprise ; much on accident.

The one essential condition is that speculation be initiated, that is, that men begin to look ahead, to anticipate demand, and to discount the future.

One man begins to produce, no longer on orders, no longer cautiously and fearfully, as if it were too much to believe that his goods will be taken off his hands, but in a sanguine spirit, assuming the initiative in production, and boldly encountering its risks. Producing more largely, his workmen have more to offer for the products of other industries, which is of itself a reason for a larger production in these branches, whose managers and proprietors respond in the same spirit. Finding the demand increasing, they act as if they believed it were about to increase still further. They produce somewhat in anticipation, and thus give their hands more to offer in exchange for the products of still other industries. From day to day the movement proceeds, gathering force as it goes, and production swells continually under the contagious influence of hope and courage, just as before it shrank and shriveled under the breath of fear and panic.

I have said that peculiarities of national character have much to do with the speedy or tardy revival of production. Nowhere ought recovery to be more rapid than in the United States. Among no people is there more of elasticity, greater alertness of action, more readiness to assume responsibilities and to run risks. Nowhere, too, does nature afford an ampler margin for subsistence, or more abundant material for the repair of mistakes and misadventures.

243. Two Examples.—The history of the panic of 1857 offers a capital illustration of the facility with which the American people recover from the sharpest contraction of productive industry, where nothing withstands the revival of trade, and where no second shock remains to be experienced. The country was in a generally sound condition, both as to capital and credit, when the blow fell. As the result, industry had scarcely shrunk to its minimum, under the influence of panic, when the enterprise and courage of merchants and manufacturers began to cause expansion. Within a few months production was again at the limits of our capital power and labor power.

When the panic of 1837 came, the country was in a wretched condition, through the misapplication of capital and the wide extension of credit.

The buoyancy of the national temper led, even at this time, to a speedy revival; but the succeeding shock of 1839 threw the country back again, and the fear and distrust thereby engendered kept the energies of the nation in a state of partial repression through a long period. Such may be the influence of a single instance of hard fortune upon reviving industry.

Quite as prejudicial to expanding production is the continual apprehension of hostile or meddlesome legislation. When the whole body of business men are sore from disasters ; when much of the industrial and commercial structure still lies in ruins, it takes but little to check the disposition again to adventure capital. That little is abundantly supplied by the popular apprehension of legislation unfavorably affecting money and credit. It need not be a great thing under a man's arms which will so increase his margin of buoyancy as to enable him to float for hours. It is a very small thing around a man's neck which will so diminish his margin of buoyancy—narrow at the best—as to drag him to the bottom.

PART IV.

DISTRIBUTION.

CHAPTER I.

THE PARTIES TO THE DISTRIBUTION OF WEALTH.

244. Distribution as a Department of Political Economy.—Under the title, Distribution, we inquire, what are the forces which divide wealth among the several persons, or classes of persons, who have taken part in its production?

In a primitive condition of society, the problem of distribution is a simple one. Three hunters join in an expedition, and at the conclusion of the chase, divide their game into three equal parts. If boys, or cripples, or men of less than ordinary force or skill, are taken into the partnership, it is easily determined what portion of a full man's share each such person shall receive.

In a highly organized community, however, the division of the product of industry into shares corresponding to the number of persons who have taken part in production, is a complicated problem.

245. The Division of the Web of Cloth.—For example, let us take the case of a cotton factory, at Lawrence, which produces in a given time a million yards of cloth. We may suppose that this is all woven in one piece, and that each person who has, in any way, contributed to making this giant web, advances in a certain order to receive his share.

The agent for the water company first appears, and cuts off some thousands of yards, inasmuch as his company furnished the power that drove the wheels below, that turned the spindles above. Then comes the owner of the land on which the mill is built, and carries off, perhaps, a piece five times as large; next, the owner of the mill, who takes the largest piece of all; next, the man who gave the use of the machinery and loaned the working capital, and now measures off many miles of the cloth as his share.

So far, all has gone smoothly. Though the manufacturer has stood by and seen the fearful inroads made upon the web by the successive claimants, little has been said, and that in a low tone and in a business-like way. Some reason is known to the manufacturer why each of these persons should receive so much and no less. Some calculation which he is able rapidly to make maintains a complete understanding between him and them.

Now, however, the scene changes; there remain but two parties as claimants to the six or seven hundred thousand yards that are left. On the one side we see a crowd composed of persons engaged in the mill as overseers, as clerks, as mechanics, as laborers, as "operatives," in all, some hundreds of men, women and children, of varying degrees of strength, skill and intelligence; on the other side, stands the manufacturer. All that these do not take, will be his; and as piece after piece is rapidly cut off, he seems to fear that not enough will remain for him, while each of them appears disaffected that his own share is not larger, deeming it especially a hardship that, after he and his comrades are served, so much will be left to the manufacturer. According to their several dispositions, some threaten that it shall not be so again; some merely grumble; others take up their little rolls of cloth and walk away with a patient air, as if they hoped for nothing better.

At last the manufacturer is left with his share. If it has been a good season, and all has gone well; if the cotton has turned out of good quality, if the weather has been propitious, with just enough of heat and of moisture for the quickest and most uniform spinning; if there have been no floods in the river, giving trouble, and no low water, so that the wheel has turned steadily and powerfully whenever the gate was lifted, the roll of cloth which the manufacturer will carry back into the warehouse will be large, and his face will wear a contented look. If, on the other hand, any one of a dozen untoward accidents, reasonably to be apprehended, has occurred, his share will be less, perhaps little, possibly nothing.

246. The Problem of Distribution.—It is under the present title that we inquire why it is that each of these claimants on the product of the cotton factory takes so much and takes no more. Of course, in the immediate instance that reason is found in the force of contract. All the other parties had agreed with the manufacturer to allow him the use of their property, or to render him their services, at certain rates. But why did they contract at those rates, and not at higher; and why will they, as they probably will, immediately proceed to make new contracts, at the same, perhaps at lower rates?

Why, in particular, is it that the division of the product is effected with so little of friction or complaint, as between the manufacturer and the water company, the owner of the ground, the owner of the mill, the owner of the machinery and of the working capital; while between the manufacturer and the "hands" there is so much of dissatisfaction and jealousy, of complaint and irritation?

247. Distinction between the Exchange of Services and of Commodities.—Among those writers who have defined political economy as the Science of Exchanges, distribution is not recognized as a separate department of inquiry, involving principles peculiar to itself. These writers find that the subjects of exchange are, broadly speaking, two, *viz.*, services and commodities, or, labor and the products of past labor. To carry forward this distinction is not consistent with the simplicity of the science which these writers have in contemplation. The difficulty is soon resolved. They discover that commodities are, after all, nothing but services which have taken on a material form, and thereafter they speak only of services, and thereby secure to political economy "one grand characteristic of the great sciences, *viz.*, simplicity." This effected, the distinction between the Distribution and the Exchange of wealth falls to the ground. There is no longer any need for the former term in political economy.

But I venture to assert that this forced simplicity, secured by compelling into a single form things having much that is not in common ; this false peace, which disregards irreconcilable differences ; this hasty generalization, by which services and commodities are made to be one and the same thing, has had the effect to render political economy signally barren through the very period when social philosophy has been most prolific, and, secondly, to forfeit nearly all popular respect for, and interest in, the so-called science of exchanges.

248. "During the present century," says the Duke of Argyle, in his Reign of Law, "two great discoveries have been made in the science of government: the one is the immense advantage of abolishing restrictions upon trade ; the other is the absolute necessity of imposing restrictions upon labor."

I do not quote this passage, here, for the sake of raising the question of Ten-Hour laws or factory inspection (pars. 471–3), but only to call attention to the clear, strong antithesis in which it places services and commodities. That statement does not exaggerate the general and still growing consent of social philosophers and legislators that the rendering of services differs so widely from the exchange of commodities that the two must stand in different relations to legislation. More and more fully has this distinction come to be recognized. If political economy denies the validity of the distinction, so much the worse for political economy, in the eyes of social philosophers and statesmen alike. Surely, the simplicity of the science may be secured at too high a cost!

Equally against the pressure of enormous vested interests, and against the protests of professional political economists, the legislation of almost every enlightened country has progressed by steady steps, through the last sixty, forty, and especially during the last twenty years, in the direction of discriminating vitally between commodities and services, allowing continually greater and greater freedom of contract in respect to the former, and bringing the contracts which involve the latter more and more completely under the authority and supervision of the State.

And yet there is complaint that statesmen and the mass of the people entertain such slight regard for political economy, whose professors, in the interest of the purity and simplicity of their science, discard from the premises of their reasoning (par. 21) all the "sympathies, apathies, and antipathies" of mankind, and insist upon treating a Manchester spinner, with a wife and six children, ignorant, fearful, and poor, as possessing the same mobility economically, and under the same subjection to the impulses of pecuniary interest, as a bale of Manchester cottons on the wharf, free to go to India or to Iceland, as the difference of a penny in the price may determine!

249. An Analogous Case.—But we shall not get a full measure of the insufficiency of the reasons given for dropping the distinction between commodities and services, in exchange, unless we ask what would be the consequences to political economy of dealing in the same spirit with the analogous case of the distinction between labor and capital, in production. Suppose the political economist were to say: Capital is but the result of the labor of the past; it is, in essence, labor which has taken on a material and more or less permanent form; whatever is true of labor must be true of capital; we will, therefore, resolve the two into one, and thus promote the simplicity of political economy. Simplicity, indeed! but at the cost of the loss of all significance, if not all sense. What sort of a political economy would that be which did not recognize the distinction between labor and capital in production? Yet the distinction has a singularly close analogy to that between services and commodities in exchange.

250. A Contest, though not a Destructive Contest.—It will be noted that the distribution of the product of industry involves what may be termed a perpetual contest between the parties to production. This contest is not a destructive one, since the interest of each of the participants requires the existence, and, by consequence, the sustentation, of all the others. Yet, within the limits consistent with this, there is opposition of interests.

251. The Parties to the Distribution of Wealth.—The contest is, in the last analysis, between individuals. We shall see that the real or supposed common interests of a number of producers may create a supposed class interest which will lead them to act in concert, with a subordination of individual preferences to the general good ; but, as a rule, the efforts of individuals are directed to a personal benefit. Inasmuch, however, as it would be impossible to work out the problem of distribution with reference to each man, woman, and child, we may aggregate individuals, according to what they have in common, into classes, larger or smaller, and may seek for the general law which governs the efforts of the members of each class towards the acquisition of wealth.

252. Classes in Distribution.—Even if we disregard petty distinctions and inconsiderable exceptions, the prime classes appearing in distribution will vary in different countries. A classification which would fully meet the facts of industrial organization in India, would omit distinctions of prime importance in England.

Inasmuch as we could not, in an elementary treatise, give the space needed to set forth the problem of distribution in each country or group of countries having a common industrial organization, we will consider for our present purpose the industrial organization of England. We take this, because it is the most highly developed organization known to industry ; because it is largely reproduced in the United States and on the continent of Europe, and in Canada and Australia, and is everywhere, among progressive peoples, more and more widely extending from year to year. Moreover, it will be easier for the reader to work out for himself the problem of distribution in countries of a lower organization, than it would be to go from the simpler to the more complex forms of industrial life.

Under the system which we have taken for the purposes of the present discussion, we have four classes of claimants upon the product of industry, and that product is accordingly divided into four grand shares. These classes and the shares respectively received by them may be expressed as follows:

1. The landlord, receiving rent.
2. The capitalist, receiving interest.
3. The employer, or entrepreneur, receiving profits.
4. The employed laborer, receiving wages.

The reason for naming these several claimants in the order just given, will appear as we make progress in the discussion of the forces which effect the distribution of wealth.

CHAPTER II.

RENT.

253. Definition of Rent.—Rent is the term applied to the remuneration received by the land-owning class for the use of the native and indestructible powers of the soil, or, as it might be expressed, for the use of natural agents.

That remuneration may be paid in money or in produce. The term land, or natural agents, must be understood to include not only arable land, but pasture, timber lands, mineral deposits, water privileges and building sites. For the present discussion, however, it will be best to take our illustrations from the occupancy and cultivation of arable land.

254. The Origin of Rent Illustrated.—Let us suppose a community, isolated from all others, to occupy a circular tract of land divided, as in the following diagram, into four sectors equal in extent but so differing in fertility that one piece will, with so many days' labor in the year given to plowing, cultivating and harvesting, yield 24 bushels of wheat per acre, while the second will yield, with the same amount of labor, but 22 bushels, the third but 20 bushels, and the fourth but 18. Now the assumption we have made as to differing degrees of fertility in the soil of the several tracts, is not an extravagant one. On the contrary, we might reasonably have assumed the degrees of fertility to differ far more widely. "A quarter of wheat," says Mr. McCulloch, "may be raised

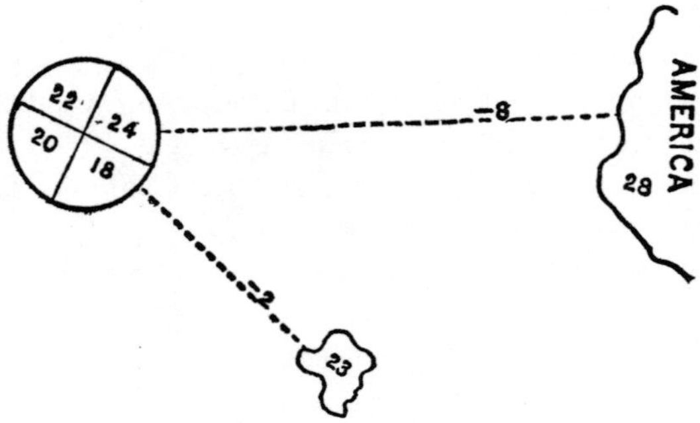

in Kent, or Essex, or in the Carse of Gowrie, for a fourth or fifth part, perhaps, of the expense necessary to raise it on the worst soils under cultivation in the least fertile parts of the kingdom."

In order to further simplify the problem, we will suppose that all the inhabitants of this community reside in a village at the center.

255. The Ante-Rent Stage of Cultivation.—Let the first case taken be when the village is yet so small that all the wheat required for the subsistence of the population can be raised upon a portion only of what we will call the 24-bushel tract. If the tract be held by a number of competing owners,* each acting for himself, seeking his individual in-

---

* If the tract were held by one person, or by several persons acting in concert, a monopoly would be established, and a rent might be exacted. What would be the limit of that rent? Two bushels an acre, inasmuch as one would do better for himself to take up for cultivation a portion of the 22-bushel tract, paying no rent, than give more than two bushels for the use of an acre of the more productive land.

But this rent of two bushels per acre, would not be paid for the whole of the first tract, but only for the number of acres actually required for cultivation in order to furnish subsistence for the community. All the owners in the combination would have to divide among themselves the aggregate sum so obtained, none obtaining so much as two bushels an

terest, no rent will be paid, or only a rent so small that for purposes of economic reasoning we may disregard it. Each owner of land in this tract will be desirous of securing for himself whatever compensation, if any, is to be paid for the use of land. But as the entire tract is not required for cultivation, and, as, consequently, only a part of the owners can receive any compensation for their land, an active competition will set in, each man offering the use of his land for less and less, in order to get something, until rent falls to a minimum, or disappears altogether.

256. Relation of Waste to Rent.—And it is here we see the significance of the word, "indestructible," in par. 253. All scientific reasoning about rent is based on the assumption that the tenant will leave the soil in as good condition as it was in when he took it. Now, it is possible for a tenant to impair the fertility of land, first, by intentional abuse, or, secondly, by taking away its productive essences, in the crops of successive years, without returning any thing to it in the shape of manures or other fertilizers.

It is only upon the above assumption that it would be true that each owner of land in the twenty-four bushel tract would prefer to lease it for a very small rent, approaching nothing, rather than not lease it at all. Unless he could be protected, by law or contract, against exhaustion of the soil, he might prefer to let his land go unoccupied. But on the assumption stated, the proposition is true that, in the situation described, no portion of the twenty-four bushel tract would bring so large a rent that it might not, for purposes of economic reasoning, be treated as *nil*.

257. Rent Emerges.—Let us now advance to the second stage. We will suppose that the population of the village has increased to such an extent that the whole of the twenty-four bushel tract will no longer raise, when cultivated as it has heretofore been, all the wheat required for the subsistence

---

acre for his individual estate. Should any one owner try to overreach the others and secure the full rent for the whole of his own land, the "ring" would be broken, competition would set in, and rents would fall to the minimum.

of the community. Cultivation will then be driven down to an inferior grade of soils. A part of the second tract, the twenty-two bushel tract, will be taken up.

Do you ask, why not increase the amount of labor upon the twenty-four bushel tract, and so raise more wheat to the acre? I answer, because of the great fact of Diminishing Returns in Agriculture, which was set forth in Part II., with so much particularity. We shall now see the whole theory of rent built upon it. The fact itself is undeniable. In every country of the world, and in every parish or township of every country, cultivation is seen descending to grades of soils below the best, because the yield from the highest grades can not be increased proportionally to an increase of labor expended thereon.

Cultivation having, in the case of the community whose industrial history we have traced so far, been driven down to the twenty-two bushel tract, rent will at once emerge. Not that rent will be paid for any portion of the latter tract, which will all be in the same condition, as regards compensation for its use, as was the first tract, when that alone was cultivated; but for the twenty-four bushel tract, and for each portion of it, rent will now be paid. Why? Because any person desiring to raise wheat may better, may he not? pay something for cultivating a portion of that tract, than cultivate a portion of the new lands for nothing.

How much will he pay? Exactly the difference between the crops to be grown on the two soils, with the same application of labor, *i. e.*, two bushels, since he can afford to pay this rent rather than move to the less productive soil. As some must so move, the landlord will be able to exact the maximum rent from the present cultivator: if not, from some other.

Let us now advance another stage, and suppose the increase of population to require the cultivation of the twenty-bushel tract. The effect of this downward movement of the limit of cultivation will be two-fold:

First, the twenty-two bushel tract will begin to bear a rent, since any cultivator can better afford to pay a certain rent for the privilege than occupy a portion of the new land for nothing. The amount of that rent will be determined by the difference in productiveness between the two tracts, being, in the case supposed, two bushels, an acre.

Secondly, the tract first cultivated now brings its owner a rent (24—20=4), not of two bushels, but of four. It is no better land than it was before; it produces no more wheat under the same application of labor and capital; yet it yields its owner a rent twice as great as before cultivation descended to the third grade of soils. That increase of rent takes place simply and solely because cultivation has so descended.

If, again, we suppose that the increasing needs of the community require the cultivation of the eighteen-bushel tract, even the twenty-bushel tract will begin to bear a rent, *viz.*, two bushels, while the rent of the next tract will rise to four bushels, and that of the most productive land to six bushels, or three times the original amount.

258. The Law of Rent.—If we have correctly traced the course of self-interest, in dealing with the occupation of land, under the necessity of a resort to inferior soils, we are prepared to state the law of rent.

1. Rent arises out of differences existing in the productiveness of different soils under cultivation at the same time, for supplying the same market.

2. The amount of rent is determined by the degree of those differences. Specifically, the rent of any piece of land is determined by the difference between its annual yield and that of the least productive land actually cultivated for the supply of the same market, under equal applications of labor and capital, it being assumed that the quality of the land as a productive agent is, in neither case, impaired or improved by such cultivation.

259. Cost of Transportation.—By productiveness throughout the foregoing discussion, has been intended net productiveness, the cost of transportation to market being first deducted.

In the illustration as thus far given, the cost of transportation has been left out of account. Let us now, however, suppose a tract to be brought under cultivation for the purpose of supplying this market, situated at so great a distance as to make the cost of transportation a considerable element in the problem of rent.

If the reader will recur to the diagram, he will see that we have marked out a tract, at some distance from our village, the path thereto bearing the legend —2, by which we have intended to signify that the cattle and men taking the grain to market will eat, going and returning, two bushels out of the produce of each acre. The net productiveness of the tract will then be, for the purpose of determining its rental, not 23 bushels, but 21. It will not be cultivated until after the first two tracts have been completely occupied. It will then be cultivated, but will bear no rent so long as its produce, combined with that of those two tracts, suffices for the sustentation of the community. But when the increasing needs of population drive cultivation down to the 20-bushel tract, the tract in question will bear a rent of one bushel, which will rise to three when cultivation seeks the 18-bushel tract.

260. A New Continent.—The reader will further note that we have connected the same community with the projecting edge of a continent, which we have named America, by a dotted line, to which we have attached the sign and figure —8. These represent that portion of the crop of the year which is given to railway companies and the owners of vessels, as a consideration for transporting the grain to the English market. The net produce of these lands is, then, 20 bushels. Though they actually yield 28 bushels to the acre, with the given application of labor, they will bear no rent till the 18-bushel tract of English land is brought under cultivation, when they will yield two bushels rent, an acre, the same as the 20-bushel English tract, the net productiveness being the same.

But suppose this American land is of vast extent, and upon it can be raised all the grain which this, or any, market requires, what will be the effect upon rents? Why this: no one will now cultivate the English 18-bushel tract. Why should one, since a greater net produce can be obtained by the same labor elsewhere? This lowest grade of soils, therefore, falls out of cultivation. With what effect upon the rent of other parcels of land? To answer this, let us recur to our formula. The rent of any piece of land is determined by the difference between its annual yield and that of the least productive land under cultivation for the purpose of supplying the same market. The 24-bushel English tract has been bringing its owner 6 bushels, an acre, rent, because, and only because, the 18-bushel tract was necessarily brought under cultivation. Now, however, that American land, with a net productiveness of 20 bushels, an acre (28—8=20) is found in unlimited amount, the margin of cultivation is pushed backwards, and the best of the English tracts brings but four bushels rent; the next best but two; the 20-bushel tract now bears no rent, as it is in competition with free American land of indefinite extent.

Again, assume that the introduction of Bessemer steel rails and various improvements in ocean navigation reduce the cost of transportation of American grain to seven bushels out of every 28, what will be the effect on English rents? Clearly the American land now has a net productiveness represented by 21 bushels, and, as it is of unlimited extent, all the English 20-bushel land is thrown out of cultivation—for who would wish to cultivate it? and the rent of the best English land is reduced to three bushels, and that of the second grade to one.

The foregoing illustration accounts sufficiently for the great economic, and, by consequence, great social change, which has been going on in the British Islands within the last few years. The reduction in the cost of transportation from the American wheat fields beyond the Mississippi to the seaboard, and from the seaboard to Liverpool, has increased the net productiveness of those fields to a degree equal to the addition of several bushels an acre to the crop. This has thrown out of cultivation much of the poorer English land, and, by lifting upward the limit of cultivation, has decreased the normal rent of all English lands, cutting deeply, in prospect, into the incomes of the land-owning class. The first effects, however, have been most severely felt by the cultivators of the soil, who, holding their farms by lease, find themselves still bound to pay the stipulated rents.

261. Relation of Rent to the Price of Land. — We have stated the economic doctrine of rent. The price of land and its rental value stand in a certain necessary relation to each other. Land has its price because, and only because, it can command a rent. But while the relation between the two is a necessary one, being no less direct than that of cause and effect, the ratio between the rent of land and the price of land, expressed in terms of produce or of money, varies widely. In some countries, where the amount of accumulated capital is large; where a high degree of civil security exists; where the rights of property are respected, and where the ownership of land carries with it social distinction and perhaps political influence, the price of land may be twenty, twenty-five or even thirty times the annual rental. In other countries, from the failure of one or all of the conditions indicated, land may not sell for more than fifteen or even ten times its rental.

262. Rent forms no part of the Price of Agricultural Produce.—From the law of rent, as it has been stated, we deduce the very important conclusion that rent forms no part of the price of agricultural produce.

No proposition which the political economist has occasion to announce is so startling, at the first hearing, as this; nor does any other contend against such persistent incredulity. And yet, no proposition can be more clearly established. We have seen (par. 132) that in the same market, at the same time, there is but one price for different equal portions of any commodity. We have also seen (par. 137) that normal price is fixed by the cost of producing that portion of the supply which is produced at the greatest disadvantage.

Apply these principles to the case in hand. England does not raise all the wheat needed for the subsistence of her population. Besides cultivating the most fertile of her own fields, she makes heavy draughts upon the United States, France, Egypt, Hungary, and the Black Sea region. For the wheat of all these countries, however, so far as it is of the same quality, there is but one price. That price is fixed by the cost of raising the million, say, of bushels which are raised at the greatest disadvantage, which means, in this case, at the greatest distance, *viz.*, on the plains of Dakota. This wheat the English must have: the proof of which is found in the fact that they do have it. Now, if they will have it, they must pay the cost of raising it, that is, must pay enough to induce men to go to that far-off country, undergo the privations of a frontier life, undertake all the risks of pioneer agriculture, and submit to enormous charges for the transportation of their product by land two thousand miles to the seaboard, and, then, three thousand miles, by sea. If the English will not pay this price, they can not have the wheat. That they get the wheat is proof that they pay this price, which, in turn, sets the price for all the wheat raised in England, and for all the wheat brought thither, whether from France, from Egypt or from the Black Sea. Wheat may be raised in Middlesex at an actual cost not exceeding two shillings a bushel; but the Middlesex farmer will not, on that account, sell his wheat below the market price, say six shillings, which price is fixed, as we have seen, by the wheat from America. The difference, four shillings, is to be profit for somebody; and we will now proceed to show that this body must be either the landlord, or the tenant, not the agricultural laborer, and not the consumer of flour.

263. What Would Happen if Rents Were Remitted?—We shall best make this appear by means of an illustration. Let us suppose that a philanthropic gentleman, whose rent roll is £20,000, being greatly moved by tales of distress, knowing that the quartern loaf is very dear, and believing this to be due to the large rents paid for the use of land, calls his tenants together, and tells them that, in consideration of the hard times and the great suffering of the poor, he has determined to remit one-half of the rent of all his farms. What would be the consequence? Doubtless all the tenants would accept the proffered terms cheerfully, and humbly thank his honor. But would they sell the wheat at any lower price? Not at all; why should they? They can get the market price for it. That price is not fixed by the cost of raising wheat on their farms, or any farms for which rent is paid. It is the no-rent land that raises that last portion of the necessary supply of wheat which fixes the price of all wheat.

But suppose, to imagine a most improbable case, that some one out of the fifty tenants on this estate were to go to the dealer in grain to whom he was accustomed to sell his crop, and say: "Mr. B., inasmuch as my landlord has remitted half my rent this year, I offer you my wheat a shilling less a bushel, in order that you may sell it at a corresponding reduction to the baker." What would the grain-dealer do? Clearly he would take the wheat, at the reduced price offered; but would he sell it to the baker for any less? Or, if he did, would the baker, getting his flour a shilling "off," put down the price of the loaf? Not if he were of the sort of baker that you and I know.

But perhaps it is said, we concede that the farmers will not sell their wheat at any lower price, on account of the remission of rent, but they will raise the wages of their laborers. Why should they? They can make presents to their laborers, just as they could make presents to grain dealers or bakers, but we are talking now about business, and, as a matter of business, why should these fifty persons raise the wages of their laborers, in consequence of the generosity of their own landlord? The laborers were willing to work, before, for the wages that were stipulated, the same wages, it may be assumed, which other laborers in the county were receiving. Why should the laborers now be unwilling to work at the same wages? And if the laborers are willing to work at the same wages, why should the farmers pay more?

264. Resume of the Subject. — These illustrations may seem very elementary, but I have known so many persons, after a complete demonstration of the proposition we are considering, go away, showing, by look or by remark, that they still clung to the notion that rent has, somehow, something to do with the price of agricultural produce, that I have thought it worth the space required to repeat the demonstration and fully illustrate the argument. I trust it has been shown, to the conviction of every reader, that rent is a matter between the landowner and the tenant, not between the landlord and the agricultural laborer, or between the landlord and the consumer of agricultural produce.

Rent is the surplus of the crop above the cost of cultivation on the least productive lands contributing to the supply of the market. Admitting the private ownership of land (pars. 493-505), that surplus, necessarily, so far as economic forces are concerned, is left in the hands of the landlord. There, so far as economic forces are concerned, it must remain. The landlord can give it away, if he pleases, just as he can give away his horse, or his house, or any thing that is his. He can give it to his tenant, just as he could give to any one else. But if he does, it becomes a pure gratuity to the tenant, who, under the operation of the principle of self-interest, will transmit it neither to the agricultural laborer nor to the consumer of food, but will retain it entire for his own enrichment.

265. Attacks on the Doctrine of Rent. — Such is the economic doctrine of wealth, which is generally known by the name of David Ricardo, though, in truth, it was announced by Anderson, a Scotch economist, who wrote at an earlier date.*

I postpone to Part VI. the consideration of attacks upon the doctrine of Rent, by certain American and French writers.

266. The Doctrine of Rent: How Far Applicable to Actual Conditions?—The law of rent which has been expounded, is true only hypothetically, that is, upon the condition assumed, *viz.*, that the owners and the occupiers of land, each for himself, fully understand their own pecuniary interests, and will unflinchingly seek and unfailingly find their best market.

How much does this mean? A great deal; more than ever was realized in any country, at any time, though it has been

*It is not, however, wholly inappropriate to join the name of Ricardo to this doctrine, on account of the great force and clearness with which he expounded and defended it. Anderson's statement of the same principle. though perfectly correct, was so made as to attract no attention, and it was not till long after Ricardo made the doctrine famous, that it became popularly known that the substance of it was contained in Anderson's work.

far more nearly approached in some than in others. Just what is implied in the above assumption?

On the landlord's part that (1) he would as soon take a new tenant as retain one whose family had been on the soil for centuries; that (2) he will entertain no other consideration than the realization of the largest possible rent; that (3) he knows all the facts which in any way bear upon the highest rate that could be charged for the use of the land without driving away all would-be tenants.

On the tenant's part, that (1) he has the means to place himself elsewhere; that (2) he could carry with him the value of his stock and fixtures, and of any improvements made during his tenancy; that (3) he knows and can intelligently canvass the varying advantages of a sufficient number of localities to make his choice practically indefinite; and that (4) neither indolence, nor inertia, nor dread of change, nor love of home, friends or country, will intervene to keep him from his best market: that is, where he can rent land, of a given degree of productiveness, at the lowest annual rate.

The recital of the foregoing conditions shows that Ricardo's law does not furnish a formula by which the rent of a single piece of land can be determined in advance. The doctrine is true only hypothetically, and the conditions assumed exist nowhere.

267. Yet this hypothetical doctrine of rent is by no means to be regarded as vain and illusory. It is, on the contrary, of vast importance. It must be fundamental in any correct theory of the distribution of wealth. No projectile ever describes a perfect parabola, since the resistance of the air and the force of the wind will interfere to prevent an absolute compliance with the law of the projectile. Yet the artillerist must always have reference to that law in pointing his piece, making such allowance for disturbing influences as existing conditions may seem to require. Any attempt to explain the partition of the product of industry which should leave Economic Rent out of account, would be either futile or deceptive.

In some countries, notably in the United States and in

England, Ricardo's law furnishes the great underlying principle according to which, with more or less of divergence from general or from local and individual causes, actual rents are primarily determined. In other countries, like those of continental Europe generally, where custom operates powerfully upon the rental of land, the doctrine is still of importance ; first, as clearly furnishing the outside limit of rent ; secondly, as establishing the proposition that the question of rent or no rent, of high rent or low rent, is purely a question between landlord and tenant, not between the employer and the employed, and not between the producer and the consumer of food.

268. Rents in the United States.—We have said that in some countries the economic doctrine of rent furnishes the principle which primarily determines actual rents. The United States offer the most striking illustration of this. So completely is the American mind imbued with the feeling that a thing is worth what it will bring ; so little sympathy is here found for the notion of classes which, by reason of weakness, must be hedged in from competition with outside forces ; so vast are the tracts of arable land not yet occupied ; so freely do our people move from place to place ; so slight are their attachments to locality, that no prejudice whatever would be created by a landlord's demanding the utmost rent which the tenant could, and in the result, would, pay. The fact that the tenant actually paid the rent demanded would be proof sufficient that he ought to pay it ; that the land was worth it, and that the landlord showed only a proper sense of his own interest in advancing the price.

Nay, should the tenant refuse to pay the increased rent and give way to another, I know not an American community where odium would attach to the landlord. It would be felt, it would be freely said : If the tenant is not willing to pay the price of the land, let some one take it who is. And what is true of the United States in this particular, is true probably in nearly equal degree of Canada and Australia, new countries exhibiting the same general conditions of social life.

Here we see the unrestrained operation of the principle of

competition, with a wholly beneficial result. The tenant and landlord, being substantially on an equality as to intelligence, enterprise and freedom of movement, seek each his own interest, yet without injury to the other.

269. English Rents.—When, however, we reach England, we find a new force entering actively to influence rents, all on the side of the tenant. Here the sentiment is universal that there are classes which, by reason of wealth, education, and social position, are bound to do and to forbear much, out of regard to the interests of classes deemed to be permanently and hopelessly weak.

The gentleman must never forget, in dealing with his servants, his laborers, his tenants, and even in some degree his trades' people, that he is dealing with inferiors and dependents, who are, in a sense, under his protection, who can not easily defend themselves against encroachment or fully assert their own interests, and that, in consequence, he is bound to act somewhat differently, it may be very differently, from what he would were he dealing with his equals.

But it is in regard to land that this sentiment operates with the greatest force. It would be impossible for an English landed proprietor to feel that freedom in regard to raising rents which characterizes the action of an American landowner. A gentleman there who should undertake to force up rents, acting on the principle that, if his present tenants could not or would not pay his price, he would find others to do it, would feel the lash of public indignation descend on his back till life was made a burden to him. Instead of gaining increase of style and state through an enlargement of his rent-roll thus obtained, his social standing would be destroyed.

With public sentiment thus acting strongly and steadily in restraint of the natural impulses of the landholding class, we should look to see a divergence of actual from theoretical rents, all on the side of the tenant's interest; and such, indeed, we find to have been the case down to the time when, perhaps ten years ago, American competition began to operate with prodigious and altogether unprecedented force. "The rent of agricultural land," wrote Prof. Thorold Rogers, "is seldom the maximum annual value of the occupancy; in many cases is considerably below such an amount."

270. Customary Rents on the Continent of Europe.—On the Continent of Europe, rents are, in general, not determined by competition, but by custom, to which Mr. Mill has assigned the same beneficent function in economics it has always performed in the sphere of politics, as "the most powerful protector of the weak against the strong." In Switzerland, France and Italy, rents were formerly fixed almost universally by the custom of the country, at a certain definite portion of the produce of the land. This species of tenure, known as the Metayer tenancy, has been fully recognized as giving to the peasantry the use of land at less than the maximum rents, as determined by the application of the purely economic formula. So strong is custom in protecting the tenant's interest, in these countries, that oftentimes it happens that, where cities have sprung up during the continuance of a family upon the soil, giving a local market for produce, and, by consequence, raising prices, the landlord, even in admitting a new family to the estate, does not attempt to exact a larger share of the produce.

"A proprietor," says Sismondi, writing of Tuscany, "would not dare to impose conditions unusual in the country; and, even in changing one metayer for another, he alters nothing of the terms of the engagement."

271. Rents in Ireland.—We have seen how far actual may be made to diverge from theoretical rents, all on the side of the tenant's interest, by the force of public sentiment. Let us now turn to a country where, in the time of which we are to speak, the population was not homogeneous; where prejudices of race and religion had engendered animosities that descended from generation to generation; where no friendly public opinion stood guard over the interests of a peasantry whose improvidence concurred with the greed of the landlord class in exciting a fierce and unremitting competition for the occupancy of the soil.

The story of the wrongs done to Ireland is so familiar that it is needless to enter into details to show why it was that in

Ireland nothing intervened between landlord and tenant to break the force of competition. It was not merely that the two classes were of different races, of different religions, and in some degree also of different speech. The confiscations and colonizations of Elizabeth, the wars of Cromwell, and lastly the Penal Code, of which the temperate Hallam says, "to have exterminated the Catholics by the sword, or expelled them, like the Moriscoes of Spain, would have been little more repugnant to justice and humanity, but incomparably more politic"—these were the prime causes which had engendered antagonisms and animosities such as have rarely, in modern times, divided the population of any land.

272. In addition hereto another and most potent cause contributed to the severity with which rents were exacted. This was absenteeism, a great part of the soil being owned by landlords who resided in England and transacted their business through local agents, or through "middlemen," who assumed the estimated rental of large estates and wrung from the peasantry whatever they could.

By a kind of natural selection, out of these agents and middlemen came to be developed a distinct species of social animal, peculiarly fierce and cunning, of preternatural acuteness to search out every possible occasion for fresh exactions, with heart of flint and face of brass. Only men with a natural aptitude for exaction, distraint and eviction were selected for such a work; years of practice made them perfect in the arts of extortion, while the consciousness of being despised and hated to the point of frenzy choked every casual thought of pity, and made absolute heartlessness both a professional virtue and a condition of self-preservation.

Such was the situation in Ireland, on the part of the landlord class, furnishing all the conditions necessary to a rigid and relentless enforcement of rent, up to the economic maximum —*i. e.*, to the extent of giving to the owner of the land the entire surplus produce above the cost of cultivation on the poorest soils.

273. How was it on the side of the peasantry? Were they prepared to supply the conditions which should prevent competition from becoming disastrous, destructive? Unfortunately, the peasantry of no country in Europe were less fitted to enter upon such a struggle with the landlord class. Sanguine, improvident even to recklessness, the Irish people clung the more closely to the land the more miserable their lot; multiplied at a rate inconsistent with the capacity of the soil for providing subsistence, and competed among themselves for the occupancy of smaller and continually smaller parcels with a passionate eagerness. Had it been a stationary population, like that of France, which entered on this struggle for the fruits of the soil, the peasantry might have had some chance; but, with a population at least fifty per cent. beyond the capabilities of the soil to support, as the art of agriculture was then practiced, while every year largely increased the number of eager, penniless competitors, misery could hardly fail to result.

In the situation described, it was a matter of course that rents were advanced to the full limit allowed by the law we have stated. But there was more than this and worse than this. Rents were demanded by the agent, or middleman, rents were even offered by the peasantry in the eagerness of their competition, in excess of the economic maximum; in excess of what could possibly be paid; in many cases in excess, incredible as it may seem, of the whole annual produce of the soil.*

274. But, it may be asked, if the tenants could not pay the rents, what harm to promise them? The landlords clearly would be disappointed; but how would the tenants suffer?

The injury done to the peasantry through this cause was threefold.

First. The whole possible produce above the bare necessities of subsistence, belonging to the landlord, the tenant had little interest in the crop or in keeping up the productiveness

---

* Cottier rents are nominal in pecuniary amount, because these rents are fixed so high that it is impossible for the cottiers ever to pay them. The nominal amount of the rent far exceeds the whole produce which the land would yield.—H. Fawcett, "Pol. Economy." This statement is probably somewhat too sweeping.

of the land. Having nothing to hope for, and being in so bad a plight that there was nothing but eviction to fear, all inspiration died out of the cultivation of the soil. What was done was always the least and the meanest that could be done.

Secondly. The promise of excessive, and indeed impossible, rents kept the tenant always in debt to his landlord. Hopeless debt differs little from slavery. The Irish cottier lived by the breath of the agent or the middleman.

Thirdly. The joint effect of the causes described was continually to lower the standard of living, and consequently the cost of cultivating the no-rent land, or lowest grade of soils, by making the peasantry reckless regarding the increase of their numbers.

275. Effects of Unequal Competition.—In the foregoing description of the state of the Irish tenantry prior to 1844, we have an illustration of the results of an unequal competition. That same force which in the United States, operating upon an intelligent, alert, active, aggressive population, under equal laws, produces effects only beneficial, in Ireland, under the conditions recited, produced disaster.

276. Actual vs. Theoretical Rents.—We see, then, that practically there may be three classes of cases in respect to rent.

First. Where, under active competition, with both parties substantially on an equality in respect to intelligence, alertness and freedom of movement, with no laws or habits or sentiments opposing the exaction of all which any thing that is the subject of bargain and sale may be worth, rents, as in the United States, conform nearly to the Ricardian formula.

Second. Where, among a population presenting wide differences of wealth and intelligence, and perhaps, also, of rank and political power, sentiments of personal kindliness and mutual regard between landlord and tenant, and a strong authoritative opinion throughout the community respecting the obligations imposed by the ownership of property, especially of landed property, serve, as in England, and in many countries of the continent of Europe, to reduce the pressure of the landowning upon the tenant class; making the landlord slow to seek occasions for raising rent; reluctant in forcing matters with the tenant to extremity, and altogether unwilling to proceed, in the case of a decent, well-meaning tenant, to distraint and eviction. Hence it comes about that rents vary widely from the Ricardian formula, always on the side of the tenantry.

Third. Where, with a tenantry ignorant, improvident, perhaps reckless in respect to family increase, and by consequence unable to offer effective resistance to an acquisitive, aggressive treatment of the question of rents, little in the way of sentiments of personal kindness on the part of landlords, and nothing in the way of an authoritative public opinion, enters to restrain the impulses which tend to advance rents. Here we have a result of ultimate injury to the economic interests of both parties and of the entire community.

277. The Rent of Pastures.—We have thus far spoken only of the rent of arable land. We have taken this first, not only because it is most important, so far as the mere amount involved is concerned, but also because the principles governing rent can be here most easily discerned. If we have done our work well, there will be little difficulty in applying the principles discovered to the rent of pastures, water privileges, building lots, mines and wood lots.

We have, throughout the foregoing extended illustration, assumed the existence of a considerable body of no-rent, arable lands, furnishing the base-line from which the rentals of the superior lands are respectively measured. To a certain extent this assumption corresponds to the facts of agriculture. More commonly, however, those lands whose net productiveness is so low that they could only be cultivated on the condition of paying no rent, are turned into pasture or grazing land. We might, therefore, say that, in many agricultural regions, the base-line for ascertaining rents, is furnished by a certain grade of pasture-lands, large tracts of which would yield but a scanty subsistence to a few cattle or sheep. Then come the more valuable pastures, which pay an appreciable rent, and, parallel with these, arable lands of moderate fertility, paying, also, an appreciable rent.

As we go upward in the scale of fertility, lands may be transferred from grazing to tillage, or from tillage to grazing, according to the demand for animal as compared with the demand for vegetable productions, at the time prevailing in the local market, or according to other conditions which we need not enter into here. Arable land is, also, often turned into pasture for the purpose of allowing it to recuperate in respect to certain properties of the soil which have been unduly drawn upon by the crops of previous years.

While, thus, a large part of the lands of any agricultural district may be used interchangeably for tillage and for grazing, it seldom happens that the best lands are used at all, or, at any rate, for more than the briefest period, as pasture. Generally speaking, the poorest lands are always used as pasture, the richest lands are always cultivated excepting, only, during intervals required for recuperation. It is in respect to the intermediate grades of soil that the alternation referred to takes place. The principle which determines the rent of pasture lands is the same as that with which we have already become familiar through our discussion of rent in its application to arable lands.

278. The Rent of Water Privileges.—Water privileges have three uses: first, for power, in connection with saw-mills, grist-mills, cotton-factories, etc.; secondly, for the supply of water, for drinking, washing, and other domestic purposes, to cities and towns; thirdly, for the irrigation of land, for the purposes of agriculture. The volume of water, the convenience of its application to the purpose for which water is, in the specific instance, required; proximity to the market, that is, the place where the water is to be used, these are the principal considerations which determine the productiveness of water-privileges for the purposes of rent. For the supply of cities and towns, the quality of the water also becomes an element of importance.

Productiveness being thus estimated, there are all degrees of productiveness among water privileges. There are the no-rent privileges, which, by reason of distance, or inconvenience of application, or of insufficient or irregular flow, are not used at all, or only used on condition that no compensation is exacted therefor. Above these, are found low-rent privileges and high-rent privileges, the measure of rent being the degree of productiveness.

279. An instructive illustration of the relation of monopoly to value is often afforded by the action of water-power companies, in regulating the prices they charge for power, according to the price of coal. In, for example, a given textile manufacturing city of New England, if coal can be delivered at four dollars a ton, the water-power company sells to a cotton or woolen-mill the right to take water sufficient to create (by its fall through a given number of feet), one-horse power, for, say, $24 a year, that amount representing the estimated cost of maintaining one-horse power, throughout a year, by the consumption of coal, at four dollars a ton. Should the price of coal fall to, say, three dollars, the water-power company would readjust its charge to meet the changed conditions of competition with steam.

Within the limits thus determined, the price of water-power is a monopoly price, being entirely irrespective of what it cost the company to acquire its rights and construct its works, and of what it may cost to keep up its service. To that monopoly, however, a limit is set by possible competition with steam-power.

280. The Rent of Building Lots.—The rent of building lots is determined by the principles already set forth. There are no-rent building lots in abundance. Every township has its squatters whose cabins, placed out of the way, on worthless land, pay no rent. Even in the neighborhood of large cities, shanties are perched on the rocks without objection from owners of land which, in another twenty or fifty years, may bear a high rent.

But something more is wanted in the case of a building, than ground to stand upon. The building must be placed with reference to its uses ; and it is the productiveness of the lot in that respect which determines the rent. Among building lots that bear a rent, the minimum may be said to be determined by the value of land for the purposes of agriculture. A man leases a hundred acres of arable land, of uniform quality, for $500, a year, and places his house upon some convenient spot, occupying, with barns and sheds, half an acre of ground. The rent of this building lot is $2.50 a year. If he were a market gardener near a large city, the rent of the lot so occupied might be $25. If, on the other hand, he were a market man instead of a market gardener, he might pay $50 for the rent of the ground on which to build his cottage in the suburbs of the city, and five times that sum as the ground rent of his little shop in the heart of the city. If a banker, he could better afford to pay $2,000 or perhaps $5,000 ground rent on State Street, or Wall Street, or Lombard Street, than occupy premises half a mile away were he permitted to do so for nothing.

The productiveness of land occupied for the purposes of manufacture or trade, has reference to the number of persons passing through the street, or to the proximity of water-privileges, or wharf-privileges, or railroad stations, or to various other facilities for either doing a greater amount of business with the same capital, or for saving expenditure upon a given amount of business. Such lots being limited in number, yet held by competing owners, their rent conforms closely to the Ricardian formula. In regard to this kind of rent, competition is, if not perfect, at least very active on both sides. No favor is shown or asked; the two parties to the bargain are regarded as equal. The landlord gets all the land will bring, if not from one tenant, then from another. The tenant expects to pay all that any man will be willing to give for the commercial advantages of occupying the ground.

281. The Rent of Mines.—The rent of mines is not governed wholly by the economic law of rent which, as stated (par. 253), has reference to the native and *indestructible* powers of the soil. Under proper care and husbandry, cultivation does not exhaust the soil. With rotation of crops, with annual manuring and an occasional season of rest, such as are provided for in most English leases, the land returns to its owner, or his representative, after 30, or 50, or 99 years, with unimpaired virtue. The enjoyment of water privileges does not exhaust the capacity of the river. The occupation of the ground for a generation does not contract the surface available for the same or a different use by another generation.

By the very nature of such deposits, the enjoyment of mining privileges diminishes the sum of the mineral in existence. The mine may be "worked out" in ten years or in twenty or in fifty, and nothing but an ugly pit be returned to the owner, at the expiry of the lease. The rent of such properties is not, therefore, regulated by the Ricardian formula, without modification. The rent must be increased sufficiently to compensate for the ultimate exhaustion of the deposits: the destruction of the value of the estate. Otherwise, the rule of rent for these properties is the same as in the case of other natural agents. The chief elements, here, in determining productiveness for the purposes of rent, are the quality of the product, the extent of the deposits, the depth of working, the distance from a market.

There are, in the United States, vast deposits of coal, for instance, near the surface, not far from a market, which will not pay for working, even if no rent be exacted, because the quality is poor, though the coal will burn, will give out light and heat, and, if delivered at the furnace free of cost, would be worth using.

There are other deposits of coal, of excellent quality, which will not pay for working by reason of the thinness of seams, or their narrow extent laterally. There are, again, vast deposits of good coal, which, by reason of their depth below the surface, are not sought by productive industry and perhaps never will be. There are still others which, by reason of distance from market are not now worth taking up at the government rates, which may in another century supply great manufacturing cities with power. These and other mines, a little more fortunate in character or location, which will just pay for working, furnish the no-rent mines. Above these are mines which pay rent, the degree of productiveness rising until the rental of a single mine becomes the income of a prince.

282. The Rent of Woodlots.—Woodlots and timber lands are, in fact, seldom rented in the United States and other new countries; first, on account of the difficulty which would be experienced in preventing waste and abuse by a tenant; and, secondly, because it is generally more profitable to cut off the whole body of wood or timber at once, than to pick from it, year by year, a certain proportion of what is standing. For these reasons, woodlots, when they reach the right condition for cutting, are commonly sold to large operators, at prices determined by the "net productiveness" of the individual tracts, reference being had to the amount and quality of timber and other wood, to the distance from market, facilities for transportation, etc.

The price at which an individual woodlot may sell, once in thirty or fifty years, may properly be conceived of as related to an annual rental, not collected at the time, but allowed to accumulate against the day of sale.

In old countries, where the value of wood and timber bears a much higher proportion to the wages of labor, than in new countries, and where the tracts so occupied are generally surrounded by dense populations, woodlots and forests are more commonly culled from year to year, instead of being cut off all at once. In such a condition, the Ricardian formula of rent would strictly apply to the several tracts supplying any given market, although, as a matter of fact, an owner would be likely to conduct the cutting of the wood and timber himself, or through his paid agents, on account of the difficulty, above referred to, of preventing waste and abuse on the part of a tenant.

283. The Rent of Buildings and of Permanent Improvements on the Land.—The so-called rent of buildings, exclusive of ground rent, is not governed at all by the economic law of rent, but by the principles which regulate the Interest on Capital, of which we are next to speak. A man owns a building lot, for which he could obtain a ground rent, that is, rent proper. Being also a capitalist, he erects a building thereon.

Why does he so? Because he believes that, in addition to the rent of the ground, he can also obtain, for the occupation of the house erected thereon, a fair remuneration for the use of his capital, a remuneration equal (damage, trouble and risk of loss being taken into account) to what he would receive were he to put his capital into the form of live stock or railroad shares, or government bonds. The building is an investment of capital. If his investment has been shrewdly made, he will receive from his tenants a sum which, in the view of the economist, consists of two parts, rent proper — ground rent—and interest. We shall see, in the next chapter, that these two elements of that remuneration are governed by widely different laws.

284. The Unearned Increment of Land.—We have seen how rent arises, under the private ownership of land, and what principles govern its amount and economic direction. We have seen that rent is purely a question between landlord and tenant, not between employer and employed, not between the producer and the consumer of agricultural produce. We have seen that, conceding the private ownership of land, rent must, so far as economic forces are concerned, remain in the hands of the owner of land; that it can only get into the hands of the tenant as a gift; that if it reaches the hands of the tenant, no economic forces will carry it into the hands of the agricultural laborer or of the consumer of food. It can only get there by a further gift or series of gifts.

We have also seen that, whenever the limit of cultivation is lowered, that is, whenever a less productive grade of soils is, by the increasing demands of population for subsistence, brought under cultivation, the rents of all previously cultivated lands are correspondingly raised, to the enrichment of their owners, not by reason of any increase in the yield of such lands, or by reason of any greater exertions put forth by the owners, but solely by reason of the necessity of cultivating a lower grade of soils.

Upon this view of rent, has arisen the question, Why should the private ownership of land be permitted to exist? at any rate, why should this incident of private ownership, the aggrandizement of the owner through the growth of the community, be longer permitted to exist? Why should not this "unearned increment of land," to use Mr. Mill's phrase, go to the community, and not to any individual?

This demand has been made very vigorously, of late years, by a school of writers which embraces more than one economist of reputation. As the elements of the question are not purely economic, but embrace considerations of political equity and political expediency, I shall reserve all remark concerning it till we reach Part VI.

CHAPTER III.

INTEREST.

285. Definition of Interest.—We have seen one share cut off from the product of industry—rent; one claimant satisfied—the landlord. The reader now sees why this topic was first treated. In economic theory, this is ever the first claim to be adjusted and paid. We can make no progress—not so much as by a single step—toward discovering the principles which govern the division of the product of industry among capitalists, employers, and laborers, until rent is taken out, until the claim of the landlord is satisfied. Hence the topic, Rent, comes first, in a treatise on the distribution of wealth.

We are now to speak of Interest: the share of the Capitalist in the product of industry.

In Part II. we inquired into the origin and office of capital. We saw that capital consists of savings out of earnings, the native powers of the earth, air and water not being regarded as capital. Wealth having been produced, some of it, much of it, must soon be consumed, in order to sustain the producing classes, and to repair the waste inevitably attendant upon production, and even upon the mere lapse of time. All of it may be so consumed, and will be, under the urgent and constantly recurring desires which wealth alone can satisfy, unless some motive for saving can be found which shall prove strong enough to withstand the impulses to immediate gratification, and to wrest a portion of wealth from the jaws of appetite. We have shown what that motive is, and how it manifests itself in a barbarous condition.

In an advanced state of society, the motive to saving is not so much found in the desire of the individual to accumulate tools and materials for his own handling, as in the desire to obtain interest from some one else, for the use of that portion of wealth whose consumption is thus postponed. To the varying strength of this motive with different men, and different races, we shall have occasion to refer further on.

286. Interest not Paid for the Use of Money.—It has been said that interest is the compensation paid for the use of capital. The usual form of statement is that interest is paid for the use of money. Broadly speaking, this is not true. Money, which is one of the many forms of capital, is, indeed, often the agent in effecting the loan of other species of capital. But in these cases, it is not the money, philosophically considered, that is borrowed: The interest paid is for the use of the capital obtained through that agency. One borrows $5,000, and gives a note for that sum, with interest. With this money he purchases live stock, machinery for his factory, or goods for his trade: these were what he wanted; these were what he really borrowed; these are what he pays interest upon. The money was solely a means to that end.

But money is not always, it is not in a majority of cases, in a highly advanced state of industrial society it is, indeed, rarely, the agent in effecting the loan of capital. The country merchant buys goods and gives his notes for two, four, and six months, promising to pay the price with interest. Interest on what? On money? No money passed in the transaction. What was borrowed was hardware and crockery, dry goods, and groceries. The young farmer buys cattle to stock his farm, and gives his note, promising to pay, with interest: not interest on money, for he has had none, but interest on the value of cows and working oxen.

287. The Rate of Interest.—Let us now inquire how the rate of interest is determined.

Since the use of capital is a matter of bargain and sale, or of exchange, what should determine the rate of interest but the demand for, and the supply of, loanable capital?

Here we see the futility of the notion, which, from time to time, obtains a strong hold on the public mind of America, and, indeed, of all new countries, that the rate of interest is to be lowered by increasing the supply of money through the issue of paper notes. Men wish to borrow that they may get control of the agencies of production: capital in its various forms. The amount to be paid for the use of capital will depend on its abundance compared with the occasions for its productive use. The issue of money will not increase the number of horses and cattle and plows, nor will it build shops and warehouses or construct machinery for manufacture or for transport.

If the people of a community be thriving and progressive, the demand for capital, to start new enterprises, or to enlarge those already established, will be very great. If the community be, also, young, having brought to new fields the social and industrial ideas, tastes and ambitions of an old society, the supply of capital will be scanty, and the rate of interest will rule high.

288. Is this high rate of interest a hardship? No, the hardship lies in the scarcity of capital. The high rate of interest becomes the active means of removing that hardship, through increasing the supply of capital available to meet the demand. A high rate of interest is not an evil, but the cure of an evil. How is this?

Capital is, as we have seen, the result of saving. Interest, then, is the reward of abstinence. A part, a large part, of all produced wealth must be at once consumed to meet the conditions of human existence; but the remaining portion may be consumed or may be accumulated, according to the will of the owner. The strength of the motive to accumulation will vary with the reward of abstinence. If that be high, the disposition to save will be strengthened, and capital will be rapidly accumulated; if that be low, that disposition will be relatively weak, and capital will increase slowly, if, indeed, the body of existing capital be not dissipated at the demands of appetite.

We do not say that the strength of the disposition will increase proportionally to the increase of remuneration; that it will, for instance, be one-fifth greater at six per cent. interest than at five per cent. Moral philosophy has reached no such precision in gauging motives. But it is certain that, among the same people, and at the same time, the higher the rate of interest the stronger will be the motives which lead to saving: the more rapid the accumulation of capital.*

So we see that a high rate of interest, instead of being the cause of an evil, is really its cure; and that to depress the rate of interest, as, for example, by force of law, would be to retard the processes by which capital is supplied.

As a high rate of interest is not in itself an evil, so a low rate of interest does not necessarily imply a condition which is a subject of congratulation. A low rate of interest may mean that, in a thriving, progressive community, the accumulation of capital has gone on so rapidly as to outrun the occasions for its productive use. It may mean that the people are so dull, indolent and unambitious, or the state of society so disordered, that commercial and manufacturing enterprises are not undertaken, and no enlargement of traditional industries is looked for. A small amount of capital more than suffices for such scanty needs.

---

* In general, taking all classes of producers into account, this will be so. Yet the effect of a reduction of the rate of interest is not wholly upon one side. Prof. Marshall very justly exhibits an effect of a reduction of the rate of interest, which, with a certain class of producers, might and probably would operate in the opposite direction.

"A high rate of interest no doubt affords a liberal reward of abstinence, and stimulates the saving of all who are ambitious of earning social position by their wealth. Again, if a man is in doubt whether to save in order to make provision for himself or his family, the expectation of a

289. The Rate of Interest tends to a Decline.—Despite the urgent and ever-recurring demands for the consumption of wealth in various forms of self-indulgence; despite the occasional reversal of the course of accumulation, in the occurrence of war; despite all the effects of misgovernment and social disorder, wealth tends strongly to increase. Since the application of steam-power to manufactures and transportation, this rate of increase has been so great as even to transcend the demand for the uses of wealth in undertaking new industrial and commercial enterprises, and thus, with some temporary exceptions, interest has tended to decline.

In this respect interest differs markedly, we may say, essentially, from rent. The latter tends to rise, with the lapse of time, the increase of population, the growth of wealth. The former tends to decline under the same conditions. This constitutes one of the two reasons why the economist insists upon treating interest and rent separately in his discussion of the distribution of the product of industry. The second of these reasons will now be stated.

290. There is not any No-Interest Capital.—We have seen (par. 255) that the whole theory of rent rests on the assumption that there is a body of no-rent lands. These serve

---

high rate of interest may induce him to save; because the higher the rate of interest, the larger the amount of future enjoyment which can be obtained by sacrificing a given amount of present enjoyment.

"But the history of the past and the observation of the present show that it is a man's temperament, much more than the rate of interest to be got for his savings, which determines whether he makes provision for his old age and for his family, or not. Most of those who make such a provision would do so equally whether the rate of interest were low or high. And when a man has once determined to provide a certain annual income, he will find that he has to save more if the rate of interest is low than if it is high. Suppose, for instance, that a man wishes to provide an income of £400 a year on which he may retire from business, or to insure £400 a year for his wife and children after his death. If the current rate of interest is 5 per cent., he need only put by £8,000 or insure his life for £8,000; but if it is four per cent., he must save £10,000 or insure his life for £10,000."

as the base from which to measure upwards the successive degrees of productiveness of the lands bearing rent.

In the theory of capital there is nothing to correspond to this. The economist does not find any no-interest capital. In theory, all capital bears an interest, and all portions of capital bear equal interest. If one portion, in fact, brings no interest to its owner, or brings an interest below that obtained by the owners of other portions, this is because of misadventure, due to accident or erroneous calculation, not to the nature of the capital itself.

Of course, it is anticipated by the political economist that the interest realized by portions of capital actually loaned will vary not a little, even within the same market, inasmuch as competition is never perfect in any sphere; but what has been stated shows how fundamentally the theory of interest differs from that of rent.

291. Is there a Minimum Rate of Interest? — We have said that the inducement to save diminishes, other things equal, as the rate of interest falls. Is there a point at which the disposition to consume wealth for purposes of comfort or luxury will equal in strength the disposition to acquire an annual income by saving wealth for productive uses, so that no further accumulation will take place, the savings out of earnings thereafter being only sufficient to make good the waste of production and keep up the stock of capital?

If there is a minimum rate of interest, it is very low. Fifteen or twenty years ago, six per cent. was the traditional rate of interest in New England, and probably few of us then thought that, if the rate were to go lower, it really would be worth while to "save." We had become so accustomed to six per cent. that it had come to seem as if there were some law of nature that fixed that rate. Six per cent.? Why of course a man would get six per cent.? Yet since that time we have seen the rate of interest steadily fall, in consequence of the vast accumulation of capital, till now loans of capital are to be had on good security at four and one-half or even four per cent., while the government borrows all it wants at three and one-half or even three. The English government has long borrowed at three per cent. The government of Holland during the most flourishing period of the republic, was even able to borrow at two per cent.

292. Income from Investments, how Computed.—Misapprehensions regarding the actual rate of interest are not infrequently occasioned by the failure to note, what would appear very plain, that the amount of interest paid upon bonds or notes, and the amount of dividends declared upon shares of corporate stock, should be compared, not with a nominal par value, but with the sum actually invested in the purchase of such bonds, stocks, notes or shares, or else with the sum for which these would at the time bring, if sold.

Thus, we read in the newspapers, that the Boston and Maine railroad, in May, 1887, declared a semi-annual dividend of five per cent., being at the rate of ten per cent., a year.

This statement, by itself, might create the impression that investment in the stock of this road would be a peculiarly profitable one. A reference, however, to the stock quotations, in another column of the same newspaper, would have shown that the shares of this railroad were then selling at about $230, on the par of $100. A person, therefore, buying a share of this stock, in April, 1887, would have received but a trifle over four per cent., per annum, which was about the rate of interest then prevailing upon "bottom mortgages."

On the other hand, a number of railroad companies, during the great speculative extension, 1868–1873, advertised to sell at seventy dollars, bonds for one hundred dollars, bearing seven per cent. interest. What, then, was the rate of interest promised on this investment? Seven per cent.? No: the rate of interest promised to be paid was ten per cent., and, even, as we shall see, more than that. The investor paid seventy dollars for a bond, to receive upon it annually seven dollars of interest, per year, until the bond should mature, and then to receive $100 in money, whereas he only paid down $70. In other words, he was, on the expiry of the bond, to receive a premium of $30, over and above an annual interest of ten per cent. The "present value" of this premium would depend on the length of time the bond had "to run."

293. False Interest: Insurance of the Principal.—A great deal that is paid under the name of interest is not interest in the true sense, but is merely a premium for the insurance of the principal sum lent. Real interest only comprises that part of the payment made which would be paid, were the return of the principal, at the date of the maturity of the obligation, a matter of reasonable certainty. Absolute assurance can be reached in no human transaction; but where the risk is so small that it amounts to nothing in the mind of the lender, as in the case of British consols, or of a "bottom mortgage," where the sum lent is only a half or a third of the value of improved real estate, we have an instance of real interest, pure and simple.

Whatever, in the same market, at the same time, is paid above this, for the use of capital, is of the nature of insurance against the risk of losing the amount lent. If the rate of real interest in London is 3 per cent., as determined by the price of consols, loans on various kinds of fair security may range from that rate up to 5 or 6 per cent.; while all the time note-brokers are "shaving" the "paper" of second and third rate dealers at from 10 to 20 per cent. discount.

294. Extra-Hazardous Risks.—The operation of the mind of the person who lends capital, at a high interest, upon poor security, is a familiar one. He sees the opportunity to obtain interest proper—the normal remuneration for forbearing to consume in immediate self-indulgence the wealth he has created, or come into possession of—without encountering any appreciable risk of losing the principal sum. But there is offered him a higher, perhaps a much higher, rate of interest, for a loan into which a chance of total loss enters. His mind balances the risk against the prize. The yearly value of the latter is definite. It is three, five or ten per cent. on the sum asked to be lent. Were he to receive this added interest for a sufficient number of years, he could even afford to lose the principal. He may receive the interest during the full term of the obligation, and then have his principal back again. He knows also that he may receive but one or two annual payments of interest, and then be compelled to recognize his investment as a total loss.

Of the degree of risk there is no measure. The ablest statistician, the first financier of the world, could give no mathematical statement of the chances for or against the ultimate repayment of the loan. The matter lies very vaguely even in the mind of the shrewdest banker or broker. He sees that there is great risk or little risk, very great risk or very little risk, or that the elements on which the ability of the borrower is to depend are altogether shrouded in uncertainty; but as to giving a mathematical expression to the value of the loan, based on the chances of loss, the man who does this is deceiving either himself or some one else.

295. With the great majority of lenders no calculation whatever, deserving of the name, enters into the negotiation of loans where more than double interest is paid. The capitalist is simply tempted beyond what he is able to bear, or else, if a man of another temper, the enhanced inducement becomes of itself a reason for refusing to lend his money, and he shuts the door upon negotiation. Look at the hundreds of millions, the thousands of millions, that have been sunk in railway shares and mining stocks by persons who had not the smallest qualifications for estimating the value of the risk, but whose prudence gave way under an offer of ten, or twelve, or twenty per cent. Writers on Interest are too much given to assuming that the losses sustained in extra-hazardous investments are balanced by the gains, and that the "average rate" is somehow maintained. The fact is, few lenders are capable of making any computation of the value of the risks they take; few even go through the form of doing so.

The only thing that can be said with assurance is that the vast majority of lenders on extra-hazardous risks are losers. The high rate of interest proves a snare. Tempted by the offer of 12 or 20 per cent., they take risks for which 40 or 50 would be inadequate. Interest is paid, dividends are declared, just long enough to complete the subscription, just long enough to secure the last gudgeon in the pool. And it is often astonishing to note the class of men who contribute to a scheme which is in its very terms an insult to common-sense. Bought wit is the best wit ; but in this matter, experience seldom suffices for wisdom. The susceptibility to humbug is perennial in the human breast. After a dance of folly, in which figure "The Periwig Company, and the Spanish-Jackass Company, and the Quicksilver-fixation Company ;" in which prospectus vies with prospectus to see which shall be the more preposterous ; and in which investor vies with investor in recklessness, there comes, indeed, a resting spell, more through exhaustion of means than through acquired prudence ; but the first tingle of reviving activity in trade starts the fever of speculation anew, and the knaves find the dupes as numerous and as credulous as ever.

296. The Wreckers of Trade.—The foregoing remarks apply to the great majority of investors who take extra-hazardous risks. Yet there are in every large commercial community those who reap enormous rates of interest with only rare losses to offset their gains. These are men with preternatural sagacity to know when it is safe to trust a rogue, how far to ride with a spendthrift towards his ruin, just the point at which to leave a tottering house whose foundations they have undermined by drains of exorbitant interest, just the moment at which to "unload" a stock ; men with the cunning to secure themselves against loss, whoever may suffer ; men who have the hardness to exact the last penny of their dues, at whatever distress to the debtor. Such men are the wreckers of trade. Their gains are great, for they reap the enormous profits of extra-hazardous risks, yet seldom lose in the principal sum lent. Rarely, indeed, is an embarrassed firm saved by their aid. Resort to them is the almost certain precursor of ruin. It serves to delay the catastrophe a little, only to make it utter and remediless at the last.

297. Double Interest.—The foregoing remarks apply only to extra-hazardous risks, where, to put it roundly, more than double interest is paid. With investments or temporary loans inside this limit, a different rule obtains. The rates of interest paid are still graded with little real appreciation of the degrees of risk taken ; the sums obtained as insurance can not be assumed to be proportioned to the hazard ; yet it is generally possible for an investor or lender to say, this is more safe than that : the adverse chances here are few and small ; are many and great there.

But there is a more marked difference between extra-hazardous and ordinary risks in the loan of capital. With the former, the rates obtained are, as a whole, taking all classes of investors or lenders together, below the actuarial value of the risks taken, and such loans and investments, in spite of the acuteness of the professional money-lending class, result, as a body, in loss. With ordinary risks, the rates of interest are, on an average, above their true value, as estimated from the basis of bottom mortgages and government loans.

For example, in England, a few years ago, the return from capital invested in government bonds was about 3.3 per cent.; while the savings banks realized on their investments, which may be assumed to have been made in a conservative spirit, 4½ per cent., and the average return to investors in railway stocks was 5 per cent. Now, here is an undeniable case of disproportion. Any shrewd and sensible man, selling £100,000 of consols, investing the proceeds in the shares of ten reputable railways, and compounding through a term of years the extra $1^7/_{10}$ per cent., per annum, would create a fund far more than sufficient to offset any losses he might sustain in an individual case. This disproportion is due first, to the estimation, higher than an actuarial value, placed by large classes of investors upon the feeling of security, the absence of all apprehensions and occasional alarms, and, secondly, to the favor extended by the courts to the investment of trust funds in government bonds.

298. Differing Rates of Interest in the Same Market.— We have laid down the proposition (par. 132) that in one market, at one time, there can be but one price for equal portions of the same commodity. The plain facts of interest seem to controvert this proposition. In the same market, at the same moment, the price paid for the use of capital may range from three per cent. upwards, to five, to ten, to twenty. Is this because between the portions of capital so loaned an economic difference exists, which creates a preference for one over the other, as when several different grades of flour are sold at several distinct prices? No, the capital loaned may be, in all economic respects, uniform. A man having $30,000 on deposit in a bank, may, on the same day, buy $10,000 worth of "governments" which pay four per cent., invest in "railways" paying six per cent. dividends, to the same amount; and loan the remainder at ten per cent. on personal security. Manifestly, between the three portions of capital loaned or invested, no economic differences existed.

To what, then, is the phenomenon noted due? In part to the cause discussed under the last head—the insurance of the principal sum lent. Twenty years ago there were on the stock market, in Lombard Street, three kinds of government securities: English consols, bringing, then, three and a quarter per cent. interest on the investment; Russian bonds bringing five and a quarter per cent., and Turkish bonds bringing ten and a half per cent. Every day large amounts of these bonds were bought by Englishmen. Doubtless, some purchasers bought portions of each kind of securities.

Inasmuch as the possibility of the English government becoming bankrupt, or tending to repudiation, is never admitted by an Englishman, the dividends received by holders of the "consols" constituted pure interest, the reward of abstinence. The added two per cent. obtained from the Russian bonds represented the value, as viewed by the purchaser, of the insurance of his capital against the risk of loss attendant on loaning it to the government of a people, possessing great natural resources, indeed, and bound together by a strong national feeling, but rude in manner, primitive in industry, with their political questions largely unsolved, and having points of possible collision with England. But while the Englishman demanded five and a quarter per cent. per annum from the Russian government, as the consideration for his loan, he exacted just twice that consideration from the Turkish government, though a government bound to Great Britain by the strongest ties of self-interest, because both the resources and the good faith of the Turkish government were reasonably suspected, and its existence was dependent on support from foreign powers.

299. Imperfect Competition in the Money Market.—We have in the foregoing paragraph used the expression, "as viewed by the purchaser." Hereby is indicated a consideration, which, while it is of importance in any market, is of especial importance in the market where capital is loaned, the so-called money-market. In quoting Prof. Jevons' statement of the reason, why, in the same market, at the same moment, all equal portions of a perfectly homogeneous commodity must bring the same price, we added that this proposition assumed perfect competition, all the conditions of a good market being fully realized. Now, perfect competition only exists where there is ample and accurate information. In bargains relating to the use of capital, so little is known by the parties respecting the supply of and the demand for capital, especially where usury laws drive borrowers and lenders to shifts and evasions; so much more are men disposed to conceal the fact and the extent of their borrowing than of their buying; so much does the repayment of the principal depend, in spite of law, upon the good faith of the borrower, that the market for the loan of capital can rarely be called a good market.

All bargains in the "money market," as the market for the loan of capital is popularly called, take place necessarily upon information imperfect at the best, often of a private and confidential nature: hence it frequently happens that, in the same market, at the same moment, loans, upon equally good security, are made at different rates; while it is not at all unlikely to occur, that, of two loans of unequal value, as to security, the more hazardous may be made at the lower rate of interest.

300. Differing Rates of Interest in Different Markets.—Of course, all that has been said of differing rates of interest in the same market holds good of different markets; but, wholly in addition of the causes which produce those differences, is reason found for different rates in distinct markets. Thus it is notorious that, for long terms of years, the loan of capital could be obtained, upon what was locally regarded as approved security, for 4 per cent. in London as freely as for 6 cent. in

New York, or 8 per cent. in Chicago, or 12 per cent. in Iowa, or Kansas.

Whence these differences? In some degree, doubtless, these successive additions of interest, as capital passed westward, were of the nature of insurance on the principal sum lent. In each case, the security might be as good as could ordinarily be obtained in that community. Security, however, is a relative term; what would be deemed ample security in one place would not pass the scrutiny of lenders in another. The older the country the greater, other things equal, the permanence of economic relations; the more does industry settle down within traditional limits, and acquire a definite and calculable rate of increase; the higher the value assigned to commercial reputation, the more carefully are the men selected who are to control the agencies of production and trade, the fewer the chances of revolutionary changes in business.

301. Disinclination of Capital to Emigrate.—But not all, or even the greater part of the differences which have been noted, are due to this cause. It is the disinclination of capital to emigrate, which allows such wide differences in the local rates of interest. This disinclination is due to various causes. In part, it is the continuing effect of old laws, now generally abrogated, discriminating against aliens. In part, it is due to the suspicion that strangers may not be fairly dealt with by courts and by officers of the law, in case of seizures or foreclosures. In part, it is due to the apprehension of the effect of international hostilities, which cause a suspension of interest-payments, if not forfeiture of the principal. In part, it is due to the fact that investments made at a distance must generally be made through an agent, upon whose good faith or sound judgment may depend the fate of the principal invested.

While these and other causes may operate, singly or in conjunction, to create local differences of interest, the main cause of such differences is found in the inertia of the owners of capital, making them ready to accept lower rates upon the spot than could perhaps be obtained with no less safety, through inquiry and effort at a distance, and, secondly, in the necessary lack of information as to prevailing rates of interest and existing degrees of security for the principal.

I remember to have read somewhere an estimate by an economist of reputation, fixing this "disinclination of capital to emigrate" at two per cent. It is doubtful, however, whether the matter is subject to any such form of statement. The disinclination to invest capital abroad must differ among men of different races; it must differ with differing conditions respecting the communication of news, and respecting international relations. Indeed, it must differ widely with differing moods of the public mind. At times, it may disappear altogether under the excitement of speculative mania, as in the days of the South Sea Bubble, and in the year preceding the English crisis of 1825. It sometimes seems to be the case that loans and investments are made abroad more freely than at home, probably because it is less easy to detect the fallacy of schemes bearing foreign names, and relating to distant lands.

CHAPTER IV.

PROFITS.

302. Definition of Profits.—We have now seen two shares cut off the product of industry—rent and interest; two claimants satisfied—the landlord and the capitalist.

We now come to inquire respecting the share of the Employer, who organizes and conducts production, deciding what shall be produced; in what amounts, of what varieties, materials and patterns; and to what persons, at what prices, and on what terms of payment, the products shall be sold.

303. The Entrepreneur or Employing Class. — We have seen that in a primitive state of industrial society the employer does not appear. When, however, the forms of production become many and complex; when the hand-tool is replaced by the machine; when many persons, of various degrees of skill, strength and intelligence, are united in the same industrial operation; when the materials consumed are gathered from distant lands, and the products, in turn, are distributed widely to consumers not known to the producer, and are sold largely upon credit; when, moreover, a few simple, standard styles give way to ever-varying fashions, in material, in form, in color: in such a state, the employer, the master, the entrepreneur, becomes a necessity of the situation. He performs a function which is indispensable to a large and varied production, and for so doing receives a remuneration which we call profits.

304. Unfortunately, as it seems to me, the entrepreneur or employing function has not been adequately treated, if, indeed, it has been in the smallest degree recognized. English and American economists, in general, have chosen to regard the capitalist as the employer of labor, that is, as employing labor merely because of the possession of capital, and to the extent only to which he possesses capital. We have just now said that, in an early stage of industrial society, the employer does not appear in distinct shape. The possession of capital there constitutes a sufficient qualification for the employment of labor.

In the later stages of industrial development, the mere possession of capital no longer constitutes the sole, or even the main qualification for employing labor. The laborer no longer looks to the employer to furnish merely food and tools and materials, but to furnish, also, technical skill, commercial knowledge and powers of administration; to assume responsibilities and provide against contingencies; to shape and direct production and to organize and control the industrial machinery. So important and difficult are these duties, so rare are the abilities they demand, that he who can discharge these will generally find the capital required. If he be the man to conduct business,* food, tools, and materials will not, under our modern system of credit, long be wanting to him. On the

* "Many employers of labor, *in some parts of England more than half*, have risen from the ranks of labor. Every artisan who has exceptional natural abilities has a chance of raising himself to a post of command." —Marshall's "Economics of Industry."

other hand, without these higher qualifications the mere possessor of capital will employ labor at the risk, almost the certainty, of total or partial loss.

The employer, the entrepreneur, thus rises to be the master of the situation. It is no longer true that a man becomes the employer of labor because he is a capitalist. Men command capital because they have the qualifications to employ labor. To men so endowed, capital and labor alike resort, for the opportunity to perform their several functions and to entitle themselves to share in the product of industry. By this is not meant that the employer is not, in any case, or to any extent, a capitalist, but that he is not an employer to the extent only to which he is a capitalist, nor is he an employer at all because he is a capitalist.

305. Use of the word Profits by English and American Economists.—As the English and American economists generally leave the entrepreneur out of their discussion of production, so they leave out of view the share of the entrepreneur in treating of the distribution of wealth. "Profits" come to mean only the remuneration for the use of capital, what we call distinctively interest ; or, if it be recognized that the man who organizes and conducts industrial operations receives something over and above the mere return upon that portion of the capital employed by him which he owns in his own right, that something is disparaged by being termed "the wages of supervision and management."

Now it is fundamental in my theory of distribution that the entrepreneur class, the employers of labor, receive a share of the product of industry which is so important, through its amount, that it can not possibly be omitted from consideration, and so widely different in the principles by which it is governed, that the term wages can not be applied thereto without inducing a wholly unnecessary and mischievous confusion of ideas, leading directly to false results.

To the entrepreneur's share of the product of industry I shall strictly apply the term profits. This use of the term, in my judgment, tends to promote clearer conceptions regarding the distribution of wealth in the modern industrial state.

306. Profits a Species of the Same Genus as Rent.—In my opinion, profits thus defined bear a strong resemblance to rent. In this view I follow Archbishop Whately, who, in the appendix to his treatise on Logic, declares that the rent of land is only a species of an extensive genus, although, as he complains, the English economists have treated it as constituting a genus by itself, and have either omitted its cognate species, or have included them under genera to which they do not properly belong. If this view is correct, the principles deduced therefrom will be of very great consequence, not only to political economy, but to social philosophy. Let us, therefore, state again the essential differences between Rent and Interest.

1st. A portion of the land cultivated for the supply of any given market, bears no rent; this we call the no-rent land. The rent paid for any piece of land is exactly measured, in theory, by its excess of advantages in production, over the advantages in production pertaining to the no-rent land. On the other hand, there is not any no-interest capital. It is true that a person lending capital may not only not obtain, in the result, any interest for its use, but may even lose the principal; but this will be due to violence or fraud, to flood or fire or stress of weather, or, else, to the unsuspected incompetency of the borrower to conduct business, all of which we may sum up in the word accident. There is no reason why such accidents should befall one portion of capital and not another, whereas there is a reason, in the nature of the case, why one piece of land should bear a rent and another not; why one piece should bear a high and another a low rent. Theoretically all capital bears interest; and, theoretically also, all capital bears the same rate of interest, exceptions being either, first, apparent only, as when an additional per cent. is charged, not as interest proper, but for the insurance of the principal, or secondly, those arising from the disinclination of capital to emigrate, from the ignorance or inertia of lenders and borrowers, or from the force of laws interfering with contracts of loan.

2nd. It follows that interest forms a part of the price of

all products, but that rent forms no part of the price of agricultural produce (for the demonstration of this theorem, see par. 262), and that the amount received by the landlord, as rent, is not paid either by the agricultural laborer, or by the consumer of the produce.

307. Profits Governed by the same Law as Rent.—Having restated the essential distinction between interest and rent, I shall now undertake to show that profits, the remuneration of the entrepreneur or employer, partake largely of the nature of rent, being a species of the same genus. So far as this is the case, profits do not form a part of the price of the products of industry, and do not cause any diminution of the wages of labor.

The successful conduct of business, under free and active competition, is due to exceptional abilities or to exceptional opportunities. Whether due to exceptional abilities or to exceptional opportunities, my proposition could be equally well established, just as it makes no difference in the theory of rent whether a piece of land owes its superior advantages for the purposes of cultivation to higher natural fertility, or to closer proximity to the market to be supplied. Yet it can not be a matter of indifference to social philosophy, whether the power to command profits be due to exceptional abilities or to exceptional opportunities; and I may, therefore, be pardoned for pausing to point out that the former are far more efficient than the latter, in securing profits.

To justify this assertion it will be enough to refer to the well-known fact that a great majority of all business houses which have achieved notable success have been founded by men who owed almost nothing to opportunity. On the other hand, nothing is more familiar than the spectacle of great houses, deeply founded, which have enjoyed high prestige, wide connections and large accumulated capital, dwindling away little by little, if not brought abruptly to their downfall, under the successors of the original founder, simply because the management which had been strong and brave and wise, became commonplace, purposeless, timid and weak. All this is so familiar that I do not fear that any American, at least, will question the assertion that exceptional abilities have far more to do with the successful conduct of business, than exceptional opportunities.

Inasmuch as it would make no difference whether profits were due to exceptional abilities or to exceptional opportunities, while the former are, in fact, much the more important factor in the successful conduct of business, I shall, hereafter, for convenience and simplicity, speak of profits as due to exceptional abilities, just as in discussing the question of the use of the land, we speak of rent as due to differences in fertility, assuming, for convenience of illustration, all the fields under view to be in equal proximity to the market.

308. A Theoretical No-Profits Stage of Production.—If the number of men of exceptional abilities were sufficient or more than sufficient to do all the business that required to be done, of all sorts and in all places ; if (2) these men, however much surpassing all other members of the industrial society, were among themselves equal in all respects which concern the conduct of business ; and if (3) this class, so constituted and so endowed, were distinguished from all not of their class so clearly and conspicuously that no one having these exceptional abilities should fail to be recognized, and no one lacking such abilities in the full measure should esteem himself capable of conducting business, or be so esteemed, for the purpose of obtaining credit, we should have a situation closely analogous to that which we described(par. 255)in the case of a community near which was found an amount of good land, of uniform quality, adequate, or more than adequate, to raise all produce required for the support of the community.

The result would be, either that this class would, by forming a combination and scrupulously adhering to its terms and its spirit, create and maintain a monopoly price for their services in conducting the business requiring to be done, which is so improbable as to be altogether out of our contemplation, or they would, by competing among themselves for the amount of business, bring down its rate to so low a point that the remuneration of each and every one of this class would be practically equal to what he would receive if employed by another.

This, which we might call the "no-profits" stage of industrial society, corresponds closely to the "no-rent" stage in the cultivation of the soil. The persons remaining in the conduct of business would earn their necessary subsistence, but no more. Economically it would make no difference to them whether they did this, as employers or employed.

309.—In fact, however, the qualifications for the conduct of business are not equal throughout all of a sufficiently numerous class. On the contrary, the range of ability is almost world-wide. First, we have those rarely-gifted persons who, in common phrase, seem to turn every thing they touch into gold; whose commercial dealings have the air of magic; who have such insight as almost to seem to have foresight; who are so resolute and firm in temper that apprehension and alarms and repeated shocks of disaster never cause them to relax their hold or change their course; who have such command over men that all with whom they have to do acquire vigor from the contact and work for them as they would not, perhaps could not, work for others.

Next below, though far below, we have that much larger class of men of business, of a high order of talent, though without genius or any thing savoring of magic, whose unqualified success is easily comprehended, even if it can not be imitated: men of natural mastery, sagacious, prompt and resolute.

Then we have the men who, on the whole, do well, or pretty well, in business: men who enjoy a harmonious union of all the qualities of the entrepreneur, though only in moderate degree, or in whom some defect, mental or moral, impairs a higher order of abilities; men who are never masters of their fortunes, are never beyond the imminence of disaster, and yet, by care and pains and diligence, win no small profits from their business, and, if frugality be added to their other virtues, accumulate in time large estates.

Lower down in the industrial order are a multitude of men who are found in the control of business enterprises for no good reason: men of checkered fortunes, sometimes doing well, but more often ill; some of them, perhaps, filling a place that would not otherwise be filled, but, more commonly in business because they have forced themselves into it under a mistaken idea of their own abilities, perhaps encouraged by the partiality of friends who have been willing to place in their hands the agencies of production, or intrust them with commercial or banking capital. The industrial careers of these men are not peculiarly happy, though the degree in which they suffer from the constant imminence of loss, perhaps of bankruptcy, is very much a matter of temperament. Some take it extremely hard, and when they fall make no effort to rise again ; others are irrepressible as Harlequin, jumping up, alert as ever, after being apparently hanged, drawn and quartered by the common executioner.

310. The No-Profits Class of Employers.—Now, in my view of the question of profits, we find, in the lower stratum of the industrial order thus rudely and hastily sketched, a "no-profits" class of employers. Notwithstanding all the magnificent premiums of business success, the men of real business power are not so many but that no small part of the posts of industry and trade are filled by men inadequately qualified, and who, consequently, have a very checkered career and realize for themselves, taking their whole lives together, a meager compensation, so meager that, for purposes of scientific reasoning, we may treat it as constituting no profits at all. Live they do, partly by legitimate toll upon the business that passes through their hands, partly at the cost of their creditors, with whom they make frequent compositions, partly at the expense of friends, or by the sacrifice of inherited means. This bare subsistence, obtained through so much of hard work, of anxiety, and often of humiliation, we regard as that minimum which, in economics, we can treat as *nil.* From this low point upwards, we measure profits.

311. Profits do not form a part of the Price of Manufactured Products.—If this view of the employing class be correctly taken, it appears that, under perfect competition, that is, where the conditions of a good market are supplied, manufacturing profits, for instance, are not obtained through any deduction from the wages of mechanical labor ; and, secondly, manufacturing profits do not constitute a part of the price of manufactured goods. All profits are drawn from a body of wealth which is created * by the exceptional abilities (or opportunities) of those employers who receive profits, measured from the level of those employers who receive no profits, just as all rents are drawn from a body of wealth, which is created by the exceptional fertility (or facilities for transportation of produce) of the rent-lands, measured from the level of the no-rent lands.

The price of manufactured goods of any particular description is determined by the cost of production of that portion of the supply which is produced at the greatest disadvantage (par. 137). If the demand for such goods is so great as to require a certain amount to be produced under the management and control of persons whose efficiency in organizing and supervising the forces of labor and capital is small, the cost of production of that portion of the stock will be large, and the price will be correspondingly high, yet, high as it is, it will not be high enough to yield to the employers of this grade any more than that scant and difficult subsistence which we have taken as the no-profits line.

The price at which these goods are to be sold, however, will determine the price of the whole supply, since, in any one market, at any one time, there is but one price for different portions of the same commodity. Hence, whatever the cost of production of those portions of the supply which are produced by employers of a higher industrial grade, they will command the same price as those portions which are produced at the greatest disadvantage. The difference, so measured, will go as profits to each individual employer, according to his own success in production.

312. Profits are not Subtracted from Wages.—Do profits, then, come out of wages? Not at all. The employers of the lowest industrial grade—the no-profits employers, as we have

* Prof. Alfred Marshall says: "The earnings of management of a manufacturer represent the value of the addition which his work makes to the total produce of capital and industry."

called them—must pay wages sufficient to hire laborers to work under their direction. These wages constitute an essential part of the cost, to the employer, of the production of the goods. The fact that these wages are so high is the reason why these employers are unable (their skill and power in organizing and energizing labor and capital being no greater than they are), to realize any profits for themselves.

The employers of the higher industrial grades will pay the same wages to their laborers. Why, in equity or in economics, should a laborer who works for a strong, prudent and skillful master, receive higher wages than one whose fortune it is to work for a vacillating, weak or reckless employer. The one laborer is as efficient as the other, and works as hard. The difference in production, which, in the one case allows rent to be paid, and in the other enables the employer to secure a profit, is due to no superiority in the quality of the labor or the capital employed, over that of the labor and the capital employed where no rents or no profits are realized. In the one case it is due to the superior fertility of the land, or its greater facilities for the transportation of produce; in the other, to the superior abilities or opportunities of him who conducts industry.

In the latter case, the employer, paying wages at the same rate to his laborers, and interest, at the same rate, to the capitalist, for so much as he has to borrow, and selling his goods, so far as they are of equal quality, at the same price as the employer who makes no profits, is yet able to accumulate a clear surplus after all obligations are discharged, which surplus is called profits. This is effected by his careful study of the sources of his materials; by his comprehension of the demands of the market; by his steadiness and self-control in the presence of temptations to extravagance or wild ventures; by his organizing force and administrative ability; by his energy, economy and prudence.

313. The No-Profits Employer.—A failure to discern the true relations of profits to wages has led to a mistaken appreciation of the interests of the community, and especially of the laboring classes, regarding the employers of labor.

While the large profits of the successful employer have been the subject of much jealousy, and almost uniformly excite in the minds of the unthinking the sense of personal wrong, there is an entire lack of jealousy exhibited towards the unsuccessful man of business, who often receives a great deal of sympathy from the laboring class.

So far as the sympathy extended towards the unsuccessful man of business is of a personal nature, flowing from a kindly disposition towards the unfortunate, it is, of course, very amiable. But there is reason to believe that this sentiment is not wholly of a good origin, but is quite as largely produced by a misapprehension of economic relations. The laborers appreciate, in some degree, the cares under which the unsuccessful employer labors, the anxieties from which he suffers, the humiliation into which he is occasionally plunged. They know he has a pretty poor time of it on the whole, and they are not envious of him. On the contrary, they use his hard lot to sharpen their envy of the man who reaps large profits from the conduct of business and the employment of labor. They compare the rich rewards of the one, who, perhaps, in time, becomes worth his millions, with the meager recompense of the other, who, at the end of a long life of labor, has little to show for it all; and the comparison tends to heighten the feeling of loss and of wrong with which the gains of the former are contemplated.

If, however, we have rightly indicated the source of profits, not only is the unsuccessful employer deserving of no special economic sympathy, but his conduct of business, his control of labor-force and capital-force is at a great cost to the laboring class, as forming a part of the general community.

We saw that rents were measured upward from the productive level of no-rent land. If, therefore, that level is lowered, rents are, (par. 257) by that fact raised. Similarly, profits are measured upwards from the level of the no-profits class of employers; and any cause which brings incomeptent persons into the conduct of business, or keeps them there against the natural tendency of trade to throw them out, increases the profits of the successful employers, as a class, by enhancing the cost of production and, consequently, the price of that portion of the supply which is produced at the greatest disadvantage. This enhancement of price is at the expense of all who consume the goods so produced; the laboring class equally with others, in theory; probably in fact more than any other, on account of their limited ability to look out for their own interests in retail trade.

314. What Causes Help to Swell the Proportion of Incompetent Employers of Labor?—Shilly-shally laws relating to insolvency do this; bad money does this; truck does this; protection, in my judgment, does this. Each of these causes enables men to escape the consequences of incompetency, and to hang miserably on to business, where they are an obstruction and a nuisance. Slavery, in like manner, enables men to control labor and direct production, who never would become, on an equal scale, the employers of free labor; and it is not more to the inefficiency of the slave than to the incompetency of the master, that the unproductiveness of chattel labor is due.

The lower the industrial quality of free labor, the more ignorant and inert the individual laborer, the lower may be the quality of the men who can just sustain themselves in the position of employers. Men become the employers of cheap labor who would never become the employers of dear labor, and who ought not to be the employers of any sort of labor. The more active becomes the competition among the wages class, the more prompt their resort to market, the more persistent their demand for every possible increase of remuneration, the greater will be the pressure brought to bear upon such employers to drop out of the place into which they have crowded themselves at the cost of the general community, and where they have been able to maintain themselves only because the working classes have failed, through ignorance or inertia, to exact their full terms.

315. Importance of this View of Profits.—It is competent to any person to dissent from the view of the origin and measure of business profits I have presented; but it can not be gainsaid that, if that view be accepted as correct, we have here the keystone of the arch, which completes the structure and binds together the other members into a symmetrical whole spanning the entire field of distribution. We shall not, however, be able to appreciate all the consequences of this theory, until we have carried our studies through the subject of wages, the remuneration of labor.

316. Getting Rid of the Employer.—In the department of Production we described the function of the entrepreneur, or employer, the person who, hiring labor on the one hand, and borrowing capital on the other, initiates industrial operations according to his own plans, and with a view to his own economic benefit. Coming down to the department of Distribution, we have, but just now, inquired how the contemplated benefit is secured by the employer, and what are the limits of that benefit, which we term profits.

It has been said, in the course of this discussion, that this benefit obtained by the employer, his profits, has been the object of not a little jealousy and envy on the part of the laborers and capitalists to whom he has paid wages or interest. Those wages and that interest the recipients would be glad to see increased by some addition derived from the source from which the employer obtains his profits. This could only be done by the laborers and the capitalists combining to perform the employer's work in production, and thereby becoming entitled, or perhaps we had better say enabled, to claim his share of the product in distribution.

317. Co-operation.—Organized and systematic efforts to get rid of the entrepreneur or employer have not been unknown. Among the many schemes for largely and rapidly improving the condition of the masses of the people, which had their birth in the period of social and political fermentation which we call the Revolution of 1848, none had fairer promise of substantial results than that known by the name of Co-operation.

Generically, co-operation is a term of wide application, and, in its use in political economy, may express the union of industrial agents in production upon any terms and under any system of organization. Since the period referred to, however, the term has come to have a limited signification, confined to an industrial organization from which the entrepreneur is excluded, and under which the product of industry is again to be divided into three principal shares, instead of four as under the entrepreneur system. I here only indicate the place which co-operation occupies in the scheme of Distribution, postponing the discussion of the scheme to Part VI.

CHAPTER V.

WAGES.

318. Definition of Wages.—We have seen three shares cut off the product of industry. Of the four principal parts* into which that product is divided, under the entrepreneur organization, as existing almost universally in England, and as rapidly extending in the United States, on the continent of Europe, and in all progressive countries, there remains but one to be treated, Wages, the remuneration of labor.

Before seeking the law which governs wages, two distinctions require to be drawn very clearly, distinctions which the reader will need to hold strongly in mind through the whole course of our future discussion, the distinction, *viz.*, between real and nominal wages, and that between the real and the nominal cost of labor.

319. Real and Nominal Wages.—Real wages are the remuneration of the laborer as reckoned in the necessaries, comforts and luxuries of life.

Real wages may differ widely, even when nominal wages are of the same amount, by reason of :

(*a*) Variations in the purchase power of money.

(*b*) Varieties in the form of payment, as when the board of the laborer, the rent of a cottage, the privilege of grazing a

---

* Certain minor shares in distribution will be treated in the next chapter. For the purposes of the present discussion they may safely be disregarded.

cow, allowances of certain quantities of food, drink or fuel, the right to take flour at miller's prices, one or more of these, are added to the money wages of the laborer. Such forms of payment are not of much importance throughout the United States, generally, at the present time ; but in many European countries they constitute elements which can not be overlooked in discussing the question of comparative wages. In England, a series of acts of Parliament, extending over four hundred years, have successively restricted the right of the employer to pay wages in aught but the coin of the realm.

(*c*) The greater opportunities in some avocations than in others for extra earnings by the laborer himself or by the members of his family. Thus, Prof. Senior says : "The earnings of the wife and children of many a Manchester weaver exceed or equal those of himself. Those of the wife and children of an agricultural laborer, or of a carpenter or coal-heaver, are generally unimportant." The true unit in the comparison of wages is evidently the family.

320. (*d*) The greater regularity of employment in some avocations than others. Varying regularity of employment may be due to (1) the nature of the individual avocation, (2) the force of the seasons, (3) social causes, (4) industrial causes, like strikes, panics, and so-called "hard times."

In illustration of the foregoing causes, we have the widely varying rates of agricultural wages from one season to another, being often, *e. g.*, more than twice as great in the third as in the first quarter of the year. This is due to both of the first two causes adduced. It is not alone the difference of the seasons which makes agricultural wages so irregular ; in part, also, it is the nature of the operations involved. After the seed has been planted, time must be given it to grow, and this would be so were there no winter. So in the fisheries, it is not alone the stress of weather which obliges the laborer to lie idle during portions of the year, but, in part, the reproductive necessities of the fish. In other avocations it is the force of the seasons alone which makes employment irregular, as, for example, in the brickmaking, quarrying, carpentering, house-painting, and other trades.

Among social causes affecting the regularity of employment, as between country and country, may be mentioned the observance of festivals and religious rites, which among some peoples occupy a hundred and more days in the year.

(*e*) The longer duration of the labor power in some avocations and some countries, than in others.

Thus, Dr. Neison has shown that the mean mortality in England between 25 and 65 years of age, is, in the clerical profession 1.12 per cent. ; in the legal, 1.57 ; in the medical, 1.81. In domestic service, the mortality among gardeners, is but .93 per cent. ; among grooms, 1.26 ; among coachmen, 1.84. Of the several branches of manufacture, paper shows a mean mortality of 1.45 ; tin, 1.61 ; iron, 1.75 ; glass, 1.83 ; lead, 2.24 ; earthenware, 2.57. Among the different kinds of mining, iron shows a mean mortality of 1.80 ; tin, 1.99 ; lead, 2.50 ; copper, 3.17.

Dr. Edward Jarvis has shown that, on the average, an Irishman who has reached the age of 20, has 28.88 years to live ; a Frenchman, 32.84 ; an Englishman, 35.55 ; a Norwegian, 39.61.

It is evident that if two persons begin to labor productively at the same period of life and continue at work until death, at the same nominal rate of wages, that one receives the higher real remuneration who lives the longer, inasmuch as the cost of his maintenance during the first unproductive years of life, must, in any philosophical view of the subject, be charged upon his wages during his period of labor.

321. Nominal and Real Cost of Labor.—Another distinction which requires to be observed is that between wages and the cost of labor.

In treating wages as high or low, we occupy the laborer's point of view. In treating the cost of labor as high or low, we occupy the point of view of the employer.

Wages are high or low according to the abundance or the scantiness of the necessaries, comforts and luxuries which the laborer can command. The cost of labor is high or low, according as the employer gets an ample or a scanty return for the wages he pays the laborer, whether these be low or high.

It is possible that an employer may pay high wages, and yet the cost of labor to him may prove to be low, by reason of the laborer's superior efficiency. On the other hand, the employer may pay wages on which the laborer can only live most miserably, and yet the employer be greatly straitened to get back these wages in the value of his product, so poor and wasteful may be the services rendered.

In Part II. we have explained at great length the causes which affect the laborer's efficiency.

It is probably true that, as a rule, the highest paid labor is that which costs the employer least. This is evidenced by the two facts that, generally speaking, employers, when they reduce their force, discharge their lowest paid laborers first; and that, generally speaking, it is the countries where the lowest real wages are paid which feel the necessity of imposing commercial restrictions to keep out the products of others. Thus, India, where the cotton spinner gets only 20 pence a week, is flooded by the cottons of England, where the spinner receives 20 shillings; and Russia, where the laborer in iron works receives but three roubles a week, has to protect herself, or thinks she must do so, against the iron of England, where the workman receives four or five times as much.

322. Relation of Wages to the Other Shares of the Product of Industry.—It has not been by accident, or whim, or from any notion respecting the comparative dignity of the several claimants to the product of industry, that rent, interest, and profits have been discussed before wages.

This order has been followed for a positive reason, which is that, in the theory of distribution here proposed, wages *equal* the product of industry *minus* the three parts already determined in their nature and amount. In this view, the laboring class receive all they help to produce, subject to deduction on the three several accounts mentioned.

323. Rent Deducted.—First, rent is to be deducted. On the lowest grade of lands there is no rent. On the more productive soils rent, at its economic maximum, equals the excess of produce after the cost of cultivating the no-rent soils has been paid. This rent does not affect the price of agricultural produce, and does not come out of the remuneration of the agricultural laborer.

We thus see that the first deduction to be made from the product of industry is of a perfectly definite nature, and that, on the assumption of active competition on both sides, the amount of that reduction is susceptible of arithmetical computation. Rent must come out before the question of wages is considered. The laborer can not get it, or any part of it, by any economic means. It must go to the land-owner, unless it be confiscated by the State, or ravished away by violence.

324. Interest Deducted.—Secondly, from the product of industry must be deducted a remuneration for the use of capital. That remuneration must be high enough to induce those who have produced wealth to save it and store it up, in the place of consuming it immediately for the gratification of personal appetites or tastes. This may imply, in one state of society, an annual rate of interest of eight per cent.; in another, of five ; in another, of three.

325. Profits Deducted.—The third and last deduction to be made from the product of industry before the laborer becomes entitled thereto, is what we have called profits, the remuneration of the entrepreneur, the employer, the man of business, the captain of industry, who sets in motion the complicated machinery of modern production.

From the importance assigned, in this work, to the entrepreneur's or employer's function, the conclusion might be hastily drawn that production would be primarily for his benefit, that he, if any one, would be the residual claimant upon the product ; that, paying the capitalist, on one side, enough, under the name of interest, to secure the use of his capital, and paying the laborer, on the other side, enough, under the name of wages, to secure his services, this man of business, captain of industry, merchant, manufacturer, or banker, would retain as his own all that remains. And so, indeed, in any individual transaction he does, owing to the force of contract, just as the farmer, under a lease, pays the owner of the soil no more in years when the yield is exceptionally large, and no less in years when the crops are short.

If, however, we have correctly indicated the source of the employer's profits, they are of the same nature as rent. As there are no-rent lands, so there is a class of employers who derive from the business they conduct a bare subsistence, at the cost of much anxiety, and perhaps also of discredit, many of them living mainly at the expense of their creditors. These we call the no-profits employers.

From this point, where profits, if any, are so small and so hardly earned that they may, for scientific purposes, be disregarded, upwards through many grades, we have employers who derive moderate profits, liberal profits, grand profits, monumental profits aggregating in a lifetime colossal fortunes, according to the degrees in which they bring courage, prudence, foresight, frugality, and authority over men, to the organization and conduct of business enterprises. If I am right in this view of the nature of the entrepreneur's function and of the source of his profits, those profits would, under full and free competition, not form a part of the price of commodities, and are not obtained by deduction from wages. In other words, these profits consist wholly of wealth created by the individual employers themselves, over and above the wealth which would have been produced, in similar industrial enterprises, by the same labor-force and capital-force under the control of employers of less efficiency.

326. The Laborer, the Residual Claimant to the Product of Industry.—These three shares being cut off the product of industry, the whole remaining body of wealth, daily or annually created, is the property of the laboring class;* their

* This is substantially the position taken by the lamented Prof. Stanley Jevons, of University College, London, who states that "The wages of a working man are ultimately coincident with what he produces, after the deduction of rent, taxes, and the interest of capital." In this matter of Wages, Prof. Jevons emphatically repudiates the doctrines generally accepted in his own country, saying: "Our English Economists have been living in a fool's paradise," and frankly ranges himself with the French economists, "from Condillac, Baudeau, and Le Trosne, through J. B. Say, DeStutt Tracy, Storch, and others, down to Bastiat and Courcelle Seneuil."

"The truth," he declares, "is with the French School, and the sooner

wages, or the remuneration of their services. So far as, by their energy in work, their economy in the use of materials, or their care in dealing with the finished product, the value of that product is increased, that increase goes to them by purely natural laws, provided only competition be full and free. Every invention in mechanics, every discovery in the chemical art, no matter by whom made, inures directly and immediately to their benefit, except so far as a limited monopoly may be created by law, for the encouragement of invention and discovery.

Unless by their own neglect of their own interests, or through inequitable laws, or social customs having the force of law, no other party can enter to make any claim on the product of industry,* nor can any one of the three parties already indicated carry away any thing in excess of its normal share, as hereinbefore defined.

327. The English Doctrine of Wages.—The view here taken of the Distribution of Wealth, under the entrepreneur organization of industry, differs widely from that held by the English economists, except as respects the single share of the landowner—Rent. According to those writers, the capitalist-employer is the residual claimant upon the product of industry. DeQuincey summed up the Ricardian doctrine in saying: "Profits are the leavings of Wages."† From the entire

---

we recognize the fact, the better it will be for all the world, except, perhaps, the few writers who are too far committed to the old erroneous doctrines to allow of renunciation." [Preface to the Second Edition of his Theory of Political Economy, 1880.]

I may remark that when, in 1874, I had occasion to trace the genesis and the literary history of the Wage Fund Theory (See *North American Review*, January, 1875), I did not find a single French economist infected by the pernicious doctrine which long held sway across the channel.

* With the exception, still, of the State and of the speculator, whom it has seemed best, for clearness of view, to remove altogether from the present discussion, and whose shares in the distribution of the product of industry will be elsewhere considered.

† "There is no other way," said Ricardo, "of keeping profits up, but by keeping wages down." "Profits," said Mr. McCulloch, "vary in-

product of the exertions and sacrifices of the industrial community, there is cut off Rent, as determined by the Ricardian formula. Next the laborer's share is ascertained in accordance with the Wage Fund,* the amount possibly to be paid in this way being irrespective alike of the number and of the industrial quality of the laboring class. The rest belongs to the capitalist-employer, as his own profits, so-called, consisting of two portions, one, due to the abstinence of the owner of capital, as such; the other due to the present, personal exertions of the employer, as such.

By this rule of distribution, no gain in the efficiency of the individual laborer, whether taking the direction of greater energy or of greater economy; no mechanical invention, no chemical discovery, however much the capability of production may be increased thereby, can profit the laborer any thing, except as it first enhances the profits of the employing class, and thereby adds to the capital of the wage fund, to be thereafter expended in purchasing labor.

328. In What Sense Wages are the Residual Share.—I have spoken of the laborer as the residual claimant upon the product of industry. That view of wages being new, even the phrase in which I have embodied it has been excepted to. Since the first edition of this treatise was published, certain writers have declared that there is no more reason for applying the term, residual, to wages than for applying it to any other share of the product of industry; that each share, in turn, comprises all which the other shares do not include.

---

versely as wages; that is, they fall when wages rise, and rise when wages fall."

In both these statements, the word profits is used to include interest, as elsewhere explained.

*A discussion of the Wage Fund Theory will be found in Part VI. A few years ago, I should not have presumed to pass by this point without undertaking a formal refutation of that theory which, till recently, had complete possession of the English Economists. The fact that, though now generally abandoned, it still holds its place in so many treatises on the shelves of our libraries, some of which are even now used as text-books in our Colleges, appears to require some notice to be taken of it.

The criticism of these writers is not just. It is competent to them to controvert the view of the origin and measure of business profits presented in the last chapter; and, in expressing their dissent therefrom, they will, of course, deny that wages constitute the residual share of the product. But no one can properly make question that, if this view of business profits be accepted, as correctly setting forth, in the large way, the facts of industry, not only is what is manifestly meant by the phrases, residual claimant, residual share, completely true, but also that those phrases themselves are perfectly accurate in the expression of that meaning.

329. Upon the theory of profits which has been expounded, the remuneration of labor, wages, is strictly the residual share of the product of industry, residual in this sense, that it is enhanced by every cause, whatever that may be, which increases the product of industry without giving to any one of the other three parties to production a claim to an increased remuneration, under the operation of the principles already stated; residual in the sense that, even if any one or all of the other parties to production become so engaged in any given increase of the product as to become entitled to an enhanced share in its distribution, their shares still remain subject to determination by positive reasons, while wages receive the benefit of all that is left over after the other claimants are satisfied.

330. The Operation of the Rule Illustrated.—Granting the correctness of the analysis we have offered, it is demonstrable that the product of industry may be increased without enhancing the share of all or of any of the other parties to distribution; and, even when the other shares are enhanced, it is possible and even probable that, on the assumption of perfect competition, the increase of product resulting from the introduction of any new force into industry will be greater than the sum of the increments by which rent, interest, and profits shall have been enhanced. If this be so, then the wages class will receive a benefit from any increase of the product of industry corresponding to that derived by the residuary legatee whenever the total value of the estate concerned is ascertained to have been, or from some unanticipated cause becomes, larger than was in contemplation of the testator when the amounts of the several specific bequests were determined upon.

331. Thus, to take the simplest possible case, let us say that the line *ax*

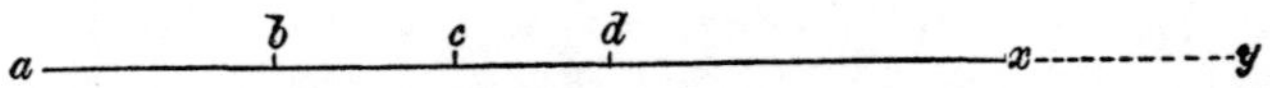

represents the amount of the production of a given community. Of this total, *ax*, let *ab* represent the share going to the land-holding class as rent; *bc*, the remuneration of the capitalist class, under the name of interest; *dx*, the portion of the produce paid in wages; and, by consequence, *cd*, the part retained by the employing class as profits. Let it now be supposed that an instantaneous improvement takes place in the industrial quality of the laboring class, by which they become so much more careful and painstaking, more adroit and alert, more observant and dexterous, as to effect a saving in the materials used in each and every stage of production, with a resulting increase of ten per cent. in the finished product over what had been accomplished by more wasteful, clumsy, heedless operatives. This assumption is certainly not an unreasonable one, as regards the extent of the possible saving to be effected through even a slight improvement in the industrial quality of a laboring population. The total product will then be represented by the line *ay*.

Our question is, To whom will go that portion of the produce which is represented by the dotted line *xy*, under the normal operation of economic forces?

I answer, If our analysis of the source of business profits is correct, this will go to the laboring class in enhanced wages.

332. To whom else should it go? To the landlord class, in higher rents? No, clearly not, since the materials employed have not been increased, but the gain to production results from a better economy of materials, in kinds and amounts as before. Hence, no greater demand is made upon the land; hence, cultivation is not driven down to inferior soils; hence, rents can not be enhanced, rent representing only and always the excess of produce on the better soils above that of the soils of the lowest net productiveness under cultivation. The line *ab*, therefore, remains unchanged.

Shall the line *bc* show any change? Shall all or any part of the gain *xy* go to the capitalist class, as interest? Again, no. An improvement in the industrial quality of the laboring class does not necessarily increase the amount of tools and supplies required in production. On the contrary, neat, intelligent, careful workmen require even fewer tools than ignorant, slovenly, heedless workmen, to perform the same kind and amount of work, since in the case of the former there will be a smaller proportion at any time broken or dulled or from any cause awaiting repair. Since, then, there is no greater demand for capital in the case supposed, there can be no increase in the rate or amount of interest; and the line *bc* will, therefore, not be lengthened.

Will the whole or any part of *xy* go to the employing class, as increased profits? If we have correctly discovered the source of business profits, this will not be the case. An improvement in the industrial quality of a given body of workmen would not require an increase in the number of employers; hence, would not, could not, enhance the aggregate amount of profits. On the contrary, an improvement in the industrial quality of the laboring class would tend, and would tend strongly, to raise the standard of business ability in the employing class; to drive out the more incompetent, thereby raising the lower limit of production in this respect, and thereby reducing the aggregate amount realized as profits.

We see, therefore, that the line *cd* will not be increased, in the case supposed; and, as we have proved the same respecting *ab* and *bc* successively, the whole of *xy* must go to lengthen the line *dx*, representing the amount previously received by the laboring class as wages.

333. We have thus far, for convenience of reasoning and simplicity of illustration, assumed that the economic effect of the improvement in the industrial quality of the body of laborers in view, is confined to an increase in the amount of the finished product through a diminution in that element of waste which enters, more or less, into all production of wealth. The same argument would hold good of an improvement in the industrial quality of the laboring population which should result in the production of goods of equal bulk and weight, but of a greater value through a higher quality, a more perfect finish, a nicer adaptation to the wants of the community. Not only is such an increase in the value of the product, which does not increase the amount of materials taken from the soil and hence has no tendency to enhance rents, possible, but *instances of this character are, more than any other, representative of the modes of production in communities of advancing civilization.* Articles are often sold for twice, thrice or ten times as much as other articles, containing the same amount of material, simply by reason of the skill and taste which has enhanced their value to the consumer. In all such cases, the increase due to the improvement in the industrial quality of the laboring classes would, under the principles laid down, go, entire, to the laborers themselves, granted only perfect competition.

334. But such an improvement in industrial quality would probably be followed, sooner or later, by an actual increase in the amount of material employed. In this case, what would be the distribution of the produce? The increase would no longer go entire to re-enforce wages. A larger amount of materials being used, a greater demand would be made thereby upon the productive powers of the soil; the lower limit of cultivation would be pushed downwards, a longer or a shorter distance, to supply the increased demand; and rent would be enhanced, as in all prosperous and progressive countries it certainly tends to be.

But the amount which would thus go to enhance rent—it might be much, it might be little—would still be limited by the Ricardian formula; and all the remainder would be applied, under the principles laid down, to increase the remuneration of labor, the portions reserved as interest and profits suffering no change.

335. But suppose, again, that the improvement in the industrial quality of the laboring class is carried to such a degree as to qualify them to use a higher order of tools, more complicated, more delicate, and hence more expensive; or to abandon the hand-tools, heretofore employed, for costly and powerful machines. Here we should have an increased demand for capital; and, by consequence, supply remaining, for the time, unchanged, interest would be enhanced. But the amount by which interest would be thus enhanced would not be the amount by which production was increased. On the contrary, the rate of interest would still be governed by the relation between the supply of and the demand for capital; and all the increase of product which was not thus taken would, under the principles laid down, go directly and exclusively to increase wages.

336. We may illustrate this by supposing a workman, who has hitherto been using a few coarse, simple, cheap and durable tools, in producing a low-grade article, to have qualified himself, by private study and practice, to use numerous, delicate and intricate tools, in doing a high order of work, in the same branch of industry. The cost of maintaining the stock of tools of the former kind might have been, including interest, repairs and occasional replacement, five dollars, a year. The cost of maintaining the stock of new tools might be fifty dollars a year. But the increased daily value of the product, due to the introduction of a superior order of workmanship, might be a dollar, or two dollars, a day. What I am insisting upon is, that, not only would the individual workman, in the given instance, if he intelligently pursued his own interest, secure higher wages, corresponding to the increased value of his production, *minus* the added cost of the service (which probably no one would deny), but that what would be true of the individual workman will be true of the working class, as a whole, so far as, by an improvement in their industrial character, they qualify themselves for a higher grade of production, higher in respect to quality or to amount.

And it is to be remembered, in this connection, that whatever the advantage which the added demand for tools or machinery may, in the immediate instance, give to the owners of existing capital, that advantage will steadily tend to decline. Thus, in the case supposed, the first equipment of the improved laborer for his new work, might cost $200, increasing the demand for capital to this extent, and thus raising somewhat the sum obtained in that community, that year, as interest. But the increase of production, might, as we have reasonably supposed, amount to even more than $200 annually ; so that the supply of capital, relatively to the demand, might, after a single year, be greater than before ; while the capability of accumulating capital during each succeeding year would be greatly enhanced.

CHAPTER VI.

WAGES.—CONTINUED.

THE CONDITIONS OF THE LABORING CLASS AS AFFECTED BY IMPERFECT COMPETITION.

337. The Economic Position of The Laboring Class.— In Chapter V. we set forth the relation of wages to the other shares of the product of industry, reaching the conclusion that, notwithstanding the formal attitude of the laboring class in industry, as hired by the entrepreneur class and working for stipulated wages, the normal operation of the laws of exchange is to make the former, in effect, the owners of the entire product, subject to the requirement of paying the definite sums charged against that product, on the three several accounts of rent, interest and profits.

338. What Will They do With it ?—This position of the laboring class would seem to be a not ineligible one, conceding that the exigencies of modern production require the maintenance of the entrepreneur class.

We have seen what is the best the laboring class can, in theory, do for themselves, under the existing organization of industry : what is the most they can claim for their services. Let us now inquire, what, in fact, this class do for themselves in this respect ; and if they fall short of realizing their full share of the product of industry, to what causes the failure is to be attributed.

The laboring class may do themselves an economic injury in either or both of two ways : first, through excessive reproduction, sexually, leading to over-population, involving the necessity of cultivating poorer and poorer soils, with the result of continually diminishing *per capita* production ; secondly, through a weak, spasmodic, or unintelligent competition with the employing class.

The consideration of the former of these causes will be postponed till we reach the department of Consumption. The latter will form the subject of the following paragraphs.

339. Imperfect Competition.—A total failure of competition is impossible. No class will be found so stolid and inert as to make no exertions whatever to change a worse for a better condition. The impulse to buy in the cheaper and to sell in the dearer market will, in some measure, actuate every body of laborers. Yet the degree in which that motive is effectual will be found to vary widely as between men of different climes, and of different races. Compare the New Englander with the East Indian. The former, inquisitive, alert, aggressive, almost destitute of attachment to locality, quick to change his avocation, if a profit shall appear, and so gifted with mechanical insight and aptitude as to acquire the rudiments of any art in an astonishingly short time; occupying a country where the transmission of intelligence is incessant, and where the transportation of passengers and freight reaches the maximum of ease, security and cheapness ; enjoying the advantage of a wide margin of living, and with no inconsiderable savings laid by from the liberal earnings of former years, is not likely to remain long ignorant of opportunities for improving his industrial conditions, whether through change of place or avocation, or likely long to allow such opportunities to remain unimproved. We get a measure of this freedom of individual movement in the census statistics, by which it appears that in 1880 nine and a half millions of the native population were living in States other than those of their birth.

340. The Immobility of Labor.—On the other hand, the East Indian, bound in fetters of caste, of superstition, of ignorance and poverty, occupying a country vast portions of which are traversed only by bullock-paths, abides in his lot, in spite of wretchedness and famine, as though rooted in the soil itself.

But we have not to go as far away as India, to find instances of a high degree of immobility in the population, in the face of strong and urgent reasons for migration. A century ago Adam Smith wrote:

"Eighteen pence a day may be reckoned the common price of labor in London and its neighborhood. At a few miles' distance, it falls to fourteen and fifteen pence. Ten pence may be reckoned its price in Edinburgh and its neighborhood. At a few miles' distance it falls to eight pence, the usual price of common labor through the greater part of the low country of Scotland, where it varies a good deal less than in England. *Such a difference of prices, which it seems is not always sufficient to transport a man from one parish to another, would necessarily occasion so great a transportation of the most bulky commodities, not only from one point to another, but from one end of the kingdom, almost from one end of the world, to another, as would soon reduce them more nearly to a level.*" So great did the resistance to the flow of labor appear to his eye, that he declared man to be "of all sorts of luggage the most difficult to be transported."

341. It might be supposed that the increase during the century in the facilities for transportation and for the diffusion of information would have done much to remove the obstructions which, in Adam Smith's day, retarded the movement of labor to its market; but the force of ignorance, fear and poverty is not so easily broken. Prof. Fawcett in his Political Economy writes: "During the winter months, an ordinary agricultural laborer in Yorkshire earns thirteen shillings a week; the wages of a Wiltshire or Dorsetshire laborer, doing the same kind of work, and working a similar number of hours, are only nine shillings a week. This great difference in wages is not counterbalanced by other considerations. Living is not more expensive in Yorkshire than in Dorsetshire, and the Dorsetshire laborer does not enjoy any particular advantages or privileges which are denied to the Yorkshire laborer."

Instances without number might be cited, showing the practical immobility of the agricultural population of England in the past; and in this respect, England may be taken as fairly representing the actual world about which the economist reasons, being in the mean between the people of North America and Australia, on the one hand, and those of Asia, on the other.

342. Change of Occupation.—So much for the movement from place to place, which is needed to meet the requirements of industrial competition. Of the movement from one avocation to another, which may be required for the same end, an even less favorable account may be given. An American will find it difficult to conceive how slow and painful is the process by which an overcrowded avocation is depleted or a growing industry re-enforced, in any of the States of Europe.

In his last and greatest work Prof. Cairnes sought to reach a measure of the rate of this movement in England. His result was substantially this: that only loss by death or disability could be relied upon to relieve the labor market in any branch of industry which was overdone, and that the sole disposable fund for supplying new laborers to new or growing branches of industry was to be found in the body of persons each year coming of age, industrially speaking. It would be easy to show that the "play" thus given to the labor market is far within the limits of those great oscillations of industry which labor must meet, fully and promptly, or suffer because it can not meet them. Moreover, it is doubtful whether Prof. Cairnes does not overrate this disposable labor fund.

So far from the members of the rising generation being perfectly free to move into avocations other than those of their parents, mill-owners are harassed by applications from their hands to take children into employment on almost any terms. The more miserable the parents' condition, the greater becomes the pressure on them to crowd their children somehow, somewhere, into service. Once in a mill, we know how little chance there is of the children afterwards taking up for themselves another way of life.

In the agricultural districts of England, gangs of children of all ages, from sixteen down to ten or even five years, were formerly organized and driven from farm to farm, and from parish to parish, to work all day under strange overseers, and to sleep at night in barns, huddled together without distinction of sex. The system of public agricultural gangs required an act of Parliament to break it up, and we have the testimony of the commission of 1867, that, in spite of the law, gangs were then still formed in some parts of the kingdom. So late as 1870, children were employed in the brickyards of England, under strange masters, at three and a half years of age. Account is given of a boy weighing 52 pounds, whose daily task covered fourteen miles ; one-half of this with a load of clay weighing forty pounds, upon his head.

Such instances show graphically the error of supposing that parents who are tied down hopelessly to an occupation which affords but the barest subsistence, can freely dispose of their children to the best advantage, among a large class of occupations. Especially when we consider that, in the development of modern industry, trades become highly localized, shall we see the practical fallacy of this assumption. Even if we suppose the parent to be advised of better opportunities opening in some trade prosecuted at a distance, yet, years before the boy or girl will be fit to send away from home, the chance of earning a few pence in the mill where the parent works, will almost irresistibly draw the child into the vortex. The truth is, that *until you secure mobility to adult labor you will fail to find it in the rising generation*, and that among an ignorant and degraded population four-fifths, perhaps nine-tenths, of all children, by what may be called a moral necessity, follow the occupations of their parents, or those with whom fortune has placed them.

343. The Industrial Effects of a Failure of Competition.—If industrial movement may be thus tardy and limited, even among a people of Teutonic blood and enjoying free institutions, it becomes a matter of serious concern to inquire what are the effects of a partial failure of competition.

And, first, let us see just what it is that we look to competition, when active and complete, to accomplish.

We have defined competition to be the operation of individual self-interest among buyers and sellers. We saw that this implied that each man acts for himself, solely, by himself, solely, in order to get the most he can from others, and to give the least he must, himself.

Now, this may seem a very unamiable thing yet, rightly viewed, perfect competition would be seen to be the order of the economic universe, as truly as gravity is the order of the physical universe, and to be not less harmonious and beneficent in operation. If free and full, unqualified, unremitting competition could be secured, the results would be more honorable to human nature, as well as practically more advantageous, in the same degree, and for the same reason that absolute justice would be more advantageous and more honorable than partial justice patched up with charity.

344. The Economic Harmonies.—When we say that through competition one reaches his best market, does this mean that in that way he does best for himself alone? On the contrary, when one reaches his best market, he does not only that which is best for himself, but that which is best for others. He not only gets more than by resorting to any other market, but, in the very act of doing so, he gives more, also. If in that market his service or commodity bears a higher price than elsewhere, this is of itself a proof that his service or commodity is there in greater demand, more needed, the subject of an intenser want, than elsewhere. Consequently, were he to resort elsewhere, he would not only receive less himself, but would satisfy a lower want on the part of others, leaving a higher want unsatisfied.

345.—But the main office of competition is to preserve individuals and classes from destruction or industrial degradation, through excessive burdens imposed by authority, through natural catastrophes affecting the sources of livelihood, or through the gradual decay of commercial demand. Deal the heaviest blow you can with a hammer into a bin of barley, and you will not injure a single grain, though the hammer be buried to your hand, because every grain moves freely from its place, and the mass simply opens to receive the intruding substance and closes around and above it. Lay one of the grains upon a rock, and your blow will smash it into a paste. Let the stoutest ship that ever rode out a hundred gales have her bow lodged in the sands, and the oncoming waves of the first storm will break her up in a few hours.

In the nature of the case, blows must fall, from time to time, upon every industrial community or class. Whether these be due to wars or failures of the harvest, or to conflagrations and floods, or to the shifting of commercial demand, or to vicious legislation, labor has an ample security against deep and permanent injury, so long as its mobility is unimpaired. On whatever spot the blow may fall, complete freedom of movement, from place to place and from avocation to avocation, will cause the original loss to be distributed over the industrial body, while the forces of repair and restoration will immediately set to work to make good what has been taken away.

346. To Him That Hath Shall be Given.—This tendency to the diffusion of all benefits to the equalization of all burdens, and to the repair of all local injuries at the expense of the vital powers of the whole industrial body, is properly the subject of admiring contemplation by social and ethical philosophers. Frederic Bastiat has, in words of deathless eloquence, described this play of industrial forces, under the title of The Economic Harmonies.

But the political economist who undertakes the explanation of the actual phenomena of the industrial world, is bound to note, not only that the assumption of full and free competition, which underlies this theory of the self-protecting power of labor, is wholly gratuitous, as applied to vast portions of the earth's population ; but, also, that, when the mobility of labor becomes in a high degree impaired, the reparative and restorative forces do not act at all. On the contrary, a new and antagonistic principle begins to operate, *viz.*, the principle that "To him that hath shall be given, and from him that hath not shall be taken away even the little that he seemeth to have."

Under the rule of this great economic as well as social law, industrial injuries once suffered tend to remain, and not to be removed. The wretch who has fallen is trampled on in the maddening struggle for place and pelf. In the case of the laborer thrown out of employment, for instance, there is always danger that self-respect, hopefulness and ambition, which we have seen (par. 76) to be most powerful factors in industrial efficiency, may fail among squalid surroundings. A less ample or nourishing diet, and less healthful conditions, submitted to for awhile, perhaps the contracting of distinctly bad habits through anxiety, disappointment and enforced idleness, may so lower his industrial power as to unfit him to render the same amount and quality of service as before. In such a case, not only is there no tendency in any economic force to repair the mischief that has been done, but even the occurrence of better times and new opportunities would not restore the shattered industrial manhood.

347. Economic Injuries Tend to Remain and to Deepen.—Irrespective of any thing catastrophic, the tendency of purely economic forces, under impaired competition, is continually to aggravate the disadvantages from which any person or class may suffer in the beginning. Defeat is an ill preparative for fresh conflicts. Every gain which one makes at the expense of another furnishes the sinews of war for further aggression ; every loss suffered diminishes the capabilities of further resistance.

This principle applies with increasing force as we go downward in the industrial scale. Emphatically is it true, that the curse of the poor is their poverty. Cheated in quantity, quality and price, in whatever they purchase, they are unable to get even as much proportionally for their little as the rich for their larger means. The tendency of purely economic forces, therefore, is to widen the differences existing in the constitution of industrial society, and to subject every person or class, who may, from any cause, be put at disadvantage, to a constantly increasing burden.

348. What may help the Laboring Class in Competition for the Product of Industry.—Granting that perfect competition would do all that has been claimed for the working classes, realizing the very ideal conditions under which they should work, but, at the same time, recognizing the fact that, in industrial society as now constituted, competition is very partial and incomplete, let us inquire what, if any thing, can be done to help the laboring classes in their competition for the product of industry.

The answer of the economists of the *laissez faire*, or Manchester school to this inquiry is a very easy one. Freedom being the ideal condition, and society suffering from lack of it, let us have all the freedom we can get, at this time, and thus prepare the way for more of it in the time to come. Let us abolish every thing in the way of restraint or regulation, every thing in the way of concert or combination in industry, which we can abolish, and trust to the future for doing away with those obstructions which are now beyond our reach.

349. Economics and Politics.—This answer is so easy as not unfairly to arouse some suspicion. Do we deal in this spirit with the question of progressive freedom in government? Does any right-thinking man, with his eyes open upon the experience of the last hundred years, allege that progress is best to be effected by indiscriminately throwing off restraints? Is it not admitted that discretion and order must be observed in removing political checks and balances and limitations? Are there not, in any well-organized society, restrictions which correspond to certain human infirmities, of which we can not now hope to rid the race, in such a way that the existence of the restrictions increases the actual degree of freedom* enjoyed by the community?

* "The modern English citizen, who lives under the burden of the revised edition of the statutes, not to speak of innumerable municipal, railroad, sanitary and other by-laws, is, after all, an infinitely freer, as

350. The Burning Theater.—But if any reader distrusts an analogy drawn between economics and politics, let us take a case from real life, where all the elements can be easily and confidently grasped. Suppose a crowded audience to be seeking to escape from a theater which has taken fire. There might be time to allow the safe discharge of all in the house. If so, the individual interest of each person clearly would coincide with the interest of the audience viewed collectively, namely, that he should fall in precisely according to his position relative to the common place of exit, and should move just so fast and no faster, according to the rate of discharge from the building into the outer air. Yet, human nature being what it is, we know that there would be great danger of a furious rush for the door, which would lead to the serious retardation of the movement of the audience as a whole, and probably to many persons being trampled upon or burned.

Suppose, now, that, at the moment of alarm, a score of resolute policemen were to present themselves, what could they do? Clearly they could not cause the audience to be discharged more quickly, safely and harmoniously than would be the case did every person in the audience truly comprehend the situation and act coolly with reference to his own interest, as above stated. As compared, however, not with what the audience ought to do, but what they probably would do, the advent of the policemen would save many limbs and lives, perhaps avert a calamity that would have filled the world with horror. With discipline thus imposed upon men in such a situation, the procedure which would be for the interest of each and of all might go forward swiftly, surely and steadily, under authoritative direction. Discipline can, indeed, create no force, but it may save much waste.

351. Registration of Land.—But if any one is still disposed to distrust analogies drawn between things inside and things outside the sphere of economics, let us take the case of a regulation prescribing the registration of real estate and the

---

well as nobler, creature, than the savage who is always under the despotism of physical want." Jevons—"The State in Relation to Labor."

recording of all transfers and mortgages of land. Such a regulation would be restrictive upon transfers. Transfers would require to be made in writing and after a definite form; certain words must be used to make the instrument effective; a certain delay must be submitted to; an office, perhaps at a distance, must be visited; copies must be made; a fee given. Yet who does not know that a regulation of this character, though in name restrictive, would in fact not retard but immensely promote the transfer of real estate. For uncertainty it would substitute the highest assurance; for the risk of losing the whole principal, it would offer a clear and indefeasible title, which would repay, many times over, the petty fee and the trouble required. The slow and costly transfer of real estate in England, where no such system exists, in comparison with the cheap and easy transfer of the same species of property in the United States, affords a measure of the force of this cause.

352. Always a Practical Question.—Perhaps enough has been said to show that the question whether a certain act, ordinance or social arrangement retards or promotes the movement of labor to its market, is a practical question, not to be determined *à priori*, except in the case of extreme measures, but to be considered and decided with reference to the existing condition of industrial society and to the actual infirmities or liabilities of the laboring population to which it was intended to apply.* A crutch operates only by restraint, and to a man of sound limbs can be only a hindrance; but it is a restraint which corresponds to the infirmity of a cripple, and may be the only means of enabling him to walk, or even of keeping him from falling hopelessly to the ground.

In application of these remarks, a brief discussion of the influence of Trades Unions and Strikes upon wages and upon the condition of the laboring class, will be found in Part VI.

353. Wages and Public Opinion.—When the writer first

---

* "The outcome of the inquiry is that we can lay down no hard and fast rules, but must treat every case, in detail, upon its merits. Specific experience is our best guide, or even express experiment where possible." Jevons—"The State in Relation to Labor."

ventured, in 1874, to urge that respect for labor and sympathy with the laboring class might become a force in determining the market rate of wages, he was greeted with derision. He has reason to believe that in the intervening years the arguments then presented have worked their way toward a conviction of the public mind that the cause thus adduced is not an unreality, but one which actually operates with perceptible force within the field of economics.

Let it be observed that what is claimed is, not that compassion and sympathy will induce employers here and there to pay wages above the market rate, but that these sentiments may become a force in determining what the market rate shall be.

354. An Analogous Case.—And, in the first place, why this incredulity on the first suggestion of the subject? Is it not true that sentiments of personal kindness and of mutual respect between classes of the community have had a very important influence, in many countries (see pars. 266–76), in determining the rates at which land should be leased? If public opinion may be a very powerful, often a predominant, force in determining the rent of land, why should we not expect that it would have at least an appreciable force in determining wages?

355. The Reason of the Case.—But let us leave analogy, and turn to the reason of the individual case. How can the sentiments we have invoked become an economic force, and thus enter into the distribution of wealth between employer and employed?

Let us recall the principle, so often insisted on, that it is only as competition is perfect that the wages class have any security that they will receive the highest remuneration which the existing conditions of industry will permit. In the failure of competition, they may be pushed down, grade by grade, in the industrial as in the social scale. Let us recall, moreover, that the failure of competition may be due to moral as much as to physical causes; that if the workman from any cause does not pursue his interest, he loses his interest, whether he refrain from bodily fear, from poverty, from ignorance, from timidity and dread of censure, or from the effects of bad political economy, which assures him that if he does not seek his interest his interest will seek him.

Now I ask, can it be doubtful that the respect and sympathy of the community must strengthen the wages class in this unceasing struggle; must give weight and force to all their reasonable demands; must make them more resolute and patient in resisting encroachment; must add to the confidence with which each individual laborer will rely on the good faith of those who are joined with him in his cause, and make it harder for any weak or doubtful comrade to succumb?

And, on the other hand, will not the consciousness that the whole community sympathize with the efforts of labor to advance its condition, by all fair means, inevitably weaken the resistance of the employing class * to claims which can be conceded, diminish the confidence with which each employer looks to his fellows to hold out to the end, and make it easier for the less resolute to retire from the contest, and grant, amid general applause, what has been demanded?

356. The Lamentable Case of Hodge.—Let us apply these principles to an individual case. Hodge thinks—Hodge is a plowman, and has been getting twelve shillings a week—that he ought to have more wages, or, rather, for Hodge would scarcely put it so abruptly, he feels that it is dreadfully hard to live on twelve shillings. He has attended a lecture delivered by Mr. Joseph Arch from a wagon on the green. He is uneasy and wants to improve his condition. So far, then, he is a hopeful subject, economically. The desire to improve one's condition is the *sine qua non* of competition. Will these stirrings of industrial ambition come to any thing? Will the discontented plowman seek and find his better market? † This is a great question, for upon the answer to it

* "Masters are always and everywhere in a sort of tacit, but constant and uniform, combination not to raise the wages of labor above their actual rate."—Adam Smith: "Wealth of Nations."

† In discussing his valuable agricultural statistics before the London Statistical Society, Mr. Fred. Purdy said: "It would appear that no commodity in this country presents so great a variation in price, at one

depends the future of Hodge, and perhaps of his sons and grandsons. Let the *Spectator* (August 4, 1872), tell how he is assisted on his way and encouraged in his weak, ignorant, doubting mind, by landlord, bishop, and judge.

"The man has been, so to speak, morally whipped for six months. He has found no friend anywhere, except in a press he can neither read nor understand. The duke has deprived him of his allotment; the bishop has recommended that his instructor should be ducked; the squire has threatened him with dismissal in winter; the magistrate has fined him for quitting work, which is just, and scolded him for listening to lectures, which is tyranny; the mayor at Evesham has prohibited him from meeting on the green; and the lawyer—witness a recent case near Chelmsford—has told him that any one who advises and helps him to emigrate is a hopeless rascal."

Now I ask, in all seriousness, is Hodge quite as likely to pursue his interest and persist in whatever that requires——which, be it observed, is no other than what the interest of the whole community requires—as if his social superiors were encouraging him to better his fortune if he finds a chance; as if the shopkeeper and the publican and the lawyer and the rector and the squire were not all ranged against him? Is it not possible that, for the lack of a little fanning, the feeble flame in Hodge's breast may die out, and he, giving up all thought of seeking his fortune elsewhere, return to his furrow, never to stray from it again?

---

time, as agricultural labor, taking the money wages of the men as the best exponent of its value. A laborer's wages in Dorset or Devon are barely half the sum given for similar services in the northern parts of England." Among the causes of this Mr. Purdy cites "the natural *vis inertiæ* of the class."

CHAPTER VII.

TWO OTHER SHARES IN DISTRIBUTION.

357. We have discussed the distribution of the product, under the entrepreneur organization of industry. We have seen that this product is divided into four principal shares, rent, interest, profits and wages, corresponding to four classes of claimants. We have now to inquire what becomes of certain portions of the product, which do not appear to go into either of the four shares enumerated. And first of the amount taken by government.

358. Taxation.—There has long been a difference of opinion among economists, whether taxation should be a title in distribution or in consumption. Prof. Senior held to the latter treatment ; Prof. Jevons favored the former.

The difference is just this : Shall we regard government as a fifth original claimant upon the product of industry, taking its share under the name of taxes, as the land-owner takes rent, the capitalist interest, the employer profits, and the laborer wages ; or shall we regard the product as divided into four shares, out of each of which is paid, as one form of the owner's consumption of his income, a sum, greater or less, for the sustentation of government, just as out of each such share are paid sums, greater or less, for shelter, food, fuel, etc.?

The question is not a very important one in a general treatise on Political Economy, and neither decision solves all the difficulties of the case, since the functions of government are so various and so widely diverse.

On the one hand, it is said that government is a great producer and should be regarded as a claimant in distribution, taking its share under the name of taxes. Government builds and keeps in repair roads and bridges and breakwaters and perhaps, also, canals and railways, for the purposes of trade and industry. Government maintains a constabulary and court-houses and jails, that the honest and industrious may work without hindrance or even fear of molestation. Government does a great many other things which minister directly to the creation of values, vastly increasing the amount of the product over what it would have been without the intervention of this agency.

On the other hand, it is said that a great part of what government does has not the production of wealth as its primary object, and that much does not even contribute indirectly to that end, as in the case of the vast military and naval expenditures of the nations of Europe, which have for their purpose, not the preservation of civil peace, but to maintain the existence or extend the power of nationalities or of dynasties. Secondly, whatever the objects of expenditure, government does not obtain its revenue through the agencies of exchange, but by forcible collection, men contributing, not because government has made it worth their while to do so, not because government is prepared to render an equivalent, but simply because government demands the contribution and will have it. For these reasons, it is urged, the revenue of the State should not be treated as a share in distribution, but as a form of consumption.

359. As has been said, the question is not free from difficulties whatever course be taken. A thoroughly consistent treatment of the subject of taxation would require the appearance of this title in more than one department of political economy.

(*a*.) The function of government in the creation of values is extensive and important, under the modern organization of industrial society. The building and maintenance of roads and bridges, of breakwaters and lighthouses, the opening of harbors, and the improvement of rivers, all directed towards a larger production of wealth, form a notable part of the industrial agencies of all progressive communities. These things, if done on the initiative and at the expense of individuals, who looked to tolls, fees, and dues for their reimbursement, would be by all deemed productive, in the fullest sense. They are not less so when done by government, with funds raised by taxation.

(*b*.) The methods of taxation, the subjects of imposition,

the agencies of collection, so far as they affect the ultimate *incidence* of taxation, that is, so far as they determine that the pressure of taxation shall finally rest here and not there, on this class and not on that, fall within the department of Distribution. The questions, *e. g.*, whether a tax on wages results in a reduction of the comforts, luxuries, and necessaries enjoyed by the laborer, or is, in the end, paid by the employer; whether a tax on rent rests upon the landlord, or is by him shifted upon the consumer of agricultural produce: these and the like are questions in Distribution.

(*c.*) The effects of the expenditure by government of a certain amount of wealth, as contrasted with the effects of the expenditure of the same amount by the classes who paid the taxes that put the treasury in funds, belong to the department of Consumption.

(*d.*) The questions, how the largest amount of revenue can be secured with the smallest cost of collection; how the needed revenue can be procured with the least irritation of the public mind; how the highest assurance can be obtained as to the proper custody and disbursement of funds; these and the like are questions in fiscal or "Cameralistic" science, and not in economics strictly considered.

(*e.*) In addition to the question (*b*), what is the ultimate incidence of any existing or projected body of taxes: who, in in the last resort pays them; whose sum of enjoyment is actually diminished by the imposition, we have a question, to which writers on taxation devote a large part of their space, *viz.*, who ought to pay the taxes of any given community: what classes should contribute to the support of the government, and in what proportions? This is purely a question in political equity.

360. The foregoing would be the true logical treatment of taxation. In an elementary treatise, however, I do not deem it worth while to deal so elaborately with this subject, and will postpone to Part VI. whatever I have to say regarding taxation, except so far as it may be desirable to speak of the influence of government expenditures when we reach the department of Consumption.

361. The Speculating Class.—Incidental to all the processes of production and exchange is the chance of gain or loss through the rise or fall of prices during the interval between buying and selling; between making and selling. This gain or loss may be slight, in any given case, or it may be considerable. There were many manufacturers in the United States who made fifty or a hundred thousand dollars, clear, by the rise of cotton, on their hands, in 1861 and 1862, and this without intentionally speculating at all, but simply through holding a large stock for the purposes of legitimate manufacturing. At other times, the daily, weekly, monthly fluctuations of prices will be very slight, now all on one side, for a long time; now, all on the other side; then, oscillating backwards and forwards across what we may call the average price.

To a certain extent, these fluctuations of price may be trusted in time to offset each other, as regards any individual merchant or manufacturer. Yet after all the effect of this is exhausted, there will still be a chance of gain or of loss, which may be so considerable as to become an important element in determining the fact of profits, or even in deciding the solvency of the merchant or manufacturer, in spite of the strictest observance of the rules of prudence, and in spite of the greatest energy and industry.

Within this field, so far as the great body of business men are concerned, fortune holds undisputed sway. They lack the faculty to discern the signs of the future. They do the best they can to produce good articles cheap, to meet the demands of the public as to fashions and styles, to keep expenses down, and to avoid losses by bad debts. When they have done this, they have done all they can for themselves; and whatever gains or losses come to them through the fluctuations of the market, come as if wholly by chance. There are other men who have a rare power to apprehend in advance the movements of the market. It is always found that when materials begin to rise, these men have a large stock on hand. Let a disastrous fall occur, these men are never caught by it. Whichever way the market turns, it seems as though the sole object were to enrich these fortunate beings.

Of course, this is speculation ; yet when it is carried on only incidentally to a legitimate manufacturing or trading business, we do not call these men speculators.

362.—In every progressive commercial community, however, is found a large and increasing number of persons who, either possessing this faculty of discerning the signs of the market, or flattering themselves they possess it, make a business of buying or selling according to their anticipations of a rise or a fall. These persons are not manufacturers ; they are not merchants, in any proper sense ; they do not buy from producers or sell to consumers ; they are neither importers, jobbers, wholesalers or retailers ; they have perhaps no stores or warehouses or stocks of goods ; possibly, would not know by sight a sample of the commodities they deal in. They simply bet upon the market, having a well or ill-founded opinion of their own shrewdness and coolness in doing so. They may lose a fortune, or make a fortune.

The difference between the two kinds of speculation may be illustrated as follows : A miller who grinds two hundred thousand bushels of grain a year, may, if he have this peculiar kind of insight, by carefully watching the market, buy his wheat at two cents a bushel less than he would have had to pay for it had he bought it from time to time as he needed it for grinding. This is speculating. Moreover, after grinding, he may hold the flour weeks, or months, until he sees his chance, and then, by going into the market at the right moment, he may sell it at ten cents a barrel more than if he had sold it as it was made. This again is speculating. Now here is a saving in materials of $4,000, and a gain on the price of the product of, say, $4,000. After making allowance for interest on the extra capital required to "carry" the wheat and the flour, and for the cost of storage, the addition made hereby to the miller's profits for the year would be a tidy sum. On the other hand, a corn-broker may buy and sell twenty thousand bushels a week, buying and selling on all sorts of time, ten days, twenty days, sixty days, six months, every transaction being a bet upon the price of corn at a future date. When the broker buys, he bets that the price will rise ; when he sells, he bets that it will fall. The men from whom he buys have as little corn as he has ; the men to whom he sells would know as little as he what to do with actual corn, were any of it to come in their way.

Of speculating as a business, two things may be said. First, it is surprising what an enormous aggregate of transactions a man of little capital and no brains to speak of, may conduct in the course of his life, and yet neither lose nor gain much if only he confines himself to small individual operations. Secondly, not less surprising are the gains of speculation when conducted by a real master. Every year an appreciable portion of the product of industry passes into the possession of the men of this class. In every highly commercial country, the largest fortunes are those made by speculation. The fortunes so made, however, are not nearly so numerous as those made by trade and industry.

363. Speculation is not wholly without its advantages to the community. If corn is likely to be scarce and, by consequence, high, four months hence, the man who now begins to buy does, in so far, call attention to that probability. By raising the price he, so to speak, advertises for an increased supply to be brought in from the outside, and for greater carefulness in husbanding the existing stock. If beef is likely to fall in price, sixty days hence, the man who now sells does what lies in him to give notice of an excess of supply, and thus affords duller-witted holders opportunity to get rid gradually of their stock, instead of encountering an utter breaking down of the market a little later. In a word, speculation while confined within moderate limits is the agent for equalizing supply and demand and rendering the fluctuations of price less sudden and abrupt than they would otherwise be.

There are causes, however, which go to render speculation extravagant, carrying it beyond all reasonable bounds, multiplying the numbers of the speculating class and vastly increasing their gains, at the expense of the sober, productive industries of a country. Foremost among these is a vicious money system. The extent to which this cause engenders speculation may be seen in the history of the "Continental" money of the American revolution, of the "Assignats" of the French revolutionary period, and of the "Greenbacks" of the war of Secession. With prices fluctuating violently and rapidly, the opportunities for acquiring large wealth by speculation are increased ten-fold, it may be a hundred-fold. This is too much for human nature: too much for honesty, too much for prudence. A subtle poison runs through the veins of the community, turning the heart to crime and the brain to folly. The face of society changes, under such an evil passion, as suddenly and as fearfully as does the face of a man stricken with a deadly fever. On every hand breaches of trust testify to the weakness of the principles of virtue under such a strain, while honest and discreet modes of obtaining a livelihood are disparaged and abandoned for those which promise quicker and larger, even if illicit, gains.

364. Loaded Dice.—Of much speculation, it must be said that it is wholly beyond economic as well as moral sympathy. If all speculation is gambling, this is gambling with the dice loaded. By means of combinations and corners, the markets are often profoundly influenced in order to produce the very fluctuations on which the grain or petroleum or stock gamblers have made their bets. The mischiefs suffered by trade and industry, originating in this source, are monstrous, even incalculable. Whether they can in any degree be repressed by law, is a grave political question, with which we are not called to deal.

CHAPTER VIII.

THE REACTION OF DISTRIBUTION UPON PRODUCTION.

365. Actual Production Compared with Productive Capability.—In a previous chapter (Chapter IV., Part 2), we considered the elements which enter into the productive capability of a community, and indicated, as the one most important question with which political economy has to deal, the inquiry, why it is that the actual production of any community falls so far short of what its land power, its labor power, and its capital power are jointly competent to effect.

It was there stated that only when we should have passed through all the departments of political economy should we be in a position fully to answer this question.

366. Even under the title, Production, however, we saw that grave liability to loss of force inheres in the industrial structure of society especially under the entrepreneur system, by which the labor power and the capital power of the community become committed to numerous highly technical employments, from which they can not readily release themselves, and, within those employments, become subjected to the direction of a comparatively small number of individuals, whose peculiarities of character, of habit, of station, seriously modify the application of capital and labor to production; whose mistaken aims, whose erroneous impulses, may divert these forces from that object; whose accidents of fortune may impair the energy of the industrial movement or paralyze it altogether.

Again, under the title, Exchange, we saw (Chapter VII., Part 3) that still further and even more grave liabilities to loss of industrial force inhere in that commercial system which, by separating producer and consumer, often by wide intervals, sometimes by half the circumference of the globe, introduces the opportunity for serious misunderstandings between these two classes; misunderstandings which, when intensified by panic, may at times result in a wide and long-continued suspension of productive activity.

367. We are now to inquire respecting the reaction of Distribution upon Production. Is here a liability to a still further loss of productive force? Discarding the terms *just* and *unjust*, or *equitable* and *inequitable*, as applied to the distribution of wealth, let us ask whether there is found, in a division of the product of industry according to certain proportions, between the several parties who have united in production, a sufficient cause for a smaller production of wealth in the future than would result from a division of the same product between the same parties in different proportions?

I think we have at various points, in our treatment of distribution, caught views of the subject which must have satisfied us that it is possible that the product of industry, in any given time and place, may be so divided among the persons and classes of persons who have contributed to its production, as to impair, in greater or less measure, the productive force up to that time existing; perhaps, even, to generate influences which shall thereafter act with increasing violence in reducing the productive capability of the community. It may be well, however, to stop a moment at this point and to treat distinctly and separately the possible reaction of distribution upon production.

368. The Landlord and the Capitalist have an Economic Advantage.—The consideration nearest at hand, in this connection, would seem to be this, *viz.*: that among the four several main classes of producers, there are wide differences as to the liability, to which these are respectively subject, of being so cut down in their remuneration, in any given time and place, as to suffer a loss of force thereby. Two of the four classes, *viz.*: landlords and capitalists, clearly occupy a position of what may be called economic advantage. They have at their command certain material agencies of production by withholding the use of which they can inflict a relatively greater injury upon others than they would themselves suffer. In the expressive phrase of children, they have their hands on "the upper end of the stick." They are in a position to make bargains for themselves to the best advantage.

It is true that, unless the landlord find a tenant, he can have no rent. Yet a landlord who has five farms to let, may put a great pressure upon each and every one of six would-be tenants. Moreover, the landlord is, in general, much more wealthy than his tenant, and is thus able to stand longer out of his remuneration, in case there comes to be a contest between the two as to the terms on which the land shall be rented. I might add that, if a given farm be not rented at all, for a season, it may not be altogether a loss to the owner.

The orchard will bring forth its crop of fruit without the intervention of a tenant; the grass will grow as thick and high as usual, on the "mowing"; the wood lots will all the time be acquiring value; the arable lands will have a rest which it might possibly have been good policy to give them, even at the sacrifice of rent.

Again it is true that, unless the capitalist lends his accumulations, he can not acquire interest; yet his loss by standing out of his interest, for a given season, may be far less than that sustained by the entrepreneur through losing the use of the capital on which he had relied. The latter person may have become so engaged that the failure to effect a loan, while it cost the capitalist but one and a half per cent. during three months, might require the entrepreneur to sell goods at a great sacrifice, or to give up some contract which promised to be highly advantageous.

Enough, perhaps, has been said to justify the assertion that the capitalist and landlord occupy positions of economic advantage, so far, at least, that they are not likely to suffer injury, except by violence or legal spoliation.

It is another question, whether the economic advantage enjoyed by these two classes is so great as to place it in their power to do an injury to other classes, that is, to cut down the shares going to those other classes, out of the product of industry, to such an extent as to impair their productive force, and, by so doing, to diminish the productive capability of the community.

369. Shall the Capitalist be Hampered?—In remarks on Usury Laws, which will be found in Part VI., I shall express the opinion that, in certain states of industrial society, the lending class have so great an advantage over the borrowing class, which, in such states of society, consists generally of distressed persons, as practically to place an individual borrower completely at the mercy of the usurer, who is able to exact a rate of interest which is not only irrespective of the economic service rendered through the loan, but soon becomes destructive of the borrower's credit and financial integrity, reducing him speedily and certainly to bankruptcy and perhaps to prison. Under conditions like these, I shall suggest that laws limiting the rate of interest, in protection of the would-be borrower, may not be as unwise and as unstatesmanlike as they have generally been considered. On the other hand, I shall undertake to show, that in advanced stages of industrial society, where commerce and manufactures are widely extended and are largely carried on by means of borrowed capital; where, therefore, borrowers are no longer distressed persons; but the most active and prosperous members of the community borrow largely, freely and of choice, as a matter of business and with a view to profit—in such stages of society laws limiting the rate of interest merely lay an extra burden upon those who are at a peculiar difficulty in borrowing. In the absence of such laws, those persons will benefit by the greater plentifulness of capital, the greater ease of borrowing and the consequently lower rate of interest, which, in general, result from freedom regarding contracts for loan, in a commercial or manufacturing community. The business classes, active, alert, aggressive in competition, will make rates of interest by which the less fortunate members of society will profit.

370. Shall the Landlord be Restrained?—In the chapter on rent, the opinion has been expressed that, in a community like the United States, or Canada, or Australia, the landlord may make the utmost out of his economic position without working industrial injury to the tenant, owing to the mobility of the population, their readiness and resourcefulness, their self-reliance and economic aggressiveness. In countries occupied by populations of a lower industrial character, we saw that, unless the constraints of law * or public opinion inter-

---

* "The land of a country presents conditions which separate it economically from the great mass of the other objects of wealth—conditions which, if they do not absolutely and under all circumstances impose upon the state the obligation of controlling private enterprise in dealing with land, at least explain why this control is, in certain stages of social progress, indispensable; and why, in fact, it has been constantly put in force whenever public opinion or custom has not been strong enough to do without it." . . . . "And not merely does economic science,

vene, the vast economic advantage possessed by the landlord class, as against a peasantry ignorant, inert and perhaps numerically in excess, is likely to operate with increasing severity, to impoverish the tenant class and to ultimately reduce their industrial efficiency, through deprivation of necessary clothing, food and shelter, as well as through the loss of hopefulness and self-respect. We saw that this might go on until almost the last stage of human misery should be reached, as in Ireland, during the period before the great famine.

371. Invidious Treatment of the Landlord and Capitalist.—What might be true in a contrary case: how far laws prohibiting or limiting the payment of rent or interest framed, not with a view to offset certain weaknesses or unfortunate liabilities on the part of the tenant or borrowing class, but drawn in a spirit hostile to the owners of land or of capital, and designed to confiscate, for the benefit of other classes, or of the community as a whole, some part or all of what would otherwise be paid on these accounts: how far such laws might impair the productive capability of the community, we shall have occasion to discuss in Part VI., under the titles, The Unearned Increment of Land, and Usury Laws. I will so far anticipate that discussion as to say, that, while in commercial or manufacturing communities, the normal effect of severe restrictions upon the payment of interest is at once to diminish the accumulation of capital for productive uses, and to prevent the existing body of capital from being applied where it will do the most good, such laws are, in such communities, so easily evaded that their practical influence is not very great.

Secondly, the effects upon the cultivation of the soil of a reduction or confiscation of rent, by legal means, are not so clear as to be beyond dispute. The theory which underlies the land laws of nearly all states that can be called civilized, is, that the private ownership of land, with the incident of the acquisition by the owner of an "unearned increment" due to

---

as expounded by its ablest teachers, dispose of *à priori* objections to a policy of intervention with regard to land, it even furnishes principles fitted to inform and guide such a policy, in a positive sense."

—PROF. JOHN E. CAIRNES.

the exertions and sacrifices of the community as a whole, is essential to industrial progress; and that not only those who are so fortunate as to be among the owners of land, but even those who have been born into the world without a title to a foot of soil, are benefited, and largely benefited, by the fact of private ownership. At the same time, it probably would not be claimed by any one that the care and pains of the individual owner, to secure the proper cultivation and preservation of his land, are proportional to his share of the product. I see no reason to believe that a reduction of rent in the case of a given tract of land, through, say, some new economic force, would diminish the care and pains taken by the owner in respect to his property, so long as his interest remained still considerable.

There have of late years appeared certain writers who claim that private ownership is not necessary to the fullest use of the soil which forms the natural endowment of any community. At least, they claim, the incident of an "unearned increment" is not necessary. They assert that all of rent proper (exclusive, that is, of the returns to actual investments of capital, in improvements) can be cut away without impairing the productive uses of the soil, though they admit that so much of the former rent might advantageously be left to the so-called owner as would constitute a reasonable commission to him, as the agent of society, for taking all needed care and pains with respect to the land. I believe this view to be altogether erroneous; but it must be confessed that the error can not be shown as clearly and strongly as in the case of the argument for prohibiting interest. I shall defer to Part VI. whatever I may have to say further on this subject.

372. Distribution as between Employer and Laborer.— So much for the possible action of distribution upon production, through causes operating to affect the shares of the product of industry going, as rent or as interest, to the owner of land or to the owner of capital.

Of much more practical importance, in these modern times, is the influence exerted upon future production by the division of the remaining product between the employing and the laboring class. I shall undertake to show that greatly to change the proportions existing between these two shares, at any time, may be to set in operation causes which will affect the future productive capability of the community, it may be to a wide extent, it may be through long periods of time.

373. Beating Down Wages.—The economists of ten or fifteen years ago, urged very strongly that a reduction of wages could not prove of ultimate injury to the laboring class. Thus Prof. Cairnes says:

"Supposing a group of employers to have succeeded, as no doubt would be perfectly possible for them, in temporarily forcing down wages, by combination in a particular trade, a portion of their wealth previously invested would now become free. How would it be employed? Unless we are to suppose the character of a large section of the community to be suddenly changed in a leading attribute, the wealth so withdrawn from wages would, in the end, and before long, be restored to wages. The same motives which led to its investment would lead to its re-investment, and, once re-invested, the interests of those concerned would cause it to be distributed amongst the several elements of capital in the same proportion as before. In this way covetousness is held in check by covetousness, and the desire for aggrandizement sets limits to its own gratification." And in a similar vein, Prof. Perry, of our own country, wrote: "If in the division between profits and wages, at the end of any industrial cycle, profits get more than their due share, these very profits will wish to become capital, and will thus become a larger demand for labor, and the next wages fund will be larger than the last."

374. Had we already discussed the principles which govern the consumption of wealth, it would be easy to show that Professors Cairnes and Perry are mistaken in their view of the necessary effects of an enlargement of profits at the expense of wages, inasmuch as a portion of such enhanced profits, instead of becoming capital (that is, wealth devoted to reproduction), might become fine horses and houses, fine clothes and opera boxes; while another portion might take the form of coming to the office one hour later in the morning and going home one hour earlier in the afternoon.

But, passing by this point, the entire argument by which the English and American economists generally have sought to establish what we may call "the economic indifference of the rate of profits," is still further defective, in that it neglects those very important considerations which relate to the possible degradation of labor: that is, the reduction of the laborer from a higher to a lower industrial grade.

375. The Degradation of Labor.—The constant imminence of this change, the smallness of the causes—often accidental in origin and temporary in duration—which may produce it, and the almost irreparable consequences of such a catastrophe, can hardly be set forth too strongly.

The assumption which underlies the statements I have quoted is that the laboring classes, while suffering economic injury from any source, will themselves remain firm in their industrial quality, and await the operation of the restorative and reparative forces which shall, in time, set them right.

The human fact, so often to be distinguished from the economic assumption, unmistakably is that there is, on the part of the working classes, unless protected in an unusual degree by political franchises, by the influence of public education, and by self-respect and social ambition, a fatal facility in submitting to industrial injuries, which too often does not allow time for the operation of the beneficent principles of relief and restoration. The industrial opportunity comes around again, it may be, but it does not find the same man it left: he is no longer capable of rendering the same service; perhaps the wages he now receives are quite as much as he earns.

376. Let us consider the possible effects of a considerable reduction of wages. If the amount previously received had allowed comforts and luxuries, and left a margin for saving, the reduction would probably be resented, in the sense that population would be reduced by migration or by abstinence from propagation, until the former wages should be, if possible, restored. But if the previous wages had been barely sufficient to furnish the necessaries of life, and especially if the body of laborers were ignorant and unambitious, the falling off in the quantity and quality of food and clothing and in the convenience and healthfulness of the shelter enjoyed would at once affect the efficiency of the individual laborer.

With less food, which is the fuel of the human machine, less force would be generated; with less clothing, more force would be wasted by cold; with scantier and meaner quarters, fouler air and diminished access to the light would prevent the food from being fully digested in the stomach and the blood from being duly oxydized in the lungs, would lower the general tone of the system and expose the subject increasingly to the ravages of disease. In all these ways the laborer would become less efficient, simply through the reduction of his wages.

377. The economists assert that whatever is taken from wages will increase capital, and hence quicken employment, and that this, in turn, will heighten wages. But we see that it is possible that what is taken from wages no man shall gain: it may be lost to the laborer and to the world. Now, so far as strictly economic forces are concerned, where enters the restorative principle? The employer is not getting excessive profits, to be expended subsequently in wages; the laborer is not under-paid; he earns now what he gets no better than he formerly did his higher wages.

This image of the degraded laborer is not a fanciful one. There are in Europe great bodies of population which have come in just this way to be pauperized and brutalized, weakened and diseased by under-feeding and foul air, hopeless and lost to all self-respect, so that they can scarcely be said to desire any better condition, and still bringing children into the world to fill their miserable places in garrets and cellars, and in time in the wards of the workhouse.

If such an injury as has been indicated may be suffered in respect to the physical powers of the laborer through the reduction of wages, quite as speedily may his usefulness be impaired through the moral effects of such a calamity. Just as the greatest possibilities of industrial efficiency lie in the creation of hopefulness, self-respect and social ambition, so the greatest possibilities of loss lie in the discouragement or destruction of these qualities. We have seen through what a scale the laborer may rise in his progress to productive power. By looking back, we see through what spaces he may fall under the force of purely industrial disasters.

378. The Argument from Self-Interest.—But we may at this point be called upon to meet an objection, founded upon the assumed sufficiency of the principle of self-interest. How, it may be asked, is it possible that employers shall fail to pay wages which will allow their laborers a liberal sustenance, if, indeed, it be for their own advantage to do so; if, by that means, the economic efficiency of the laborers will be thereby increased?

I answer, first, that the assumption of the sufficiency of self-interest to secure wise action is grotesquely wide of the miserable truth regarding human nature, to whatever department of activity we have reference. Mankind, always less than wise and too often foolish to the point of stupidity, on the one hand, or of fanaticism on the other, whether in politics or in domestic life, in hygiene or in religion, do not all at once become wise when industrial concerns are in question.

The argument for feeding a hired laborer liberally, that he may work efficiently, applies with equal force to the maintenance of a slave; yet we know too well that everywhere the lust of immediate gain has always despoiled the slave of a part, often a large part, of the food and clothing necessary to his highest efficiency. The same argument would apply to the case of live-stock. Yet it is almost impossible, by any amount of preaching and teaching, by any number of fairs and premiums, to keep a body of farmers up to the point of feeding cattle well and treating them well. The world over, the rule regarding the care of live-stock is niggardliness of expenditure, working deep and lasting prejudice to production.

The foregoing would be a sufficient answer to the objection I have anticipated. On every hand we see true self-interest sacrificed to greed: why should it not be so in the case of the wages of hired labor?

But another and additional reason appears. It is that the

employer has none of that security which the owner of stock or the master of a slave possesses, that what goes in food shall come back in work. A man buying an underfed slave or ox knows that when he shall have brought his property into good condition the advantage will all be his ; but the free laborer may at any time carry to another employer whatever of bone and sinew and nervous energy he may have gained through liberal subsistence. There is, as yet, no law which gives the employer compensation for "unexhausted improvements" in the person of his hired man.

379. Beating Down Profits.—The foregoing comprises all I should three or four years ago have deemed it necessary to say, regarding the division of the product of industry between employers and employed, as affecting the future productive capability of a community. The normal position of the employer is so clearly one of advantage, in competition with the employed, that it would have seemed scarcely worth while to inquire into the industrial effects of a pressure put upon the employing class so severe as to reduce the profits of business below the point required to secure the fullest employment of the land power, labor power and capital power of the community.* Even the introduction of Trade Unions into the field of industry can scarcely be said to have done more than offset

* Oddly enough, many economists who have been serenely confident that any possible reduction of wages, under pressure from the employing class, would not injure the body of laborers, holding that whatever might thus for the time be taken from wages must infallibly, and before long, be restored to wages, [see remarks of Profs. Cairnes and Perry above], have manifested the greatest anxiety lest profits should be unduly reduced through the encroachments of wages. Not a few of these writers have formally warned the laboring class against demanding higher wages, lest they should so reduce the profits of business as to impair or destroy the employer's interest in production. It is difficult to see the consistency of these two opinions. If what is unduly taken from wages, by pressure from the employing class, is certain to be restored to wages, why may it not be that whatever is unduly taken from profits, by pressure from the laboring class, shall, in the end, be restored to profits ? If the economic harmonies exist, they surely must "work both ways."

the naturally great advantage enjoyed by the employing class, in competition for the product of industry.

Within the last few years, however, attempts have been made, among us in the United States, to establish confederations of labor, more far-reaching, more thoroughly organized, more authoritatively controlled, than the now familiar Trade Unions. Should the avowed purposes of those most conspicuously engaged in these efforts be accomplished, in whole or in any considerable degree, it would appear that the economic advantage might not only be shifted from the employing to the laboring class, but might there be so much enhanced as to require us to contemplate an extensive reduction of profits as a possible cause of impairment to the productive capability of the community. The further consideration of this topic will be postponed to Part VI., where we shall speak of the Knights of Labor.

380. The Doctrine of Laissez Faire.—If such liabilities to an impairment of the productive capability of the community lie in the distribution of wealth, what becomes of the characteristic doctrine of the so-called Manchester School, *laissez faire:* hands off: leave economic forces to work, alike unaided and unhindered, in the assurance that the interests of individuals will be found to harmonize so far with the interests of the community as to secure the highest welfare of each and of all?

On this point my views can not be expressed so well by phrases of my own devising, as in the language of an eminent English economist.

"There is no evidence," says Prof. Cairnes, "either in what we know of the conduct of men, in the present stage of their development, or yet in the large experience we have had of the working of *laissez faire*, to warrant the assumption that lies at the root of this doctrine.

"Human beings know and follow their interests according to their lights and dispositions; but not necessarily, nor in practice always, in that sense in which the interest of the individual is co-incident with that of others and of the whole. It follows that there is no security that the economic phenomena of society, as at present constituted, will arrange themselves spontaneously in the way which is most for the common good.

"In other words, *laissez faire* falls to the ground as a scientific doctrine. I say as a scientific doctrine ; for let us be careful not to overstep the limits of our argument. It is one thing to repudiate the scientific authority of *laissez faire,* freedom of contract, and so forth ; it is a totally different thing to set up the opposite principle of state control, the doctrine of paternal government. For my part, I accept neither one doctrine nor the other ; and, as a practical rule, I hold *laissez faire* to be incomparably the safer guide. Only let us remember that it is a practical rule, and not a doctrine of science ; a rule in the main sound, but, like most other sound practical rules, liable to numerous exceptions ; above all, a rule which must never, for a moment, be allowed to stand in the way of the candid consideration of any promising proposal of social or industrial reform."

PART V.—CONSUMPTION.

CHAPTER I.

SUBSISTENCE: POPULATION.

381. What is Consumption?—By the term consumption, in economics, we express the use made of wealth. This does not necessarily imply the destruction of the form or material of the commodities so used, or even the exhaustion of the value which had at some time been imparted to them. In general, however, the use of wealth involves, in a greater or less degree, loss of substance and change of form, with a decline, rapid or slow, in that power in exchange which we call value.

"That almost all that is produced is destroyed, is true; but we can not admit that it is produced for the purpose of being destroyed. It is produced for the purpose of being made use of. Its destruction is an incident to its use; not only not intended, but, as far as possible, avoided."* That destruction may, in exceptional cases, be practically avoided altogether. An intaglio is consumed, in the economic sense, when it finds its place in the British Museum, where it may remain unimpaired through uncounted centuries. Certain hewn stones were consumed, in the economic sense, twenty-five hundred years ago, when they were lifted into their place in a Roman aqueduct. As hewn stones, simply, they had been commodities, having a variety of possible uses. They might have been wrought into the fortifications of the city, or used in building

* Prof. N. W. Senior.

a temple, or an amphitheater, or a private palace. But when once they were applied to a definite use, they were, in the economic sense, consumed. They ceased to be merely hewn stones, to be sold by themselves, and subject indifferently to many uses ; they became inseparable parts of something else.

Iron ore is consumed, *i. e.*, applied to the end in view in its production, when thrown into the furnace, and here takes place almost instantaneously not only a great chemical change, but a complete loss of form. The iron bar or plate is in turn consumed, when it is fitted into a bridge, without undergoing any chemical or mechanical change at the time, to be thereafter subject only to slow agencies of decay in the atmosphere, or to effects of attrition which, from one year to another, would be imperceptible.

382. Consumption as a Department of Political Economy.—Why should the economist interest himself, at all, in questions relating to consumption? Why, having traced wealth through its production, distribution and exchange, should he not leave it in the hands of the consumer without further inquiry, satisfied with its having reached the end for which it was created? So have many, indeed most, economists dealt with the uses of wealth, declining to recognize consumption as a department of political economy.

It is, of course, competent to any writer on economics thus to limit the scope of his inquiry ; but I can not but deem it a subject of much regret that the fascinations of the mathematical treatment of economic questions, and the ambition to make political economy an exact science, should have led to the practical excision of the whole department of consumption from so many recent works. For, after all, the chief interest of political economy to the ordinary reader, its chief value to the student of history, must be in the explanation it affords of the advance or the decline in the productive power of nations and communities ; and it is only in the consumption of wealth that we find the reasons for the rise of some and the fall of others, from age to age.* It is in the use made of the exist-

* The late Prof. Jevons, in the introduction to his "Theory of Political Economy." after noting the close analogy to the science of Statical

ing body of wealth that the wealth of the next generation is determined. It matters far less for the future greatness of a nation what is the sum of its wealth to-day, than what are the habits of its people in the daily consumption of that wealth; to what uses those means are devoted. That wealth may be applied to ends which inspire social ambition, which restrict population within limits consistent with a high *per capita* production, which increase the efficiency of the laborer and supply instrumentalities for rendering his labor still more productive, or it may be applied to ends which allow the increase of population in the degree that involves poverty, squalor and disease; to ends which debauch the laborer morally and physically, striking at both his power and his disposition to work hard and continuously. When it is remembered that statisticians estimate the wealth of England at only five or six times the amount of its annual production, it will appear of how much more importance, in the large view of a nation's future, is the direction of its expenditures than the absolute amount of its accumulations, at any given time. The completeness with which the French people, through their temperance, frugality and industry, combined with the strict repression of population, made up in a few years the terrific losses and fines of the German war, affords a very striking illustration of the virtue there is in the labor power of a country to replace its capital, if only a right consumption of the annual product be assured.

383. Subsistence.—The primary use of wealth is for subsistence. In the earliest stages of human society, man, like the lower animals, had only one want. Like the lower animals, he gathered his food, whether fish or flesh or nuts or berries, where he chanced to find it, and ate it without preparation. Long, however, before he began to cultivate food, even in the simplest way, he began to cook it. The discovery

---

Mechanics presented by the Theory of Economy proposed by him, significantly says: "But I believe that Dynamical branches of the science of Economy may remain to be developed, on the consideration of which I have not at all entered." Elsewhere Prof. Jevons says: "We, first of all, need a theory of the Consumption of Wealth."

of fire and its application to the preparation of food, is made by some writers upon primitive society to mark the boundary between the purely savage and the barbarous condition.

Man is the only animal that has attained the capability of preparing food for consumption. All other species are content with the animal or vegetable material. Man, even in the lowest of existent communities, demands for his subsistence something more than the raw material. It must be prepared or manufactured for his uses, though this may be by very rude and simple processes.

384. Clothing and Shelter.—At what stage in the evolution of the human kind, clothing and shelter, other than that furnished by the casual cave or by the foliage of the forest, became a requirement of the theretofore naked man, exposed unsheltered to the storm, we need not inquire. At moderate elevations throughout the zone in which the human race originated, that requirement has never been onerous. The amount of effort there involved in providing the bamboo hut, the wigwam of poles and boughs, or the tent of skins, for protection against the rainy season, and in preparing the scanty garment of pelts or of cloth, demanded by comfort or by the awakened sense of decency, has never been great. Food still remains, in those regions, the one great requirement of human existence.

When, however, mankind spread over higher altitudes or zones further removed from the equator, as tribes were driven up the mountain sides by victorious enemies, or were crowded toward the arctic or antarctic circles by the increasing scarcity of the casual food of the chase, of the fishery, or of the natural forest, the requirement of clothing, of shelter, and last of all, of fuel, came to be of increasing urgency and severity. Within certain limits, however, clothing, shelter and fuel are, in the higher latitudes, interchangeable with food, in the human economy. One of the prime purposes of food being there the maintenance of the warmth of the body, that occasion may, in part, be served indifferently by a certain amount of food, or by clothing of a certain thickness applied to the frame, or by the combustion of a certain amount of fuel within an inclosure, or of a larger amount of fuel in the open air.

And here, as on the ten thousand occasions of a higher civilization, it is found that the greatest economy resides in the largest capitalization of labor. A dress of skins, which may have cost the effort of a week, will, during the time it lasts, more than replace, for purposes of warmth, food which would have required the efforts of many months. A hut which may have been a season in building, may save more in the food required for health and comfort, during the lifetime of the builder, than could have been obtained by the hunting or the fishing of years.

385. Now let us suppose that, within some geographical division, the conditions of production are such that each adult male is able by steady labor to secure for himself considerably more, in the way of food, clothing, shelter and fuel, than is required for his own subsistence in health and strength to labor and in physical comfort, meaning, by this last, not much, only a freedom from pain and discomfort. It does not matter, whether the laboring population under consideration obtain the means of subsistence, as hunters, as fishermen, as herdsmen, or as agriculturists. The question we have to ask is, what will these laborers do with the wealth they produce, after the strict needs of subsistence are met; how will they consume it?

386. The Wife.—In the first instance, it may be assumed that each laborer will undertake the support of one adult female, and this, not out of charity, or compassion, not by the force of any legal arrangement, not with any reference to the continuance of the tribe, but in obedience to a natural instinct second only, in the demand it makes upon men, to the craving for food. The latter satisfied, the former asserts itself, irrepressibly, among all classes and conditions of men, in all states of human society.

The woman with whose subsistence the laborer's income or annual production of wealth thus becomes charged, will, in greater or less degree, add to the means of the family thus formed. She will spin and weave, fashioning the fibrous materials which the man has gathered, into garments, blankets, and nets. She will, in various ways, prepare the flesh, the fish, or the vegetable food, which the head of the family supplies, rendering it more palatable, more nutritious, more wholesome, or less perishable, according to the nature of the subject matter. She will bring water from the spring or brook. She will keep the hut or tent in a certain order and decency.

While, thus, the female, in an early stage of industrial society, adds something to the family means, both by what she makes and by what she saves from waste, we may assume that, speaking broadly, she does not produce as much as she consumes. The margin of subsistence which the hunter, the fisherman, the herdsman, the tiller of the soil enjoys, is smaller after he has taken a wife than before. Nor is the contribution made by the wife to the joint revenue of the family in any degree a determining cause of the formation of the family.

We have, thus, the two earliest forms of the consumption of wealth, first, in the sustentation of the individual laborer, and secondly, in the maintenance of the wife. Let us suppose, for the further purposes of this discussion, that the production by the head of the family, increased by the wife's contribution, amounts to three and a half times what is necessary to support one adult person in health and strength to labor, and in physical comfort, according to the definition of that term already given. We have, then, to be deducted from this amount the subsistence of both husband and wife.

387. The Child.—Now, we have to note the third great form of consumption, in the order of nature. The association of husband and wife is followed, in the vast majority of cases, by offspring. Races that are comparatively infertile, for what reason physiology can not say with confidence, are known to history, and some such are to-day in occupation of portions of the earth's surface; while, among prolific races, are here and there found individuals who are sterile, from causes which physiology is equally unprepared to explain. The proportion of these exceptional cases among laboring populations is very small. We may, therefore, disregard them in our argument.

The appearance of the child makes a new and imperative demand upon the revenue of the family. In the immediate instance, it diminishes the ability of the mother to render her accustomed services in the household and reduces her contribution to the joint income. Then and afterwards, for a long time, it causes a steady draft upon the resources of the father in the way of food and clothing.

The demand thus made upon the family income is, within the limits of the father's ability, met, in general, fully and even cheerfully. It is not in obedience to the requirements of law, or because of any patriotic desire to make good the numbers of the community, or contribute to the strength of the state, or, on the other hand, from the consideration that these babes may, after the lapse of years, themselves become producers, and possibly, in time, become his support in his old age, that the father unquestioningly gives up to his children that margin of subsistence, which, as a married man without children, he might have enjoyed. It is in obedience to a purely individual feeling, of an instinctive character, so generally planted in the human mind that, in spite of instances of parental neglect or cruelty, we may speak of it as universal.

Here we have the third form in which wealth is consumed. It will be remembered that, thus far, we have supposed nothing to be done with the wealth produced in the primitive community which has for its object display, luxury, or even the gratification of appetite beyond the actual requirements of subsistence. That wealth is applied to the support, first of the productive laborer, secondly, of the wife, taken in obedience to a natural craving which may be termed a universal instinct of mankind, and, thirdly, of the children springing from that union.

388. **Children in Excess.**—Let us suppose that, with three children, of various ages, the subsistence which can be provided by the head of the family is fully taken up. These five persons, male and female, old and young, consume all that can be produced, which we have assumed to be equal to the sustentation

of three and a half adults. If, now, other children are to appear to claim a support at the hands of the husband and father, what will be the result? Clearly, a reduction in the standard of living. There will no longer be food, clothing, shelter and fuel adequate to maintain each and every member in health and strength, and without pain or discomfort resulting from deprivation of things needful. The new-comers will, indeed, under the impulse of the parental instinct, be admitted to an equal participation in the family income; but the share of each member of the family will be diminished. The pinch may come earliest and most severely at one point rather than another; food may be denied, or fuel, or clothing, or shelter, according to circumstances; but, in one way or another, something less than what is necessary to maintain the members of the family in health and strength and comfort, is supplied. Of this the effects may be grouped in three forms: first, the reduction of vital force and labor power; secondly, the diminution, perhaps the disappearance, of the subsistence fund heretofore laid up against the occurrence of bad seasons or the disability of the head of the family through accident or sickness, thirdly, the generation of infirmities and diseases of a transmissible character.

389. The Effort of Nature to Restore Equilibrium.—Now let us, further, suppose this increase in the number of children beyond the limits of subsistence to have taken place uniformly throughout the tribe, but to have taken place once for all, not from a persistent but from a purely transient cause: will there be any effort of nature to restore the condition of general health, strength and comfort, which has been for the time lost?

It is, indeed, true that nature will make an effort, first, through disease, which will have a greater destructive power upon an ill-sustained than upon a well-sustained community, especially in the case of children and of the aged; secondly, through an impairment of the reproductive power of the adult; and, thirdly, through famine breaking upon a population whose store laid up against drought or flood or fire or the ravages of insects, has been, once for all, eaten up. But this effort of nature will be unequal to the work to be done. The history of a thousand tribes shows that there is not sufficient force in famine or disease to prevent the permanent reduction of a community, through excess of numbers, from a condition of physical well-being to one of inadequate subsistence with consequent impairment of vital force and labor power.

390. Solidarity of the Family.—Of late years, with the growing interest in biological investigation, there has been manifested a disposition, in certain quarters, to glorify privation and famine, as agents in the uplifting of the human condition, the doctrine of the "survival of the fittest" being applied to societies of men without due consideration of a most important difference existing between men and other species of animals.

It is the solidarity of the family which prevents the law of the survival of the fittest from exerting that power in raising the standard of size and strength and functional vigor among men, which it exerts throughout the vegetable and the animal kingdoms, generally. In the vegetable kingdom I suppose there are no traces of this solidarity of parent and offspring, although not being a botanist I can not speak with assurance. In the animal kingdom, exclusive of man, the solidarity of the family exists, indeed, but to a limited extent only, and for a brief period. The mother protects and nourishes her offspring most sedulously and devotedly; drains her life-blood for its support, and will die in its defense; but, in general, when the offspring is weaned the connection is broken. The lives become separated. The young must thereafter be their own providers and protectors. Mother and child become competitors for food in the same field or forest; may even tear and kill one another in the struggle for existence. Thus the principle of survival obtains leave to operate. If the conditions of existence become hard, if subsistence is inadequate, the weak, the deformed, the sick, are run over, trampled on, killed out, while the fittest survive, acquire all the nourishment which is to be had, grow continually larger and stronger, breed only among themselves, and thus the standard of size and strength rises from generation to generation.

With man, however, the conditions of the struggle for existence are greatly changed. Generally speaking, that struggle is between families as units, not between individuals. Within the family, the young and old, the weak and the strong, male and female, are bound together by natural instincts, which are too strong for pain, for hunger, for death itself. If want or famine pinch, all suffer together. So far as any preference is given, it is to the younger and the weaker. The parent denies himself that the cries of the child may be hushed. If one member of the family fall sick, instead of being neglected, or even trampled on, as among the lower orders of animals, he commands the tenderest care of all. This, clearly, is not a condition under which the principle of "the survival of the fittest," however fierce may be "the struggle for existence," can operate among men, to raise the standard of size and strength and functional vigor. Instead of the natural elimination of the weakest and the worst, it is here the best who, from sexual or parental love, bare their breasts to receive the blows of fortune.

391. The Capabilities of the Procreative Force.—We have thus far inquired respecting the effects of an increase of the number of children in any community beyond the limits of subsistence, assuming for the moment the increase to be due to purely transient and adventitious causes. How is it as to the degree of activity and persistence in the procreative force, in the presence of a threatened reduction in the standard of living below the point of health, strength and freedom from discomfort?

But, first, of the reproductive capability of mankind. It is evident that the mere fact of children being born to parents does not, of itself, insure or threaten any increase of numbers from generation to generation. With the limits set to human life, reproduction in a certain degree may be only sufficient to make good the loss by death. It may be even less than is necessary to this end. Hence we must inquire what is the normal relation between births and deaths.

In his celebrated treatise on "Population," Mr. Malthus assumed a birth rate sufficient to yield, in spite of occasional celibacy and exceptional sterility, in excess of four children to a family. There is reason to believe that in any colony of European blood, planted on new land, of reasonably salubrious quality, within the temperate zone, this rate of increase would be reached, and, in the majority of cases, exceeded. That rate of reproduction alone, however, would be sufficient to secure an appreciable increase of each generation over the one preceding, were the facts of infant and of adult mortality but moderately favorable to the growth of population.

392. Geometrical Progression.—Now, if we may assume for the members of successive generations an undiminished degree of fecundity, we have here all the conditions of a geometrical progression. And the possibilities of geometrical progression, when persisted in for a long time, become simply tremendous, whether in population, in wealth, or in any other direction.

What is the characteristic of geometrical, as contrasted with arithmetical, increase? It is that, in the former case, *the increase itself increases:* the fecundity of the original stock is transmitted through all that is successively derived from it. Thus, to take a series of ten terms, we might have

Arithmetical: 2, 4, 6, 8, 10, 12, 14, 16, 18, 20.

Geometrical: 2, 4, 8, 16, 32, 64, 128, 256, 512, 1024.

Here, in the arithmetical series, the difference between the ninth and tenth terms is the same as that between the first and second, *viz.*, 2. In the geometrical series, the difference between the first and second terms is, also, 2; while, between the ninth and the tenth, it is 512. It would require more than five hundred terms to carry the arithmetical series to the point which, in the geometrical series, is reached in ten terms. It would require more than a million terms to carry the former series to the point reached by the latter in twenty-one terms; a thousand million terms to carry the former series to the point reached by the latter in thirty-one terms.

These tremendous leaps in the geometrical series, are due to the fact that the increase between the first and second terms becomes itself the cause of a proportional increase between the second and third terms; which increase, in turn, becomes the cause of corresponding increase between the third and fourth, and so on to the end. Whereas, of the arithmetical series we may say that the entire increase comes out of the original stock, which continues to propagate at a constant rate, while all the successive increments so produced remain barren.

393. Population Increases by Geometrical Progression.—Now it is according to the former and not the latter law, that population increases; and as we said, the consequences of a persistence in a geometrical ratio, through a considerable period of time, are simply tremendous. "The elephant," says Mr. Darwin, "is reckoned the slowest breeder of all known animals, and I have taken some pains to estimate its probable minimum rate of natural increase. It will be safest to assume that it begins breeding when thirty years old, and goes on breeding till ninety years, bringing forth six young in the interval, and surviving till one hundred years old; if this be so, after a period of from seven hundred and forty to seven hundred and fifty years, there would be alive *nearly nineteen million elephants descended from the first pair!*"

Man, though a slow breeder, as compared with many of the lower animals, has a rate of reproduction far exceeding that of the elephant. Population has shown the capability, over a vast extent of territory, on more than one continent and through considerable periods of time, of doubling once in twenty-five years. With this capability we may say that, if "neither evil, nor the fear of evil" checked the population of the United States, it would, in a century and a-half, amount to three thousand two hundred millions. Of course this consummation could never be reached. Such a population would be impossible under the conditions of human existence.

394. The Persistence of the Procreative Force.—Such being the capabilities of the procreative force, when operating unrestrained, let us inquire what virtue there is in the fear of a reduction of the standard of living below the point of health and physical comfort, to check population at that line.

It is commonly assumed, in discussions relating to wages, that the laboring class will more and more withhold their increase as the conditions of life become harder and harder; and that any economic injuries which they may suffer, from whatever cause, will, in the order of nature, be in this way repaired. Instead of it being true, however, that the laboring class tend thus to resist and resent any lowering of the standard of subsistence, the fact is that never is the procreative force more active than when the conditions of life become meager and squalid; when the reserve of the summer against the winter, of the good year against the bad, is swept away by the clamorous necessities of to-day; when alike enjoyment of the present and hope for the future are at their lowest point. Never had the marrying age been earlier, or christenings more frequent in Ireland than when, just upon the verge of the great famine, Earl Devon's Commission, in 1844, thus described the condition of the peasantry: "In many districts, their daily food is the potato; their only beverage, water; their cabins are seldom a protection against the weather; a bed or a blanket is a rare luxury; and, in nearly all, their pig and manure heap constitute their only property."

The state of the population of India and China affords a conclusive proof that there is not sufficient virtue in economic forces to keep population above the plane of extreme misery, if once it falls below the plane of comfort and decency. On the contrary, a moral weakness or recklessness is induced which tends strongly and swiftly to carry population to the point of industrial distress. Then, indeed, famine makes its appearance, as periodically in India, to set bounds to increase of numbers; but, for the reasons that have been stated, this force does not operate, as in the animal kingdom exclusive of man, to cut off only the least active, aggressive, intelligent, or self-reliant. The effect of famine, and of the diseases generated by famine, operating upon population across the barrier imposed by the solidarity of the family, is to lower the physical tone, to taint the blood, and weaken the will-power of the entire body, making it increasingly difficult, from generation to generation, to restore the lost conditions of economic well-being.

CHAPTER II.

THE APPEARANCE OF NEW ECONOMIC WANTS.

395. An Ascending Scale of Personal Consumption.—We have thus far dwelt on the effects of an increase of numbers beyond the limits of subsistence, as the latter are determined by the law of diminishing returns in agriculture. We have seen, that since the procreative force increases rather than diminishes in the face of poverty and squalor, there is no natural resting-place for population, if once it passes below the plane of ample subsistence, until it reaches the point where it meets the "positive checks" of famine and disease and, it may be added, of war.* This principle of population, to which we give the name, Malthusianism, was first clearly enunciated and fully illustrated by Mr. Malthus, in the last year of the last century, although intimated in the writings of earlier economists, especially of the Italian Ortes.

Let us now consider the relations of subsistence and population, on an ascending scale of personal consumption. We have seen that population will go on increasing as fast and as far as food is provided to support it, all increase of wealth surely taking the form of an increase of numbers, unless other and more imperative demands are made upon the income of the family. But let us suppose that, at the point where a competent subsistence is provided to maintain the whole population in health and strength to labor, and in freedom from all discomfort resulting from privation of things absolutely necessary, the want of something beyond this comes to be strongly felt by the individual members of the community.†

---

* "It is impossible," says Senior, "that a positive check so goading and remorseless as famine, should prevail without bringing in her train all the others. Pestilence is her uniform companion, and murder and war are her followers."

† "The much greater number and the longer continuance of his wants," says Prof. Roscher, "are amongst the most striking differences between man and the brute. While the lower animals have no wants but neces-

396. Diversity of Early Economic Desires.—What that want may be does not matter for the purposes of the present discussion ; and, indeed, it would not be likely to be the same in the case of all communities. In one, the first want felt, after the absolute requirements for the support of life and laboring power are satisfied, is of ornament and decoration. Even when men are hardly covered from the cold and scantily nourished, the passion for display makes its appearance in forms that are ludicrous enough to the eye of the civilized man, but which have a most serious meaning to the barbarian and engross his faculties as completely as widely different objects do the faculties of the Parisian. In another community, the first want felt after the claims of immediate bare subsistence are met, is of a store for the future and a provision against the caprices of the seasons and the casualties of life. Just as the ant—the ant of fable, at least, if not of the naturalist—differs from the butterfly, so have certain tribes of men, in the earliest condition to which we can trace them, differed from others in this respect of care for the coming time. The first want emerging in the life of another community may be of wealth to be expended in worship and in honor of the national or local deity. Millions of men may consent to live squalidly that a few temples may shine like the sun, their altars smoke with unending sacrifices, their priests walk resplendent with embroidered and jeweled vestments. In still other communities, the new want may take the form of a love, no longer of ornament, but of comely dress, or of desire for a diversified diet, or of a taste for leisure, or of a craving for some costly drug or drink, like the opium of the East Indian and the Chinaman or the fire-water of the North American Indian.

Writers on economics have, indeed, endeavored to establish something like an order of natural succession for the various wants emerging in human experience : thus Prof. Senior says

---

sities, and while their aggregate wants, even in the longest series of generations, admit of no qualitative increase, the circle of man's wants is susceptible of indefinite extension. And, indeed, every advance in culture made by man finds expression in an increase in the number and in the keenness of his rational wants."

that man's "first object is to vary his food;" "the next desire is variety of dress;" "last comes the desire to build, to ornament and to furnish;" I deem it, however, more consonant with what is known of communities having only a small margin of living, to hold that the appearance of economic desires, beyond the need of bare subsistence, is governed by the moral and social characteristics of each race or tribe of men.

397. Economic Wants Antagonize the Procreative Force.—Whatever be the passion or desire which is first developed in the mind of any community, it makes a demand upon the existing body of goods, or upon the current production of wealth, which at once antagonizes the strong and urgent disposition, which has been indicated, to the consumption of wealth in the support of an increasing population. The newly awakened passion or desire can not be gratified out of the existing fund of wealth, unless the procreative force receive a check. Whether this shall be done or not, is a question upon the answer to which depends the whole economic future of the community.

Any economic want may act in restraint of population in one or more of three ways: first, by diminishing the numbers of the marrying class, inducing celibacy among those who do not find the way to obtain an income adequate to the support of a family; secondly, by procrastinating marriage; and thirdly, by diminishing the birth-rate within the married state. The forces which operate in restraint of population may take any one of these three ways, or take them all, in which latter case the reduction of the ratio of increase will be very marked. If for example, the number of married pairs in a given community were brought down from 100 to 80, by the spread of celibacy; if, through later marriages, the child-bearing period for each married pair were reduced from twenty years to fifteen, and if the interval between births were extended from two years to three, the number of children born under the latter state of things would be, to the number born under the former state, as 40 to 100.

398. A Diversified Diet.—Whatever be the want most commonly felt, after the requirements of mere subsistence are met, there can, I think, be no question that the want which has been efficient on the largest scale, at once in promoting labor for its gratification, and in restricting the increase of population, is the craving for a diversified diet. Once let the traditional sole diet of the barbarian, be it fish, or flesh, or grain, be crossed with some other species of food, exciting thus the pleasure which resides in variety, and an economic force has been introduced into the life of the community which is capable of producing mighty results.

Without claiming to speak with authority as a student of sociology, I should say that this has been the lever by which more tribes and races of men have been raised and kept, one degree, at least, above the condition of a population pressing all the time, at all points, upon the limits of subsistence, than by any other.

A diversified diet, although doubtless it contributes, in a degree, to health and vigor, is yet a pure luxury in the sense that it is never sought on the former account, but wholly because of the gratification of appetite thereby secured. It will seem strange to those who have not studied the question of population, that an appetite for objects of luxury should be spoken of as having greater power to overcome the disposition to indolence and the disposition to excessive procreation, than the fear of privation and actual misery. Yet so it is ; and as we go up the scale of human wants and desires, as viewed by the moralist, we shall find that, in general, the higher the want or desire, ethically considered, the stronger it proves to be. Mere sentiments, involving no gratification to any bodily sense, impel men to exertions the most painful and protracted, and hold in check the most masterful passion of the human kind, that passion which defies abject physical want and laughs in the face of famine and pestilence.

399. Decencies.—Of narrower range in its application to tribes and races of men than the desire of a diversified diet, but of greater intensity and persistency within that range, is the desire of what we may call decencies, meaning thereby those things which are prescribed or required by public opinion. It is evident that the term decencies, in economics, must have a very various application to different communities and to different classes within the same community.

"The question whether a given commodity is to be considered as a decency or a luxury, is obviously one to which no answer can be given, unless the place, the time and the rank of the individual using it be specified. The dress which in England was only decent a hundred years ago, would be almost extravagant now; while the house and furniture which now would afford merely decent accommodations to a gentleman, would then have been luxurious for a peer.

"The causes which entitle a commodity to be called a necessary, are more permanent and more general. They depend partly upon the habits in which the individual in question has been brought up, partly on the nature of his occupation, on the lightness or severity of the labors and hardships that he has to undergo, and partly on the climate in which he lives.

"Shoes are necessaries to all the inhabitants of England. Our habits are such that there is not an individual whose health would not suffer from the want of them. To the lowest class of the inhabitants of Scotland they are luxuries. Custom enables them to go barefoot without inconvenience and without degradation. When a Scotchman rises from the lowest to the middling classes of society, they become to him decencies. He wears them to preserve, not his feet, but his station in life. To the highest class, who have been accustomed to them from infancy, they are as much necessaries as they are to all classes in England.

"To the highest classes in Turkey, wine is a luxury, and tobacco a decency. In Europe, it is the reverse. The Turk drinks and the European smokes, not in obedience but in opposition both to the rules of health and to the forms of society. But wine in Europe and the pipe in Turkey are among the refreshments to which a guest is entitled, and which it would be as indecent to refuse in the one country as to offer in the other.

"A carriage is a decency to a woman of fashion, a necessary to a physician, and a luxury to a tradesman." *

* N. W. Senior.

400. The Desire of Decencies the Great Preventive Check to Population.—Whatever dignity the moralist may assign to the disposition to conform to the prevailing sentiments of the community, the economist must recognize this as the most effective motive which operates either to urge men to labor for the production of wealth, or to check the increase of population after the condition of "diminishing returns" has been reached. It is in the latter respect that we have here especially to do with it. "The great preventive check," says the wise economist so oft quoted in this chapter, "is the fear of losing decencies." If by this is to be understood the check which is of greatest potency where it operates at all, the remark is perfectly just. But, in fact, it is only in few communities that this cause operates with sufficient force to restrict population within the limits of the highest *per capita* production. In England, among the working classes reproduction has gone on with the least possible regard to its effect upon the standard of living. In France, on the other hand, even the peasantry are so fully alive to the inexpediency of a rapid multiplication, and are so temperate and prudent, that the excess of births over deaths has been reduced to a minimum. In the States of the American Union, the increase of population was, until recently, everywhere encouraged by the fact that the country had not reached the condition of diminishing returns, but, on the contrary, as is always the case before that condition is reached, foreign immigration and native growth in numbers alike added to the power and wealth of the several communities. Within the past twenty-five years, the rate of natural increase in the Northeastern States has encountered a decided check, due to the rising standard of living in communities whose productive capabilities are already fully developed.

401. Influence of a Popular Tenure of the Soil Upon Population.—There can be no question that the influence exerted upon population by a popular tenure of the soil is very conservative. The reasons therefor are thus stated by M. Sismondi:

"In the countries in which cultivation by small proprietors

still continues, population increases regularly and rapidly until it has attained its natural limits: that is to say, inheritances continue to be divided and subdivided among several sons as long as, by an increase of labor, each family can extract an equal income from a smaller portion of land. A father who possessed a vast extent of natural pasture, divides it among his sons, and they turn it into fields and meadows; his sons divide it among their sons, who abolish fallows; each improvement in agricultural knowledge admits of another step in the subdivision of property.

"But there is no danger that the proprietor will bring up children to make beggars of them.

"He knows exactly what inheritance he has to leave them; he knows that the law* will divide it equally among them; he sees the limits beyond which partition would make them descend from the rank which he himself has filled; and a just family pride, common to the peasant and the prince, makes him abstain from summoning into life children for whom he can not properly provide. If more are born, at least they do not marry, or they agree among themselves which of the several brothers shall perpetuate the family."

The power of population strictly to limit itself, under the impulse to preserve family estates from undue subdivision, by the means adverted to in the closing sentence of the paragraph quoted, is strikingly illustrated by Prof. Cliffe Leslie in the facts which he adduces regarding the population of Auvergne, in France. In the mountains, it appears, the people cling with remarkable tenacity to the conservation of the inheritance unbroken. The daughters willingly consent to take vows and renounce all part in the common estate; or, if they contract marriage, agree to leave to the head of the family their individual shares of the inheritance. It is the same with the sons, of whom some become priests; others emigrate, consenting never to claim any part of the property. One of the sons remains at home, working with the father and

* The law of so-called partible succession, prevailing widely over the western part of Continental Europe.

mother, and becomes in time the proprietor of the ancestral estate. Thus the principle of equal partition, established by law, is eluded by the connivance of the family, it seldom occurring that the other children assert their claims, so fully accepted is this usage in the manners of the mountains.

Prof. Leslie, after giving the foregoing as the substance of an official report, adds: "The renunciation by the emigrants of their share in the family property certainly shows, if not an extraordinary imperviousness to new ideas, an extraordinary tenacity of old ones; and, in particular, of two ideas which are among the oldest in human society—subordination to the male head of the family, and conservation of the family property unbroken."

From the *London Times*,* I take the following testimony to the influence of an extensive ownership of land in antagonizing the procreative force, and in winning for improved living, comfort, luxury, and security of condition, what would otherwise be usurped and wasted upon increase of population, with resulting squalor and poverty:

"Over the greater part of France the standard of comfort and well-being has been increasing ever since the termination of the great war, in 1815. The country had been so drained and impoverished by the wars of Napoleon and by a century and a half of bad government, that the general misery of the population was indescribable, and the poverty even of the landed proprietors and middle classes was very great. . . . . For many years comfort and well-being, and even luxury, have made their way into the households of all classes in France. The standard of living has risen enormously. The habits of saving and thrift have not been neglected. In the art of managing and regularizing their lives, the French people are unrivaled and the object of every family is to live well and to save, at the same time, so as to be able to leave their sons and daughters in as good a position as themselves, at all events, and in a better, if possible. . . . . Among people with such habits and such views of life, the risk and expenditure

*January 25, 1883.

attendant upon a large family are naturally regarded with horror. 'Since two or three children give us sufficient enjoyment of the pleasures of paternity, why,' the greater number of Frenchmen argue, 'should we have more? With two or three children we can live comfortably, and save sufficient to leave our children as well off as ourselves; a greater number would involve curtailment of enjoyments both for ourselves and our children.'"

402. Attacks Upon the Doctrine of Malthus.—The views respecting the relations of population and subsistence contained in the foregoing paragraphs are essentially those which are known as Malthusian. Mr. Malthus unquestionably committed some errors of statement and faults of reasoning in his original enunciation of the principles of population, as is likely to be the case on the first promulgation of great economic or social laws; and during his whole life he was closely followed by criticism and abuse. Since Mr. Malthus' death has taken all personal interest out of the controversy over the principles of population, and Malthusianism has come to be merely a name for a body of doctrine, the views here presented have been a butt for the headless arrows of beginners in economics and of sundry sentimental sociologists.

Meanwhile the doctrine (1) that there resides in nearly all races and tribes of men a strong, urgent, persistent disposition to carry the increase of population beyond the limits of adequate subsistence; (2) that very few, even among the noblest of modern communities, have shown the capability to check reproduction at the line of the highest *per capita* production of food, clothing, shelter and fuel; (3) that, if this line be once over-passed, the procreative force proceeds thereafter with augmented force; (4) that, if the desire of luxuries and decencies does not prevail to stop the increase of population, the fear of losing necessaries, and even the actual experience of privation and suffering almost certainly will fail to do so; (5) that, through the dominion of this imperious instinct, nearly all the communities of men are under the constant imminence of being swept away into misery, squalor and disease, this doctrine which we term Malthusianism has stood unshattered, impregnable, amid all the controversy that has raged around it.

403. Prof. Senior's Statement.—I can not forbear again to quote this eminently wise economist, to whose criticisms, indeed, Mr. Malthus owed the correction of some of the faults of his original statement of the principles of population. Prof. Senior says:

"Although we believe that, as civilization advances, the pressure of population upon subsistence is a decreasing evil, we are far from denying the prevalence of this pressure in all long settled countries: indeed, in all countries except those which are the seats of colonies applying the knowledge of an old country to an unoccupied territory.

"We believe that there are few portions of Europe the inhabitants of which would not be richer if their numbers were fewer, and would not be richer hereafter if they were now to retard the rate at which their population is increasing."

CHAPTER III.

CONSUMPTION: THE DYNAMICS OF WEALTH.

404. The Potato Philosophy of Wages.—We have, thus far, spoken of economic wants, mainly in their effects as retarding the increase of numbers. Until an adequate check, of a sufficiently persistent character, has been secured here, the economist who fully appreciates the consequences of over-population can hardly fail to recognize almost every economic want, whatever its origin or its object, and however little either may be approved by the moralist or physiologist, as being better than none.

It has been from this point of view, that the English writers have insisted so strongly that cheap food is a thing to be deprecated.

Thus Mr. J. R. McCulloch says:—"When the standard of natural or necessary wages is high—when wheat and beef, for example, form the principal part of the food of the laborer, and porter and beer the principal part of his drink, he can bear to retrench in a season of scarcity. Such a man has room to fall; he can resort to cheaper sorts of food—to barley, oats, rice and potatoes. But he who is habitually fed on the cheapest food has nothing to resort to, when deprived of it. Laborers placed in this situation are absolutely cut off from every resource. You can take from an Englishman; but you can not take from an Irishman. The latter is already so low, he can fall no lower; he is placed on the very verge of existence; his wages, being regulated by the price of potatoes,* will not buy wheat, or barley, or oats; and whenever, therefore, the supply of potatoes fails, it is next to impossible that he should escape falling a sacrifice to famine."

And Prof. Thorold Rogers says: "A community which subsists habitually on dear food is in a position of peculiar advantage, when compared with another which lives on cheap food, one for instance, which lives on wheat, as contrasted with another which lives on rice or potatoes; and this, quite apart from the prudence or incautiousness of the people."

405. Better Things Than Dear Food.—Clearly, the basis of this reasoning is the Malthusian doctrine. These economists recognize the strong probability, the almost certainty, that a people will carry their increase closely up to the limits of subsistence according to the kind of food they use, whatever that may be. If it be the lowest and cheapest, like rice in India and potatoes in Ireland, the failure of the crop means starvation, no adequate reserve being expected to be provided, on a sufficient scale, by the population of any country. If the kind of food be higher and dearer, the masses may, in the event of a failure of the crop or crops concerned, fall back for the time upon the lower and the cheaper.

* Dr. Travers Twiss states that it was calculated prior to the famine, that two-thirds of the population of Ireland lived wholly on potatoes. Sir Arch. Alison says: "Three times the number of persons can be fed on an acre of potatoes who can be maintained on an acre of wheat in ordinary seasons."

But suppose this danger of an increase of numbers, fast following up subsistence, crowding all the time upon the limits of food, to be once for all passed. Suppose we have a community which will accept the opportunity of living upon cheap food and apply the saving to the permanent enlargement of their capital, or to other forms of enjoyment, to dress, to better lodgings, to luxuries, perhaps to expenditures upon education and culture. What harm, then, would Mr. McCulloch or Prof. Rogers find in cheap food, be it potatoes, or rice, or the Indian corn of America? Surely none. The more is saved from the cost of food, the more can be spent upon making homes ample and comfortable, healthful and decent, the more can be spent upon school-houses and churches, upon books and periodicals, upon literature and music and art. The wife may be let to stay at home and keep the house; the children be given their time, to acquire an education and to secure for themselves a thorough preparation for their work in life.

Let me not be understood as quarreling with this potato philosophy of wages so far as the assumption which underlies it, *viz.*, that population will inevitably keep close up to the limits of subsistence on the kind of food, whatever that may be, which forms the popular diet, is justified by the facts of society, as it very widely is. I only claim that, in any country whose people had shown the capability of setting bounds to the increase of population by the exercise of their own judgment and will, cheap food would become a means of increasing the comforts and luxuries enjoyed by that people in other directions of expenditure, or of enlarging the capital and improving the productive agencies at their command.

406. The Dynamics of Wealth.--As a means of checking the increase of numbers, which otherwise would surely carry population to the point of misery, famine and pestilence, the appearance of almost any economic want must be greeted as a good, without much respect to the origin or object of that want. But the moment the capability of the self-limitation of population is assured, the economist discovers wide differences between the various demands for the consumption of the existing body of wealth, made by the differing appetites and desires of different communities, or of different classes in the same community, as regards the influence of those various forms of consuming wealth upon the power and the disposition to create values in the future.*

It is here we find the body of economic literature most deficient. We need a new Adam Smith, or another Hume, to write the economics of consumption in which would be found the real Dynamics of Wealth ; to trace to their effects upon production the forces which are set in motion by the uses made of wealth ; to show how certain forms of consumption clear the mind, strengthen the hand and elevate the aims of the individual economic agent, while promoting that social order and mutual confidence which are favorable conditions for the complete development and harmonious action of the industrial system ; how other forms of consumption debase and debauch man as an economic agent, and introduce disorder and waste into the complicated mechanism of the productive agencies. Here is the opportunity for some great moral philosopher, strictly confining himself to the study of the economic effects of these causes, denying himself all regard to purely ethical, political or theological considerations, to write what shall be the most important chapter of political economy, now, alas, almost a blank.

407. Two Popular Fallacies Concerning Consumption.— In a preceding chapter, we discussed the question, how it is that there can be, at any time, with abounding natural resources, unemployed labor power, unemployed capital power, no lack of disposition on the part of the owners of capital to secure a return from the productive use of their property, no lack of dis-

* When we remember that the expenditure of the people of Great Britain, annually, for alcoholic beverages, reaches the enormous sum of £180,000,000, or $900,000,000, four-fifths, at least, of which is spent in a way that is not only without any beneficial effect, but is positively injurious, a large part of it going to the destruction of moral, intellectual and physical power, we get a rude measure of the force which a wiser consumption of wealth might introduce into the economic life of that country.

position on the part of laborers to earn wages by work, and yet an enforced idleness, with resulting poverty and squalor. Two popular explanations of this condition of things are always sure to be offered during the continuance of "hard times," one of which finds its expression in the sounding phrase, "over-production," while the other emphasizes its supposed antagonism to the theory of the over-productionists, by the use of the term "under-consumption."

A brief reference to the conditions under which wealth is produced, will suffice to show that, like all condensed phrases, each of these large words signifies more than one thing ; that, in certain senses, each phrase embodies a great deal of arrant nonsense ; that, taken otherwise, each embodies a vital truth ; and, finally, that, so far as either means any thing at all, that meaning is exactly identical with what is expressed by the other.

408. Over-production.—All producers are also consumers. Men produce only because they desire to consume. They produce only so much as they desire to consume. Any given producer may, however, desire to realize his enjoyment either now, or at a future time ; either in satisfying his own personal wants and appetites, or in satisfying those of friends, children or beneficiaries.

The idea of over-production, therefore, involves the absurdity of supposing that men will labor to produce that which they have not the desire to consume.

But passing over this initial absurdity, we observe in the use of this phrase, a vague notion that the amount of necessaries, comforts, and luxuries, which a community, at any given stage of its progress, is prepared to consume is a definite amount ; and that, if the amount produced is somewhat rapidly increased, the capacity for consumption will be outrun, and men will stand, without appetite, before a mass of good things, for which they know no uses and with which they are, for the time, utterly at a loss to deal.

The fallacy of this will sufficiently appear if we ask, not who are the men able and willing to make away with a vastly greater body of wealth than they find themselves in possession of, but who are the men who would not be found willing and able to do this? Is there any mechanic or laborer, receiving wages to the amount of $300 or $500 a year, who could not, and would not gladly, spend $600 or $1,000? Is there any merchant or professional man or man of leisure, with an income of $3,000 or $5,000, or $10,000, who could not easily give account of an income of $6,000, or $10,000, or $20,000? It is absurd to suppose that the limit of consumption can be reached. What with houses and horses, clothes, equipage, and travel, costly viands and drinks, any civilized community could instantly double, quadruple, or decuple its consumption of wealth were the wealth provided.

409. Under-consumption.—In like manner, the phrase, under-consumption, involves an initial absurdity, when applied in explanation of so-called "hard times." Thus, during the period of 1876–9, it was said that the people of the United States were suffering from under-consumption; yet, not for a long period, if ever, had consumption followed so quickly upon production; had the food earned been so quickly eaten; had the margin of saving been so small, as during the years referred to. A strange term, truly, to apply to such a condition: this under-consumption!

But passing by this initial absurdity, we find that beneath the phrase, under-consumption, lurks the notion that, somehow or other, wealth when once produced is in danger of getting in the way, so that other wealth can not be produced until this be first eaten or drunk or burned up, or by some means gotten rid of. As a matter of fact, there has never been any accumulation of wealth on the earth's surface so great as to impede the further production of wealth, and there is not likely to be. Were men willing to produce wealth without consuming it, they could go on forever. Of course, men will not, in general, produce more than they desire, sooner or later, to consume.

410. Over-production and under-consumption mean the same thing, and that is under-production. This is, of course, a mere jangle of words, until the phrases are qualified, as they should be. Over-production, as alleged by those who would explain hard times, is *partial over-production*, production, that is, which has gone on in certain lines, generally under speculative impulses, until it has exceeded the normal, or even, possibly, a highly stimulated demand. This excess of supply in certain lines leads to the accumulation of vast stocks of unsalable goods,* which involves *partial under-consumption*, these stocks melting slowly away through a period extending over months, it may be, years. Meanwhile, *general under-production* is the result. The bodies of labor and capital which have been called into the over-done branches of industry, can not readily, if at all, be transferred to other branches ; they remain where they are, half employed, waiting for the renewal of demand. In the dreary interval, producing little, they have little with which to purchase the products of others, who are consequently compelled to restrict their production proportionally, as was shown in pars. 237–40.

In this way it is we vindicate our paradox that over-production means nothing more or less than under-production, or, for that matter, than under-consumption. There is no over-production possible, except a partial over-production, an over-production in certain lines, which inevitably involves a lowering of the scale of production as a whole : that is, partial over-production involves general under-production.

It is under-production which makes hard times. Over-production, general over-production, is impossible, and, were it to occur, were the creation of wealth to outrun men's capacity to consume, no one would be injured thereby. But under-production is an unmistakable evil. It means less wealth produced, and consequently fewer of the comforts and necessaries of life, on the average, to each member of the community. To large classes it means hunger, cold and squalor ; debility, sickness and premature death.

411. The Destruction of Wealth.—We have already adverted to the fact of the extensive destruction of wealth, by

* The result is the same if the distorted production of the past has taken the form of an excess of machinery and plant in some lines or in many lines of manufacture, or an excess of the means of transportation.

accident or by natural causes, as affording an explanation, in part, of the comparatively slow progress of accumulation, even in the states whose land power, labor power and capital power are greatest. We have now to deal with the same fact, in our theory of consumption.

A most stubborn belief appears among the non-agricultural masses of every community where wages or labor or wealth is a topic of familiar discussion, to the effect that the destruction of wealth in some way increases production. Laboring people generally hold to this ; our servants believe it religiously, and justify themselves, secretly or openly, for all their breakage and wastage by the plea that it "makes trade good." Even cultivated persons are not free from an instinctive feeling that the abrupt removal of the existing body of wealth quickens industrial activity and promotes the general welfare, though it may be at the cost, for the time, of individuals.

Frederic Bastiat, in one of his capital little essays, has dealt with this notion so cleverly that there can be no excuse for any writer using his own phrases on this theme.

412. The Broken Pane.—"Have you ever had occasion to witness the fury of the honest burgess, Jacques Bonhomme, when his scapegrace son has broken a pane of glass? If you have, you can not fail to have observed that all the bystanders, were there thirty of them, lay their heads together to offer the unfortunate proprietor this never-failing consolation, that there is good in every misfortune, and that such accidents give a fillip to trade. Every body must live. If no windows were broken, what would become of the glaziers? Now, this formula of condolence contains a theory which it is proper to lay hold of in this very simple case, because it is exactly the same theory which unfortunately governs the greater part of our economic institutions.

"Assuming that it becomes necessary to expend six francs in repairing the damage, if you mean to say that the accident brings in six francs to the glazier, and to that extent encourages his trade, I grant it fairly and frankly, and admit that you reason justly.

"The glazier arrives, does his work, pockets his money, rubs his hands, and blesses the scapegrace son. *That is what we see.*

"But if, by way of deduction, you come to conclude, as is too often done, that it is a good thing to break windows—that it makes money circulate—and that encouragement to trade in general is the result, I am obliged to cry, halt! Your theory stops at what we see, and takes no account of *what we don't see.*

"*We don't see* that since our burgess has been obliged to spend his six francs on one thing, he can no longer spend them on another.

"*We don't see* that if he had not this pane to replace, he would have replaced, for example, his shoes, which are down at the heels; or have placed a new book on his shelf. In short, he would have employed his six francs in a way in which he can not now employ them. Let us see, then, how the account stands with trade in general. The pane being broken, the glazier's trade is benefited to the extent of six francs. *That is what we see.*

"If the pane had not been broken, the shoemaker's or some other trade would have been encouraged to the extent of six francs. *That is what we don't see.* And if we take into account what we don't see, which is a negative fact, as well as what we do see, which is a positive fact, we shall discover that trade in general, or the aggregate of national industry, has no interest, one way or other, whether windows are broken or not.

"Let us see, again, how the account stands with Jacques Bonhomme. On the last hypothesis, that of the pane being broken, he spends six francs, and gets neither more nor less than he had before, namely, the use and enjoyment of a pane of glass. On the other hypothesis, namely, that the accident had not happened, he would have expended six francs on shoes, and would have had the enjoyment both of the shoes and of the pane of glass.

"Now as the good burgess, Jacques Bonhomme, constitutes a fraction of society at large, we are forced to conclude that society, taken in the aggregate, and after all accounts of labor and enjoyment have been squared, has lost the value of the pane which has been broken."

413. Destruction sometimes the Removal of Obstruction.—It is, of course, possible to conceive a situation where the destruction of wealth may have the direct effect to secure a larger production of wealth. Thus, a man may occupy a certain water privilege with an antiquated mill, which he can not make up his mind to tear down. To destroy the mill seems to him like waste, or, even if he appreciates the fact that the erection of a new and more commodious structure, with modern appliances, would be true economy, he can not bring himself to incur the initial expense just at this time ; he procrastinates in the matter, and so perhaps goes on, year after year, cramped in his operations, perhaps unable even to undertake production in certain lines, for which there is an advantageous opening. Now, in such a case, it might happen that the burning down of the old mill would lead to the immediate erection of a new one which would pay for itself in a short time, and the net result, thereafter, be the substitution of a powerful and efficient agent of production for one that was inadequate and outworn.

Undoubtedly, too, the destruction by fire of the old and crooked parts of certain cities, filled with rookeries and tumble-down houses, almost impassable to traffic and repulsive of aspect, has led to an actual increase of wealth within a short time thereafter. The quarter destroyed may have been long a nuisance and an obstruction to the growth of the city and the development of its trade ; but the inertia of property owners, their blindness to their large, their permanent interests, their reluctance to make great capital expenditures, and especially the fact that it was of no use for a single property owner to try to improve the quarter by tearing down his rookeries, so long as the general character of the neighborhood remained what it had been, these causes might have long withstood the needed improvements. The fire comes, resolves all doubts, burns up the accumulated foulness of generations, leaves the ground open to building, and, six months or a year thereafter, a new and elegant quarter has arisen from the ashes. Not all, not by any means the larger part, of this represents the production of wealth in the interval. The greater share represents the transplanting of wealth previously existing. Yet, in addition, there may, as we said, conceivably have been a large creation of values due to the improvement of commercial sites and commercial avenues heretofore neglected.

Such instances of the destruction of wealth leading to a larger production are comparatively rare. In the vast majority of cases, that destruction, however rejoiced over by shallow persons who are influenced only by "what they see," or by selfish persons who secure an immediate individual advantage from the loss of others, is a public misfortune.

414. Government Expenditure.—On the part of many, perhaps most, persons who favor large government expenditures, the actuating motive is found in the opinion we have already dealt with, that wasteful and even destructive consumption "makes trade good," "encourages industry," "raises wages," etc. To this shallow notion we need pay no further attention. Something which is at least less obviously false is intended in the proposition laid down by more than one economist of reputation, that government expenditures, within moderate limits, are industrially beneficial.

This view may be stated in the language of Mr. McCulloch, one of the most careful of the English economists of the last generation :—

"A moderate increase of taxation has the same effect on the habits and industry of a nation that an increase of his family or of his necessary and unavoidable expenses has upon a private individual. . . . .

"But we must be on our guard against an abuse of this doctrine. To render an increase of taxation productive of greater exertions, economy and invention, it should be slowly and gradually brought about, and it should never be carried to such a height as to incapacitate individuals from making the sacrifices it imposes by such an increase of industry and economy as it may be in their power to make, without requiring any very violent change in their habits. The increase of taxation must not be such as to make it impracticable to overcome its influence, or to induce the belief that it is impracticable. Difficulties that are seen to be surmountable sharpen the inventive power and are readily grappled with ; but an apparently insurmountable difficulty, or such an excessive weight of taxation as it was deemed impossible to meet, would not stimulate, but destroy exertion. Instead of producing new efforts of ingenuity and economy, it would produce only despair. Whenever taxation becomes so heavy* that the produce it takes from individuals can no longer be replaced by fresh efforts, they uniformly cease to be made ; the population becomes dispirited, industry is paralyzed and the country rapidly declines."

And to the same effect Jeremy Bentham writes : "By raising money as other money is raised, by taxes (the amount of which is taken by individuals out of their expenditure on the score of maintenance), government has it in its power to accelerate to an unexampled degree the augmentation of the mass of real wealth."

415. Such is the claim in behalf of government expenditure. What is to be said of it? Let us proceed by way of an example. Let us take a large population spread over a vast extent of country, like India, which possesses almost illimitable facilities for the improvement of the soil through irrigation, and whose broad spaces demand numerous and extensive lines of artificial communication, by canal or railway. Let it be supposed that the people occupying this country are what the people of India now are, in numbers, in character, in habits of living and of working. Alike under the influence of sexual passion and of religious superstition,† they continually tend to increase up to the limits of subsistence, even to the verge of

---

* I can not forbear to quote the words of Bacon: "The blessing of Judah and Issachar will never meet: that the same people should be both the lion's whelp and the ass between burdens ; neither will it be that a people overlaid with taxes should ever become valiant and martial."

† The early marriages of India are attributed to the religious beliefs of the people, as they hold that the welfare of the soul after death depends greatly on the performance of the burial rites by male offspring of the deceased.

famine ; not only accumulating no capital, but laying by no store for future wants ; having neither the genius for organization nor the capacity of self-denial which would be required to initiate the simplest local improvements.

Now, we may imagine such a population ruled by a benevolent, disinterested despot of the highest order of intelligence, a Napoleon devoted to the arts of peace. We may imagine this ruler, by a system of taxation that shall be as just between individuals and as judicious in its seasons and methods as human wisdom can make it, first, drawing from the crops of good years a store against the occurrence of bad harvests ; then, by a gradually increasing stringency of exaction, adding to the cost of living in such a way as to discourage the growth of population, while applying the proceeds to great public improvements which enable the food supply of the empire to be readily equalized in the event of local scarcity; which guard the crops against the effects of periodical drought ; which afford rapid and cheap passage to the products of inland districts.

And as the productive power of the country increased under such an administration, we can imagine the high-minded ruler, intent on his benevolent purpose, still drawing away from the people, by taxation, all the surplus above the necessary cost of subsistence for the present population, which might otherwise be applied to the increase of population, and, with the means thus acquired, providing capital in its various forms for the use of the frugal and the temperate, perfecting communications, protecting the health and lives of his subjects by sanitary arrangements, and, at last, undertaking the elementary education of the whole body of the people.

All this, it is clear, an absolute ruler of the character indicated might do for his people ;* and not a little of this many

---

* This is, in fact, involved in the theory of the British administration of India. The reasons are well stated in the following paragraph from the *Times* of 1879 :

"In England the remission of taxation is urged with great force, because it is said that taxes remitted will fructify in the pockets of the people. No result of this kind can be expected in India. If the condia benevolent and able ruler has done for his people. The "forced frugality," to use Bentham's phrase, which his taxes have imposed, has at once repressed population and stimulated industry among the existing body of laborers. His wise expenditures upon public works and in public education has sown the seed from which has sprung many a golden harvest.

416. But while we see, thus, what an ideal monarch might do for a people indolent, unambitious, sensual, by applying a portion of the wealth they created to ends more useful, elevating and satisfying than their individual tastes and appetites would have selected, we are forced also to remember how large a part of the wealth raised by taxation has, in all ages, been spent in war, pomp and folly; how strong is the temptation to extravagance and even to corruption in government expenditure; how much of what the people pay the treasury does not receive; how much of what the treasury disburses does not reach its intended object. These considerations are strong enough to justify, in a large degree if not wholly, that unwillingness to intrust to government the consumption of the wealth of the community, much beyond what is necessary to secure domestic tranquillity and the administration of justice between man and man, which is so peculiarly American.

Yet it is possible that this feeling may be carried too far. When one contrasts the highways, the bridges, the streets, the harbors, the breakwaters, the lighthouses, and other aids to transportation and commerce, which government provides, with the best that could reasonably be looked for from individual or associated effort, without the taxing power; when one contrasts our system of public education with the best

tions of living are made easier there, as they would be by a remission of taxes, the consequences would not be an improvement in the well-being of the people, but an increase of their numbers. Our duty, therefore, as guardians and governors of the people, charged with the responsibility of keeping alive in times of famine a vast population with no reserved resources of its own, is to save for those who do not save for themselves, to keep a margin of income over expenditure so that we may have in hand a fund upon which to draw in the recurrent periods of distress. This is a leading principle in Indian finance. Whoever forgets this neglects the primary duty of an Indian administrator."

that voluntary contributions or private munificence ever supplied; when one contrasts the sanitary arrangements for supplying pure air and pure water to our crowded cities with the condition of things which exists where these matters are left to unofficial action; he will find occasion to qualify in no small degree his assent to the proposition that, under a well-ordered constitution, government is only a policeman, to keep people from breaking each other's heads or picking each other's pockets.

PART VI.—SOME APPLICATIONS OF ECONOMIC PRINCIPLES.

It has seemed best to reserve to this portion of our work the discussion of some topics which involve the application of economic principles to questions of law or governmental policy, into which considerations of political equity or political expediency will intrude themselves so that they can hardly be shut out; and also to place here some matters of economic detail which might have unduly interrupted the course of our argument, had they been dealt with at the points with which they are logically connected.

Throughout this part, therefore, I may be found to adduce considerations not strictly economic, with a freedom I have not allowed myself heretofore.

The topics to be treated under this title are:

1. Usury Laws.
2. Industrial Co-operation.
3. Political Money.
4. Pauperism.
5. The Doctrine of the Wage-Fund.
6. The Multiple or Tabular Standard.
7. Trade Unions and Strikes.
8. The Knights of Labor.
9. Attacks on the Doctrine of Rent.
10. Nationalization of the Land.
11. The Banking Functions.
12. The National Banking System of the United States.
13. Foreign Exchanges.
14. Bi-Metallism.

15. The Revenue of the State.
16. Taxation.
17. "Protection" *vs.* Freedom of Production.
18. Socialism.

I.

USURY LAWS.

471. The Prejudice against Taking Interest.—It has already been said (par. 36) that it is not the province of the economist to justify the existing order of things, or to establish the morality or the political equity of laws or institutions affecting property; yet we shall get so good a side-light upon the economic principles governing the loan of capital, in briefly considering the objections that have been raised against interest, or the taking of usury, as it is invidiously called, that it may be worth our while to step out of the direct path for a moment, at this point.

For many centuries, and even within a comparatively recent period, the Christian Church proscribed the taking of interest as a moral offense, and the laws of nearly all civilized countries made it a crime, while the voice of publicists and of ethical writers, alike, was raised against it as a wicked and pernicious practice. Whence came this general consent in denouncing that which is to-day accepted as right in morals and as practically beneficial, by all except a few fanatics?

The origin of the prejudice against usury is commonly attributed to a mistaken apprehension of a provision of the Mosaical Code forbidding the receipt of interest from any member of the chosen race, and to a passage in the works of Aristotle, those works which once had so profound and pervasive an influence in forming the political philosophy of Europe, to the effect that *as money does not produce money* nothing more than the return of the principal sum lent can equitably be claimed by the lender.

418. Does Money Produce Money?—Of the theological argument it is not necessary to say much here. The inhibition of usury, as between one Hebrew and another, was doubtless a feature in the general policy adopted for keeping the peculiar people apart from their profane neighbors and intensifying their community of feeling. The dictum of Aristotle, claiming no divine authority but professing to found itself on reason, remained unchallenged for ages amid all the political speculations of Europe. Mr. McCulloch attributes to John Calvin the high honor of having first detected the fallacy of this argument against usury, discerning that, while money does not produce money, that which may be purchased with money does produce after its kind, and that herein is a perfect justification for the payment of interest.

Money, does, indeed, not produce money, but capital produce, capital. If a man borrows money he may with it buy grain which, when sown, will bring forth "some thirty, some sixty and some an hundred fold." He may purchase cattle, of which a small herd will in a few years become a mighty one. If he employs it in trade or in manufactures, his production may be so largely increased thereby that he may pay a liberal reward to the lender, and yet be better off than if he had not borrowed.

407. The Movement Toward Reform.—England led the movement toward a more enlightened policy. By an act of 1546 * lenders were allowed to receive interest, though at a rate not to exceed ten per cent. During a brief reaction under Edward VI. this law was repealed, but a statute of Elizabeth restored the right to take interest. Subsequent statutes reduced the rate of legal interest successively to 8, 6 and 5 per

---

* 37, Henry VIII. Though thus legalized, public sentiment and particularly the opinions of the clergy remained in a high degree hostile to usury. "I do wish," said Dr. Wilson, in his Discourse upon Usury, published more than twenty years after the act of Henry VIII., "some penal law of death to be made against usurers, as well as against thieves and murderers, for that they deserve death much more than such men do; for these usurers destroy and devour up, not only whole families, but also whole countries, and bring all folks to beggary that have to do with them."

cent. (Queen Anne), at which last point it remained till the present reign, when all restrictions on loans were abolished.

Among the States of the American Union, Massachusetts has made contracts of loans as free as those of purchase and sale.

Interest is now allowed to be paid on loans in all civilized countries, the prohibition of usury having fallen utterly out of the sympathies of this age. Money-lending, or the taking of interest when payment for goods or lands is forborne, has passed beyond all stigma; and the profession of the banker, who organizes and conducts the borrowing and the lending of whole communities, is among the most honorable known to modern society. Yet there still survives an opinion, very widely spread, that the taking of interest should be under the regulation of the State, to prevent the abuses which are apprehended from the power of the money-lender over the needy and necessitous borrower: that, to use Bacon's phrase, "the tooth of usury be grinded, that it bite not too much."

This opinion finds expression in the statutes of nearly all nations and of almost every State of the American Union, and even the general banking law of the United States provides that the associations (National Banks) to be organized thereunder may receive interest at the rate allowed by the laws of the State, Territory or District where they are located, and no more, and that, where no local rate is fixed by law, the rate of interest shall not exceed seven per cent., to be, however, taken in advance (discounted).

420. Laws Regulating Interest.—All civilized nations having legalized the taking of interest on loans, the term, usury laws, as applied to existing legislation, has reference, not to the prohibition of interest but to its regulation, generally through the means of a prescribed maximum rate which it is made unlawful to exceed. As has been stated, such laws still stand on the statute books of highly civilized states. What shall be said of them? As a substitute for the laws that forbade the taking of interest they must be regarded as in the nature of enlightened legislation, and I am not sure that, even when considered without comparison with pre-existing legislation, these laws were, in an earlier time, wholly without justification. They were enacted in the interest of the would-be borrower, who was regarded as unable to sustain, without grave injury, which might also work injury to the community, the competition to which he was subjected in his efforts to secure the loan of capital. And in the ages in which these laws were enacted, this assumption was not without reason.

421. Usury Laws in Early Ages.—Borrowers were, then, generally persons embarrassed or distressed, whether by their own fault or by misfortune. Trade and manufactures were not, as so largely now, carried on by means of borrowed capital. The man who asked a loan was presumably in circumstances which put him very much at the mercy of the money lender, just as a man in times of famine is at the mercy of the dealer in food, who may make unreasonable, extortionate and cruel terms.

And the money lender in those days was not, in general, a nice sort of person. The recent outbreaks in Roumelia, Roumania and Russia testify to the natural feelings of a simple-minded, ignorant, passive, and more or less stupid people, who see houses and lands and cattle and goods and even standing crops pass with fatal certainty out of the hands of the many into the hands of a class in whom the faculty of acquisition is developed to such a degree as to make them, in comparison with a peasantry like that of the Slavonic States, as wolves among sheep.

We allow all men to walk our streets indifferently, because men are so constituted physically as to be substantially equal, so far as contact is concerned. We brush each other and sometimes run full against each other, and yet give and take no harm. But suppose one-half the people of our cities were as fragile and brittle as glass, while the other half, divided on the line of sex, or otherwise, were as heavy and as hard as iron, would not the law require the latter to go by separate streets, and protect the weaker part of the community from a contact that would be fatal?

I am not at all sure that economic reasons would not justify the legislature in interfering to save by any practicable means one class in the community from the effects of such one-sided competition as existed between borrower and lender in the ages referred to ; nor am I sure that the kind of laws referred to were wholly without the beneficent effects they were intended to have.

422. Evasion of Usury Laws.—Even in the ages when the taking of interest, in any form, was strictly prohibited under the most cruel penalties, usury laws were very frequently evaded, through a great variety of artifices and contrivances. In modern times, the laws prescribing a maximum rate of interest, generally under penalties of moderate severity, are, it may be said as a rule, violated or evaded, whenever the use of capital* becomes more valuable than the consideration allowed by law to be paid, be that five per cent., or six, or seven, or more.

The most important means of evading the usury laws are the following :

First. *Fictitious Deposits in Bank.*—Every successful merchant and manufacturer will, of course, keep a considerable deposit to his credit in the bank or banks with which he habitually deals. He will do this to protect himself against the failure of remittances from his own correspondents, to enable him to meet unanticipated demands, perhaps to take advantage of exceptionally good bargains suddenly offering.

What we have now in mind is the keeping of deposits in bank, in excess of what the merchant or manufacturer would naturally maintain for his own purposes, as an inducement to the bank to loan him capital in emergencies.† Thus, we

---

* The reader is referred to par. 286 for the demonstration that interest is paid for the use of capital, not always, not generally, not often, for the use of money, as such. In the present article, however, in writing of usury laws and the means of evading them, I shall use the phrases of the so-called Money Market, more properly the market for the loan of capital ; and shall speak of money being scarce, money being worth such a per cent., *etc.*, meaning always thereby, capital.

† Samuel Jones Lloyd, afterwards Lord Overstone, in his testimony before the British Commons Committee of 1841, said : "The compensation to the banker for his loss in advancing money upon discount, at a

might suppose that a certain merchant or manufacturer finds it for his interest to keep "a line of deposits," in a certain bank, averaging twenty thousand dollars. This he might deem sufficient for all his own purposes. In order, however, to make sure that the bank will discount his notes when "money is scarce," he may think it worth while to maintain an average deposit of fifty thousand dollars. He gives the bank the use, all the time, of thirty thousand dollars, with the implied understanding that the bank, on its part, will loan him all it possibly can, in periods of financial difficulty. This course is pursued to a very great extent. It is natural that wealthy merchants and manufacturers should in this way protect themselves against emergencies; but this only makes it all the harder for those who can not afford to keep large deposits in ordinary times to borrow what they may absolutely require in periods of pressure or distress.

Second. *Commissions.*—Suppose the law to prescribe that interest shall not be taken above six per cent. per annum. A merchant has occasion to borrow ten thousand dollars for two months. On this the maximum legal interest would be one hundred dollars. But the demand for capital, at the time, is so great, or the supply of it so small, owing to the prevalence of speculation or to the existence of commercial distrust, that no one is willing to lend ten thousand dollars, two months, for so little as one hundred dollars. Our merchant goes to a broker and says: "I wish to borrow so-and-so, and I will give you one per cent. for negotiating the loan." Now, one per cent. commission on ten thousand dollars is one hundred dollars: so that the would-be borrower really promises to pay at the rate of twelve per cent. per annum. Since he is in this frame of mind, there is no longer any difficulty about getting the loan. The probabilities are that the broker divides his commission with the lender.

Third. *Fictitious or "Dry" Exchange.**— Let us suppose

rate below its real value, would be found in the value of the accounts kept with him by the parties to whom such advances were made."

*In his standard work on usury, Plowden states that "Dry Exchange" was sometimes carried, in his day, to a very great extent. The borrower the would-be borrower, in the case referred to, goes to his bank and offers his note for ten thousand dollars, payable in sixty days. The cashier says, "We can not discount this note ; but if you will make it payable in New York, we will try to put it through for you." This is done. At maturity, the note is paid in New York. The bank charges one-half per cent. "exchange," theoretically for bringing the money home, though it may be that the bank would at the time rather have its money in New York than in Boston. Now, one-half per cent. exchange on ten thousand dollars is fifty dollars, which is three per cent. on a loan of that amount for two months. This added to the six per cent. interest which the bank is authorized to charge, makes nine per cent. received by the bank in this transaction.

Both the first and the third of these modes of evading usury laws are completely within the law. A man has a right to keep as large deposits as he pleases in his bank ; the bank has a right to charge whatever rate of exchange may be mutually agreed upon for bringing money from a foreign country or a distant city. Dividing the commission between the broker and the lender is unlawful ; but it can be so easily and secretly done as to be practically beyond any danger of incurring penalties.

Fourth. *Loans for Unnecessarily Long Periods.*—To illustrate this mode of defeating the intention of usury laws, let us return to the case of the merchant, who, in time of commercial trouble, has occasion to borrow ten thousand dollars for two months. He offers his note for that amount, on that time, to a bill broker, who replies : "I can not get this discounted for you ; but, if you will make out your note for a year* I

"draws" on an imaginary person in a foreign country. After the expiration of the time the bill is to run, comes a "protest" from that country for the non-payment of the bill, with the re-exchange of the money thence to the place where the money was drawn, the paper having, in fact, never been out of the country. "The borrower," says this writer, "being thus charged with exchange, re-exchange, protest and incidental expense, pays in all, some twenty or thirty per cent."

*A witness before the Commons Committee of 1841, testified that he once

will get you the money, at the legal rate." This is done. The lender sacrifices his chance of getting his eight or ten per cent. through some roundabout method, during two months, for the sake of placing his capital, at the maximum legal rate, for an entire year. He believes that the stringency in the market, which now makes "money" really worth eight or ten per cent. will soon be over. In that case, interest will probably fall below the legal rate; perhaps during a greater part of the year capital may be "a drug," at three or four per cent. The lender may thus be better off in making the borrower pay six per cent. for twelve months, than if he had taken from him eight or ten per cent. for two months, to have his capital thrown back on his hands at the expiration of that time.

423. Economic Effects of Laws Prescribing a Maximum Rate of Interest.—Such are the most important of the means resorted to for evading the laws establishing a maximum rate of interest. It must not be thought that, because usury laws may thus be evaded, they have, therefore, no economic effect. On the contrary, they exert a very considerable influence.

(*a.*) These underhand or roundabout modes of doing business must cost somebody something.

Now, the person on whom this charge is likely to rest is he who, in the time and place, occupies the position of relative economic disadvantage. This, it is needless to say, is, in times of financial trouble, the borrower, who must have the money or submit to great loss, perhaps to ruin.

(*b.*) More important, still, among the effects of usury laws, is the destruction of an open market for the loan of capital, and the preventing of a quotable rate of interest. When the actual rate goes above the legal rate, and borrowers and lenders are driven to roundabout and underhand methods of making up the difference, nobody knows "what money is worth." The borrower, under a terrible necessity to secure

---

negotiated in a period of stringency a loan of £100,000 to a mercantile house, for the term of seven years, although the borrowers only wanted the use of the capital for a few months, and would have been glad to take it for that time, at a high rate of interest, had this been permitted by the law.

a loan, lest his notes should "go to protest," and he be financially dishonored and perhaps ruined, is practically blindfolded, at the moment of his greatest weakness and need. The more anxious he is, the more completely is he at the mercy of the lenders, who, in such a case, have a common interest in creating the impression that "money" is very scarce and fast growing scarcer. Every borrower who becomes frightened spreads fear on every side around him, until perchance a panic prevails, and borrowers submit to every degree of extortion.

(*c*.) Even more important than the loss to the borrowing class through the most exorbitant rates of interest, is the sacrifice of stocks of goods, securities, bonds, etc., to which many merchants are driven, in times of commercial distress, through the difficulties and delays interposed by the laws regulating the loan of capital.* Many a man in such a case, either because he has not the time to negotiate a loan by artifice, or because his credit is not of the best, or because he is driven to desperation, will sell goods consciously at a great disadvantage. Oftentimes, such a man has to submit to a sacrifice of five, ten, or fifteen per cent. of the value which the goods had a week before, and which they perhaps will have a month later. Now, to sacrifice only five per cent. on a body of goods, in order to get through one month of financial stringency, is equivalent to borrowing capital for that length of time, at the rate of sixty per cent., per annum ! How much more would it have been for this man's advantage, had the law permitted him to go into an open market for the loan of capital, and there pay whatever its use was, at the time, worth, were that nine, or twelve, or fifteen, or eighteen per cent. !

424. Usury Laws in Communities Mainly Non-Commercial.—We have spoken of the relations of the borrower to the

* It is to this Lord Bacon alludes when he says, "Were it not for this easy borrowing upon interest, men's necessities would draw upon them a most sudden undoing, in that they would be forced to sell their means (be it lands or goods) far underfoot ; and so *whereas usury doth but gnaw upon them, bad markets would swallow them quite up*."

lender of capital, in a primitive condition of industrial society, before business has come to be carried on by loans of capital, and while borrowers are generally distressed persons. We have, also, referred to the relations of the borrower and the lender, in communities having a high commercial and financial organization. Intermediate between these two conditions is a state of society, such as characterizes extensive regions of the United States, to-day, where agriculture is prosperous, where industry has made some progress, yet where the community still remains mainly non-commercial. This state of society is commonly left out of account by writers who oppose usury laws. I do not, however, deem it candid to omit communities of this character altogether from consideration, or to assume that conclusions which we may have drawn from the study of a highly advanced commercial society will apply to these, without qualification.

On the whole, I do not think that the question of the effect of usury laws in a mainly agricultural community, in modern times, is quite so simple as most writers have treated it as being.* On the one hand, I have no doubt that the fixing of a legal rate of interest has a certain effect upon the disposition of owners of capital in lending that capital. We have seen (par. 147) that the moral and intellectual elements of supply and demand are very potential in exchange. I have no doubt whatever, that the current rate of interest, in a country where a rate is fixed by law, sometimes affords an example of the operation of this force.

Again, I have no doubt that the influence of penalties threatened for exceeding a certain rate of interest, in a community chiefly non-commercial and of simple industrial organization and where the element of personal acquaintance largely enters into all relations of man with man, is distinctly felt in inducing some persons to accept the legal rate, if that be

* "It is in vain," says John Locke, "to go about effectually to reduce the price of interest by a law; and you may as rationally hope to set a fixed rate upon the hire of houses, or ships, as of money." And elsewhere this eminent philosopher calls a law to regulate the rate of interest "a law to hedge-in the cuckoo."

fixed tolerably near the ordinary market rate, so that the temptation to evade the law is not overwhelming. On the other hand, it is equally clear that such provisions of law may be evaded by the various means recited, and probably will be evaded whenever the inducement offered is very great; and that, so far as borrowers are driven to shifts to disguise excess of usury, they are likely to find themselves worse off than they would be in an open market.

Just where the balance would be, in such a community as has been described, so far as the interests of the ordinary agricultural borrower, or small country trader or mechanic, are concerned, I confess I do not feel confident; and I doubt if any man knows enough to say rightly even to which side the balance might incline in a community composed of men of different race, or of different traditions and social habits, from those whom he has been accustomed personally to observe.

425. Usury Laws in Highly Commercial Communities.—But in any modern commercial community of large and varied and complicated industrial concerns, the case is a simple one.

In an advanced state of industrial society, where borrowing is no longer the resort of the embarrassed and distressed, alone, or mainly, but, on the contrary, the most flourishing trade and manufactures are carried on chiefly by means of borrowed capital; where, in the usual course of prosperous business, notes are made and are paid by the thousands, every day, usury laws become purely mischievous.

First, because the vastly greater interests of trade and industry would properly outweigh, were society called to choose between them, the interests of distressed and embarrassed individuals; and,

Secondly, because such persons will, in fact, benefit by the greater plentifulness of capital, the greater ease of borrowing, and the consequently lower rate of interest, which, in general, result from freedom regarding contracts for loan. The business classes, active, alert, aggressive in competition, make rates of interest by which the less fortunate profit.

II.

INDUSTRIAL CO-OPERATION.

427. The Objects of Co-operation.—In Part IV. we have shown the place in the scheme of distribution that is to be occupied by what is termed co-operation, should that project be, in any appreciable degree, realized. We said that the object of co-operation, in the technical sense in which that word has been used by economic writers, and even popularly used, since the Revolution of 1848, is to get rid of the "entrepreneur," or employer, as an industrial agent.

It is evident that if the parties to production, other than the landlord, are to be thus reduced to two, that function may be performed either by the capitalist class or by the laboring class. The capitalists may, as such, become employers of labor: that is, each capitalist may become an employer because he is a capitalist, and in the degree in which he possesses capital. Whereas, now, only a small fraction of the owners of capital are also employers of labor. In this case, interest and profits would be united. In the other case, the laborers may become self-employed, taking all the responsibilities of production, borrowing capital according to their occasions for its productive use, and paying a remuneration therefor on the principles heretofore determined. In this case, wages and profits would be united.

The latter is the change in industrial organization which is in contemplation when co-operation is urged. It is in the interest of the laboring classes, not of the owners of capital, that the employer is to be extruded from the industrial system and his profits brought to re-enforce wages. The whole significance of co-operation, as a scheme of industrial reform, lies in this: that the laboring classes expect to divide among themselves the large amount of wealth which they now see going, day by day, into the possession of their employers, as profits.

427. Mistaken Conception of the Economists.—But, although the laboring classes fully understand this, and know precisely what co-operation, if effected, would mean to them, the political economists, unfortunately, by reason of that incomplete analysis of the productive agencies to which we have before adverted (par. 304), are unable to give an intelligible, or even self-consistent account of co-operation. Not more than two or three English or American economists* have given a definition of co-operation which will bear examination. Why is this? Because, having persistently refused to regard the function of the employer, they can not, consistently with their own analysis of production, give account of a scheme whose whole object is the elimination of that "functionary," as Prof. Rogers calls him. Yet, seeing, as they must, that co-operation really attempts something, and would, if effected, essentially change the existing organization of industry, they hit upon the utterly erroneous explanation that co-operation is to get rid of the capitalist! Hardly an economist but blunders at this point.

428. Prof. Cairnes's Statement.—Take a writer so justly celebrated for clearness of thinking as the late Prof. Cairnes. The frequency with which he has been quoted in these pages is evidence of the high respect in which his work is held by the writer. Yet Prof. Cairnes stumbles at the very threshold of the subject. "The characteristic feature of co-operation," he says, "looked at from the economic point of view, is that *it combines in the same persons the two capacities of laborer and capitalist.*"

Now, it is not at all of the essence of co-operation that the laborers should be capitalists; that they should furnish any portion of the capital required for conducting the operations to be undertaken under this system. It is, of course, probable that some, perhaps most, of the co-operators would, in fact (though, as we have said, this is not of the essence of the

---

* Prof. Thorold Rogers defines co-operation justly, as "a scheme . . . by which the laborer can *unite the functions and earn the wages of laborer and employer, by superseding the necessity of using the services of the latter functionary.*"

Prof. Amasa Walker had previously given expression to the same conception of co-operation.

scheme), own small amounts of capital; and the aggregate sum so held would be put into the co-operative business, and, by that amount, the sum to be borrowed of outsiders would be reduced. Yet, in order to secure justice between those co-operators who had and those who had not capital to put in the business, between those who had much and those who had little, it would be necessary that each associate who put capital into the business should be remunerated for his abstinence and for the risk of his principal, by a payment over and above what an associate contributing only through his labor would receive.

In other words, the co-operative company would pay interest to its own members for the use of whatever capital they could command, and would borrow, on interest, the remaining capital required, just as the employer now does. The co-operative workmen who were so fortunate as to possess capital would lend it to their own company, instead of lending it, as now, through the agency of the bank or the savings institution, to employers of labor, perhaps to their own employers.

Just so far as a laboring man joining a co-operative association had the courage and faith and self-control to save out of his earnings, he would become a capitalist, exactly as if he were not a co-operator. If, however, he chose to indulge himself by eating and drinking up all he earned, he would remain no capitalist, in spite of co-operation. Co-operation can not make a man a capitalist. Nothing can do that but saving, and while co-operation might, and doubtless would, encourage frugality, no scheme of man's devising is going to radically change man's nature so that a large proportion of the community will not consume all their incomes—be those incomes large or small.

We see, thus, how erroneous is Prof. Cairnes's definition. The aim of co-operation is to get rid of the employer, and divide his profits among his former workmen, who are to become, for the future, self-employed: to organize themselves, in their own way, for industrial purposes, and carry forward production on their own account and at their own risk.

429. The Benefits Aimed at by Co-operation.—Such being

the nature of co-operation, let us inquire what advantages might reasonably be looked for from it, provided it were found practicable.

Let us begin by taking the laborer's point of view:

First. To secure for the laboring class that large amount of wealth, which, as we have seen, goes annually in profits to the employer.

Second. To secure for the laborer the opportunity to produce independently of the will of an employer. Under the existing industrial system, it remains with the entrepreneur to decide, not only what shall be produced, and how and when and in what amounts, but also whether any production at all shall take place.

It is true that the employer may, out of compassion, carry on production for a while where no profit to himself appears, rather than leave his working people to suffer. It is also true that his selfish interests may induce him to carry on production for a while, under similar conditions, in order to keep his customers from going to others. But neither of these considerations can be relied upon to any great extent or for any long period, nor can both together be relied upon at all as against the apprehension of considerable loss on the part of the employer. In a state of the market which causes the employer to doubt whether, after paying out large sums for materials and labor, he will get his money back in the price of the products, a suspension of production to the extent of a third or a half is the most natural course for him to adopt.

But while a body of laborers can not reasonably complain that their employer curtails production on the first intimation of commercial disorder or of diminishing demand, co-operation would place it within their power to keep up production on their own responsibility, remaining at work and selling their product for what it would bring. It would no longer be the interest of the one employer, but that of the many workmen, which should decide whether production were to proceed or not.

430. Co-operation from the Point of View of the General Economic Interest.—The foregoing are the two chief benefits which the laboring class have looked to co-operation to secure for them. In addition to these, the political economist beholds in co-operation three sources of advantage. First : Co-operation would, by the very terms of the case, do away with strikes. The employer disappearing, the workman becoming self-employed, these destructive contests would disappear also. Second : The workman would be incited to greater industry and to greater carefulness in dealing with materials and with machinery. Third : In no small degree frugality would be encouraged. It can not be doubted that a co-operative laborer having the opportunity to invest his savings at once in his own business would feel a much stronger inducement to frugality than does the wage laborer.

431. Co-operation, from a Still Higher Point of View. —We may leave to the moralist or the statesman the additional consideration that co-operation would clearly tend to improve the moral, social and political character of the workman, by giving him a larger stake in society, making his remuneration directly dependent on his own exertions, and admitting him to a participation in the deliberations and decisions of industry.

432. The Difficulties of Co-operation.—The advantages which would attend the successful establishment of co-operation being so many and so great, it may be asked why has this scheme, proposed so long ago, sanctioned by the highest economic authority, appealing directly to the self-interest of the laboring classes, advertised extensively in discussions relating to labor and wages, not been immediately successful, on a large scale ? How is it, that, on the contrary, co-operation can hardly be said to have escaped failure, when one considers the great number of enterprises of this character which have been started and the few that have survived ?

Co-operative enterprises may be divided into two classes—one attempting what we may call Productive co-operation ; the other what we may call Consumptive * co-operation. In enterprises of the former class, the laborer seeks to make for himself an income ; in the latter he seeks to expend or consume

* By many called Distributive.

that income to the best advantage : to make each dollar of his daily or weekly earnings go as far as possible in providing subsistence for himself and family. Of course, all the agencies of transportation and exchange are, as we have stated, productive ; yet in the difference of aim which has been shown to exist between the two classes of co-operative establishments, is found the justification of the distinction indicated.

433. Consumptive Co-operation has had no inconsiderable degree of success in England, in the way of shops for the sale of flour, meats, groceries and other articles of domestic consumption, at which subscribers or members of the associations establishing such shops buy goods at, perhaps, the usual prices of retail trade, generally for cash, the profits of the year or the season, after deducting the expenses of supervision and management, being divided among the members, either equally or in the proportion of their purchases.

In the United States, the indifference of the people, even of the poorer classes, towards small savings and that same unwillingness to take pains to secure a sound administration of trusts which has permitted municipal and State governments to fall so largely into the hands of unworthy persons, have combined to limit very narrowly the application of the scheme of consumptive co-operation. Here and there, "union" stores (the word store being used very generally in the United States in the sense in which the English use the word shop), "Granger" stores, or "Sovereigns of Industry" stores, fill a small place, generally for a brief period, in the general system of exchange ; but these have never become highly important agencies in our public economy.

434. Productive Co-operation.— But while consumptive co-operation has had a degree of success which at least proves it to be a practicable scheme, given only a reasonable degree of popular interest in its maintenance, the history of productive co-operation alike in France, where it may be said to have originated, in England, and in the United States, has been of the most discouraging character. Of numberless enterprises undertaken within the last forty years by associations of laborers, with the encouragement and often the active assistance of philanthropists and political economists, and enjoying the benefit of a vast amount of gratuitous advertisement,* scarcely any remain. Mr. Frederick Harrison, reviewing the history of co-operative enterprises in England, indicates the co-operative cotton mills as the only true instances of the application of this principle on any important scale. "Some of the mills," he says, "never got to work at all; some took the simple form of joint-stock companies in few hands; others passed into the hands of small capitalists, or the shares were concentrated among the promoters. In fact, there is now, I believe, no co-operative cotton mill, owned by working men, in active operation, on any scale, with the notable exception of Rochdale."

"Here and there," Mr. Harrison continues, "an association of bootmakers, hatters, painters or gilders, is carried on, upon a small scale, with varying success. But small bodies of handicraftsmen (or, rather, artists), working in common, with moderate capital, plant and premises, obviously establish nothing."

435. The Difficulties of Productive Co-operation.—With such a statement, from a distinguished labor champion, we repeat our inquiry, Why is it that co-operation, in the view of the many and great advantages which it offers, has had such partial and doubtful success? The answer is at hand. The difficulties of productive co-operation are directly as its advantages. The arbitrary powers wielded and the vast profits enjoyed by the employing class make the working classes desire, naturally enough, to bring about an industrial order in which they shall no longer be subject to such exercise of authority, and in which they shall themselves reap the large sums of wealth which they see passing into the hands of their employers. Yet when a body of laborers set up for themselves,

---

* Within the last three or four years, a fresh crop of co-operative enterprises has sprung up, especially in the United States. Time has not yet served to determine the question of success or failure. The fullest accounts of these enterprises will be found in the publications of the American Economic Association.

the result very soon shows that the reason why the employer wields such despotic power and enjoys such large revenues, is that he performs a part in modern industrial society which is of supreme importance, in which any thing less than the highest abilities of organization and administration involve comparative, if not absolute, failure.

The time may come, when a body of laborers, joined together for the purpose of co-operative production, will give as intelligent a direction, as close a supervision, as rigid a discipline, as energetic an impulse, as the present successful man of business gives to the enterprises on which his fortunes and his reputation are staked ; but, for one, though believing thoroughly so far as politics are concerned, in a government of the people, by the people, for the people, I see nothing which indicates that, within any near future, industry is to become less despotic than it now is. The power of the master in production, "the captain of industry," has steadily increased throughout the present century, with the increasing complexity of commercial relations, with the greater concentration of capital, with improvements in apparatus and machinery, with the multiplication of styles and fashions, with the localization and specialization of manufactures.

436. I shall be heartily glad to see the working classes rise to the height of the occasion, and vindicate their right to rule in industry by showing their power to do it. But meanwhile it must be distinctly understood, that nothing costs the working classes so much as the bad or commonplace conduct of business; that industry must be energetically, economically, and wisely managed, no matter who is to do it ; and that co-operation will be successful only as it results in the production of equally good articles, at equally low prices, as those produced under entrepreneur management.

If we have made our analysis of profits correctly, it appears (par. 312) that the gains of the employer are not taken from the earnings of the laboring class, but measure the difference in production between the commonplace or bad, and the able, and shrewd, and strong management of business. When associated laborers are able to manage business as ably, strongly and shrewdly as private employers, they can dismiss the entrepreneur, and keep his gains themselves.

437. A Possible Field for Industrial Co-operation.—I have spoken thus strongly of the difficulties of productive co-operation, because I believe that only harm will come to the interests of the working classes from slurring over those difficulties, as is so often, with the best intentions, done by writers on economics. In speaking thus, however, of the evil liabilities which beset such enterprises, I have reference to industry as a whole, and especially to its larger branches, which supply general markets, and which are subject to competition at once far-reaching and searching. In the last sentence quoted from Mr. Frederick Harrison, we find indicated the outlines of a possible field of co-operation, within which most of the difficulties which attend such enterprises on a larger scale, are not encountered, or are encountered in greatly diminished force. Where (1) a branch of industry is of such a nature that it can best be carried on by a small group of workmen ; where (2) the workmen so engaged are substantially on a level as regards strength and skill ; where (3) the initial expenditure for tools and materials is small, and, especially, where (4) the goods are to be produced mainly or wholly for the local market, the difficulties of the co-operative system sink to a minimum and the advantages rise to a maximum. It is in such branches of industry, therefore, that the experiment of productive co-operation should first be tried. Success can be achieved here, if anywhere. Should success be here achieved, advantage may be taken of the experience thus accumulated and of the training thus acquired, to undertake progressively larger enterprises. On the other hand, should the difficulties of productive co-operation prevent a decided success within the nearer and easier field, it would be worse than futile to attempt to inaugurate that system on a more ambitious scale.

438. Profit-Sharing.—The obstacles which beset productive co-operation are not those which are encountered by the scheme of Profit-Sharing, which has been highly recommended by many writers and which has been undertaken of late years, not, indeed, on a large scale, but in numerous instances. The advantages of this scheme, illustrated by many examples of at least partial and temporary success, will be found stated in the work under the title, Profit-Sharing, by Mr. Sedley Taylor. Fresh literature on the subject is now almost daily appearing in newspapers, magazines, pamphlets and official reports. The matter is one of economic and administrative detail, too minute to be treated in an elementary work of this character.

The object sought is to interest workmen in increasing production and in reducing waste and breakage, through a payment to them of a portion of the employer's profits. It is, also, held that this system would have the effect to promote good feeling between master and man, and to diminish the resort to strikes and labor contests, although, in fact, it has not always served, when tried, to prevent the workmen concerned from joining others of the same trade when such contests have once begun.

The difficulties of profit-sharing are found (1) in the smallness of the amount which can thus be distributed among the workmen, without unduly diminishing the employer's interest in production ; (2) in the suspicions likely to arise regarding the employer's good faith in declaring the amount thus subject to distribution, unless the workmen, or a committee of them, are to be allowed such access to the employer's books and accounts as few business men would willingly concede, and (3) in the perplexing question, what shall be done, under such a system, in the not infrequent cases where the employer realizes, not a profit, but a loss.

The last of these difficulties is, perhaps, the greatest. The employer is, not unnaturally, disposed to hold that, if the workmen share in his gains, they should also share in his losses ; or, at least, that his gains and losses, through a considerable period of time, should be set off against each other, and that only the balance of gain for such a period should be subject to the rule of distribution. Such a postponement of the dividend, however, taken in connection with the smallness of the amount which, at the most, could thus be divided, would reduce the interest of the workmen in the system, to such an extent as to practically deprive the arrangement of nearly all influence over their actions, if it did not lead to its early abandonment.

III.

POLITICAL MONEY.

439. Inconvertible Paper Money is, by Distinction, Political Money.—In all modern societies, money is at once an economic agent and a political institution. The selection by the State of a money metal, the adoption of denominations and devices for its coinage, the establishment of a standard of purity in the coin, and the conferring of the legal-tender property upon the money pieces so formed, are acts of legislation or administration which give to all forms of money with which we are familiar something of a political character.

But there is one kind of money which owes its existence and acceptance as the common medium of exchange so completely to legislation or to the act of the ruler, that it may be called, by eminence, political money. This is the inconvertible paper money of which we wrote in Chapter 5, Part III. In comparison herewith, the other forms of money known to modern commerce may be regarded as having so little of a political character as to justify their being called economic money.

The essential difference between what we here call economic and what we call political money, is that the supply of the former, under free coinage, is limited by natural conditions of production, while the supply of the latter is released from all such conditions, and is made to depend upon law or the will of the ruler. It requires more labor, in general twice as much labor, to raise two thousand ounces of gold or silver from the mine as to raise one thousand ounces, to be coined into money; but it costs no more labor to print two million dollars of paper money, or ten millions, or fifty, than to print one million. To multiply the amount of such money, it is only necessary to print the word fifty, or ten, or two, instead of the word one.

By some, this capability of increase at will, independently of the expenditure of labor or capital, has been regarded as a prime advantage, and such money has been denominated by these advocates of government issues, political money,—that character being attributed to it as meritorious. It is, then, from the friends of such money that I borrow the term. Accepting the challenge contained in this title, let us proceed to inquire further regarding government paper money, applying to it the test to which all political institutions and arrangements are rightly subjected.

440. The Favorable Possibilities of Political Money.—I have already, with a frankness that has, on other occasions, been severely blamed, admitted that government paper money may, for a time at least, irrespective of redemption, pass in circulation without depreciation; performing perfectly the function of a medium of exchange, registering the comparative values of the several commodities in the market with all the facility and accuracy that could be desired, and serving as a standard of deferred payments well or ill according as its own amount is regulated. Prof. Jevons states that between 1789 and 1809 the value of gold fell 46 per cent.; that from 1809 to 1849 it rose 145 per cent.; while between 1849 and 1874 it fell at least 20 per cent. It is certainly conceivable that paper money might be so regulated in amount as to fluctuate less in value than did gold during the eighty-five years covered by Prof. Jevons' computation.

441. The Liability to Evil Inhering in Political Money.—In the case of every proposed political institution or arrangement, however, we are bound to investigate, not its possibilities only, but also its probabilities. It is not enough to show that it might conceivably be so established and maintained as to yield results of good. It must also appear that its successful working does not depend upon an exercise of prudence, virtue and self control, beyond what is reasonably and fairly to be expected of men in masses, and of rulers and legislators as we find them; and the consequences of its possible perversion or abuse must be weighed against the advantages which might be derived from its legitimate application and employment.

Paper money, then, as a political institution or arrangement, must submit to this test. The man who advocates government issues, without being prepared to show reasonable ground for believing that they will not be so abused as to accomplish more of evil than of benefit, is not entitled to be listened to. After the experiences of the past hundred years intelligent men rightly refuse to take the trouble even to discuss political schemes which assume an impossible virtue, or which disregard the actual conditions under which alone they could be set to work.

In the case of government paper money the liability to abuse is found in the tendency to over-issue ; to this end the fiscal exigencies of government (par. 444) are likely to combine with a popular craving (par. 445) for a money of diminishing value.

We have already (par. 220) shown that the smallest degree of depreciation, even, as Mr. Bagehot says, the mere liability to depreciation without its reality, may unsettle the exchanges between the paper money country and those with which it trades, in a degree to work very injurious effects. But what we have here to consider is the liability to extensive over-issues, with an altogether new series of consequences to trade and industry.

442. Two Motives Operating to Produce Expansion.— This liability arises from the fact that, where the principle of inconvertible paper has once been adopted, two powerful motives tend to produce expansion, with no adequate restraining force in operation. When once the traditional fear of paper money is worn off, the only safeguard against over-issue is found in far-reaching, conscientious, disinterested and courageous statesmanship. All the selfish interests that make themselves felt, all the passions of the hour and the appetites that clamor for indulgence, favor expansion. There is an unremitting pressure on that side, which now and then rises to furious impulses against the frail barrier that withstands inflation.

How far is it wise for any moderate advantage to call into being forces which are only to be kept from becoming in the highest degree destructive by being constantly watched and unremittingly opposed? Is it good policy—is it consistent with ordinary common sense—to invoke, for the accomplishment of a definite and at the best not considerable good, agencies respecting which it is confessed that the least relaxation of vigilance, a momentary indulgence of human weakness, one false motion, will lead to serious, perhaps irreparable disaster?

443. Time no Safeguard.—Nor does the liability to over-issue diminish with the lapse of time. Moderation in the issue of government paper money does not form a political habit which becomes a security against abuse. On the contrary, the longer the *régime* of inconvertible paper money lasts, the greater the danger. The popular mind becomes accustomed to the sight and the thought of it; the fear of it is worn off; a generation comes upon the stage that has not known metallic money, or bank money convertible into coin on demand.

In 1690, the Colony of Massachusetts issued paper money to pay the charges of the disastrous expedition of Sir Wm. Phipps. At first, over-issue took place and depreciation set in; but by prompt action the excess was called in and redeemed, and the notes brought to par. They so remained for nearly twenty years. When, however, in 1710, the second expedition against Canada took place, the colony fell, without an apparent struggle, into the gulf of irredeemable paper; the money of Massachusetts became a weltering chaos; trade was brought into the utmost confusion; production to the utmost weakness. From this miserable condition the colony did not emerge for nearly forty years, till, in 1749, the paper was bought up at 11 : 1 in silver and burned.

Russia first issued paper money in 1768, and for nearly twenty years kept her notes at par, only to fall at the end of that period into an abyss of discredit and depreciation from which her trade and finances have not yet recovered.

Twice since the Revolution of 1848 Austria has stood on the very verge of specie payments, only to be thrown backward into insolvency by the imminence of war.

The danger of over-issue never ceases to threaten inconvertible paper money. The path winds along the edge of a precipice. Vigilance can not for a moment be relaxed. The prudence and self-restraint of years count for nothing against any new onset of popular passion or in the face of a sudden exigency of government.

444. The Fiscal Motive.—The exigencies of the public treasury constitute, perhaps, the most formidable of the two dangers which menace the integrity of a paper money circulation.

"Real money," said Edmund Burke, "can hardly ever multiply too much in any country, because it will always, as it increases, be a certain sign of the increase of trade, of which it is the measure, and consequently of the soundness and vigor of the whole body. But this paper money may and does increase, without any increase of trade, *nay, often when trade greatly declines*, for it is not the measure of the trade of the nation, but of the necessity of the government. It is absurd and must be ruinous, that the same cause which naturally exhausts the wealth of a nation should likewise be the only productive cause of money."*

The two most marked instances of continence in the issue of irredeemable paper are those afforded by the Bank of England during the period of the Restriction, and by the Bank of France in 1848, and again in 1871. No one can question that the prudence and self-restraint here shown were due mainly to the fact that, in neither case, would the profit of fresh issues have inured to the benefit of the government. At the same time, it would not be candid to omit to mention the loyal observance by the Congress of the United States of the pledge it gave the country in 1864, that the greenbacks should not exceed $400,000,000.

---

* In the same vein, Alexander Hamilton: "In great and trying emergencies there is almost a moral certainty of its becoming mischievous. The stamping of paper is an operation so much easier than the levying of taxes, that a government in the practice of paper emissions would rarely fail to indulge itself too far in the employment of this resource."

445. Scaling Down Debts.—In all free governments, or governments much subject to popular impulses, a second danger of over-issue arises from the appetite which is engendered in the masses of the people for further emissions for the purpose of scaling down debts, "making trade good," and enabling works of construction and extensive public improvements to be undertaken, for which taxation could not easily provide the means.

The intrusion of the debtor class into the legislature with their impudent demands for issues to scale down debts is a familiar spectacle. Even the sterling virtue of early New England did not save those primitive communities from the fiercest impulses of political dishonesty, when once the paper money passion had been aroused. "Parties," says the historian Douglass, "were no longer Whigs and Tories, but creditors and debtors. Governors were elected and turned out as the different interests happened to prevail."

The same feature appeared early in the history of the French Revolutionary paper money. We have seen it in our own country during the present generation, an active, aggressive, vehement, virulent force, engendered by the desire of paying debts, wiping off scores, raising mortgages, in depreciated money.

Paying debts is always a disagreeable necessity. For one man who would steal to acquire property, in the first instance, a score will do that which is no better than stealing, in order to retain property which has passed into their hands and which they have come to look upon as theirs, though not paid for.

It is the view of not a few sound economists * that a grad-

---

* Thus M. Chevalier says: "Such a change will benefit those who live by current labor: it will injure those who live upon the fruits of past labor, whether their fathers' or their own. In this it will work in the same direction with most of the developments which are brought about by that great law of civilization to which we give the noble name of progress."

And Mr. J. R. McCulloch declares that "though, like a fall of rain after a long course of dry weather, it may be prejudicial to certain classes, it

ually progressive depreciation of metallic money, from age to age, might be advantageous to society as a whole, both relieving industry in some measure from the weight of burdens derived from the past, and giving a certain fillip to industrial enterprise.

But here the injury to the creditor class is not the work of man, but of God; like the death of a miserly bad man which brings his wealth into the hands of a generous, philanthropic, public-spirited heir, at which change of ownership men may properly rejoice. But had the heir procured the death of the miser, the aspect of the case would have been entirely different. No plea of public spirit or benevolence in the disposition of the wealth could compensate society for that deep and damning wrong.

A reduction in the burden of obligations, accomplished by the act of a legislature, in the issue of paper for the purpose of enabling the debtor to pay in a depreciated money, has no virtue in it to promote industry or encourage enterprise. It carries with it the sting of injustice and fraud. It draws after it retributive agencies which curse the people and the age. Having reference exclusively to economic interests, we may confidently say that the man who advocates the scaling down of debts, for the sake of encouraging trade and production, shows himself so ignorant of history as to be a wholly unfit adviser as to the present and the future.

IV.

PAUPERISM.

446. The Impotent vs. the Able-Bodied Poor.—The relief of the impotent poor, whether by private or by public charity, is, so far as political economy is concerned with it, a question relating to the consumption of wealth. It is so much a matter of course, under our modern civilization, that the very young and the very old, the crippled and deformed,

is beneficial to an incomparably greater number, including all who are actively engaged in industrial pursuits, and is, speaking generally, of great public or national advantage."

who are unable to earn their own maintenance, shall not be allowed to starve, that the matter of relief to these classes becomes one of administrative detail, that does not require even to be alluded to in an elementary treatise on economics. The experience of that country from which we derive our law and much of our administrative machinery, is, however, so instructive as to the influence for mischief upon the entire laboring population and upon the future production of wealth, that may be wrought by ill considered provisions for the distribution of alms to the able-bodied poor, as to make it worth while briefly to recite that experience here ; and thereupon to define the limits outside which the consumption of wealth for this purpose becomes prejudicial.

We shall get at our subject most directly by inquiring, why is it that the laborer works at all. Clearly that he may eat. If he may eat without it, he will not work. The neglect or contempt of this very obvious truth by the British Parliament, during the latter part of the eighteenth and the early part of the nineteenth century, brought the working classes of the kingdom almost to the verge of ruin, created a vast body of hopeless and hereditary pauperism, and engendered vices in the industrial system which have been productive of evil down to the present day.

447. Establishment of the English Pauper System.— By statute of the 27th year of Henry VIII., the giving of alms was prohibited, and collections for the impotent poor were required to be made in each parish. By 1st Edward VI., bishops were authorized to proceed at law against persons who should refuse to contribute for this purpose, or should dissuade others from contributing. By 5th Elizabeth, Justices of the Peace were made judges of what constituted a reasonable contribution. By 14th Elizabeth, regular compulsory contributions were exacted. But the act of 43d Elizabeth created the permanent pauper system of England.

The increasing necessity for legal provisions for the poor, during the period covered by this recital, is attributed by judicious writers, first, to the destruction of the abbeys and monasteries, which had, in earlier times, disbursed vast revenues in charity; and, secondly, to the effects of the flood of new silver from the mines of Spanish America, which, by rapidly raising prices and thus reducing the purchasing power of fixed incomes, had caused large numbers to be thrown out of employment.

By the act of 43d Elizabeth, every person in the kingdom was given a legal right to public relief, if required; but voluntary pauperism was severely dealt with, and the able-bodied were compelled to work. At first, the body of inhabitants were to be taxed for the objects of this statute; but subsequent legislation threw the burden entirely upon the landowners, where it remains to this day, with the exception that partial grants are now made out of the Imperial revenues to meet the charges of maintaining certain classes of paupers, such as the insane.

448. Removal of the Workhouse Test.—The principle of requiring the able-bodied poor to work continued for generations to be fundamental in the English pauper system; and for the better enforcement of this requisition parishes or unions of parishes were, by an act of 9th George I., authorized to build workhouses, residence in which might be made a condition of relief. Moreover, from the days of Elizabeth to that of George III., the spirit which actuated the administration of the poor laws was jealous and severe. Doubtless in that administration unnecessary harshness was sometimes practiced; but, on the whole, the effect on the working classes was wholesome, for it was made undesirable to become a pauper.

On the accession of George III., a different theory came to direct legislation relating to poor relief, and a widely different temper of administration began to prevail. Six successive acts, passed in the first years of that reign, intimated the changed spirit in which pauperism was thereafter to be dealt with. In the 22nd year of George III., the act known as Gilbert's act gave a fuller expression to this spirit. By that act the workhouse was no longer to be used as a test of voluntary pauperism: the 29th section provided that "no person shall be sent to such poor-house except such as are become indigent by old age, sickness or infirmities, and are unable to acquire a maintenance by their labor ; except such orphan children as shall be sent thither by order of the guardian or guardians of the poor, with the approbation of the visitor, and except such children as shall necessarily go with their mothers thither for sustenance."

With respect to the rest of the poor, the act by its 32d section provided "That where there shall be in any parish, township or place, any poor person or persons, who shall be able and willing to work but who can not get employment, the guardian of the poor of such parish, etc., on application made to him by or on behalf of such poor person, is required to agree for the labor of such poor person or persons at any work or employment suited to his or her strength and capacity, in any parish or place near the place of his or her residence, and to maintain, or cause such person or persons to be properly maintained, lodged and provided for, until such employment shall be procured, and during the time of such work, and to *receive the money to be earned by such work or labor, and apply it in such maintenance as far as the same will go, and make up the deficiency, if any.*"

By the repeal of the workhouse test, and by the additional most injudicious provision which we have placed in italics, a deadly blow was struck at the manhood and industrial self-sufficiency of the working classes of England.

449. "The act," says Sir George Nicholls, in his History of the English Poor Law, "appears to assume that there can never be a lack of profitable employment, and it makes the guardian of the parish answerable for finding it near the laborer's own residence, where, if it existed at all, the laborer might surely, by due diligence, find it himself. But why, it may be asked, should he use such diligence when the guardian is bound to find it for him, and take the whole responsibility of bargaining for wages and making up to him all deficiency? He is certain of employment. He is certain of receiving, either from the parish or his employer, sufficient for the maintenance of himself and his family ; and if he earns a surplus, he is certain of its being paid over to him. There may be uncertainty with others, and in other occupations. The farmer, the lawyer, the merchant, the manufacturer, however industrious and observant, may labor under uncertainties in their several callings; not so the laborer. He bears, as it were, a charmed life in this respect, and is made secure, and that, too, without the exercise of care or forethought. Could a more certain way be devised for lowering character, destroying self-reliance, and discouraging, if not absolutely preventing, improvement?"

450. The Logical Outcome.—By 1832 the false and vicious principle on which Gilbert's act was based had been carried logically out to its limits in almost universal pauperism. The condition of the person who threw himself flat upon public charity was better than that of the laborer who struggled on to preserve his manhood in self-support. The commissioners appointed in that year to investigate the workings of the poor law, found that, where the independent laborer was able to earn by his week's work but 122 ounces of solid food, the pauper had 151 ounces given him in idleness. The former had only to abandon his effort to provide for himself, to be better provided for than was possible through his own exertions. The drone was better clothed, better lodged and better fed than the worker.

All the incidents of this bad system were unnecessarily bad. The allowance for each additional child was so much out of proportion to the allowance for adults, that the more numerous a man's children the better his condition, and thus the rapid increase of an already pauperized population was encouraged. Moreover, the allowance in the case of illegitimate children was even greater than for those born in wedlock. The British Parliament had turned itself into a society for the promotion of vice. "The English law," said Commissioner Cowell, in his report, "has abolished female chastity." "In many rural districts," writes Miss Martineau in her History of the Peace, "it was scarcely possible to meet a young woman who was respectable, so tempting was the parish allowance for infants in a time of great pressure." "It may safely be affirmed," said the Poor Law Commissioners of 1831, "that the virtue of female chastity does not exist among the lower orders of England, except to a certain degree among domestic servants, who know that they hold their situations by that tenure and are more prudent in consequence."

SUCH MAY BE THE EFFECTS OF FOOLISH LAWS. THE LEGISLATOR MAY THINK IT HARD THAT HIS POWER FOR GOOD IS SO CLOSELY RESTRICTED ; BUT HE HAS NO REASON TO COMPLAIN OF ANY LIMITS UPON HIS POWER FOR EVIL. ON THE CONTRARY, IT WOULD SEEM THAT THERE IS NO RACE OF MEN, WHOM A FEW LAWS RESPECTING INDUSTRY, TRADE AND FINANCE, PASSED BY COUNTRY SQUIRES OR LABOR DEMAGOGUES, IN DEFIANCE OF ECONOMIC PRINCIPLES, COULD NOT IN HALF A GENERATION TRANSFORM INTO BEASTS.

451. Poor Law Reform.—We have seen what a system the English squirearchy substituted for the economic law that he that would eat must work. The natural effects of this system were wrought speedily and effectually. The disposition to labor was cut up by the roots ; all restraints upon increase of population disappeared under a premium upon births ; self-respect and social decency vanished before a money-premium on bastardy. The amount expended in the relief and maintenance of the poor rose to enormous and even ruinous sums. In some instances landowners relinquished their estates in order to escape the monstrous rates levied upon them, in support of local paupers.

In this exigency, which, in truth, constituted one of the gravest crises of English history, Parliament, by the Poor Law Amendment Act (4th and 5th, William IV.) returned to the principle of the act of Elizabeth. The workhouse test was restored ; allowances in aid of wages were abolished ; paid overseers were appointed, and a central system was created for the due supervision of the system. Illegitimacy was discouraged by punishing the father, instead of rewarding the mother ; and the law of pauper settlement* was modified so as to facilitate the migration of laborers in search of employment.

---

* The law of parochial settlement was enacted in the reign of Charles II. While other restrictions upon the movements of population gradually gave way, during the two centuries following, before the expansion of industrial enterprise and the liberalizing tendencies of modern

By this great legislative reform the burden of pauperism, in spite of the continuing effects of the old evil system, was reduced in three years, by an average amount, the kingdom over, of forty-five per cent.

452. The Principle that Should Govern Poor Relief.—The moral of this episode in the industrial history of England is easily drawn. It is of the highest consequence that pauperism shall not be made inviting; that, on the contrary, the laborer shall be stimulated to the utmost possible exertions to achieve self-support, only accepting relief as an alternative to actual starvation. It is not, to this end, necessary that any brutality of administration shall deter the worthy poor who have no other recourse; but, it should be the prime object of legislation to make the situation of the pauper less agreeable than that of the independent laborer, and that, by no small interval. The workhouse test for all the able-bodied poor, and genuine hard work, up to the limit of strength, are imperatively demanded by the interests of productive labor. Wherever there is a possible choice between self-support and public support, the inclination to labor for one's own subsistence should be quickened by something of a penalty upon the pauper condition, though not in the way of cruelty or positive privation. "All," says Mr. Geo. W. Hastings, "who have administered the Poor Law must know the fatal readiness with which those hovering on the brink of pauperism believe that they can not earn a living, and the marvelous way in which, if the test be firmly applied, the means of subsistence will be found somehow."

---

thought, the mischievous tendencies of the Law of Settlement were given a wider scope and an increased severity, from reign to reign. Migration within the Kingdom was practically prohibited. If the laborer, in search of employment crossed the boundaries of that one of the fifteen thousand parishes of England in which he belonged, he was liable to be apprehended and returned to the place of his settlement. Parish officers were perpetually incited by the fears of the rate-payers to the utmost zeal in hunting down and running out all possible claimants for public charity, on whom, if unmolested, residence would confer a right to support. "Where," says Prof. Rogers, "an employer wished to engage a servant

V.

THE DOCTRINE OF THE WAGE-FUND.

453. The Doctrine Stated.—In opening the subject of Wages, I passed by without discussion the once generally received doctrine—generally received, that is, in England and America—of a fund set apart for the payment of wages, and proceeded at once to state affirmatively the views I hold regarding the laborer's share in the product of industry.

Inasmuch, however, as the student will find this doctrine explicitly taught in the great majority of all the systematic treatises on the shelves of our libraries, it seems important that it should be dealt with critically.

The doctrine of a Wage-Fund is, in substance, as follows: There is, in any country, at any time, an amount of wealth set apart by economic forces for the payment of wages. The ratio between the aggregate capital and the portion thus devoted to the payment of wages, is not necessarily the same in different countries at the same time, or in the same country at different times. That ratio may vary with the conditions of industry and the habits of the people; but at any given time, the amount of the wage-fund, under the conditions existing, is determined in the amount of capital.* Were the amount of that capital greater, the wage-fund would be greater, and greater in precisely the same proportion. Were the amount of that capital smaller, the wage-fund would be smaller, and smaller in precisely the same proportion.

---

from a foreign parish, he was not permitted to do so unless he entered into a recognizance, often to a considerable amount, to the effect that the new-comer should not obtain a settlement, else the bond to be good against the employer. Parochial registers are full of such acknowledgments."

* "There is supposed to be, at any given instant, a sum of wealth which is unconditionally devoted to the payment of wages of labor. This sum is not regarded as unalterable, for it is augmented by saving and increases with the progress of wealth; but it is reasoned upon as, at any given moment, a predetermined amount."—*J. S. Mill: The Fortnightly. May*, 1869.

The wage-fund, therefore, may be greater or less at another time ; but at the time taken, it is definite. The amount of it can not be increased by force of law, or of public opinion, or through sympathy and compassion on the part of employers, or as the result of appeals or efforts on the part of the working classes.*

The sum so destined to the payment of wages is distributed by competition. If one obtains more, another must, for that reason, receive less, or be kept out of employment. Laborers are paid out of this sum, and out of this alone. The whole of it is distributed without loss, and the average amount received by each laborer is, therefore, determined precisely by the ratio existing between the wage-fund and the number of laborers, or, as some writers have preferred to call it, between capital and population.†

The wage-fund, at any given time, being thus determined, the rate of wages will be according to the number of persons then applying for employment.‡ If these be more, wages will be low ; if these be fewer, wages will be high.

It thus appears that the wage-fund—the aggregate amount

---

* "That which pays for labor in every country is a certain portion of actually accumulated capital, which can not be increased by the proposed action of government, nor by the influence of public opinion, nor by combinations among the workmen themselves. There is, also, in every country, a certain number of laborers, and this number can not be diminished by the proposed action of government, nor by public opinion, nor by combinations among themselves. There is to be a division now, among all these laborers, of the portion of capital actually there present." —*Prof. A. L. Perry, Pol. Econ.* In the later editions of his treatise, Prof. Perry modifies his statement.

† "The circulating capital of a country is its wage-fund. Hence, if we desire to calculate the average money wages received by each laborer, we have simply to divide the amount of this capital by the number of the laboring population."—*Prof. H. Fawcett: The Economic Position of the British Laborer.*

‡ "More than that amount (the wage-fund), it is assumed, the wages-receiving class can not possibly divide among them ; that amount, and no less, they can not but obtain: so that, the sum to be divided being fixed, the wages of each depend solely on the divisor, the number of participants.—*J. S. Mill: The Fortnightly. May*, 1869.

to be distributed as wages—is, at any given time, irrespective alike of the number and of the industrial quality of the wages class. The average rate of wages is determined exclusively by a comparison of the amount of that fund with the number of that class. The industrial quality of the laborers has nothing to do, at the time, with their wages.

454. The Doctrine Examined.—What shall we say of this doctrine of a Wage-Fund? Several objections may be urged against it, any one of which would be fatal.

First. The doctrine assumes that wages are always and necessarily paid out of capital, the results of past accumulation. As a matter of fact, wages in England, where this theory of wages originated, were, at one time, early in the century, paid, financially speaking, out of capital generally, if not universally. That condition of things has continued to the present time.

Why was this? Was it of the essence of the matter, or an accident?

I answer, wages were advanced by capital in England, because capital had there been accumulated to so great extent that employers were able to lay down the whole of the wages to be paid as soon as the service was rendered, even before the products were harvested or marketed, while, at the same time, wages were and had been so low that the laborers had been able to save little or nothing out of their earnings in the past, and were consequently obliged to look to their employers for subsistence, almost from the moment they began to work.

But during the same period a very different relation between laborer and employer, as regarded the payment of wages, existed in the United States. Employers were paying their laborers by the year, giving them their wages, in full, only when the crops were harvested or the goods marketed, making meanwhile such advances as their means allowed, or as were required by the varying wants of their workmen, no small part of whom had saved enough out of the liberal earnings of former years to support themselves and their families until the year's wages should be paid.

In other words, the *industrial* conditions were more favorable to the payment of wages in the United States, while in England the *financial* conditions were more favorable. But it is the industrial conditions which determine the amount of wages, the necessaries, comforts and luxuries which the laborer receives for his services. The financial conditions only determine the manner and time of payment, whether at once or on a future day, whether in money or in goods.

455. Wages may be advanced out of Capital, but are paid out of the Product.—But even if, in fact, all wages were laid down by the employer as soon as services were rendered, before the crops were harvested or the goods marketed, it would not follow that the existence of capital furnished the reason for the employment of labor, or that the amount of that capital furnished the measure of the wages to be paid.

An employer pays wages to purchase labor, not to expend a fund of which he may be in possession. He purchases labor, not because he wishes to keep it employed, but as a means to the production of wealth. He produces wealth, not for the sake of producing it, but with a view to a profit to himself, individually, in that production.

If a person have wealth, that, of itself, constitutes no reason why he should expend any portion of it on labor, on machinery, or on materials. It is only as he sees that he can increase that wealth through production, that the impulse to employ it in those directions is felt. But for the profits by which he hopes thus to increase his store, it would be alike easier and safer for him to keep his wealth at rest than to put it in motion for the benefit of others. The mere fact that the employer has capital at his command, no more constitutes a reason why he should use it in production, when he can get no profits, than the fact that the laborer has arms and legs constitutes a reason why he should work when he can get no wages.

We repeat: the employer purchases labor with a view to the product of labor. The kind and amount of that product determine what wages he can afford to pay. He must, in the long run, pay less than that product, less by a sum which is to constitute his own profits. If the product is to be greater, he can afford to pay more ; if it is to be smaller, he must, for his own interest, pay less.

It is, then, for the sake of future production that the laborers are employed, not at all because the employer has possession of a fund which he must disburse. IT IS THE VALUE OF THE PRODUCT, SUCH AS IT IS LIKELY TO PROVE, WHICH DETERMINES THE AMOUNT OF THE WAGES THAT CAN BE PAID. Thus, it is production, not capital, which furnishes the motive for employment and the measure of wages.

In saying that production furnishes the measure of wages, it is, of course, not to be understood that wages equal the product of industry. The advocate of the wage-fund asserts that capital furnishes the measure of wages, meaning that the amount to be paid in wages is some part of the aggregate capital of the country, the ratio between the two varying from time to time, indeed, but being, for any given moment, fixed by the existing conditions of industry. So I say, production furnishes the measure of wages, meaning that the amount to be paid in wages is some part of the product of industry, the ratio between the two varying, probably, from time to time, from causes innumerable, but being, for any given moment, fixed by existing conditions.

456. No Wage-Fund Irrespective of the Industrial Quality of the Laborers.—But if production furnishes the measure of wages, the amount so to be paid can not be irrespective of the industrial quality of the laboring class. If we assume that upon a cultivated island are tools and carts and animals for draught, and other forms of capital adequate for a thousand laborers, the production will vary within a very wide range according to the industrial quality of the laborers using that capital. If we suppose them to be East Indians, we shall have a certain annual product ; if we suppose Russian peasants to be substituted for East Indians, we shall have twice or three times that product ; if we suppose Englishmen to be substituted for Russians, we shall have the product again multiplied two or three fold. An Englishman will do from three to thirty times as much work in a day as a

Bengalee, according as the nature of the work makes smaller or larger demands upon the skill and strength of the laborer. By the wage-fund theory, the rate of wages would remain the same through these changes, inasmuch as the aggregate capital of the Island and the number of laborers in the market would be unchanged, the only difference being found in the substitution of more efficient for less efficient laborers. According to the view here advanced, on the contrary, the amount to be paid in wages should and would rise with the increased production due to the higher industrial quality of the laboring population. Whether it would rise in exact proportion thereto is not the question we are now considering.

457. No Wage-Fund Irrespective of the Number of Laborers.—But, further, if production furnishes the measure of wages, the amount to be so paid cannot be irrespective of the numbers of the laboring class.

By the wage-fund theory, the amount that can and will be paid in wages is a predetermined dividend, the number of laborers being the divisor, and the average wages the quotient. Just in proportion as the number of laborers is diminished will the average wages be raised; just in proportion as the number of laborers is increased, will the average wages be lowered. "There is no use," writes one of the expositors of this doctrine, "in arguing against any one of the four fundamental rules of arithmetic. The question of wages is a question of division. It is complained that the quotient is too small. Well, then, how many ways are there to make a quotient larger? Two ways. Enlarge your dividend, the divisor remaining the same, and the quotient will be larger; lessen your divisor, the dividend remaining the same, and the quotient will be larger."

This theory, that the number of laborers constitutes the divisor of a predetermined dividend, is manifestly erroneous, because it leaves out of account the influence upon production of the condition of Diminishing Returns, or the reverse, in agriculture, as well as the mechanical effects of the division of labor.

Let us, first, suppose that the island occupied by the body

of one thousand laborers before referred to, contains a great breadth of choice arable land, of which the laborers have been hitherto able to cultivate but a small portion. If, now, the number of laborers be increased twenty per cent. with a corresponding increase of capital, production will be more than proportionally increased (see par. 50), through the effect of the division of labor and the union of forces in production. Here, again, we find the wage-fund theory at fault. So great is the virtue of this cause that an increase of laborers—before the condition of diminishing returns is reached—might be followed by an increase of production even in the lack of a proportional increase of capital, or indeed, of any increase at all.

458. But now let us take the condition of diminishing returns in agriculture, that state where, if anywhere, it might be supposed the wage-fund theory would hold good. In such a condition, the soil, as we have seen (par. 51), fails to respond adequately to new applications of labor; the product falls off, not absolutely, but relatively; and, thus, while the aggregate crops are larger through the incoming of new laborers, the actual amount falling to each laborer is diminished. Wages fall. But does this happen in accordance with the economic doctrine we are considering? No; *per capita* wages fall, because *per capita* production is diminished, although often this is coincident with an actual increase of capital.

It would be brutal to inflict further blows upon a body so exanimate as the theory of the Wage-Fund. The natural and the literary history of this doctrine will be found at length in an article in the *North American Review*, for January, 1875.

VI.

THE MULTIPLE OR TABULAR STANDARD OF DEFERRED PAYMENTS.

459. We saw (par. 191) that, with a view to avoiding the fluctuations to which even the precious metals are subject, through long periods of time, it has been proposed by writers

of eminence to create a multiple or tabular standard of value. This is to be done by joining together a number of articles, of importance in the economy of daily life, in such a way that the fluctuations of value in the several constituent articles shall largely neutralize each other.

460. The details of the scheme as proposed by these writers may be stated as follows. A number of articles in general use, corn, beef, potatoes, wool, cotton, silk, tea, sugar, coffee, indigo, timber, iron, coal, and others, shall be taken, in a definite quantity of each, so many pounds or bushels or cords or yards, to form the standard required. The value of these articles, in the quantities specified and all of standard quality, shall be ascertained monthly or weekly by government, and the total sum which would at the time purchase this bill of goods shall be, thereupon, officially promulgated. Persons may then, if they choose, make their contracts for future payments in terms of this multiple or tabular standard.

For example, suppose I sell a house to-day, the value of which, as agreed upon between myself and the purchaser, is $20,000, one-half to be paid down at the time, two-tenths to be paid in two years, three-tenths in five years, with interest on the last two sums. One-half of the purchase money, being payable at once, is paid in money, $10,000 in gold or bank notes. For the rest, the purchaser and I look at the last published statement of the government commissioner, and find the value of a unit of the tabular standard to be $12.50; that is, $12.50 will now purchase the bill of goods which form the standard. The purchaser then gives me two notes, one for 320 units of the tabular standard, payable in two years, and one for 480 units, payable in five years, with interest at six per cent., per annum, meanwhile. At the end of the first year, the two parties interested look in the official gazette, and find the value of the unit at the time to be $12.75. There is then to be paid one year's interest on each note, amounting, in the case of the first note, to 19.2 units, which obligation is discharged by the payment of $244.80 in current money; and, in the case of the second note, to 28.8 units, which obligation is discharged by the payment of $367.20.

At the end of the second year the value of a unit of the tabular standard might be ascertained to be $13, or $12.25 ; in the latter case the interest on the first note is discharged by the payment of $235.20, and that on the second note by the payment of $352.80. If, however, the value of a unit has been ascertained to be $13, the interest on the first note will be $249.60, and that on the second note $374.40.

But the principal of the first note, 320 units, is now to be paid. A similar computation shows that, if the value of the tabular standard is $12.25, the maker of the note must pay $3,920 to discharge his obligation ; if the value of the unit be $13, he must pay $4,160.

461. What has been Effected?—Now, without waiting for the maturity of the second note, let us see what the use of the tabular standard has thus far effected. When I sold my house, two years before, I gave the purchaser two years' credit for two-tenths of the price. Had I taken the money at the time, it would have bought me so many pounds of beef, so many bushels of corn, so much iron, coal, etc. Now, at the end of the second year, what I receive as the stipulated two-tenths payment for the house will bring me precisely the same amount of beef, corn, iron, coal, etc. Meanwhile the debtor has paid me, every year, as interest, enough to enable me to purchase six parts in a hundred of this entire list of commodities. The purchaser has had the advantage of obtaining credit, to that extent, but has derived no unearned benefit from the delay of payment ; and, on the other hand, has been protected from any loss through that source.

462. It is to be observed regarding the proposed tabular standard, first, that it is not obligatory upon any one to use it. Persons buying and selling still make their contracts in terms of money if they please. The government merely affords them the opportunity to make their contracts payable in units of the tabular standard, if it be worth their while to do so. Secondly, the only machinery required for the operation of this system would be a commission to ascertain the current prices of the articles on the official list and to publish the same. No new method of accounting would be introduced. Interest and principal could be computed as easily as under the present system. The courts would enforce the obligation of contracts on precisely the same principles when expressed in units of the tabular standard, as when expressed in dollars or pounds sterling. Thirdly, no new medium of exchange would be introduced. The creditor would not be obliged to receive, at the maturity of the note, so many cart-loads of vegetable, animal and mineral products, to be hawked about for sale. The payment, at the maturity of the obligation, would be made in money. The only effect of the introduction of the tabular standard would be to decide how much money at that date constituted the equivalent, in the power to purchase the necessaries, comforts and luxuries of life, of the money which would have been paid had the sale been for cash. In short, it is a means of giving and taking credit without receiving an unearned advantage or suffering an undeserved injury through fluctuations in the value of money.

463. Is it Practicable?—Such being the contemplated advantages of the system of a tabular or multiple standard, the question whether the use made of the system, if established, would be worth the small degree of effort necessary to establish it, is a question which could only be answered after trial. The mere fact that the scheme is sound and the advantages of its adoption unquestionable, would not of itself be sufficient to secure any considerable application of this standard to the actual operations of trade. It took hundreds of years for the Arabic figures to drive the abominably clumsy Roman figures out of the counting rooms of great merchants and bankers. The slow progress of the metric system, even in this age of innovations and of quick communication, affords a measure of the difficulty of supplanting one habit of trade by another, however much superior.

The practical limits of this system, were it to be once introduced and tried, are fairly a matter of doubt. Prof. Jevons deemed it practicable to extend this mode of determining the claim of the creditor, the obligation of the debtor, to ordinary commercial paper having three months or more to run.

I do not myself apprehend that the system would trench, in any considerable degree, on the field of so-called commerce. The merchant, buying every day and selling every day, giving notes with one hand and taking them with the other, may fairly look to see his losses, through fluctuations in the purchase power of money, offset by his gains through the same source; or, in a worse result, he is in a position, by greater energy and economy, to make good his capital. It is essential, or at least highly important to the conduct of business, in the modern organization of industrial society, that the merchant or manufacturer shall be able to tell just where he stands, at any time; to strike an exact balance between assets and liabilities. But this would not be possible with the tabular standard. A note for 400 units, payable in September, might not offset a note for 400 units receivable in August or October. The difference might be small; it might also be large. It would thus be impracticable for the man of business to cast up, at a moment, the results of any given transaction, or ascertain precisely his own standing. By the very description of the system, every note given or taken would have to be liquidated.

Commerce will not tolerate any such obstruction; and the scheme, so far as this application is concerned, may be dismissed at once. Commerce will do the best it can with the use of money and of credit expressed in terms of money. Nothing is more characteristic of the commercial spirit than the disposition to take the evil with the good, roughly to strike the average of gain and loss, promptly to charge-off bad debts, always looking on towards the future, never regretting the past. This spirit leads, doubtless, into many errors, but it is the very life of commerce.

464. For what classes of contracts, then, might the multiple tender be advantageously employed?

Certainly the need of such a standard of deferred payments is most imperative in the case of those who are not in the way of repairing any losses they may suffer through fluctuations in the value of money; upon whom the full effects of depreciation fall directly and remain without relief. And while the advantages of such safeguards upon the value of debts here rise to their maximum, the obstruction sinks here to a minimum. In permanent investments of property not the least inconvenience will be encountered by the scheme of a multiple tender, which might be extended to the cases of all who have definitively retired from active life, carrying away with them all they will ever have to support old age and provide for their children; to the cases of trustees and guardians, under a solemn responsibility in the care of estates, where loss is more to be dreaded than gain to be desired; to the cases of institutions whose funds are sequestered from the stock of active capital, for pious and charitable uses. The funds of savings banks might be put under the same safeguard, and government loans might also be issued in terms of the multiple tender.

VII.

TRADE UNIONS AND STRIKES.

465. Wholly a Practical Question.—It has been shown (pars. 348–56) under the title of Distribution, that the question, whether any law or institution does or does not promote the freedom of industrial movement enjoyed by the community, is a question not to be decided *à priori*. Consideration must be had of the actual effects of such a law or institution, comparison being made not between the state which will result therefrom and an ideal state of perfect economic mobility, but between the new condition and the condition which does exist or probably would exist without that law or institution.

Let us take the case of Trade Unions, so called, which undertake, through agreements among themselves and perhaps simultaneous strikes against their employers, to fix wages, regulate the hours of labor, and control many of the various details of industry. To the first suggestions of such associations, the economist promptly and properly objects that all combinations in the sphere of economics are opposed to competition. The objection is well taken, and it remains for the advocate of trade unions to show sufficient cause for thus obstructing competition.

The economist further alleges that such associations are liable, are even likely, to fall under the control of demagogues, who will use their power to bully or harass employers, to make unreasonable demands, and to precipitate labor contests, in which the interests of all classes will be sacrificed to the self importance of a few managers. This point, again, is well taken. That liability, that likelihood, exists, and the advocate of trade unions is bound to show no small degree of practical benefit resulting from such associations, to offset the mischief they are almost certain to commit in the ways indicated.

466. On the other hand, the advocate of trade unions alleges that these associations, though in form opposed to competition, and though subject to many abuses, do yet, in certain states of industrial society, assist the laborers as a class to assert their interests in the distribution of the product of industry. This claim is not, on the face of it, unreasonable.

We have seen (pars. 343–5) that competition, perfect competition, affords the ideal condition for the distribution of wealth. But as we saw in the case of the audience in a theater that had taken fire, the action of men in concert and under discipline, while it can never be wiser than that of men acting coolly and intelligently for themselves, may be far wiser than the action of men stricken with panic and hurried into a senseless, furious rush. Respecting trade unions, the question is not, whether joint action is superior to the individual action of persons enlightened as to their industrial interests, but whether joint action may not be better than the tumultuous action of a mass, each pursuing his individual interest with more or less of ignorance, fear and passion.

Now, with a body of employers, few, rich and powerful, having a friendly understanding among themselves and acting aggressively for the reduction of wages or the extension of the hours of work, and, on the other side, a body of laborers, numerous, ignorant, poor, mutually distrustful, while each feels under a terrible necessity to secure employment, who shall say that such a body of laborers might not be better able to resist the destructive pressure from the employing body, if organized and disciplined, with a common purse and with mutual obligations enforced by the public opinion of their class?

I said, destructive pressure, for we saw that the pressure of competition, if it be unequal, may lead to the degradation of the laboring class (pars. 345–7), just as the waves over which and through which a ship rides unharmed, when herself free to move, become crushing and destructive, let once the ship's bow be jammed between rocks or lodged in the sands.

467. II. Strikes.—The question of the economic influence of strikes is a distinct question. There have been trades unions which seldom or never resorted to strikes. Some of the greatest strikes have occurred without the agency of organized trade unions. For myself I entertain no doubt that the early strikes in England, which followed the repeal, in 1824, of the Combination acts, were essential to the breaking up of the power of custom and fear over the minds of the working classes of the Kingdom. For centuries it had been a crime, by statute, for workmen to combine to raise wages or shorten the hours of labor, while masters were left perfectly free to combine to lower wages or lengthen the hours of labor. The beginning of the century found the laboring classes of England almost destitute of political franchises, unaccustomed to discussion and the free communication of thought, tax-ridden, poverty-stricken, illiterate. What else than the series of fierce revolts, the rebellions of down-trodden labor, which followed Huskisson's act of 1824, could, in an equal period of time, or, indeed, at smaller cost, have taught the employers of England to respect their laborers, and have taught the laborers of England to respect themselves; could have made the latter equally confident and self-reliant in pressing home a just demand, or made the former equally solicitous to refuse no demand that could reasonably be conceded?

For, be it remarked, perfect competition, which affords the only absolute security possible for equitable and beneficial distribution, requires that each and every man for himself shall unremittingly seek and unfailingly find his best market. If for any reason, whether from physical obstruction or legal inhibition, or from his own poverty or weakness of will or ignorance, or through distrust of his fellows or a habit of submission to his employer or his social superiors, any man fails, in fact, to reject the lower price and to seize the higher price, the rule of competition is violated; all immunity from deep and permanent economic injury is lost; the man may be crushed in his spirit, in his health, in his habits of life, and may thus sink finally and hopelessly to a lower industrial grade. The history of mankind is full of examples of large populations broken down by a competition to which they were unequal, until they have become pauperized, brutalized and diseased beyond the power of any purely economic causes to raise them upwards and restore them to industrial manhood.

468. Strikes are the Insurrections of Labor.—In claiming that strikes may, in certain states of industrial society, in their ultimate effect really aid the laboring classes, let me not be misunderstood. To strikes I assign the same function in industry which insurrections have performed in the sphere of politics. Had it not been for the constant imminence of insurrection, England would not through several centuries have made any progress towards freedom, or even have maintained its inherited liberties.

Strikes are the insurrections of labor. They are, wholly, a destructive agency. They have no creative power, no healing virtue. Yet, as insurrections have played a most important part in the political elevation of downtrodden people, through the fear they have engendered in the minds of oppressors, or through the demolition of out-worn institutions which have become first senseless and then pernicious, so strikes may exert a most powerful and salutary influence in breaking up a crust of custom which has formed over the remuneration of a body of laborers, or in breaking through combinations of employers * to withstand a legitimate advance of wages.

* "Masters are always and everywhere in a sort of tacit, but constant and uniform, combination not to raise the wages of labor above their actual rate."—*Adam Smith.*

Doubtless even more important than the specific objects realized by strikes, has been the permanent impression produced upon the minds and the temper of both employers and employed. The men have acquired confidence in themselves and trust in each other ; the masters have been taught respect for their men, and a reasonable fear of them.

Nothing quickens the sense of justice and equity like the consciousness that unjust and inequitable demands or acts are likely to be promptly resented and strenuously resisted. Nothing is so potent to clarify the judgment and sober the temper, in questions of right or wrong, as to know that a mistake will lead to a hard and a long fight.

469. What is the Failure of a Strike?—Nor must it be thought that because strikes often, perhaps we might say commonly, fail of their immediate object, they are, therefore, nugatory. Many an insurrection has been put down speedily, perhaps with great slaughter, which has been followed by remission of taxes, by redress of grievances, by extension of charters and franchises. It may be considered doubtful whether the successful or the unsuccessful insurrections of England have done more to advance English liberties. Of the rising of the peasantry against Richard II., which was suppressed in a few days, Prof. Thorold Rogers says : "The rebellion was put down, but the demands of the villains* were silently and effectually accorded. As they were masters for a week of the position, the dread of another servile war promoted the liberty of the serf." Even an unsuccessful strike may make employers more moderate, considerate and conciliatory, as they recall the anxieties, the struggles and the sacrifices of the conflict.

470. Better than Strikes.—Yet, as insurrections mark off the first stages of the movement towards political freedom, so strikes belong to the first stages of the elevation of masses of labor, long abused and deeply debased. Happy is that people, and proud may they be, who can enlarge their franchises and perfect their political forms without bloodshed or the

---

* Persons holding land by a servile tenure.

threat of violence, the long debate of reason resulting in the glad consent of all. In like manner, no body of laborers can get for themselves by extreme measures so much of honor and of profit as they will when, through cultivating moderation, good temper and the spirit of equity. they attain the capability of conducting their probably unavoidable disputes with the employing class to a successful conclusion without recourse to the brutal and destructive agency of strikes. With political rights such as are enjoyed by all classes in the United States, with universal education, free land, the quick communication of ideas, the cheap transportation of persons and effects, the abundant opportunities offered for accumulating and investing savings, it is a shame to us, as a people, that we have not yet made for ourselves a better way out of our industrial disputes.

471. III. Factory Acts.—We should apply the same tests to any existing or projected legislation intended for the relief of the laboring classes, such as acts restricting the hours of labor, providing for the safety of operatives against accidents from machinery, directing the sanitary inspection of workshops and factories, prohibiting the employment of children of tender age or of women underground, or in work unsuited to their sex, or immediately before or after confinement. The one question in regard to each such measure is not whether its intention is philanthropic or otherwise ; not even whether it does or does not, in form, violate the principle of competition ; but whether it does, in effect,* and in the large, the long, result, leave the laboring classes better off or worse off, as to the ability and disposition to seek and to find their best market ; whether, in fact, in the condition of industrial society then and there existing, it promotes or retards competition.

The beginning of the present century found children of

---

* "In discussing these matters, we need, above all things, discrimination. One hundred modes of government interference might be mentioned of which fifty might be very desirable and fifty condemnable. In each case, as I contend, we must look to the peculiar aim, purpose, means and circumstances of the case."—*Prof. Jevons: The State in Relation to Labor.*

five, and even of three years of age, in England, working in factories and brick-yards; women working underground in mines, harnessed with mules to carts, drawing heavy loads; found the hours of labor whatever the avarice of individual mill-owners might exact, were it thirteen, or fourteen or fifteen; found no guards about machinery to protect life and limb; found the air of the factory fouler than language could describe, even could human ears bear to hear the story.

472. English Factory Legislation.—The factory legislation of England, the necessity and economic justification of which the Duke of Argyll has called (par. 248) one of the great discoveries of the century in the science of government, began in 1802, with an act which limited the hours of labor in woolen and cotton mills to twelve, exclusive of meal times, imposed many sanitary regulations upon the working and sleeping rooms of operatives, required the instruction of children during the first four years of apprenticeship, and provided an official inspection of establishments for the due execution of the law. Further legislation was had in 1816 and 1831; while in 1833 was passed the important act known as 3d and 4th William IV. (ch. 103), which forbade night work in the case of all persons under eighteen years, and limited the labor of such persons to twelve hours, inclusive of an hour and a half for meals; prohibited the employment of children under nine years of age—while, between the ages of nine and thirteen, the hours of labor were reduced to eight; prescribed a certain number of half-holidays, and required medical certificates of health on the admission of children to factories. Numerous acts have enlarged the scope of these provisions and extended them to other classes of workshops and factories; while, with the good faith and thoroughness characteristic of English administration of law, a rigid and relentless inspection compels a punctilious compliance with these provisions in every workshop and factory of the kingdom. The principle of the English Factory acts has been slowly extended over the greater part of Europe.

473. Economists Oppose Factory Legislation.—Unfortunately for political economy, its professors in the Universities, in Parliament, and in the press, generally ranged themselves in opposition to this legislation. Acting upon a series of arbitrary assumptions which fell far short of the facts of human nature, the English economists insisted upon attributing to the individual initiative of the laborer, however miserable and blind and weak, however overborne by circumstances and bound to his place and work by poverty, ignorance and inertia, all that economic virtue which belongs to the individual initiative of the laborer when fully alive to his own interest, alert in seeking the highest price for his services or commodities, and able to move freely to his best market without hindrance from any source, whether within or without himself. They asserted that labor was fully competent to protect itself against abuses, if left free by law. They asserted that all restrictions upon industry are obstructive, failing to see that while restriction and regulation are obstructive as against an imagined condition of perfect practical freedom, these may actually increase the ease and readiness of movement in a state where obstructions exist on every hand. They argued that to limit the power of the operative to sell his labor must, in the end, diminish the price he will get for it, not seeing that, just as a crutch, while it is only a hindrance and a burden to a sound man, may keep a cripple from falling to the ground, and may even enable him slowly and feebly to walk, so a restriction upon contracts for labor may correspond to an infirmity of the laboring classes under certain moral and physical conditions, in such a way as to give them a greater freedom of movement than they would have without it.

I said that it was unfortunate for political economy that the professional economists of England opposed the factory acts. This had the effect to set both men of affairs and the masses of the people against political economy. The latter were alienated by what they deemed either indifference to human suffering or subserviency to the interests of capital. The former saw how far wrong the pursuit of this so-called science could carry intelligent men, on a practical question. To them this seemed to justify the contempt so generally entertained by men of affairs for "theorists." The cause of the trouble was not that the economists were theorists, but that they were bad theorists. Their theories did not cover the facts of the case they had undertaken to deal with. The economic men* they had created for the purposes of their reasoning were no more like Englishmen than were the Houyhnhnms of Jonathan Swift.

That legislation prohibiting factory labor in excess of what is compatible with health and strength, having due respect to conditions of age and sex, requiring the observance of sanitary principles, and protecting working people against abuses as to the time and form of paying wages* may be practically beneficial in a high degree, has long passed beyond controversy among the statesmen of nearly all civilized countries. If political economy objects to such legislation, so much the worse, as I said before, for political economy. But I hope there has been shown sufficient reason for holding that no such opposition of principle exists; and that both the largest production and the most equitable distribution of wealth may be subserved by legal regulations wisely conceived to meet the grave and perhaps incurable infirmities of manufacturing populations.

---

* See par. 21.

† A long series of parliamentary battles have been fought over the question of Truck, that is, the payment of wages in commodities instead of the money of the realm. By the act of 1833, this practice (except in the form of giving "board" as a part of wages) was prohibited in respect to mining and manufacturing industry generally.

VIII.

THE KNIGHTS OF LABOR.

474. Their Relations to Trade Unions.—The public mind of England and, though in a less degree, of America, has become accustomed to the idea of the organization of bodies of laborers, for mutual support and for the promotion of their common interests. Beginning fifty or sixty years ago, the modern trade union has worked its way, against a deep prejudice on the part of employers and of economists, alike, to very general acceptance. I believe it to be true that the best publicists and the most judicious men of business in England concede that the trade unions of the kingdom, whatever errors may have been committed in the course of their development, now fully justify themselves by their acts. In the United States, I have, within the past year or two, been assured by three prominent railroad presidents that they would greatly prefer dealing with the locomotive engineers as members of their brotherhood, to dealing with them individually; and that they believed the influence of this organization to be, over the whole country, good. Generally speaking, however, employers among us are less fully reconciled to the existence and activity of trade unions than are employers in England, probably because trade unions, with us, are in a stage which in England was passed almost a generation ago; perhaps, also, because such associations are less needed here than there.

Within the past three or four years, a new development in the organization of the laboring class has taken place in the United States, in the form of a general confederation of trade unions, re-enforced by large numbers of persons not attached to any union, under the title, Knights of Labor. The essential object of the new confederation is to bring to bear upon employers, either in strikes or during those discussions, regarding hours of work, rates of wages, etc., which might be expected to result in strikes, a pressure more severe, more unremitting, more far-reaching, than any isolated body of laborers or even the most formidable trade unions could hope to produce and maintain. By drawing the whole laboring class* of the country into one mighty confederation, whose trade districts and assembly districts, while they provide for the local needs, or the characteristic trade requirements, of their several constituencies, shall yet be subject to the legislation of a general labor congress and to the executive authority of a supreme council, it is intended to inaugurate a new era in the so-called "conflict of labor and capital."

In principle, this organization does not differ from the smallest trade union. The distinction between the two is one purely of degree. In practical effect, however, the Knights of Labor, if they shall accomplish as much as one-half their declared purposes, will produce a veritable revolution in industry: a change, no longer of degree, but of kind.

The difference is just here. Up to this time the labor organizations, the trade unions, have, on the whole, not done more than offset the great economic advantage which the employers of labor enjoy in the increasing struggle over the product of industry. When I say the labor organizations have not done more than this, I do not overlook the fact that they have, at times, done a great deal which was aside from this; have wrought much mischief, in bad blood or under the guidance of demagogues, through acts which were reprehended not less by their own wiser members than by the general sense of the community. What I mean to say is, that, irrespective of such sporadic acts of folly, the power given to the working classes by their organizations, added to the power which those classes would have wielded, if unorganized, has not been more than enough to secure the full, attentive and respectful consideration of their interests and claims. It has not been enough, speaking broadly, to overbear the master's rightful authority,

* In fact, the Knights of Labor, at their maximum, included about ten per cent. of the laboring population, agricultural or mechanical. Within the large factory industries, however, the proportion was very much greater, the "Knights" having almost complete control of many trades.

to interfere with his necessary control of his business, to render it unsafe for him to undertake contracts, much less to transfer the initiative in production from him to his workmen.

475. The Laborer must look out for his own Interest.—The reader who has carefully followed the course of discussion in this treatise will not have failed to apprehend the opinion of the writer, not only that an active and even eager pursuit of their own interests by the working classes is a condition of their realizing the utmost economic good that might be brought to them, but that it is, not less, for the interest, the particular, selfish interest of the employing class themselves, that they should have to do with men who are acute and alert in searching out opportunities for the improvement of their own condition, with men who are bold and persistent in following up every possible advantage. I believe that the industrial republic has as little need as has the political republic, of citizens who have no opinions for themselves as to their rights and interests, but thankfully receive whatever, in the time and place, may be offered them. I believe it is eminently for the prosperity and growth of the community that each and every member, whatever his place in the industrial order, should strongly desire to improve his condition, and should seek to do so by all means which are compatible with industrial peace. I have even, under a preceding title (Strikes), expressed the opinion that, on rare occasions and for manifestly good reasons, industrial warfare itself may result in the better adjustment of economic relations.

476. The Balance of Power between Employers and Employed.—The accomplishment of the avowed purposes of the Knights of Labor, however, would lead to the complete subjugation and subjection of the employing class, a result, which, in my view, would be fraught with the most mischievous consequences. Up to this time the trade unions have, in general, brought to bear a sufficient pressure to make employers carefully considerate of the wishes and interests of their laborers, anxious to avoid all causes of offense, willing to concede whatever they possibly can. This is as it should be.

No good comes from the exercise of unchecked and irresponsible power in industry, any more than in government.

On the other hand, the trade unions, up to this time, while they have been able to make themselves heard and considered, while they have had all the power necessary to cause the employer to be desirous and even anxious to concede every reasonable demand, have yet, in the main, shown a sense of responsibility for the fairness and reasonableness of their demands. They have known at the outset, or have learned as the result of unsuccessful contests, that there is a limit to their power; that, in making excessive and exorbitant claims, they are likely to be beaten; and that every defeat on such an issue weakens themselves and strengthens their antagonists for any future contest. In a word, while, under the conditions which subsisted until within the last three or four years, many employers were, by force of temperament, unreasonably arbitrary, and large bodies of laborers were, on their side, often unreasonably exacting, something approaching an equilibrium had been reached between the powers of the two parties, securing industrial peace to as great a degree as might fairly be expected under the rightful and desirable ambition and self-assertion, the fortunately growing ambition and self-assertion, of the working classes.

477. The Subjugation of the Employer.—On the other hand, such a confederation of labor as is now proposed and attempted would utterly destroy the balance of industrial power, leaving the employer only the choice between conceding any and all demands, however unreasonable, or ceasing to produce. And this object is distinctly avowed by the leaders in this movement, some of whom have carried their scheme out to its full logical consequences, declaring it to be their purpose to bring about a state of things, in which, while the employer shall still occupy his formal attitude in production, he shall be, in effect, only the paid, doubtless the well-paid, agent of what they are pleased to call "the productive classes." The employer is still to remain the superintendent of the industrial operations; he is still to risk his own capital and the borrowed capital for which he has made himself responsible; he is still to exert his technical, administrative and financial skill in the conduct of the business over which he is placed; he is still to exercise authority, so far as permitted, over the *personnel* of the works or factory. But the real initiative in production is to rest, not with him, but with the council or committee or executive officer, not, indeed, of his own laborers, but of those of the whole country; he is to engage no one and to discharge no one, without consent; others are to decide for him all questions relating to the quality of work or the conduct of his workmen; the hours and general conditions of labor, the rates of wages and the times and modes of payment, are to be determined by the general parliament of labor or under its authority.

Beyond this, I do not understand that it is the present purpose of the promoters of this movement to go. For example, if I rightly understand the matter, the employer, having produced goods under the conditions recited, will be left free to dispose of them at his pleasure, selling them to whom he will, at such prices and on such terms of payment as he choose, unless, indeed, that be prevented by some "boycott," * placed upon some person or class of persons, or upon some kind of goods, or upon the product of certain machines, under authority of the parliament of labor or of its executive officers, for some industrial, political, social or personal reason.

478. Difficulties Attendant on the Scheme.—Of course, no "long headed" man, and there are many such among the promoters of this movement, expects that any one of the present employers of labor will find the conditions thus imposed agreeable, or will submit to them if he has any choice, short of leaving business. They anticipate that many employers will refuse to submit to such conditions and will relinquish production,

* The designation of this new weapon of industrial and social warfare is derived from an Irish gentleman, one Captain Boycott, against whom it was, a few years ago, so conspicuously employed by his hostile tenants as to cause his name to be permanently affixed thereto. To boycott is simply to place under a ban. No person who respects the authority which lays the boycott will deal with a person thus placed under the ban, or with any person who does deal with him.

perhaps with consequences immediately injurious to their laborers and to the community. They anticipate that others will resist violently, throwing their whole energies and fortunes into the contest, fighting with fury, as if for life, and only ceasing their struggles when bound hand and foot. But they expect that still others will submit, more or less unwillingly, to the terms imposed upon them, and will consent to carry on business under the new *régime.* The next generation of employers they look to see made up of men bred and trained under the new conditions, men who, born into such a state of things, and not knowing any other, except historically, as belonging to a bad past age, when the rights of labor were not respected, will accept the situation as cheerfully as the Frenchman of to-day accepts the great Revolution. Such men, it is believed, will be both glad and proud to wield the limited, delegated powers then pertaining to the position of the employer of labor; and will, in good faith and good feeling, execute the laws and decrees of the parliament of labor or of its supreme or local council or of any committee thereto authorized.

Probably, also, none of the more clear sighted of the promoters of this movement anticipate that the legislation of their congress or the decrees of their standing councils or the acts of their executive officers will, at first or for a long time, be free from much that is visionary and unpractical, or even from the influence of personal piques, jealousies and animosities. They doubtless anticipate that much that is futile will be attempted, and that much that is mischievous will be accomplished. No intelligent person could possibly believe that such tremendous and far-reaching powers could be placed, all at once, in the hands of a few men without grave abuses being generated; or that a machine so gigantic could be set up and put to working without much jarring and friction, and an occasional accident, even if a permanent breaking-down be avoided.

The men who are concerned in this movement are shrewd enough to see that the sense of the entire helplessness of the employing class must inevitably affect, and affect profoundly, the judgment and the will of the soundest, wisest, and most fair-minded representatives whom the body of laborers could select, rendering them less sound, less wise and less fair-minded than they would be in dealing with a body of employers who were not helpless, but had the power to resist and to strike back, if crowded too far. These men, also, are shrewd enough to see that there is great likelihood that the sense of the helplessness of the employing class will so operate, at least in the first instance, upon the minds of the body of laborers as to cause them to select, as their representatives, not the soundest, wisest and most fair-minded of their class, but those who are extreme, arbitrary and arrogant in character and in manners, and who will fast become more and more so, through the exercise of such tremendous powers.

All this, any clear-minded person must see, on the first contemplation of such a scheme ; all this, doubtless, the leaders of the Knights of Labor fully realize ; but were these probabilities presented as an objection to that scheme, they would answer, that the education of the mass of laborers, to use, without abuse, such and so great industrial powers, is, in their belief, practicable, in time, in such time as would be taken for accomplishing any other great moral and intellectual advance; and that such an education and training of the mass of laborers would itself be a social and political gain, far transcending in value even the industrial blessings which the most sanguine could look for from the fullest success of the proposed scheme of democracy in industry.

479. Another View of the Knights of Labor.—I have sought to state, fully and fairly, what I understand to be the purpose of the leading promoters of the organization known as the Knights of Labor. Probably many, even among the leaders in this movement, probably most of the members of the organization, regard it as an effort to give encouragement and moral support to the constituent trade unions and to bodies of labor heretofore isolated ; as a means of stimulating the self-respect and self-assertion of the laboring class, of promoting their mutual acquaintance, of strengthening the feeling of a common interest among them, rather than as a serious attempt to reverse the relations heretofore subsisting between employer and employed and to transfer the initiative in production and the control of industry from the former to the latter class. In this narrower sphere, it is conceivable that an organization like the Knights of Labor might become a great educational force ; a useful agency for directing the efforts of its members toward the improvement of their condition ; a source of much inspiration, through the deliberations and debates of earnest men, representing the better sense and higher purposes of vast bodies of laborers, in the main, right-minded, honest and patriotic. Indeed, it is not improbable that, should the confederation relinquish its larger designs, it will assume this less ambitious but more useful function. How fully and how long it would, in such a capacity, be supported by the efforts and contributions of its present members, we need not consider.

480. Can Profits be Confiscated?—Reverting to the larger scheme, openly avowed and vigorously advocated, of those who would make the Knights of Labor all that has been described, let us ask, how far the object aimed at is desirable ; how far it is, in itself, practicable ; how far such an organization is suited to accomplish that object.

In the first place, can one be mistaken in deeming it the main object of this industrial enterprise to secure to the laboring class the benefit of a part, perhaps the greater part, of the profits now realized by the body of employers, which the laborers regard as excessive ? If this be, indeed, the main object of the association, the aim is, if I have rightly indicated the origin and measure of business profits, a mistaken one. Profits are not obtained by deduction from wages ; they are purely the creation of the employers themselves. The mass of profits represents the wealth produced by able, skillful, resolute and far-seeing men of business, over and above that which is produced, with the same amount of labor power and capital power, by employers who fail in one or more of the qualities necessary to success.

If this view of the source of the employer's gains be just, it is not possible to wrest profits to the benefit of the body of laborers. The employers may, indeed, be prevented from realizing them, by strikes and industrial disturbances ;

but no part of the profits which they would otherwise have made, will, for that reason, go to any other class in the community. On the contrary, the community as a whole, and the working classes in especial, will be worse off for the impairment or destruction of *the employer's interest in production, i. e.*, his profits.

Are there, then, no means by which the working class can operate, at once to reduce the amount going to the employing class as profits, and in the same degree to enhance their own wages? I answer, yes: there are such means. These have been pointed out in paragraphs 310 to 314. In just so far as the laboring classes, by their influence upon legislation or administration, or by their own direct action, contribute towards elevating the standard of the employing class, thus raising the lower limit of production in this respect, in just so far will they increase, not only the relative share, but the positive amount, coming to them in wages. It does not need to be said that treating employers as public enemies, levying industrial warfare upon them, concerting schemes to harass them and take them at every accidental disadvantage, rendering it unsafe for them to undertake contracts on a large scale and over long periods of time, and subjecting them to insults and indignities, as so many labor leaders seem to think it a matter of class duty to do, is not a way to effect the desired result. Such courses must not only reduce the *average* standard of business ability, by driving out the ablest men, but must introduce into the employment of labor whole classes of persons of lower and still lower grades of efficiency, to the great and lasting injury of the community and of the working classes, first of all, last of all, most of all.

481. Will the Machine Work?—So much for what I understand to be the main object of this industrial movement. A few words only will be needed regarding the suitability of the agencies to be employed.

One might cherish grave doubts regarding the practicability of breeding a race of conductors of business, who, possessing energy, intelligence, forethought and resolution, will rather like to execute the legislation of a parliament of labor; will cheerfully accept the condition of being ordered about by a committee of their own hands, or of a local council; will be unhesitatingly ready to embark capital in enterprises over which they have practically no control. One might entertain grave doubts as to the capability of the working classes, after any course of education, however long, painful and costly, maintaining a parliament of labor which shall be competent to deal with concerns a hundred times as large, important and difficult as those which come before the American Congress, without making a mess of it, compared with which the muddle into which Congress manages to get our industry and finances would be clearness and order and system and light. But it is probably not necessary to go so far into the matter as to inquire what might come to pass should the Knights of Labor pursue their designs through a considerable period of time. It is in the highest degree improbable that the organization itself could maintain activity long on such a scale as has been projected.

The very vastness of the scheme foredooms it to failure. The attempt to embrace so much under a single rule; to legislate in detail for so many conflicting interests; to regulate, from a central point, conditions of life and labor so widely diverse as those of city and of country, of east and of west, of agriculturist and of artisan, of common and of skilled labor, of the producer of materials and of him who uses those materials in the production of still higher classes of commodities, must result in failure. The restiveness shown by many trade unions, the open revolt of some, the early establishment of a rival Confederation, already intimate the essential weakness of the scheme, at least if it is to be administered in the masterful spirit of the last two years.

482. Is the Scheme "American"?—Nor do I believe that, if it were left to the suffrage of the laboring classes in America themselves, one in twenty of those who were born upon the soil would vote to bring about such a subjection of the employing class to the will of their workmen or to a general parliament of labor. The American well knows that there is neither hardship nor indignity in working for another man, in his shop, at his task, with his tools, on his terms. He knows that industry, to be successfully conducted, must be controlled by its responsible head. He sees all around him men who have risen from the ranks of labor to become the conductors of business, no one hindering them, all applauding their efforts and rejoicing in their success. He knows that for himself and his children the way is open clear up to the top. The American workingman can be reasoned with, and that not on a low plane only ; he is capable of understanding and appreciating almost any consideration relating to the market ; his spirit is that of civility, reciprocity and fair play ; he cordially and intelligently accepts, in its full economic bearings, the maxim, "live and let live." Had it been left to our native population alone, not one of those violent and reckless attacks upon production and transportation, which have, within the past two or three years, shocked the whole industrial system and have come near to produce a general crisis of trade, would ever have taken place.

IX.

ATTACKS ON THE DOCTRINE OF RENT.

483. Bastiat.—A doctrine of such far-reaching consequences as Ricardo's doctrine of Rent has not been allowed to stand without suffering many and vehement assaults. The French Bastiat has, in his eloquent and witty work, "The Harmonies of Political Economy," undertaken to demonstrate that Rent, proper, economic rent, does not exist ; that it is purely a fiction jointly maintained by the economists and the communists ;* that all which the landlord receives for the use of his land is nothing but the proper remuneration for the labor and capital expended in inclosing the land, providing means of access, draining, manuring and otherwise improving the soil, erecting buildings for sheltering the produce, housing the laborers, etc. Inasmuch as Bastiat's objections to Ricardo's doctrine were far

* In stigmatizing this doctrine he continually joins together the names of "Ricardo and Proudhon."

more strongly and clearly stated by the late Mr. Henry C. Carey, of Philadelphia, I pass at once to the consideration of the views of the latter.

484. Carey.—Mr. Carey's attack is twofold. His first argument is founded on a "comparison of the *cost* and *value* of existing landed capital." To use his own phraseology, "*There is not throughout the United States, a county, township, town, or city, that would sell for cost; or one whose rents are equal to the interest upon the labor and capital expended.*"* And Mr. Carey draws what he regards as the logical inference from this alleged fact: "If we show that the land heretofore appropriated is not only not worth as much labor as it has cost to produce it in its present condition, but that it could not be reproduced by the labor that its present value would purchase, it will be obvious to the reader that its whole value is due to that which has been applied to its improvement."†

Now, it appears to me ‡ not only that this is not "obvious," but that something very like an Irish bull is to be found here. The trouble with this argument is its superabundance of proof. The effect is much the same as that which results from a superabundance of powder in charging a gun.

Had Mr. Carey been able to show that, in any case taken, a county, township, town, or city was worth exactly as much in labor as it had cost, the coincidence of amounts would at least have suggested, if it did not create a proper presumption to that effect, that the labor expended was the cause of the value existing; but when Ricardo's critic asserts that any farm and any collection of farms, has cost more, often far more, than it is worth, he furnishes the means for his own refutation.

Suppose the present value of a piece of land to be represented by 100 units, while the value of the labor it has cost to "produce" the farms found thereon, is represented by 125. Now, says Mr. Carey, inasmuch as the land is not at present worth more than 100, while the labor invested in it was worth

---

* Carey: The Past, Present and Future, p. 60.

† Carey: Political Economy, vol. I., p. 102.

‡ This discussion of Mr. Carey's propositions is abridged from my work, "Land and Its Rent," published in 1883.

125, it is clear that nothing but the labor has entered to give value to the land!

But how so? What has become of the 25 which was in excess of the 100? Lost, says Mr. Carey, since, "as labor is improved in its quality by the aid of improved instruments, all previously accumulated capital tends to fall below its cost in labor."*

Ah! but if that 25 can be lost and has been lost, how can you show that another 25 has not been lost, and still another 25, through the operation of the same cause? How can you prove that proper economic rent does not enter? How, indeed, can you prove that the present value of the land is due, in any part whatever, to the labor expended in the past?

John Smith's barn has been broken into, over night, by a burglar who sawed a hole through the door to effect his entrance. Mr. Carey, in the interest of justice, appears next morning among the excited throng of neighbors, and produces a board taken from James Brown's woodshed, which, though not corresponding to the guilty hole in size or shape, is yet *large enough*, as he explains, to allow just such a piece to be cut out of it, thus conclusively proving James Brown to have been the robber of John Smith's barn!

485. How the Value of Agricultural Improvements should be Estimated.—An argument that breaks down thus, under the slightest strain, can not be worth further notice on its own account; yet we may find matter of not a little economic interest in following out the question here raised, as to the relation between what Mr. Carey calls the cost of producing farms and the value of farms when "produced."

First. To begin with, all statements regarding the amount so invested in any country or district are based on comparatively little information. The data are few and meager, even for making estimates. Accomplished statisticians, accustomed to deal with computations relating to agriculture, like Mr. Robert Giffen, Professor Thorold Rogers, or Sir James Caird, would scarcely presume to claim approximate accuracy for any estimates they might make regarding the

* Political Economy, vol. I., p. 35.

amount of labor involved in bringing even a limited agricultural region into its present state of productiveness.

Second. Again, wholly in addition to the difficulty encountered in estimating the amount of labor involved, would be the difficulty of computing the money value of that labor. While some great works of improvement are effected by bodies of hired laborers working through the year or through the agricultural season, most farm improvements are effected in the off season, when the wages of hired labor are very low,—perhaps only one-half what they would be at another period of the year; and probably the greater part are effected by the labor of the owner or occupier of the land and his family, in fragments of the day which would not otherwise be utilized, or in portions of the year when little or nothing of the current work of the farm can be done.

Third. The element of interest can properly be introduced into such computations only in respect to a very small proportion of agricultural investments.

In general, where capital is applied, it is in the expectation of an immediate improvement of the productive power of the land, the annual increase of the produce being relied upon to furnish at least the annual interest upon the investment, so that, speaking broadly, in any comparison between the cost and the value of landed property, only the first cost of the improvements should be set against the ultimate value.

There are cases, of course, where capital is applied to the land in the view alone of a distant increase of value. Here, within moderate limits of time, the inclusion of interest is not unreasonable. But even here, and even within comparatively brief periods, the application of the principle of geometric progression, in the form of compound interest, is of very doubtful propriety. Geometrical increase is rarely attained and never long maintained in things human. Contemplating an actual instance of such increase within the field of industry, the most unreasonable expectation which can be formed concerning it, is that it will continue. That it should continue long, is not so much unlikely as impossible.

Sir Archibald Alison, in his discussion of the British Sink-ing Fund, states that "a penny laid out at compound interest at the birth of our Saviour would in the year 1775 have amounted to a solid mass of gold eighteen hundred times the whole weight of the globe." So, doubtless, it might be shown that the value of Adam's first day's work in the Garden, properly compounded during six thousand years, would amount to more than the present value of all the lands of the world, and consequently that all the work that has been done since, in bringing the soil under cultivation, has been thrown away!

The incredibility of geometric increase through any considerable period of time can not be too strongly impressed upon the student of economics. The produce of a single acre of wheat, sown over and over for fourteen years, would cover all the solid land on this planet. The spawn of certain fish would suffice in even fewer years, if reproduction went on in geometrical progression, to fill to the brim the basin of every pond, lake, river, sea, and ocean.

Hence we see the utter inconsequence of computations into which compound interest is allowed to enter, except in strict subordination to common-sense. Probably there is no way in which a man can so quickly and so conclusively show himself unfit to be listened to, as by appealing to geometrical progression for the proof of an economic or social theory.

Fourth. But the consideration of greatest importance in computing the cost of "producing" farms, is that, in general, agricultural improvements are compensated, and are expected to be compensated, upon the principle of those annuities in which a certain number of annual payments both yield due interest on the purchase money and extinguish the capital itself, as when a man for $1,000 (on which the normal interest would be $50 or $60) purchases the right to receive $120 a year for a certain term, with no claim on the principal thereafter.

Now, is this so, or is it not? Let us satisfy our minds on this point; for if the proposition just now stated is correct, it disposes effectually of the argument against the economic doctrine of rent derived from the fact of expenditures in "producing" farms.

That this proposition is correct, is, I think, proved conclusively by the fact, abundantly established by English experience, that *there are few classes of improvements known to agriculture which a tenant for 33 years will not make at his own expense,* notwithstanding the certainty that he will cease to enjoy the benefit of them at the expiry of his lease.

Do not the several considerations adduced, and especially the last, take away all the force of this labored argument against the doctrine of rent?

486. Mr. Carey's Historical Argument.—But Mr. Carey was not satisfied with one refutation of Ricardo's law. He attempted and, to the satisfaction of his disciples, achieved, a second demonstration of its falsity. That this subsidiary argument against the doctrine of rent should have been for a moment admitted, affords a striking proof of the weakness and vagueness with which economic questions, especially those affecting the land, have been discussed.

"It will," Mr. Carey says,* "be perceived that the whole system (of Ricardo) is based upon the assertion of the existence of a single fact, namely, that, in the commencement of cultivation, when population is small and land consequently abundant, the soils capable of yielding the largest return to any given quantity of labor alone are cultivated.

"That fact exists, or it does not. If it has no existence, the system falls to the ground. *That it does not exist, that it never has existed in any country whatsoever, and that it is contrary to the nature of things that it should have existed, or can exist, we propose now to show.*

"We shall commence," he says, "our examination with the United States. Their first settlement is recent; and, the work being still in progress, we can readily trace the settler and mark his course of operation. If we find him invariably occupying the high and thin lands requiring little clearing and no drainage, those which can yield but a small return to labor, and as invariably traveling down the hills and clearing and draining the lower and richer lands, as population and wealth

* Past, Present, and Future, p. 23.

increase, then will the theory we have offered be confirmed by practice,—American practice, at least.

"If, however, we can thence follow him into Mexico and through South America, into Britain, and through France, Germany, Italy, Greece, and Egypt, into Asia and Australia, and show that such has been his invariable course of action, then may it be believed that when population is small and land consequently abundant, the work of cultivation is, and always must be, commenced upon the poorer soils; that, with the growth of population and wealth, other soils, yielding a larger return to labor, are always brought into activity, with a constantly increasing return to the labor expended upon them."

487. All this is Irrelevant to the Doctrine of Rent.— I will not say, with Prof. Roscher, that Mr. Carey's lengthy exposition is "rank with inexact science and unhistorical history." It does not matter a particle, so far as the validity of Ricardo's doctrine is concerned, whether Mr. Carey has correctly apprehended or grossly misapprehended the facts of human history, in the respect under consideration.

Let it be conceded that the order of settlement in all new countries is that which Mr. Carey has indicated,—the newcomers taking up light, dry, sandy soils, which will yield a quick return to the labor of the colonists, aided by their scanty capitals; and that it is only when wealth has been in some measure accumulated, after the first severe struggle to maintain existence, that deeper and richer, but cold and wet soils, are opened, the forests cleared, the swamps, rich with the vegetable mold of centuries, drained. What, pray, does all this prove, so far as the doctrine under consideration is concerned? It is absolutely indifferent to the matter at issue.

It is true that Ricardo assumed, for the purpose of illustrating his doctrine, that the soils first cultivated, within any considerable country, were those most productive. It also appears from the context, that Mr. Ricardo really supposed that this was the historical order of occupation. Yet *the economic law of rent has reference alone to lands under cultivation* AT THE SAME TIME; and would have precisely as much validity if every thing which Mr. Carey has contended for, regarding the actual order of settlement and cultivation, were conceded, as if the hypothesis of Ricardo were historically accurate.

488. Is this History indeed Historical ?—I have said that the complete establishment of Mr. Carey's historical order would not effect the validity of Ricardo's law of rent ; and that, therefore, one might, for argument's sake, concede the accuracy of the narrative concerning the early settlement of Europe, Asia, and America, which occupies so large a portion of his treatises.

But while the historical order of settlement is thus of no consequence as affecting the economic law of rent, it must be admitted that important consequences would follow the establishment of the proposition that "the work of cultivation is and *always must be* commenced upon the poorer soils ; that, with the growth of population and wealth, other soils yielding a larger return to labor are *always* brought into activity ;" or, as the author elsewhere expresses it, that the settler *invariably* travels down the hills, clearing and draining the lower and richer lands, as population and wealth increase.

What are the economic consequences which, as we have said, would follow the establishment of Mr. Carey's proposition ? These : that, instead of the increase of population lowering the margin of cultivation, and thus enhancing the aggregate body of rents,* it would be shown to have the effect, by stimulating the cultivation of better lands, to throw out the poorer (the first cultivated) soils, and thus to raise the lower limit of cultivation, and thus at once to diminish the share of the produce going as rent to the landlord, and to increase the average produce, per capita, of the community. Rents will still be determined by the Ricardian formula ; but the importance of rent as a factor in the distribution of wealth will be diminished.

In view of the importance of these consequences, let us proceed to examine Mr. Carey's sweeping assertions regarding the actual order of settlement and occupation, for the purposes of agriculture. Let us see whether this history be indeed historical or not.

---

* See par. 257.

In the first place, we note that the detailed accounts relate, in the main, either to the settlement and cultivation of countries in ages when military necessities were a controlling force, or else to the very earliest stages of settlement and cultivation of the land, under circumstances which made the needs of immediate subsistence peculiarly urgent, as in the new States of the American Union, eighty, sixty, forty years ago.

It would take more time than we have at command to go through the history of the settlement of Britain, Italy, Greece, Germany, and other ancient countries, and attempt to analyze the influences which determined the selection of lands for habitation and cultivation. When we contrast the sites of nearly all ancient and medieval cities, built upon the towering rock, with the utterly indefensible sites of our modern cities, we can well understand that not economic but political and military exigencies may have given a strong preference to high and rugged ground, even for agriculture, in the days of almost universal warfare. The crops, indeed, raised on such ground would neither be so ample, nor obtained with so little effort and sacrifice, as those which might have been raised in the fertile valleys below, but they would be in a less degree subject to be swept away by occasional forays of armed bands.

Fortunately, we do not need to enter into an analysis involving so much time and labor, and perplexed by so many uncertainties regarding the facts with which we should have to deal. If the forces which in those days determined population to high and poor soils were exclusively or even predominantly economic forces, we shall not fail to find them operating to control the occupation of new countries in these times of general peace. Let us then consider the course of settlement in the United States. Mr. Carey himself expresses his preference for investigation in this field. "Their first settlement," he says, "is recent, and, the work being still in progress, we can readily trace the settler, and mark his course of operation." *

---

* Past, Present, and Future, p. 24.

489. Take the Case of Ohio.—And, to further narrow the field, let us confine our view to the State of Ohio. This State is as favorable as any to the theory under consideration. "The early settlers," says Mr. Carey, "of Ohio, Indiana, and Illinois uniformly selected the higher grounds, leaving the richer lands for their successors." *

The settlement of Ohio may be said to have been in progress all the time between 1802, when its inhabitants were fewer than 50,000, and 1832, when its population had reached 1,000,000 : in progress in this sense, that not until the latter date had settlers found their way into every corner and county of the new State.

Now let it be conceded that throughout this period Mr. Carey's statement regarding the course of occupation holds good substantially. I say, substantially, because to justify the assertion that the settlers "uniformly" selected the higher grounds would require a greater amount of particular and local knowledge than any one man ever possessed.

How much, then, would there be in this fact, admitted for the sake of argument, which should be in contravention of the economic doctrine of rent? These early settlers of Ohio were, in the first instance, necessarily controlled in their "location" by considerations relating to the transportation of their products and to communication with the settlements they had left behind. Now, advantages of situation, as we have before seen, enter just as fully into the net productiveness of any tract of land, according to Ricardo's doctrine, as advantages arising from superior fertility. Even in illustrating the origin of rent (par. 259) we assumed the existence of a very productive tract, situated at so great a distance that it would not be occupied until cultivation had been driven to descend through several successive stages within the territory immediately surrounding the market.

But, secondly, the early settlers of Ohio were largely compelled by the immediate exigencies of pioneer life to do something different from that which would have been the most advantageous had they possessed an ample store

* Past, Present, and Future, p. 32.

of necessaries and of the utensils and materials of industry. New-comers must needs do, not what they would, but what they can; they must raise a quick crop, by little labor; and it is natural enough that they should generally seek the side-hill, which is self-drained, and the open country, which does not require clearing, and the thin, dry soil, which gives a speedy, though not a large return.

They still seek that land which will be most productive under the circumstances in which they find themselves placed; for, as Professor Johnston* has well said, that which would be rich land for a rich man may be poor land for a poor man.

490. But the question I wish now to raise is, whether, when the first exigencies of pioneer life were passed, when some store had been accumulated, when population had become sufficiently dense to allow a reasonable degree of co-operation in labor, when time had been afforded to lay out roads and bridges and to perfect the means of transportation, when the capabilities and resources of the land had become thoroughly known, — whether *then* it remained true that cultivators in Ohio neglected the best soils for those of an inferior quality?

If not, the fabric so laboriously reared for assaulting the stronghold of the economists, tumbles to the ground, of its own weight. How much does it matter that the people of Ohio, while they were first spreading loosely over the State, took up lands as is asserted, unless it can be proved, or at least a strong presumption can be established, that they continued to take up poorer soils, in preference to the best? Mr. Carey asserts that the hypothetical order of settlement is "universally false"; that is, it is false as applied not to one but to all stages of the history of any community. As this matter is important, let us formulate it somewhat rigidly.

Let us suppose the possibly cultivable lands of Ohio to form seven distinct grades, 1 to 7, No. 1 being the poorest, No. 7 the richest. Let us divide the economic life of Ohio, beginning in 1802 and ending — when? into seven generations, with continually increasing population.

---

*A distinguished agricultural chemist of Great Britain, author of "Notes on North America."

Now, according to the view we are considering, generation No. 1, the first settlers, will take up lands No. 1, the poorest of all; generation No. 2 will take up lands No. 2, the next to the poorest; generation No. 3 will take up lands No. 3, and so on.

This, or something very like it, must take place, or our "law" breaks down; for should generation No. 3, say, have the presumption to take up lands No. 6, and generation No. 4 be thereby encouraged to take up lands No. 7, why then generation No. 5 will be compelled to take up lands No. 5, that is, lands poorer than those which had been brought in by the two generations preceding, while generation No. 6 will be driven to take up lands No. 4, far down on the scale of fertility; and generation No. 7, the flower of civilization, will actually have to "decline upon" lands No. 3, which, according to Mr. Carey, generation No. 3 should, in conscience, have taken up. In other words, we should have cultivation driven down to inferior soils, a state of things respecting which Ricardo's critic declares that it not only never has existed in any country whatsoever, but that it is contrary to the nature of things that it should have existed or can exist.

In view of such possible results, what an appalling responsibility rests upon the people of any generation in the matter of not taking up any better land than they ought! In the first place, think what a degree of virtue it requires, that they should deliberately deny themselves the enjoyment of the really best land around them, in order that the coming generations, with increasing numbers, should have the privilege of first occupying these, as Mr. Carey says they *must* do! Even more remarkable than this, think of the degree of intelligence that is required to point out to the men of any generation just the share of the lands of the State which Mr. Carey's theory will permit them to occupy, they being necessarily ignorant as to what the future population of the State is to be, or through how many generations or centuries the increase of population upon the territory is to be continued!

491. But let us return to Ohio. We have seen what is required to make this "historical law" true. How far do the probabilities of the case favor the application of that law throughout the settlement of that State?

We may believe that there were, in Ohio, in 1832, when the population was 1,000,000, about 4,000,000 acres of improved land in farms. By 1850, when the population had risen to 2,000,000, these 4,000,000 acres had become 10,000,000. Did the addition thus made to the inclosed and improved lands of the State include a fair proportion of the best lands within its limits, or were the new lands, also, thin, dry, sandy soils, only not quite so poor as those brought in between 1802 and 1832, — soils giving little root to grasses or to grain, but raising a small crop easily and quickly? Unless the latter was the case, this great historical law becomes little better than arrant nonsense.

There is a popular belief throughout the Eastern States of this Union, that, in the eighteen years covered by this period, — 1832–50, — there was an immense amount of "clearing" done in Ohio; and the virtues of the "pioneer's ax" have been celebrated in song and story. Is this all a mistake? Or, if the people of Ohio really did cut down the primeval timber over thousands of square miles, did they, as they ought, take pains to cut down only timber which grew over comparatively poor soils, so as not to interfere with the rights vested in unborn generations by Mr. Carey's "law"?

Between 1850 and 1880, again, the population of Ohio increased to 3,000,000, and the number of acres of improved lands rose to 18,000,000. Were the 8,000,000 acres improved for the first time during this period, all, or substantially all, of a quality next above those previously brought in, but still below the best? Did this added territory embrace lands only a little less thin, a little less shallow, than those occupied in 1850? Did this vast annexation still leave the really good lands of the State uncultivated, only to be improved when the population shall reach 5,000,000 or 10,000,000?

492. I do not care to contest Mr. Carey's assertion that the first generation of settlers in any American State have spread themselves loosely over the soil, picking out the spots which offered the greatest facilities for the transportation of produce and for communication with the older settlements, perhaps giving a certain preference to naturally cleared, self-drained land. But that the second generation, in any American State, north of Mason and Dixon's line at least, have shrunk from the real problem of their economic life, have failed to grapple with the obstacles which withstood their acquisition of the richest resources of nature, have neglected to subdue the soil, the best soil they could find, with ax and spade, strenuously, manfully, with incessant toil, with unflinching courage, I, for one, do not believe; and Mr. Carey has not adduced a scintilla of evidence to prove a proposition so contrary to all we have ever learned of the character and life of the Western people. In the absence of any such statistical demonstration, common fame and common sense give the flattest contradiction to this hypothesis.

With this we may safely leave the argument against the Ricardian doctrine of rent. The person who denies the truth of the Ricardian law in effect declares that men habitually rent or sell highly fertile and comparatively infertile fields, rich corn lands and mountain pastures, at the same price; that men habitually rent or sell lands near a market at the same price with lands the most distant from the market. If he does not mean to assert this, he does not in the smallest degree traverse the path of Ricardo's argument. If he does mean to assert this, he puts himself on the level of the person who should assert that men habitually sell two bushels or ten bushels of wheat, indifferently, at one and the same price.

X.

THE NATIONALIZATION OF THE LAND.

493. The Law of Rent Re-stated.—We have seen what is the nature of Rent. It represents the surplus of the produce over the cost of cultivation on the poorest lands actually contributing to the supply of the market at the time.

We saw (par. 262–4) that, conceding the private ownership of land, rent is merely a question between landlord and tenant; that so far as economic forces are concerned, rent must remain in the hands of the landlord; that, setting violence aside, it can only come into the hands of the tenant by gift from the landlord; that, were it, by virtue of the landlord's generosity, to reach the tenant, it would, so far as economic forces are concerned, go no further. It could only be carried to the agricultural laborer or to the consumer of agricultural produce, by another gift or series of gifts.

494. The Equities of Rent, as between Landlord and Tenant.—So much for the economics of rent; let us look a moment at the equities of it.

Certainly, as between the landlord and the tenant, the latter can set up no claim to any portion of rent. This is shown in the following way: It is, as we have seen, of the very essence of rent that it represents, and is measured by, the surplus of produce over the cost of cultivation on the poorest (or most distant) lands under cultivation for the supply of the same market. Now, these poorest or most distant lands have occupiers who must be presumed to be industrially, and, if you please, morally, just as meritorious as those who cultivate the better lands or the lands nearer the market. The several classes of tenants are only put on an equality when rent is exacted according to the Ricardian formula. It would clearly be inequitable that one body of occupiers should receive back, in the price of their products, only the actual cost of cultivation, while another should receive large sums in addition to this, as would be the case were rents to be remitted.

495. As between Landlord and the Agricultural Laborer.—In the same way it may be shown that the agricultural laborers on lands which bear a rent have no claim, in equity, to any portion of that rent. Why should they receive any more for their services than the laborers who cultivate the no-rent lands?

Clearly, then, as against either the tenant or the agricultural laborer, the landlord has an easy case. He can prove that neither of the two has any claim whatever to any part of what he receives as rent.

496. As between the Landlord and the Community at Large.—But suppose the issue to be raised between the landlord and the whole community, can the acquisition by individuals of the surplus of the produce above the cost of cultivation on the poorest soils, be so successfully defended on grounds either of political equity or of political expediency?

As this question has within the past few years become a "burning" question, I think it but right to present the argument of those who urge that "the unearned increment of land" should go to the State and not to individuals. This argument can not be better presented than in the language of John Stuart Mill, who, in his later days, became President of the English Land Tenure Reform Association, whose professed object was to agitate this question.

497. Mr. Mill's Argument.—"Suppose," says Mr. Mill, "that there is a kind of income which constantly tends to increase without any exertion or sacrifice on the part of the owners, these owners constituting a class in the community whom the natural course of things progressively enriches, consistently with complete passiveness on their own part. In such a case there would be no violation of the principles on which private property is founded, if the State should appropriate this increase of wealth, or any part of it, as it arises. This would not properly be taking any thing from any body; it would merely be applying an accession of wealth, created by circumstances, to the benefit of society, instead of allowing it to become an unearned appendage to the riches of a particular class.

"Now this is actually the case with rent. The ordinary progress of a society which increases in wealth, is at all times tending to augment the income of landlords; to give them both a greater amount and a greater proportion of the wealth of the community, independently of any trouble or outlay incurred by themselves. They grow richer, as it were, in their sleep, without working, risking or economizing."

In the paper from which the foregoing paragraphs are extracted, Mr. Mill expressly excepted the present value of the land in possession of individuals at the time the system of the public acquisition of the increment of the land should go into effect. Such an act should, in his view, have reference only to future increase.

In another place, while expressing a general respect for the rights of property, Mr. Mill proceeds:

"Some people ask, But why single out the land? Does not all property rise in value with the increase of prosperity? I answer, No. All other property fluctuates in value, now up, now down. I defy any one to show any kind of property, not partaking of the soil, and sufficiently important to be worth considering, which tends steadily upward, without any thing being done by the owners to give it increased value. So far from it, that the other of the two kinds of property that yield income, namely, capital, instead of increasing, actually diminishes in value as society advances. The poorer the country, or the further back we go in history, the higher we find the interest of money to be. Land alone—using land as a general term for the whole material of the earth—has the privilege of steadily rising in value from natural causes; and the reason is that land is strictly limited in quantity; the supply does not increase to meet the constant increase of demand . . .

"Well would it have been if this diversion of the public wealth had been foreseen and guarded against long ago; let us at least prevent any more gigantic fortunes* from being built up in a similar manner. The Association claims for the State the right to impose special taxation upon the land, equivalent to its special advantage."

"Those countries are fortunate," remarks Mr. Mill, "or would be fortunate, if decently governed, in which, as in a

---

* "If the Grosvenor, Portman and Portland estates belonged to the municipality of London, the gigantic incomes of those estates *would probably suffice for the whole expense of the local government of the capital.* But these gigantic incomes are still swelling; by the growth of London they may again be doubled in as short a time as they have doubled already."—*Ibid.* Prof. Adolph Wagner, of the University of Berlin, advocates the assumption by the State of all urban real estate, while deprecating the extension of the principle to agricultural land.

great part of the East, the land has not been allowed to become the permanent property of individuals, and the State consequently is the sole landlord. So far as the public expenditure is covered by the proceeds of the land, those countries are untaxed, for it is the same thing as being untaxed to pay to the State only what would have to be paid to private landlords if the land were appropriated.

"The principle that the land belongs to the Sovereign, and that the expenses of government should be defrayed by it, is recognized in the theory of our own ancient institutions. The nearest thing to an absolute proprietor whom our laws know of, is the freeholder, who is a tenant of the Crown, bound originally to personal service, in the field or at the plow, and when that obligation was remitted, subject to a land tax intended to be equivalent to it."

498. The Feudal Burdens of Land in England.—In the paragraph last quoted, Mr. Mill contemplates the feudal obligations of the tenant by military and other service as approximately the equivalent of an annual rent, which would be made, rudely indeed, to increase with the increasing value of land due to the growth of population and the progress of trade and manufactures. The chief of these obligations, as formulated by law and custom in England, are thus stated by Sir Edward S. Creasy, in his work on "The English Constitution."

The king, as feudal lord of his barons, and other military tenants, had a right to exact from them military service, or a pecuniary payment in lieu thereof; and it seems to have been optional with the king to claim the money, whether the vassal wished to serve in person or not, and even to exact both money and personal service. This war tax is called escuage or scutage, and the constant wars and troubles of the times always furnished a ready pretext for demanding it. Other exactions of money payments, under the name of aids, were continually practiced. Besides these, the heir, on succeeding to his estate, was required to pay a sum of money to the lord, under the title of a "relief." If the heir was a minor, the lord took possession of the land, as guardian, and used or abused it as he pleased, till the heir obtained his majority.

Even then the heir was obliged to pay a fine on suing out his livery, that is, on obtaining the delivery of the land from his guardian to him. The lord also had the right of nominating and tendering a wife to his male ward, or a husband to his female ward. And if the ward declined to marry the person so selected, the ward forfeited to the lord such a sum of money as the alliance was considered worth. The lord was entitled to a fine upon alienation: that is, if the tenant disposed of the land, or any part of it, to any third party. If the tenant died without heirs the land reverted to the lord. This was termed escheat (par. 573), and, as the right of devising real property did not exist in England after the Conquest, till Henry VIII's time, escheats were numerous. The lord also claimed to take back the land whenever the tenant committed any of a numerous list of crimes or acts of feudal misconduct. Such criminality or misconduct on the tenant's part was held to work a forfeiture.

499. Composition for the Feudal Burdens Upon Land.—On the restoration of Charles II., the land-owning class secured their release from the strictly feudal burdens, the consideration received by the Crown being solely an excise upon beer; and thus the vast possibilities of revenue to be derived from the composition of the feudal obligations of the landowning class were sacrificed. In the revolution of 1688, however, there was, as Mr. Mill notes, a reaction against this sacrifice of the rights of the public revenue. Indeed, the revolution of 1688 was, in Mr. Mill's view, "a revolution made by the towns against the country gentlemen. One of the fruits of it was a tax on the land of four shillings in the pound, which, at that time, may have been an equivalent for the burdens which had been taken off the landlords."

In 1692, accordingly, the lands of England were valued for the purposes of the land tax.

This land tax was to be a tax, not upon the community, not upon raw produce, not upon commercial agencies and manufacturing operations, but solely a tax upon landlords, in reduction of their rents: a resumption by the State, for its own benefit and for the corresponding relief of other classes, of a portion of the rents arising from the increase of population and the progress of trade and manufactures.

The following is Mr. Ricardo's statement of the incidence of a land tax:

"A land tax, levied in proportion to the rent of land,* and varying with every variation of rents, is, in effect, a tax on rent, and, as such a tax will not apply to that land which yields no rent, nor to the produce of that capital which is employed on the land with a view to profit merely and which never pays rent, it will not, in any way, affect the price of raw produce, but will fall wholly on the landlords."

But if the revolution of 1688 was, indeed, as Mr. Mill conceives it, a revolt of the towns against the country gentlemen, the force of that movement was soon exhausted. The landowners resumed control of English legislation; *the valuation of* 1692 *has remained to this day as the basis of the land tax*, while the rate of that tax was in 1798 made permanent at 4 shillings in the pound on the valuation of that date. It was by this series of acts that the right of the State to participate in the increase of the rental value of the lands of the kingdom was relinquished, in consideration of an annual payment, forever, of about £2,000,000.

500. Mr. Cobden's Denunciation.—It was to this relinquishment of the rights of the revenue by parliaments composed of country gentlemen, for the benefit of landlords, at the expense of the general community, that Richard Cobden alluded in his somewhat threatening speech of December 17, 1845.

"I warn ministers and I warn landowners and the aristocracy of this country against forcing upon the attention of the middle and industrious classes the subject of taxation.

"If they make it understood by the people of this country how the landowners here one hundred and fifty years ago deprived the sovereign of his feudal rights over them; how the aristocracy retained their feudal rights over the minor copyholders: how

* On the other hand, Mr Ricardo says, "If a land tax be imposed on all cultivated land, however moderate that tax may be, it will be a tax on produce, and will therefore raise the price of produce."

they made a bargain with the king to give him four shillings in the pound upon their landed rentals, as a quit charge for having dispensed with these rights of feudal service from them; if the country understand, as well as I think I understand, how afterwards this landed aristocracy passed a law to make the valuation of their rental final, the bargain originally being that they should pay four shillings in the pound of the yearly rateable value of their rental, as it was worth to let for, and then stopped the progress of the rent by a law making the valuation final; that the land has gone on increasing ten-fold in many parts of Scotland, and five-fold in many parts of England, while the land tax has remained the same as it was one hundred and fifty years ago; . . . if they force these things to be understood, they will be making as rueful a bargain as they have already made by resisting the abolition of the Corn Law."

501. Mr. Mill's Land-Tenure Reform Agitation.— What Mr. Cobden thus threatened in 1845, Mr. Mill undertook about 1870: an agitation of the whole question of taxation, and an active inquiry into the right of the landlord class to receive the progressive increase of rents.

The following is an extract from the programme of the Land-Tenure Reform Association, of which Mr. Mill was President:

"(IV.) To claim for the benefit of the State, the Interception by Taxation of the Future Unearned Increase of the Rent of Land (so far as the same can be ascertained), or a great part of that increase, which is continually taking place without any effort or outlay by the proprietors, merely through the growth of population and wealth; reserving to owners the option of relinquishing their property to the State, at the market value which it may have acquired at the time when this principle may be adopted by the Legislature."

502. What Shall be Said of the Equity of this Proposal? —In their appeal alike to history and to political equity, I can not see that the Land-Tenure Reformers, under Mr. Mill's leadership, were wrong. That (1), by the original Teutonic constitutions the land belonged to the tribe or the community, and not to individuals, and was generally cultivated and enjoyed in common or by rotation of tenure, that (2), even when permanence of individual possession was established and titles were created, the occupation of land was charged with duties to the State, both of fiscal contribution and of personal service, which were onerous, and which tended to increase as the needs of the State increased and as the rental value of the land increased; that (3), in Europe, generally, when the occupiers of land were released from these duties to the State, it was upon a consideration wholly inadequate or upon no consideration at all; while that release was conceded by the land-owning class, as the ruling class, to themselves as parties in interest, in a way which in this age would be regarded as corrupt; and that (4), the unqualified ownership of land, thus established, enables the land-owning class to reap an unearned benefit, at the expense of the community: these propositions seem to me indisputable.

503. What of its Expediency?—As a measure of political expediency, however, the scheme of the assumption by the State of the increment of land, appears to me fatally defective.

In the first place, it must be observed that a large part, at best, of the possible mischief has already been done, beyond repair, in the surrender of the rights of the community to individuals. As that surrender is now generations, even centuries old, and as much of the land has changed owners, sometimes over and over again in the interval, many of the present possessors having paid the full price of to-day, in good faith, under existing arrangements which were fully sanctioned by law, it would be simple robbery* for the State to reassert its interest in the land without fully indemnifying owners. This the English Land-Tenure Reform Association, in their programme already quoted, fully acknowledged. They proposed to "reserve to owners the option of relinquishing their property to the State at the market value which it may have

* It will be seen from what follows that it is only in this respect that Mr. Henry George's proposal differs from that of Mr. Mill.

acquired at the time when this principle may be adopted by the Legislature."

It is only, then, to the future increase in the value of land that this scheme would apply. Such a limitation of its scope would not only greatly reduce the importance of the benefit to be derived by the State in every community, but would deprive it of all significance in many communities* where land has doubtless already reached its maximum value.

But, secondly, government could, by the confession of the Association, not realize through this scheme all that is left after the foregoing deduction has been made. Inasmuch as the State is bound to be very careful and solicitous not to do injustice, the appraisement of the present rental value, or capital value of estates, in the administration of such a scheme, must be very conservative. This, again, is admitted by Mr. Mill. "It is not necessary," he says, "to enforce the rights of the State to the utmost farthing. A large margin should be allowed for possible miscalculation."† Yet such an allowance would diminish, by just so much, the inducement to the State to assert its interest in the lands now held by individuals.

504. How About Depreciating Property ?—Thirdly, it is clear, that the State, if it will claim the benefit of all increase in the value of lands resulting from the growth of demand, due to general causes affecting the increase of the community in numbers or productive power, is bound in equity, to make good all losses arising from the decrease in the value of lands which results from the decline of demand due to general causes acting in the opposite direction. If the so-called proprietor of land is not to be allowed to reap any gain not brought about by his own exertions, he must, in simple fairness, be protected against losses which no vigilance or effort of his

* For example, all over England, Ireland and Scotland, agricultural rents have been steadily *falling* through the past ten years or more. So it has been in many of the States of the American Union.

† No one who has studied with care, as Mr. Mill had done, the question of "Unexhausted Improvements" as an element in tenant right, could fail to appreciate the appalling difficulties which would attend the appraisement of real estate for a purpose like that in view of the Land-Tenure Reform Association.

could have averted. "Heads I win: tails you lose," is not a game at which the State can, in fairness or decency, play with its citizens.

The range of this consideration is not a narrow one. In almost every community, even the most flourishing, the phenomenon of declining values is seen side by side with that of rising values. Notwithstanding the large increase during the past twenty years in the aggregate value of real estate in the city of Boston, for instance, there are extensive sections where houses will not bring any thing near their price at the beginning of this period. Now if, in 1867, the principle of collecting for public uses all excess of rents above those prevailing at that date, or, at the option of the owner, paying the capital value of the property and assuming the ownership, had been adopted by competent authority in and for the city of Boston, the city would now be paying to thousands of property holders considerable annuities, representing deficiencies in rental value which have occurred since 1867, or else it would, which is more probable, have come into possession of street on street of houses and stores whose owners preferred to surrender their property at their capital value in 1867.

505. Fourthly :—Practical objections might be multiplied ; but it will be sufficient to refer to the official jobbery, trickery, and corruption which would be involved in the management by the state of all the landed property of the country, either in an attempt to administer it productively, or in the occasional re-valuation and re-leasing of it in parcels to suit the occasions of individuals. To my view, the condition of things that would result would be simply intolerable. When we contemplate the history of even petty transactions of a like character, on the part of our national government, or of the several state governments, it seems impossible to believe that any inducement should ever draw the American people, traditionally jealous of the enlargement of governmental powers, on to the adoption of such a measure.

MR. HENRY GEORGE'S CRUSADE.

506. The proposals for the nationalization of the land, offered as we have stated, by Mr. Mill in 1870, while they received much serious consideration from economists and publicists, aroused no popular excitement. In 1879, Mr. Henry George, then of San Francisco, published a work entitled "Progress and Poverty," which, about 1883, began to command public attention in an extraordinary degree. During and since that year, the agitation of the question of the public or private ownership of the soil, has gone forward with increasing vehemence, until now (1887), both in Great Britain and in the United States, large bands of enthusiastic disciples, call themselves by the name of the author of "Progress and Poverty."

Mr. George's practical proposals require but brief notice. They differ from those of Mr. Mill* only in the single respect that, while Mr. Mill, like an honest man, contemplated the full compensation of the existing body of owners of land, according to the value of their several properties, at the time the scheme should be adopted and proclaimed by adequate authority, Mr. George repudiates any such obligation on the part of the State, and proposes to confiscate the entire value of the land. The attempted justification for this precious price of villainy is found in the mere, bald assertion of Mr. Henry George, that the State never had the power to give a title to any parcel of land to any person, for any purpose ; and that, therefore, all land titles are, from the beginning, void. Under this scheme, alike the man who cultivates broad tracts for profit, and the man who occupies a corner with his humble dwelling ; the man who inherited land from his ancestors, and the man who has bought land with the savings from years of labor, would find themselves despoiled without redress or recompense. Even where the government itself sold the land and put the proceeds into its treasury, Mr. George would have the government confiscate the property, without refunding the price !

Mr. George is, indeed, good enough to say that he will

* Neither Mr. Mill nor Mr. George proposes that the title of land shall pass to the state. They agree on the plan of advancing the taxes upon the land so as to confiscate the successive increments of value.

allow improvements on the land to remain the property of those who made them, although, as he justly remarks, improvements made by any person on land not his own, appertain to the land and pass with it. The gratification naturally felt at this magnanimous proposal is, however, qualified by the reflection that, if the sovereign authority of a nation, with the full concurrence and glad consent of all its citizens, generation after generation, can not, as Mr. George assures us, avail to give the faintest title to the smallest parcel of land, possibly Mr. George's single permission to the unhappy intruder to retain possession of his improvements might not prove conclusive. In another generation, or perhaps another year, some new apostle of a regenerated humanity might become a candidate for the Mayoralty of New York, on the issue of confiscating land improvements.

So much for Mr. George's practical proposals. I will not insult my readers by discussing a project so steeped in infamy.

507. Mr. George's View of Rent.—In supporting these proposals, however, Mr. George has put forward a theory of the relation of Rent to the other shares of the product of industry, which has imposed upon so many persons that I deem it worth while to state and refute it here. Mr. George's view of Rent, as a factor in distribution, affords the key to the collocation of the words, Progress and Poverty, in the title of his work. The subject of that work is Rent; and Progress and Poverty is, in his opinion, an appropriate title for a treatise on that subject, inasmuch as, according to his theory, all social and industrial progress does, so long as land remains private property, that is, so long as rent is paid to any but the State, not only naturally but necessarily and inevitably, cause poverty to increase, at a constantly accelerating ratio. To use his own language: "*Irrespective of the increase of population, the effect of improvements in methods of production and exchange is to increase rent.*" The proof of this proposition is as follows:—

"Demand is not a fixed quantity that increases only as population increases. In each individual it rises with his power of getting the things demanded. . . .

"The amount of wealth produced is nowhere commensurate with the desire for wealth; and desire mounts with every additional opportunity for gratification.

"This being the case, the effect of labor-saving improvements will be to increase the production of wealth. Now, for the production of wealth, two things are required, labor and land. Therefore, the effect of labor-saving improvements will be to extend the demand for land, and wherever the limit of the quality of land in use is reached, to bring into cultivation lands of less natural productiveness, or to extend cultivation on the same lands to a point of lower natural productiveness. And thus, while the primary effect of labor-saving improvements is to increase the power of labor, the secondary effect is to extend cultivation, and, where this lowers the margin of cultivation, to increase rent. . . .

"Thus, where land is entirely appropriated, as in England, or where it is either appropriated or is capable of appropriation as rapidly as it is needed for use, as in the United States, the ultimate effect of labor-saving machinery or improvements is to increase rent, without increasing wages or interest.

"It is important that this be fully understood, for it shows that effects attributed by current theories to increase of population are really due to the progress of invention, and explains the otherwise perplexing fact that labor-saving machinery everywhere fails to benefit laborers."

And he concludes, after repeating and further illustrating this view of the effect of productive improvements and inventions, with the following italicized proposition: "Wealth, in all its forms, being the product of labor applied to land, or the products of land, any increase in the power of labor, the demand for wealth being unsatisfied, will be utilized in procuring more wealth, and thus increase the demand for land." And so, to use his own phrase, labor can not reap the benefits which advancing civilization brings, because they are "intercepted," that is, intercepted by rent.

That it may not be supposed that I am misrepresenting Mr. George, or omitting any qualification of his propositions, I quote another extended paragraph.

"*Land being necessary to labor,* and being reduced to private ownership, *every increase in the productive power of labor but increases rent,*—the price that labor must pay for the opportunity to utilize its powers; and thus *all the advantages* gained by the march of progress *go to the owners of land and wages do not increase.* Wages *can not* increase ; for, the greater the earnings of labor, the greater the price that labor must pay out of its earnings for the opportunity to make any earnings at all. The mere laborer has thus no more interest in the general advance of productive power than the Cuban slave has in advance in the price of sugar. And just as an advance in the price of sugar may make the condition of the slave worse, by inducing the master to drive him harder, so may the condition of the free laborer be positively, as well as relatively, changed for the worse by the increase in the productive power of his labor. For, begotten of the continuous advance of rents, arises a speculative tendency which discounts the effect of future improvements by a still further advance of rent."

508. The Second Count of the Indictment.—The last sentence introduces Mr. George's second count in his arraignment of rent, as the great social criminal.

Please carefully to note the point. The necessary, immediate and direct effect of any addition, from whatever source, to the productive power of labor, is to increase rents by just that amount, so that nothing is left to go either into enhanced wages or enhanced profits, the landlord taking the entire increase, whatever that may be.

But now another force enters, actually to deplete the already starving laborer. This is the speculative advance in land, owing to the expectation of further increments of value at the expense of the community.

"We have," says Mr. George, "hitherto assumed, as is generally assumed in elucidations of the theory of rent, that the *actual margin* of cultivation always coincides with what may be termed the *necessary margin* of cultivation,—that is to say, we have assumed that cultivation extends to less productive points only as it becomes necessary from the fact that natural opportunities are at the more productive points fully utilized. This, probably, is the case in stationary or very slowly progressing communities; but in rapidly progressing communities, where the swift and steady increase of rent gives confidence to calculations of further increase, it is not the case. In such communities, the confident expectation of increased prices produces, to a greater or less extent, the effects of a combination among land-holders, and tends to the withholding of land from use, in expectation of higher prices, thus forcing the margin of cultivation farther than required by the necessities of production."

509. The Third Count.—But this is not the end of the mischief attending the private ownership of land. We have now the third and final count in this arraignment. The speculative holding of land, just described, becomes, in turn, the cause of incessant industrial disturbance, and of those great periodic convulsions of production and trade which involve the laboring classes, poor, inert, and unapt to travel or to change of occupation, in the deepest distress.

"Production," says Mr. George, in explanation of an assumed industrial crisis, "has somewhere been checked, and this reduction in the supply of some things has shown itself in cessation of demand for others, the check propagating itself through the whole framework of industry and exchange. *Now, the industrial pyramid manifestly rests on the land.*

"The primary and fundamental occupations, which create a demand for all others, are evidently those which extract wealth from nature, and hence, if we trace from one exchange point to another, and from one occupation to another, this check to production, which shows itself in decreased purchasing power, we must ultimately find it in some obstacle which checks labor in expending itself on land.

"And that obstacle, it is clear, is the speculative advance in rent, or the value of land, which produces the same effects as (in fact, it is) a lock-out of labor and capital by landowners. This check to production, beginning at the basis of interlaced industry, propagates itself from exchange point to exchange point, cessation of supply becoming failure of demand, until, so to speak, the whole machine is thrown out of gear, and the spectacle is everwhere presented of labor going to waste while laborers suffer from want."

510. This concludes Mr George's arraignment of private property in land.* If these successive counts can be sustained, he is fully borne out in his conclusion that "the necessary result of material progress—land being private property—is, *no matter what the increase in population*, to force laborers to wages which give but a bare living;" or, as he elsewhere expresses it, that "material progress does not merely fail to relieve poverty, it actually produces it;" or, again, that, "whatever be the increase of productive power, rent steadily tends to swallow up the gain and *more than the gain;*" or, again, that "the ownership of the land on which and from which a man must live, is virtually the ownership of the man himself, and in acknowledging the right of some individuals to the exclusive use and enjoyment of the earth, we condemn other individuals to slavery, as fully and as completely as though we had formally made them chattels."

To a man who believed but a small fraction of this, the conclusion which Mr. George announces at the close of the following paragraph would appear irresistible :—

"As long as this institution exists, no increase in productive power can permanently benefit the masses, but, on the contrary, must tend to still further depress their condition. . . . Poverty deepens as wealth increases, and wages are forced down while productive power grows, because *land*, which is the source of all wealth and the field of all labor, is monopolized. To extirpate poverty, to make wages what justice commands they should be, the full earnings of the laborer, we must therefore substitute for the individual ownership of land a common ownership."

511. Examination of Mr. George's Propositions.—I believe I have presented, in the foregoing extracts, every essential feature of Mr. George's economic system, without suppression or perversion. Let us now take up, in inverse order,

---

* The paragraphs following are condensed from my work, Land and Its Rent.

Mr. George's three capital propositions. And, first, how much is there in the view that commercial disturbance and industrial depression are chiefly due to the speculative holding of land?

That land, in its own degree, shares with other species of property in the speculative impulses of exchange, is a matter of course. Every body knows it; no one ever thought of denying it. Mr. George makes no point against private property in land, however, unless he can show that it is, of all species of property, peculiarly the subject of speculative impulses. Now, this is so far from being either self-evident or established by adequate induction, that the contrary is the general opinion of economic writers. Of all species of property, land, especially agricultural land, starts latest and stops earliest in any upward movement of prices, as induced, for instance, by a paper-money inflation, which perhaps affords the best opportunity for the study of purely speculative impulses.

512. We now come to Mr. George's second count. The allegation that the enhancement of the value of land, above what should be regarded as the capitalized value of its present productive or income-yielding power, withdraws large bodies of land from cultivation, thus driving labor and capital to poorer and more distant soils, in order to secure the needed subsistence of the community, can only be characterized, so far as all the agricultural* uses of land are concerned, as a baseless assumption, for which not a particle of proper statistical proof can be adduced, and which is directly contrary to the reason of the case.

Because, forsooth, a man is holding a tract of land in the hope of a rise in its value, years hence, does that constitute any reason why he should refuse to rent it, this year or next, and get from it what he can, were it no more than enough to pay his taxes and a part of the interest on the money borrowed to "carry" the property? How unreasonable to assume that

---

* It will be observed that in the extracts quoted it is *cultivation* which is spoken of.

men owning good productive land will refuse to allow it to be cultivated now, simply because they can not get for it a rent which corresponds to what they look forward ultimately to realize as its capital price!

Undoubtedly the speculative treatment of building lots does cause a certain amount of city real estate to be held out of use. Nobody needed Mr. George to tell him this; but that the amount of land so reserved is such as seriously to retard the development of population, trade, or manufactures, except in a craze like that which seized the people of San Francisco in 1868,* seems highly improbable.

513. Progress and Poverty?—Let us now proceed to deal with Mr. George's main proposition, the proposition to which the others are subsidiary. If this be established, it really does not matter much whether the others are true or not, since the condition of humanity under the grinding pressure of this main force will be about as bad as it could be; while, if this be disproved, Mr. George's whole system must break down ridiculously, leaving it to matter little whether the minor evils attributed to the private ownership of land be found to have any real existence or not. This it is which constitutes the original feature of Mr. George's book, the proposition, namely, that, "irrespective of the increase in population, the effect of improvements in methods of production and exchange is to increase rent;" this effect being carried so far that "all the advantages gained by the march of progress go to the owners of land, and wages do not increase," the laboring man having "no more interest in the general advance of productive power than the Cuban slave has in advance in the price of sugar," capital also, in its turn, suffering, and to an equal extent, since, as Mr. George states, the effect of labor-saving machinery or improvements is to increase rent without increasing *either wages or interest.*

---

* This episode, consequent on the fast approaching completion of the first trans-continental railway, appears to have profoundly affected Mr. George's mind, and have produced in him the belief that what there and then took place, under extraordinary circumstances, is a common incident of land ownership.

Now this is not only false, but ridiculously false, blunder being piled on blunder, to reach a conclusion so monstrous.

514. In the first place, the proposition is contradicted by plain facts of common observation and by unimpeachable testimony of industrial statistics. The laborer has gained in wages through the labor-saving inventions and improvements of modern times. Speaking of England, Sir James Caird says: "The laborer's earning power in procuring the staff of life cost him five days' work to pay for a bushel of wheat in 1770, four days' in 1840, and two and a half days' in 1870." So much for bread. "Thirty years ago," says Sir James, "probably not one-third of the people of this country consumed animal food more than once a week. Now, nearly all of them eat it in meat or cheese or butter, once a day." The same high authority adds: "The laborer is better lodged than he ever was before." We need no one to tell us that the laborer's power to purchase manufactured articles has increased, since 1770, much more rapidly than his power to purchase agricultural produce, whether animal or vegetable.

To the assertion of Mr. George that even the capitalist gains nothing by inventions and improvements in the agencies of trade or manufactures, because the landlord usurps and absorbs all possible increase of productive power, what better answer can we give than that of Professor Emile de Lavelèye, himself a qualified advocate of the state ownership of land?

"Who occupy the pretty houses and villas which are springing up in every direction in all prosperous towns? Certainly, more than two-thirds of these occupants are fresh capitalists. The value of capital engaged in industrial enterprise exceeds that of land itself, and *its power of accumulation is far greater than that of ground rents*. . . . We see, then, that the increase of profits and of interest takes a much larger proportion of the total value of labor, and is a more general and powerful cause of inequality, than the increase of rent." *

515. So much for industrial statistics and facts of common observation. Let us now turn to the reason of the case. And,

---

* "Contemporary Review," November, 1882.

first, let us recite Mr. George's own argument. "The effect," he says, "of labor-saving improvements will be to increase the production of wealth. Now, for the production of wealth, two things are required—labor and land. *Therefore* the effect of labor-saving improvements will be to extend the demand for land."

A pretty piece of reasoning this! Two things are needed for the production of wealth, land and labor; *therefore* an increase of production will "extend" the demand for land, forsooth! But *why not also for labor*, since both are concerned in production?

But Mr. George is further in error, even, than would so far appear. He has got the thing exactly wrong. It is not only true that an increased production of wealth *may* involve an enhanced demand for labor as well as for land; but it is also incontestably true that the increased production of wealth rarely if ever causes an increased demand for land without a corresponding demand for labor, while, on the contrary, an increased production of wealth may cause an enormous increase in the demand for labor without enhancing the demand for the products of the soil in any degree whatsoever.

Here is a pound of raw cotton, the production of which makes a certain demand, or drain, upon the land. To that cotton may be applied the labor of one operative for half an hour, worth, say, five cents. Successive demands for the production of wealth may lead to the application of, first, a full hour's labor, then of two hours', then of three, four, or five; finer and finer fabrics being successively produced, until at last the pound of cotton has been wrought into the most exquisite articles. Mr. George says that the whole effect of any increase in the production of wealth is to enhance the demand for land. Here is a large increase of production, twofold, threefold, tenfold, with no additional demand, or drain, upon the soil.

516. But I go further, and assert, without fear of contradiction, that not only is no increase in the demand for land necessarily involved in an increased production of wealth, but that the enhancement of the demand for land, in the progress of society, habitually falls short of the enhancement of the demand for labor, the increase of production taking two great forms,—one which involves no increase whatever in the materials derived from the soil; the other in which the increased demand for land falls short, generally far short, often almost infinitely short, of the increased demand for labor.

Let us look around. I have cited one instance, that of the use made in the mill of a pound of cotton, manufactured successively into fabrics worth, perhaps, twenty cents a pound, then thirty, then fifty, then one dollar. This is not an extreme case.

Here is the rude furniture of a laborer's cottage, worth perhaps $30. The same amount of wood may be made into furniture worth $200 for the home of the clerk, or into furniture worth $2,000 for the home of the banker. The steel that would be needed to make a cheap scythe worth eighty cents may be rendered into watch-springs, or surgical or philosophical instruments worth $100 or $200. A gentleman of means goes to Delmonico's, and pays two, three or five dollars for a dinner which makes no heavier drain upon the productive essences of the soil than a dinner of corned beef and cabbage for which a laborer pays twenty-five cents. A part of the difference between the prices of the two dinners, to be sure, represents the cost of an expensive business "stand" on Fifth Avenue; but by far the greater part represents service of one kind or another, at one stage or another, in making the dishes exquisite in appearance and flavor, in serving them neatly and elegantly with all the appliances of taste and fashion. Our gentleman, before dining, had perhaps been measured for a pair of boots for which he was to pay $12 or $15, yet containing no more leather, and so making no more draught upon the productive essences of the soil, in the way of nourishing the animal from which the leather was cut, than the laborer's $3 pair of "stogies"; he had also ordered a suit of clothes for $60 or $75, at his tailor's, no thicker, no warmer, containing no more fiber, than the laborer's $15 tweeds. In all these cases (and they fairly represent the facts of personal con sumption in modern society) the main cause for the excess of value in products of higher price is not the use of a larger quantity of material, involving a greater demand or drain upon the productive essences of the soil, but the application of *more labor* to the same quantity of material.

517. How Far Mr. George is in Error.—In contradiction, then, of Mr. George's proposition that the entire effect of an increase of production is expended in raising rents, neither wages nor the interest of capital deriving any gain whatsoever therefrom, rent indeed absorbing the entire gain," and more than the gain," we have seen,—

1. That an increase of production *may* enhance the demand for labor equally with the demand for land.

2. That, in fact, in those forms of production which especially characterize modern society, the rate of enhancement of the demand for labor tends to far exceed the rate of enhancement of the demand for land.

3. That an increased demand for the production of wealth may, and in a vast body of instances does, enhance the demand for labor without enhancing the demand for land in any, the slightest, degree, the whole effect being expended in the elaboration of the same amount of material.

4. We have now only to show, in the fourth place, that, instead of all improvements and inventions increasing the demand for land, as Mr. George declares, the most numerous and most important classes of improvements and inventions actually operate powerfully, directly, and exclusively, in reducing the demand for land,—we have, I say, only to show this, to convict this writer of the grossest incompetence for economic reasoning. This it will be easy to do.

518. Influence, upon Rents, of Improvements in Transportation.—With few exceptions, all improvements and inventions fall naturally under one or another of three great classes,—first, those which affect manufacturing industry; second, those which affect transportation; third, those which affect the cultivation of the soil.

Of these three classes it has always been admitted by economists that the first tends to enhance the demand for land,

and thus to raise rents, although, as we have just now seen, not necessarily, or indeed usually, without also enhancing the demand for labor and capital, and thus raising wages and interest. The two remaining classes of improvements and inventions tend directly, and indeed operate exclusively,* to reduce the demand for land, leaving, thus, the whole advantage of such improvements and inventions to be acquired by either labor or capital, or, in one proportion or another, by both labor and capital.

And, first, of improvements in transportation. I need not waste time in calling to mind the mighty strides which invention has made, during the past fifty years, in this direction, substituting for the sailing vessel of 400 tons, which carried its petty cargo of wheat in forty or sixty days from New York to Liverpool, the steamship of 5,000 tons, which makes the passage in nine days or twelve ; substituting for the tedious wagon carriage which in forty or fifty miles, perhaps in twenty or thirty only, ate up the whole value of the freight, carriage by steam cars, drawn on steel rails, which, allowing for transport from Dakota to New York, leaves enough of the value of the freight to pay for the ocean passage and for the support of the producer upon those distant plains. Add the telegraph and the fast mail, for transmitting orders and transacting sales, and one will hardly question the assertion that the greatest of all the classes of improvements and inventions effected within the last half-century, has been that which relates to transportation.

Is it the effect of improvements of this class to enhance rents? Absolutely and exclusively the reverse. Whatever quickens and cheapens transport, acts directly in the reduction of rents, and can not act in any other way, since it throws out of cultivation the poorer lands previously in use for the supply of the market, enabling the better soils at a distance to take their place, thus raising the lower limit, or, as it is called, the "margin" of cultivation, and thus reducing rents.

* "Irrespective of the increase of population," to use Mr. George's own voluntary qualification.

519. Influence, upon Rents, of Improvements in Agriculture.—But, secondly, take the case of agricultural improvements and inventions. Here the effect on rents is not so simple. Yet it is perfectly demonstrable that, of the two groups * into which such inventions or improvements are divided, all of one kind diminish rent in a certain degree, while all of the other kind diminish it in a much higher degree.

The two kinds of agricultural improvements and inventions referred to are :

First, those which do not actually increase the amount of produce, but diminish the labor and expense by which that amount is obtained, such as the improved construction of tools, or the introduction of new instruments which spare manual labor.

Second, those which enable the land to yield a greater absolute produce, such as the disuse of fallows by means of the rotation of crops, the introduction of new vegetable species, the introduction of new and more powerful fertilizing agents or a better application of familiar manures, and mechanical inventions, like sub-soil plowing or tile-draining.

Now, improvements or inventions of the first class, as, by the supposition, they do not increase the produce of the land, so they do not, supposing them to be equally applicable to all grades of soil, diminish the share of that produce going to the landlords as rent. But while the actual number of pounds, bushels, etc., of agricultural products going to the owners of the soil remains the same, in the face of such improvements and inventions, those products are *cheapened* through the saving of labor in their production. Thus, while rents remain the same, *in kind*, their money value, or power to purchase the products of other branches of industry or the services of other classes of producers, is diminished in just so far as such improvements are effectual.

520. Next, it is clear that those agricultural improvements and inventions which enable a given area to yield a greater quantity of produce, act even more directly in diminution of

* As justly characterized by Mr. J. S. Mill.

rent. Take, for illustration, the disuse of fallows by rotation of crops. Formerly it was thought necessary to let even the best land lie out of cultivation one year in three or four. On the contrary, it is now perfectly established that, if crops be duly varied, land may be continuously cultivated without exhaustion. It is evident that this discovery is equivalent to increasing the capacity of any tract by one-half or one-third: so that, for a given amount of agricultural produce required for the sustentation of the community and for the raw materials of manufacture, such an improvement would allow vast bodies of the poorer grades of soil to be thrown out of cultivation, thus diminishing (paragraph 257) the aggregate amount to be received, as rents, by landlords, in that community. A similar effect, in a greater or less degree, would be produced by the introduction of new and more powerful fertilizers, or by sub-soil plowing and under-drainage.

521. Summing up.—We thus see that all real agricultural inventions and improvements tend, as all improvements and inventions in transportation tend, directly and exclusively, to diminish rents. So that of the three grand classes into which industrial improvements and inventions are divided, two act in a direction exactly opposite to that in which Mr. George's theory would require them to act. Of the third grand class of improvements and inventions, viz., those relating to manufactures, we have admitted that some do, by calling for larger amounts of raw material, enhance the demand for land; but we have shown, that in these very cases, the increase in the demand for labor is almost always equal to the increase in the demand for land, is often greater, is sometimes vastly greater. We have, also, shown that there are other, still more numerous and more important, improvements and inventions in manufactures which do not enhance the land in any degree, while they call for greater and still greater applications of labor to the same amounts of material.

Can any thing more be required to show how groundless and preposterous is the view of the hitherto unsuspected importance of rent as a factor in the distribution of wealth, which Mr. George has presented as a marvelous discovery in economics, and upon which he has built his pretentious superstructure: the necessary relation of Progress to Ever Increasing Poverty? That such an argument should for a moment have imposed upon anybody, is enough to give one a new conception of the intellectual capabilities of mankind.

XI.

THE BANKING FUNCTIONS.

522. "The trade or profession of banking," says Lord Liverpool, "has been exercised in all countries and all ages. It existed in the republic of Greece and in ancient Rome. There were, in all these States, men who received money as a deposit, repaid it upon the drafts of those who had intrusted them with it, and derived their profits from having this money in their custody."

1st. Financiering.—In modern times, the first banks appear in Italy. Mr. Bagehot states that the earliest of these "were finance companies. The Bank of St. George, at Genoa, and other banks founded in imitation of it, were at first only companies to make loans to, and to float loans for, the governments of the cities in which they were founded."

"Financiering," then, may be regarded as the first banking function developed, in modern times. In the reign of William and Mary certain capitalists made a loan of £1,200,000 to the English government, receiving, in consideration therefor, a charter constituting them the Governor and Company of the Bank of England. Robert Morris's Bank of North America had a very similar origin. Under the present National Banking system of the United States, the bank begins by lending all, or nearly all, its capital to the government. The great war loans of the United States, 1861-5, were, in the main, "floated" by the banks.

523. 2d. Book Credits of the Bank of Amsterdam.—The next banking function historically developed was that of giving the people good money in place of a medley of worn and clipped coins, of a great diversity of coinages, belonging to many nations. It was to serve this office that the banks of Northern Europe were created.

"Before 1609," says Adam Smith, "the great quantity of clipped and worn foreign coin which the extensive trade of Amsterdam brought from all parts of Europe, reduced the value of its currency about 9 per cent. below that of good money, fresh from the mint. Such money no sooner appeared than it was melted down or carried away, as it always is in such circumstances.* The merchants, with plenty of currency, could not always find a sufficient quantity of good money to pay their bills of exchange; and the value of those bills, in spite of several regulations which were made to prevent it, became in a great measure uncertain.

"In order to remedy these inconveniences, a bank was established, in 1609, under the guarantee of the city. This bank received both foreign coin and the light and worn coin of the country, at its real intrinsic value in the good standard money of the country, deducting only so much as was necessary for defraying the expense of coinage and the other necessary expenses of management. For the value which remained after this small deduction was made, it gave a credit on its books. This credit was called bank-money, which, as it represented money exactly according to the standard of the mint, was always of the same real value, and intrinsically worth more than current money. It was at the same time enacted "that all bills drawn upon or negotiated at Amsterdam, of the value of 60 guilders or upwards, should be paid in bank money, which at once took away all uncertainty in the value of those bills."

It will be observed that Adam Smith calls these credits inscribed upon the books of the Bank of Amsterdam, "bank-money;" but this money, if it is to be called so, will be seen to differ widely from the bank money of to-day, already described: 1st. It did not circulate from hand to hand, as the ordinary medium of effecting exchanges; 2d. It was never in excess of the amount of metallic money actually in the vaults on deposit.

* See statement of Gresham's Law, par. 181.

524. 3d. Cancellation of Indebtedness.—The next banking function, which we are called upon to notice, is the Cancellation of Indebtedness.

An enormous volume of indebtedness at all times exists in any highly progressive country, which has to be paid and renewed from day to day. The labor and loss of time involved in collecting debts and paying moneys, with the probable delay and disappointment involved therein, would be almost intolerable unless some special agency were established for doing this work upon a large scale and with all the advantages which we have found to result from the application of the division of labor. This function the bank performs.

If, in any great city, many banks are required to carry on this function, these banks, in turn, establish a common agency for settling their mutual obligations, called a Clearing House.*

The transactions of such an institution in New York or London may amount to thirty or forty thousand millions of dollars a year. This vast body of indebtedness is adjusted through the labor of a hundredth part as many clerks and messengers, and the use of a hundredth part as much actual money as would have been required, had each person who had money owing to him been obliged to attend to the collection himself, or through his own clerks or messengers.

525. 4th. Exchange.—The next banking function is to remit money and conduct exchange.

What is termed "Exchange," is merely the principle of the cancellation of indebtedness between individuals of the same city, carried out to trading communities and nations. We shall speak, under a subsequent title, of the principles regulating Foreign Exchanges.

This function, again, the bank to a great extent performs, and in so doing renders the trading community an immense service. If every merchant who had to pay money in another city or country were obliged to find out, for himself, some

* The subject of the Clearing House and, indeed, all the agencies and instrumentalities of trade will be found treated most lucidly and justly in Prof. Jevons' work "Money and the Mechanism of Exchange."

person who had the right to receive money at that place, at that time, and perhaps in the same sum, an inconceivable amount of inconvenience and delay, of vexation and disappointment, often resulting in commercial discredit, would be experienced.

If we may accept Mr. Henry Thornton's account * of the rise of the country banks of England, it was through the gradual growth of exchange-operations between country shopkeepers and those of the cities, that these institutions came, almost unnoticed, into existence.

526.—5th.—Safe Deposit.—The fifth banking function is to serve as a place of safe deposit. Mr. Francis, in his History of the Bank of England, attributes the rise of the city banks primarily to the need of this service. In the unguarded and unlighted London which Macaulay so graphically describes in his memorable Third Chapter, robberies and burglaries were of frequent occurrence. No man's home was safe, if known to contain any considerable amount of treasure, unless barricaded and defended by armed servants. The goldsmiths, having in the way of their trade to keep large quantities of gold and silver, had strong houses strongly guarded. To them, men of smaller means, private gentlemen, or shopkeepers, intrusted what they dared not keep at home, paying, at first, for the privilege.

In the course of time, the goldsmiths found that this custody of funds afforded a legitimate opportunity for realizing a profit, through loaning some part of these deposits. Then the depositors were no longer required to pay for the safe keeping. In time, the bankers came, perhaps, to pay interest on the deposits, themselves, which they loaned out to others, at higher rates, while the depositors received certificates of the value of what they had left with the goldsmiths. The certificates soon began to circulate from hand to hand. "These," says Mr. Francis, "may be considered the first kind of bank notes issued in England." In this way the goldsmiths' street in London, Lombard Street, came to be the bankers' street, the greatest banking street of the world.

* In his famous work on Paper Credit, published in 1802.

The ordinary bank is still, to a great extent, a place of safe deposit for money, family jewels, deeds, and bonds, although special institutions for safe deposit are now found in many large cities.

527.—6th. Deposit and Discount.—The sixth and the chief of the legitimate functions of the modern bank is to serve as an intermediary in the loan of capital, in aid of commerce and manufactures and other private enterprises, not merely to loan its own capital, as in the case of the Bank of Genoa and others that have been spoken of, or to conduct loans for government, or for great corporations.

The technical terms, deposit and discount, serve to characterize this function. It is in this way that banks make their largest contribution to the advancement of commerce and industry. This office of banking is, however, as much overrated by some as it is underrated by others. Men who are not versed in economic principles, when they see the wonderful effects wrought by gathering into one great reservoir the wealth of ten thousand individuals, much of which would otherwise be hoarded or unwisely applied, and conducting it thence, as occasions require, in various directions, through channels judiciously devised to secure the highest and most effective irrigation of the field of industry, are apt to imagine that the bank in some way creates capital. This is a wholly mistaken notion. The bank adds to the wealth of the community only by economizing and directing capital to the best ends.

So important is this function that most European writers, when they speak of banking, have only in mind deposit and discount, all other functions being held to be minor and subordinate.

528.—7th. Issue of Paper Money.—To an American, however, the word, banking, is more likely to bring up the notion of paper money. The issue of such money is the seventh and the last of the banking functions which we have occasion to consider.

That the making of money is not necessarily connected with deposit and discount, is abundantly established by the consent of all writers of authority in this field, as well as by the example of many of the greatest deposit banks of the world. "Issuing," says Mr. Nicholson, "is creating money; banking is managing money after it has been issued."

"A bank of issue," says Lord Overstone, "is intrusted with the creation of the circulating medium; a bank of deposit and discount is concerned only with the use, distribution or application of that circulating medium. The principles upon which these two branches of business ought to be conducted are perfectly distinct, and never can be reduced to one and the same rule."

The great London joint-stock banks, a single one of which holds deposits rising into tens of millions, and whose ordinary dividends are three times as great as those of the Bank of England, never issue a note.

In this country, however, the word bank, through much of our history, has to most people signified little more than a place where paper money was manufactured.

529. The Banking Agencies.—Such are the banking functions. The agencies by which the functions are performed may be grouped under four heads: (1), state banks; (2), joint-stock banks; (3), private banks; (4), bill-brokers and dealers in exchange. These agents enter in very different proportions to effect the banking work to be done in different countries. In this country, so large a part of the banking work was, from the beginning of the country till the outbreak of the war of secession, done by joint-stock banks, that it may be broadly said that this was the sole banking agency known to our people, although, in a few cities, private banking houses of high reputation were early started and well maintained, and the business of bill-broking was not unrecognized. Under another title, we shall give a brief sketch of the present "National Banking System" of the United States.

XII.

THE PRESENT BANKING SYSTEM OF THE UNITED STATES.

530.—The National Banking System of the U. S.*— No bank, in the modern sense of that term, was established in America during the colonial period. The word, bank, was indeed sometimes used, with reference, however, to a batch of paper money issued from a colonial treasury. During the revolution the eminent financier, Robert Morris, established a bank in aid of the continental finances. In 1790 there were three banks in the United States; the Bank of North America, in Philadelphia, established, as related, by Robert Morris, but then under a charter from the state of Pennsylvania; the Bank of New York, in the city of that name; and the Bank of Massachusetts, in Boston. In 1791 was created the first Bank of the United States, with a capital of ten millions of dollars, having a charter for twenty years, with power to issue notes payable on demand in specie. So completely without regulation and without inspection was the so-called paper money of the United States in that period, that it is impossible to recover the facts of banking capital, circulation, deposits or specie. Scarcely a statistical fragment survives. There is reason to suppose that the officers of many banks did not themselves know the liabilities of their own institutions. The paper money issued by such an institution, was, in every economic sense, inconvertible. The pretense of conversion could only be maintained by a stringent public opinion, hostile to the presentation of bank notes for redemption, by bank retaliations, and even, in frontier communities, by "lynch law."

531. On the refusal of Congress to re-charter the bank of the United States, a large number of the state banks sprang into existence, almost all of the usual American "joint-stock" type, on the principle of limited liability. In not a single state were the banks subject to regulation or even supervision,

---

* The first part of this article is condensed from the twelfth chapter of my work on Money, Trade and Industry.

to make sure that they did their duty or that they did not commit injury. The language of Mr. J. R. McCulloch, regarding the American banking system of that day, is hardly extravagant. "Had a committee of clever men been selected to devise means by which the public might be tempted to engage in all manner of absurd projects, and be most easily duped and swindled, we do not know that they could have hit upon any thing half so likely to effect their object as the existing American banking system. It has no redeeming quality about it, but is, from beginning to end, a compound of quackery and imposture."

532. The outbreak of war with England caused the suspension of specie payments by nearly all banks except those of New England ; but this was followed by an enormous increase of issues, so that the outstanding notes, which had been estimated at twenty millions in 1811, rose, according to Secretary Crawford, to somewhere between sixty-two and seventy millions in 1813, and to somewhere between ninety-nine and a hundred and ten millions in 1815. The fact that it was impossible for the secretary of the treasury to tell, within eleven millions, the amount of the notes outstanding, is fairly characteristic of the monetary system at this time. The circulating paper was of every degree of value down to utter worthlessness. Many banks were ably managed by honest men, with reasonable regard to the public interest. Many were organized and conducted by sharpers and swindlers, as a means of wholesale robbery.*

At the close of the war, in 1815, the depreciation of bank paper reached, in some cases, fifteen, twenty and even twenty-five per cent. The excess of circulating paper had also been promoted by the extensive issue of United States treasury

---

* Prof. Sumner, in his History of American Currency, states that the Farmers' Exchange bank, of Gloucester, Mass., was organized with a nominal capital of one million dollars. Only $19,141.46 was ever paid in ; and of this the directors subsequently withdrew their own subscriptions, leaving $3,081.11. One man bought out eleven directors for $1,300 each and then loaned himself $760,265. When the bank failed it had $86.46 in specie. The bank notes outstanding were estimated at $580,000

notes. These were not of forced circulation; they failed to be paid at maturity, and added greatly to commercial distrust and distress. Throughout 1816 the banks continued to issue their discredited notes, while floods of unchartered scrip were poured out, in bills of all denominations from six cents upward.

533. The evils of the financial situation led to the establishment, in 1816, of the second Bank of the United States, with a capital of thirty-five millions, of which the United States government owned one-fifth, and with a charter having twenty years to run. Before 1836, however, the bank had been broken down by the relentless attacks of President Jackson, and it was finally driven to take refuge under a Pennsylvania charter. Our space will not serve to discuss how far the failure of the second United States Bank to perform its anticipated office of regulating the paper circulation and of preventing excessive and improper issues by the state banks, was due to its original constitution; how far to false management; how far to circumstances; how far to persecution by the administration. Suffice it to say that the paper money of the country, during this period, was a weltering chaos. The wildly extravagant issues of really inconvertible paper money, supplied the motive and the means for every species of extravagant, wanton and irresponsible speculation. Words could scarcely exaggerate the extent to which the distortion of production and the misapplication of capital were carried.* The whole head was sick and the whole heart faint.

---

* "That the evils of this period were due chiefly to vices of paper money banking seems too clear to be questioned. The opening up of the western country would inevitably have led to much wild adventure, commercially and industrially; but it was the 'elasticity' of the circulation, the facility of local issue, without the reality, or scarcely the pretense, of redemption, which made the banks, even the best of them, reckless as to the character of the enterprises to which they gave assistance; while the money thus put into circulation, without 'reflux,' enhanced prices, and still further stimulated both speculative investments and speculative trading. When the courage of the better class of banks gave way, hundreds of 'wild cat' or 'coon-box banks,' so called, without capital,

The retribution came in the panic of 1837, in the second and heavier shock of 1839, and in the long and dreary prostration of industry which followed.

534. The experiences of this period led, in several states, to legislation designed to place the issue of bank notes on a sounder basis. In 1838 the free banking system of New York was established, under which all circulating notes were to be secured by deposit, with the state comptroller, of United States or New York stocks or bonds, and of mortgages on improved or productive real estate. A little later a law was passed requiring each bank to redeem its notes at some agency in New York city, Albany or Troy. Subsequent acts increased the proportion of securities to notes issued, and furnished further guaranties to holders.

This is the scheme of secured circulation, known as the New York system, which came to be imitated, more or less fully; and on which, to a considerable extent, the banking laws of the United States are framed.

The plan of basing a circulation upon securities is not to be altogether approved. It does not give convertibility, in the sense of preventing excessive issues, even in the view of the advocates of the "banking principle." * It does not so much as secure the perfect acceptability of the notes, as a medium of exchange, since the receiver desires to be assured that the notes will, at any moment, be worth what he has taken them for, whereas the New York system only gives him a pledge that, should the bank fail to redeem its notes, he will, at some future date, after the bank shall have been wound up and the securities disposed of by the comptroller, receive the face value of all the notes which he may then hold.

---

without a constituency, with no past and no expectations of a future, whose managers risked nothing and had nothing to lose, came forward with loans of notes to speculators who planned to build cities in the wilderness, or contractors who proposed to construct roads and bridges without materials, tools, or money to pay wages. Again, as in early New England, a bank meant a batch of paper money."—Walker: Money, Trade and Industry.

* See paragraphs 224–6.

535. But while this system can not be accepted as based upon perfectly sound principles of money, or even of banking policy, it proved at the time so great a check on reckless paper money banking, and it has had so great an effect in educating the public mind to more correct views of the banking function and of the responsibilities attaching to note issues, that it deserves to be treated with much consideration by the historian of American money. The painful experiences of 1837–40, and the active discussion of the principles of money and banking which they called forth ; the growth of a public sentiment condemning an excess of paper issues, and the formulation of precepts, more or less carefully observed by bank managers ; a vast improvement in the commercial morality of the country, due partly to education, and even more to the development of manufactures which, to a vastly greater degree than agriculture, rest on good faith and commercial honesty ; the shortening of the terms of credit ;* these causes, together with the legislation which has been described and the development of the Suffolk bank system † in New England, served to place the paper money issues of the United States on an improved basis between 1840 and 1860. The rapid improvement of trade and industry after the panic of 1857, already alluded to (par. 243), affords a striking proof of the comparative soundness of credit, trade and industry in the later period.

536. Early in the war of secession, the treasury being in great distress, Secretary Chase initiated the movement which resulted in the establishment of the present banking system of the United States. This system was to be essentially modeled on that established in New York by the law of 1838, all note issues being secured by an abundant deposit, at

---

* Prior to 1837 commercial credits were often extended to twelve and even eighteen months.

† This was a system, gradually developed, by which substantially all the banks of New England were brought to maintain a deposit with the Suffolk Bank of Boston, in consideration of which that bank bound itself to redeem their notes on presentation.

the Treasury Department in Washington, of United States stocks. Indeed, it was this feature which furnished the real motive to the scheme. The Treasury was to sell to the banks some hundreds of millions of bonds, as the basis for their note circulation, while all notes of state banks not coming under the new system were to be "taxed out of circulation."

As a measure of fiscal resource, the national bank law was essentially a failure. Owing to the delay in securing the desired legislation * and in transmuting the existing state banks into national banks, it was not until the war was nearly over and until the credit of the United States had become so well established as to give the Treasury the ability to borrow freely, at home or abroad, that the new national banks began to call for bonds in large amounts, as a basis of circulation.

537. But while that banking system failed to answer the expectations of Secretary Chase as a fiscal resource, it resulted in placing the paper money banking of the country on a more secure and convenient basis than it had ever before occupied. In all previous periods of our national history the bank money of some sections had been liable to a discount—often a considerable discount—if offered far away from the place of issue; while, in addition to the actual losses sustained by holders, the annoyance resulting from the frequent refusal to receive banknotes by those who did not know about the individual bank whose name and devices they bore, was almost intolerable. Under the existing system, a national banknote from Texas or Minnesota, if not suspected to be counterfeit, passes as readily in Massachussetts or Pennsylvania as the notes of local banks. By the new law, the United States Comptroller of the Currency, whose office was then created, was authorized to permit the establishment, for a term not exceeding twenty years, of banking associations consisting of not less than five persons, with a minimum capital, except in small places, of one hundred thousand dollars. Such associations were required

* The act establishing the national banking system bears date February, 1863.

to deposit, with the Treasury Department, United States bonds to the extent of at least one-third their capital, for which there should be issued to them circulating notes in amount equal to ninety per cent. of the market value of their bonds, but not beyond ninety per cent. of the par value of such bonds. The issue of currency, under this act, was to be limited to three hundred millions, that amount to be apportioned among the States according to population and banking capital.

In 1882, a new law was passed, providing for extending the charters of national banks.

538. The operation of the law regarding the deposit of United States bonds as a basis of circulation, may be illustrated as follows: A national bank expends $160,000 in the purchase of bonds, then selling at 80 per cent. of their par or face value. The bank would then hold bonds to the amount (at par) of $200,000. On the deposit of these, the treasury department would issue circulating notes thereon to the extent of ninety per cent., not of their par, but of their market value, viz.: one hundred and forty-four thousand dollars. These notes, bearing its own corporate title and its characteristic devices, the bank would issue in the discount of commercial paper. This might, in fact, constitute the greater part of what the bank had, at the outset, to loan—its own promises to pay. If we suppose the bank to keep out the whole body of notes received from the treasury on loans bearing interest at an average rate of five per cent., the annual income from this source will be $7,200. In addition thereto, the bank will receive from the treasury department, semi-annually or quarterly, drafts for the amount of the interest falling due on the bonds held for the redemption of the notes. If the rate of interest on the bonds were four per cent. (on the par value, of course), the amount so received would be $8,000 a year, making the aggregate income on both accounts, $15,200. This would be a return of 9½ per cent. on the amount—$160,000—expended in the purchase of the bonds. In addition thereto, would be the expectation of profit arising from the fact that, at the maturity of the bonds, be that five, fifteen, thirty or fifty years hence, the government is bound to pay the face value of the bonds, whereas the bank purchased them at eighty per cent. Now, the "present value" of twenty (100-80) dollars, at five per cent. interest, is considerable if payable in five years, is worth considering if payable in fifteen years, is inconsiderable if payable in thirty or fifty years : so that this element may amount to much, little or nothing, according to the term which the bonds have to run.

If, in a second case, the bank invested the same sum—$160,000, in United States bonds, at par, it would receive bonds to the amount of $160,000, on which the treasury department would issue $144,000 worth of circulating notes, as before, being ninety per cent., this time, alike of the market and of the par value of the bonds held for redemption. Making the same assumptions as before, regarding the average rate of interest realized by the bank on its loans, and the rate of interest on the bonds themselves, we should have the income from the former source, $7,200, and from the latter source, $6,400 ; an aggregate of $13,600, being eight and a half per cent. on the amount invested, with no longer any expectation of profit from the difference between the amount of purchase money and the principal of the bonds to be paid at maturity.

If, in a third case, we suppose that the bank expends the same amount, as before, in the purchase of United States bonds, bearing a premium of twenty-five per cent. (and the bonds of the United States have almost always been at a premium, greater or less, at times rising, on some classes of bonds, to the rate assumed), the face value of the bonds so purchased would be but $128,000, on which the treasury department would issue notes to the amount of $115,200, being ninety per cent. of the face value of the bonds, though but seventy-two per cent., this time, of their market value. On the same assumption as to interest, etc., as before, the bank would receive from the loan of its notes $5,760 ; from the government, as interest on the bonds, $5,120 ; an aggregate of $10,880, or only six and eight-tenths per cent. on the $160,000 invested. In this case, moreover, there must be taken into account an ultimate loss of one-fifth of the purchase money. Although the bank has paid $125 for each $100 bond, the government will, at maturity, pay only the face value, namely, $100. The "present value" of the amount thus to be, sooner or later, lost, is to be determined by the same principles which would be applied to obtaining the "present value" of the amount to be ultimately gained, had the bank purchased bonds at a discount. As we said before, their "present value" would be much, little or practically nothing, according to the term which the bonds had to run.

539. The profit to the banks, under the present system, largely depends, it will be seen, upon two elements : the rate of interest on the bonds themselves, and the premium or discount at which the bonds can be, at any given time, purchased. During the war, a bank could purchase, for $100,000 in greenbacks, an equal amount of six per cent. bonds, payable, principal and interest, in gold. Depositing these in the treasury, it would receive $90,000 in circulating notes, which it would loan at such rates of interest as the commercial demands of the time allowed, and would receive each year, as interest, $6,000 in gold, which it could sell at twenty-five, fifty or even a hundred per cent. advance in greenbacks, according to the enormously high, though fluctuating, war premiums on gold then prevailing. The gradual decline and finally the disappearance of the premium on gold *; the reduction in the rate of interest on government bonds from six per cent. to five, to four and a half, and ultimately to three and a half and even three per cent., through successive refunding operations ; and lastly the appearance of high premiums upon bonds bearing the reduced rates of interest, these three causes have concurred to diminish, point by point, the profit, to the bank, in buying United States bonds and depositing them with the treasury department, as the basis of note circulation, until, at the present time (1887), many banks are surrendering their circulation, finding it more to their interest to use the capital at their command in other ways. The number of

* Specie payments were resumed on January 1, 1879.

national banks at the present time in existence, is about two thousand nine hundred. These are, of course, distributed very irregularly over the surface of the country.

540. The money of the United States now consists of gold coin (twenty, ten, five, two and a half or one dollar pieces), legal tender for debts in any amount; (2) of silver dollars, legal tender in any amount; (3) of subsidiary silver coins (fifty, twenty-five, twenty, ten or five cent. pieces), legal tender in small amounts as change; (4) of copper or nickel coins (five, three, two or one cent pieces); (5) of "greenbacks," of various denominations, from one dollar to one thousand dollars; (6) of "gold notes" and (7) of "silver notes," of various denominations, issued solely upon the deposit, at the several sub-treasuries,* of equivalent amounts of gold or silver; (8) of national banknotes, issued as hereinbefore described. In this highly complex mass, the proportion of banknotes is continually diminishing, owing to the reduction in the profits of banknote circulation already accounted for. This fact constitutes one of the gravest features of the financial situation, and threatens the country with the speedy loss of all the advantages thus far enjoyed under the national banking system.

XIII.

FOREIGN EXCHANGES.

541. Meaning of Exchange.—Formerly, when debts were paid by the merchants of one country to those of another, it was almost always necessary actually to change the money of the debtor country into that of the creditor country. Thus, if a merchant in Paris had occasion to pay a debt to a mer-

---

* After the destruction of the second United States Bank and the crisis of 1837-9, the United States government adopted the policy of keeping its funds in its own treasury at Washington, or in the custody of "assistant treasurers," appointed in the great commercial cities. The offices of the assistant treasurers are popularly called "sub-treasuries." The origin and development of the sub-treasury system will afford an admirable economic exercise for advanced students.

chant in Antwerp, it was necessary first to compute the quantity of "*fine*" (*i. e.* pure) silver contained in the amount of Antwerp money due under the contract ; then to find out how many French coins (their weight and fineness being known) would be required to make up that amount of pure silver. This being ascertained, the Paris merchant paid down the French money (*plus* the premium, or *minus* the discount, of which we shall speak later) and received the Paris banker's order upon some Antwerp banker to pay the Antwerp merchant the amount of Antwerp money due him. It was with reference to this changing of one kind of money into another, that the term exchange was first applied to this class of transactions. It came in time, however, to be equally applied to transactions between cities under the same government, having the same kinds of money, where, hence, no actual changing of money pieces was required.

At the present time, this changing of money pieces plays a very much less important part in exchange. Instead of many states having independent authority to coin money, there is now but one coining authority in all Italy. The money of Germany is now uniform in weight and fineness. France, Italy, Belgium, Switzerland, Greece and Austria have certain money coins which may be said to be in common, *i. e.*, they contain the same amount of pure metal, though under different denominations and with different inscriptions. The vast extension of the British empire has made the "sovereign" current money over a large part of the globe.

542. What is Exchange?—In essence, where a man *buys exchange*—he buys the right to have paid to him, or his agent, or his creditor, a certain amount of fine gold or silver, to be delivered in some other place mentioned in the contract. If I buy in New York "exchange on London," some one who has gold in London, or who has a right to demand gold there, sells me his claim to receive a definite amount of that metal, in London, at a definite time, or at my convenience if we so agree. I may then, either go to London and get the metal, as, for instance, if I am starting out on a European tour, or I may send an order, by post or telegraph, for some one else to get it there, as, for instance, if I have bought cotton goods or pictures in London, and have agreed to pay for them in this way.

543. Par of Exchange.—Now, we may suppose that, in order to induce some person to sell me "exchange on London," I have to pay him, not in goods, but in a certain amount of gold in New York, where we both live. How much gold shall I pay him in New York to induce him to give me the right to receive a certain amount, say 1,000 ounces, of gold in London? Shall I have to pay him 1,000 ounces, or more, or less? That depends on whether exchange is at par (equality), or above par, or below par.

Exchange between two places is at par, when, by paying a certain amount of money metal, or its equivalent, in one place, you can purchase the right to receive an equal amount of the same metal in the other. I say, the same metal, for there can be no par of exchange between countries having gold money and countries having silver money, unless, indeed, the bi-metallists (par. 563) shall make good the claim that their system will establish and maintain a certain definite ratio between the values of the two metals.

Exchange is above par or below par, when the right to receive elsewhere a given amount of gold or silver, is to be purchased by paying, in the one case, a larger, and, in the other case, a smaller amount of the same money metal, in the place where the transaction is effected.

Exchange will be at par when the sums of the payments to be made to and from any two places, within a given time, exactly balance each other. If the sum of the payments to be made within a limited period by the merchants of one place, say New York, to the merchants of another place, say London, is greater than the sum of the payments to be made in New York by the merchants of London, then exchange on London will be above par in New York; that is, a New York merchant having to pay a debt, within that period, in London, will have to pay down more than 1,000 ounces of gold in New York to buy the right to have paid to him, or to his creditor, 1,000 ounces of gold in London.

544. The upward limit of the premium * on bills of exchange is the cost of remitting specie. The New York merchant, in the case supposed, will not pay more, in addition to 1,000 ounces, than the cost of sending 1,000 ounces from New York to London, interest, freight, insurance, and commissions being taken into account. If the holders of bills demand a premium above this, the New York merchant will send the metal, and in that way pay his debt. Within the limit thus assigned, the premium on bills rises or falls with the fluctuations of the market, according to the law of supply and demand.

While, thus, exchange on London is at a premium in New York, exchange on New York will, conversely, be at a corresponding discount in London. If a New York merchant, owing 1,000 ounces of gold in London, has to pay somewhat more than that amount, a London merchant, owing 1,000 ounces in New York, will be able to purchase the right to receive that amount there for something less than 1,000 ounces. The downward limit † of the discount on bills of exchange is, again, fixed by the cost of remitting specie.

545. The Balance of Trade.—We have said that exchange between two places will be at par when the sum of the payments falling due on the one side is equal to the sum of the payments falling due at the same time on the other side. It may happen —it frequently does happen—in the trade between countries A and B, that country A may at one season of the year have the larger payments to make, while in another season the relations will be reversed. The exports from the United States, for example, tend to take place predominantly in the few months following the harvest. At that time the United States becomes chiefly a creditor country. The merchants of other countries have large amounts to pay in New York, on account of produce received; and consequently exchange on New York is at a

* Except, of course, in great and sudden emergencies, like the outbreak of a war, or the occurrence of a commercial crisis.

† Except in great and sudden emergencies, as indicated in a previous note.

premium in London, Paris, Amsterdam, etc. Conversely, exchange on London, Paris, Amsterdam, etc., is at a corresponding discount in New York. During the other half of the year, the United States generally import more largely than they export, and the course of exchange is reversed. Bills on London are at a premium in New York, on account of large payments to be made abroad; bills on New York are at a discount in London. The discrepancy thus arising from the nature of the industry of any given country, between the times at which its payments are chiefly to be made and those at which it is to receive the bulk of the amounts due to it, on account of its own exports, is, in a degree, often very largely, removed by bills drawn, as the phrase is, in blank. These are bills which do not discharge a debt, but create a debt. Exporters often draw such bills, generally with permission obtained in advance, upon those to whom they habitually sell or consign their shipments, in anticipation of the goods being actually dispatched. Such a course is liable to very grave abuses, being often resorted to, not merely in promotion of reckless and outrageous speculation, but even for the purposes of downright swindling; and the courts and newspapers are much given to reflecting severely upon this practice, in general, whenever some case of its perversion is brought to light. Yet this system of credits, when kept within bounds, confined to proper parties, and, as Mr. Goschen says, "jealously and even suspiciously watched," serves a very important purpose in equalizing the income and outgo of nations and in diminishing the extent to which shipments of specie require to be made.

The point we have now reached introduces the vexed question of the Balance of Trade. Few subjects are more complicated or more generally misunderstood. The question, whether a year's commercial transactions have, in the net result, brought a nation more in debt to other nations than they, in the aggregate, have come to owe to it, is commonly decided, offhand, by simple reference to the custom-house statistics of the values of exports from and imports into that country. Such a test is altogether fallacious. The statistics of exports and imports, if fairly well collected and compiled, are of great value; but it is necessary, first, to make correction for their internal errors, and, secondly, to take into account several elements which the custom-house statistics do not undertake to include.

546. Errors in Commercial Statistics.—The official statements of imports and exports are more or less disturbed by errors from two exactly opposite sources. If the goods imported or exported are subject to duties at the custom house, the importer or exporter comes under a very strong temptation to misrepresent their value or amount. If, on the other hand, the goods are free of duty, both the custom-house officials and the merchants are liable to become very careless in making the required statements as to the quantity of such goods, and still more careless regarding statements of value.

How far these two causes together may result in vitiating the official statistics of imports and exports, will, of course, depend greatly upon the organization of the civil service, upon the general morality of the trading and official classes, and upon the integrity and severity with which the laws are enforced; but it is not possible under any organization or administration wholly to eliminate errors of importance, from one or both of these sources. Imported goods subject to duty will be largely undervalued, in spite of all the vigilance of honest officials. Exports are probably even more grossly undervalued, because being, by the fiscal system of most nations, free of duty, even the most honest officials are likely to attach little importance to the statements of value, since they are aware that no revenue interest of the government is concerned therein.

In addition to these general causes, affecting, though in very different degrees, the commercial statistics of all nations, there are apt to be special liabilities to error affecting the commercial statistics of any given country. Thus, with regard to the United States, it is found that while a reasonable degree of care and pains is taken to ascertain the values of goods exported by ocean-going vessels, the statement of our exports by rail, by ferry-boat, or by small river and lake vessels to Canada and Mexico, are exceedingly defective, so much so as to be almost wholly worthless. It is notorious that many millions are omitted yearly from our statistics on these accounts.

547. Elements not included in Custom House Statistics.—Passing now to elements, other than internal errors in custom-house statistics, which require to be taken into account, in order to reach the true balance of trade, I will briefly mention the most important. The reader who desires to pursue the subject, will find it treated in a most interesting and instructive manner in Mr. Goschen's work on Foreign Exchanges.

The principal elements to be considered are, first, the exportation or importation of government securities, shares and bonds of corporations, titles to property, etc. This is an element, which, at times, may rise to an enormous importance; at other times, it may sink into insignificance. It may be considerable as between certain countries, while as between either of those countries and any other, it may amount to little or nothing.

During the war of secession the United States sold its bonds in Europe * to the amount of hundreds of millions of dollars, bringing back arms, ammunition, clothing and other supplies. The latter went into the statistics of imports; while the statistics of exports took no account of the former. As these bonds had many years to run, the value of the goods so imported did not enter into the amount to be paid for abroad in those years. In the same way, many of our great railroads have been built mainly or wholly with foreign capital, shares in the stock of those railroads, or more commonly, first-mortgage bonds, being sent abroad without passing through our custom-houses, while rails and other supplies were brought back through the custom-house, thus swelling our tables of imports. In like manner, large quantities of foreign goods, of all sorts, have been sent to us year after year, in consideration of which foreigners have received from us, not our corn, cotton or petroleum, but the titles to mines, to agricultural and grazing lands, mortgages on western farms, the bonds of cities and counties, etc.

* "To contract a foreign loan is [with regard to the Balance of Trade] equivalent to an increase of exportation."—Goschen.

The aggregate amount of such securities and titles exported from the United States has been enormous, though the movement has been very irregular from year to year. Nor has the current been all one way. When our government began to refund its debt at a lower rate of interest—at three and a half or three per cent., instead of six or seven per cent., nearly all our national bonds which had been held in Europe were returned. Now and then some large mass of railroad or city bonds are sent back, at maturity, for redemption,—the proceeds to be reinvested in other securities, of which the custom-house would not take notice, or to be "drawn against" in payment for corn or cotton, of which the custom-house would take notice.

While the element which we have been considering is of enormous importance to the United States, as affecting the balance of trade within any given year, England is the nation whose commercial statistics need most to be supplemented from this source. Hers has been the greater part of the capital which has come to us from Europe, for loan or investment; and for the last forty years she has been doing a similar work in every part of the world, building railroads in Canada, Australia, Mexico, South America, India and Persia, even in France, Germany and Russia, providing capital, out of her superabundance, for every species of enterprise in any land that promised a profit, and even furnishing the means with which half the wars of the present generation have been waged.

548. Interest on Government Securities.—But while, as we have said, it is true that in these modern times, enormous amounts of imports or of exports of merchandise are, in the case of any given country, set off, not against equal amounts of exports or of imports of merchandise, but against shares, stocks, bonds, or mortgages, sent abroad or brought home, as the case may be, it is also true, that dividends or interest on such shares, bonds, etc., become due annually, semi-annually, or quarterly, immediately thereafter, and require, therefore, to be added to the amounts which the debtor nations have to pay; which the creditor nations have to receive, thus affecting at once the course of exchange. Some nations have to pay millions annually, others, tens of millions, on this account. Those nations, which, in some past period have spent vast sums in great wars or on costly public improvements, without paying for them at the time through taxation, now find a certain portion of their exports of merchandise going every year to pay the interest on their debts. Against this is set nothing of which the custom-house takes notice. No goods come back to pay for these exports : only some packages of canceled coupons.

549. Expenses of Fleets on Foreign Stations, etc.—Another item which should be added to the imports of a country, in making up its current accounts with other nations, consists of the expenses of its fleets on foreign stations, or of its armies, if in occupation of other countries. In the case of great naval nations, this item is not of small importance. For a little while after vessels of war leave the home ports, their petty expenses may be met with gold taken from home, which may or may not have passed the custom-house ; but subsequently, the expenses of the fleet will be met by bills of exchange, which will be just so much added to the volume of bills which represent the commercial imports of the home country.

The expenses of foreign embassies and legations and of the consular service stand in the same relation to the imports of the country represented.

550. Expenses of Foreign Travel.—In like manner the sums expended by tourists and travelers abroad constitute a very considerable item in those accounts which go to determine the balance of trade. The good things eaten or drunk by our citizens abroad are as much a part of our imports, for the purposes of such a computation, as if they had been brought to the United States in vessels and had been consumed here. Every year, many millions are expended by our citizens abroad, out of the proceeds of bills of exchange. Mr. Goschen states that several millions sterling are annually expended by the rich Russian nobility in traveling or in foreign residence.

551. Tributes, War Indemnities, Etc.—From whatever motive an independent country, a colony or a province may have occasion to make payments to another power, or to the sovereign or mother country, whether that motive be found in protection extended, in privileges conceded, in fear of hostility, or as a fine for past conduct, such payments affect exchanges in all respects as if they were on account of foreign goods imported. Yet, here, again, we have an element of which the statistics of commerce take no account. Whenever these payments are regular, they affect the course of exchange no more, if not less, than ordinary commercial payments. Thus, trade and exchange adjust themselves to the tribute paid by Java to Holland with perhaps even more of exactness and certainty than as if the payments were on account of goods imported into Java for the improvement of its agriculture, or for starting manufactures. On the other hand, an extraordinary payment of this character, is likely to produce great and far reaching, and it may be long enduring effects upon the market of exchange. The gigantic war indemnity paid by France to Germany, in 1871,* notwithstanding the transcendent financial skill with which the negotiations were conducted, set in motion forces which were felt by trade and industry to the remotest parts of the earth.

552. Freight, Insurance, Profits, Commissions, Etc.—But we have not yet reached the largest of the elements which determine the balance of trade, of which ordinary commercial statistics take no account. Let us suppose, for illustration, that country A imports from country B goods, whose value, at the ports of B, is one hundred and fifty millions of dollars, and exports to B goods, whose value, at its own ports, is correctly stated at one hundred millions. Now, here is an apparent difference of fifty millions of dollars. If, however, we can reach the facts regarding the carriage, insurance, etc., of these goods, amounting in the aggregate to two hundred

* A study of the methods used in the payment of this indemnity, and of its financial and industrial effects, will constitute an admirable exercise for a pupil well-grounded in economic principles.

and fifty millions of dollars, we may find the apparent balance greatly modified, in the way either of increase or reduction. Suppose, for example, that country A owns all the shipping engaged in this traffic; the charges for freight on its own exports might easily reach ten or fifteen millions of dollars, which would require to be added to the custom-house valuation, in order to make up the true balance between the two countries. On the other hand, the ten or fifteen per cent. charged for carriage on its imports would be paid to its own citizens. In the same way country A might do all the insurance business relating to both sides of the traffic; and its merchants and factors might conduct all, or nearly all, the commercial operations involved. In such a case the premiums for insurance, the commissions and profits of trade would go still further to reduce the apparent balance between the two countries. On the other hand that apparent balance might have been greatly extended by the fact that all the shipping merchants and most of the importers, factors and insurers engaged in the traffic belonged to country B.

The suppositions above made are not in themselves unreasonable. It generally happens that, in the commerce between two nations, one or the other does by far the larger part, often, practically, the whole carrying business,* as well as obtains an altogether disproportionate share of the premiums of insurance, and of the profits and commissions of traffic.

553. It is not necessary to extend our enumeration to minor items of the accounts between trading nations, in order to show the reader how greatly the ordinary statistics of imports and exports must be corrected and supplemented before we can reach a decision as to the amounts by which the payments to be made in any given period by one country to any other country or to all other countries, exceed the payments due to itself. Mr. Goschen states that Russia has more than once, in times of peace, as I understand it, so far fallen behind in

* "An exclusively maritime country could discharge its obligations to other countries which supply it with necessaries, simply by becoming their carrier, without exporting any produce or manufactures to them in return."—Goschen.

her dealings with other countries, as to be obliged to contract a foreign loan, exporting public securities made for the purpose, as a means of restoring the balance. Of course, such a temporary expedient in the end serves to increase the commercial and financial difficulties of a country.

554. Our illustrations have thus far been drawn mainly from the commercial transactions of two countries, real or supposed. We have perhaps sufficiently shown that, of the amount of payments falling due on one side or the other in a given period, only the balance will require to be discharged in money, the principle of cancellation being applied to all but that excess.

Even this, however, would involve a very much larger use of money in the adjustment of national balances than actually takes place. Although the total exports of a country will always tend to approach its total imports, yet its exports to and imports from any single country may be very unequal. Thus, the United States import tea, silk, etc., to an enormous value, from China, while exporting very little to China. Again, our imports from England are very large, but our exports to that country are vastly greater still. If the United States adjusted its accounts with each foreign country separately, the balances requiring to be paid in money during a year would rise into hundreds of millions of dollars.

555. To further reduce the balances to be paid in money; to still further extend the principle of the cancellation of indebtedness, resort is had to a common market of exchange for all the nations. If, for example, the United States imports from Great Britain manufactured goods to the value of one hundred millions, and exports to Great Britain two hundred and fifty millions, it uses its favorable balance of one hundred and fifty millions in London as a sort of bank on which to draw for the payment of its indebtedness to many other countries from which it imports more than it exports to them. For example, it pays its Chinese creditors in accepted bills drawn on London importers of American wheat, cotton or petroleum. These bills Chinese merchants, having to pay for large amounts of English manufactures, are glad to get possession of; and thus an additional body of indebtedness is canceled. The operation of this force is greatly accelerated by the course of events which have made London the great settling place for the transactions of international commerce.* Prof. Jevons, in his work on "Money and the Mechanism of Exchange," stated that there were then (1875) no less than sixty important colonial and foreign banks which had their own London offices or houses; and that there were, in addition, fully one thousand foreign and colonial houses in correspondence with London bankers. Here, then, in this Exchange of the World, as Edmund Burke called it, a hundred years ago, meet all the claims of all the creditors in the world, and all the acknowledgments of all the debtors in the world, which have not been adjusted nearer home. In the portfolios of the London banker or exchange broker are found bills representing the shipment of every kind of agricultural produce, of every class of manufactured goods, not to or from England merely, but from the country of production, however distant, to every other country known to commerce. And these bills are of all amounts, from the pettiest sums up to thousands of pounds sterling, falling due at all dates from to-morrow up to this day six months. From this varied mass to pick out accepted bills, recognized obligations which, in amount and time of maturity, shall cancel each other, is a work to which the highest intelligence is applied. Although the aggregate profits are large, the amount of exchanges thus effected is so enormous that the percentage charged for the negotiation is very small.

556. It is by this complicated agency that the balance of payments between nations, requiring to be made in money, is reduced to a minimum. Out of hundreds or thousands of millions of "exchange" negotiated, the bodies of indebtedness which bankers or brokers can not find means to offset

* Of this Mr. Goschen says the "primary cause is to be found in the stupendous and never-ceasing exports of England, which have for effect that every country in the world, being in constant receipt of English manufactures, is under the necessity of making remittance to pay for them, either in bullion, in produce, or in bills."

amount to but a few millions. Except for the continuous production of the precious metals in certain countries which thereby become gold or silver-exporting countries, and except for the acts of government in replacing metal money by paper money, or, conversely, in resuming specie payments after periods of suspension, or, again, in changing "the standard," from silver to gold or gold to silver, the amount of metal money which would be required to go, now here and now there, to make up for local and temporary failures of coincidence between the amounts to be received and the amounts to be paid, in international trade, would be almost inconsiderable, in comparison either with the aggregate of commercial transactions or with the total body of the precious metals in use.

557. Operating Upon the Exchanges.— The peculiarly important and responsible position which London occupies, as the center of the exchange transactions of the world, has led to the establishment of a well-recognized policy of dealing with the outflow of gold from that point, whenever such a movement is caused by what is called "an unfavorable turn of the exchanges."

In spite of the great perfection to which the cancellation of international indebtedness is there carried, it will at times happen that a "drain" of bullion continues so long as to cause acute alarm as to the integrity of the financial system of the kingdom. When the act of 1844 was passed, it was believed that the provisions of this law, to the effect that no bank note (beyond the fixed amount of fifteen million pounds) should be issued except on the actual deposit of an equivalent amount of specie, and that, conversely, no specie should be withdrawn except upon the surrender of an equivalent amount of notes, would have the effect, automatically, to check a drain, from whatever cause proceeding. Inasmuch, however, as the painful experiences of several commercial crises showed that this force could not always be relied upon as sufficient,* the directors of the Bank of England have adopted

* Bagehot's "Lombard Street" will be found most interesting and instructive to an advanced student in economics and finance.

the policy of raising the rate of discount, sharply and rapidly, whenever signs of a considerable export of gold shall appear. Of course, the decree of the directors can absolutely control the rate of discount only upon the capital which the Bank itself has to loan; but the moral influence of such an act upon the joint-stock and private banks and upon individual capitalists is naturally very great, and the general rate of interest is at once appreciably affected.

In doing this, the object of the directors of the Bank, who deem themselves, by the force of tradition, though not of law,* largely responsible for the financial integrity of the kingdom, is so to raise the rate of interest, or of discount, as to induce foreign creditors, who have the right, at the time, to demand gold from England, to leave that gold for awhile in England, thus checking a "drain" which is considered dangerous. By raising the rate of interest at once, from three or four to six or eight † per cent., the profit on the investment of funds in England is made so great that any foreign creditor, who is not absolutely required by his financial circumstances to draw his money away to his own country, feels a strong inducement to leave it still longer in England.

It is in this way that the financial authorities of the kingdom seek to "tide over" a highly unfavorable state of the exchanges; and it may be said that the policy, although involving a resort to means which are altogether artificial and highly exceptional in finance, uniformly proves successful. "The fact," said Mr. Goschen, "has been that almost every advance in the bank rate of discount is followed by a turn of the exchanges in favor of England. Foreign creditors give their English debtors a respite, and prefer to wait longer for remittances, gaining interest meanwhile at the profitable English rate."

558. The Special Case of England and the United States.— We have said all that the limits of our space will allow concern-

---

* Walker: Money, Trade and Industry, pages 292–98.

† The Bank has, in pursuance of this policy, more than once raised the rate of discount as high as eleven per cent.

ing foreign exchange in general. A word may, however, be added regarding the exchange between England and the United States. The valuation, in American money, of the English pound sterling, has been several times changed. Prior to 1792, the pound sterling was valued at $4.44 4-9, according to the bullion standard of the Spanish dollar, then universally current among us. From that date down to 1834, the American dollar was worth 97⅓ cents in gold, at which rate a pound sterling was worth $4.56½ cents. By the coinage act of 1834 our standard was so reduced that the bullion contained in the American dollar was worth only 91¼ cents, so that the pound sterling became worth about $4.87. The United States custom-house valuation of the "sovereign," that is, the coin representing the English pound sterling, was, however, fixed at $4.84. By this difference in bullion value between our dollar and the English standard money, a fictitious par of exchange was created between England and the United States, so that an American stock or bond worth $100 in New York, would be quoted in London at about $109, whenever the amounts respectively to be paid and received between the two countries were equal.

By an act of Congress of January, 1874, the custom-house valuation of the English sovereign was again changed, this time to $4.87 65/100, at which point it now remains. The London stock exchange responded to this action, the same year, by valuing the American dollar at four English shillings, equivalent to about 97⅓ cents of our money, from which it results that American stocks or bonds worth $100 are quoted in London at about $102.75, subject to variations on account of the fluctuations in commercial transactions.

XIV.

BI-METALLISM.

559. The question of Bi-metallism is to be decided solely upon the principles which have been laid down in Part III., as governing the value of money; but the question is one of so much popular interest and has been so confused by the passionate controversy waged over it, that it may be worth while to set the points at issue fairly forth, for the assistance of the beginner in economics.

And first let us depict the situation, in view of which the controversy has arisen.

560. The Gold-Using Countries.—We find one group of States, of great importance in international commerce, whose habits of trade make gold money, or bank notes predicated upon a reserve of gold money, the most agreeable and convenient medium of exchange. These are rich countries, having vast accumulations of wealth, derived from the industry of the past. In them, because their productive power is large, wages are high. In them, trade and industry are organized with a great degree of complexity and minuteness. It is not needful for our present purpose to name all the countries of this group ; but clearly it embraces England, France, Belgium and Holland, in Europe, and on this continent, the United States.

It is admitted, that, in these countries, the use of silver as the ordinary money of trade would be attended with great inconvenience, and would meet so much prejudice on the part of the people as to render it inexpedient for any government to propose the introduction of that metal as the sole money of full legal-tender power. These countries, however, use a large amount of silver as fractionary money, for the purpose of making change in transactions, and for retail purchases.

561. The Silver-Using Countries.—On the other hand, we find a group of countries, embracing an aggregate number of inhabitants several times greater than those previously mentioned, in which the facts of industry and the habits of the people respecting exchange are such as to make gold an impossible money. Such countries, beyond a doubt, are China and India, where the ordinary wages of labor range from two to eight cents a day. There are other countries —some in Europe and some in America—settled by the people of Southern Europe, in which wages range from twelve to thirty cents a day, in some of which the ordinary use of gold as money can not be pronounced exactly impossible ; yet where reasons, both of practical convenience and of sentiment and habit, give a decided preference to silver for that purpose: a preference so decided that it is not reasonable to anticipate that these countries will soon, if ever, pass over from the silver-using to the gold-using group of countries. The group of countries in respect to which we have spoken of the use of silver money as more consonant with the facts of industry and the habits of the people than the use of gold, comprise the Spanish American states, Russia, and most, if not all, of the southern states of Europe.

I have said that it is not necessary for our present purpose that all commercial countries should be named on the one side or the other of the dividing line drawn. Controversy might easily arise as to the proper location of Italy or Germany,* perhaps also of Austria; but we have no call to undertake the question. It is enough if it appear not only that there is one great group of states which, in fact, use gold as their principal money, and another great group which use silver, but that the preference for the one metal or the other is so far determined by economic causes, such as the rate of wages, the degree of accumulated wealth, etc., as to make it highly probable that the two money metals will continue to be used, as now, each within a wide field that is peculiar to itself.

562. What the Bi-Metallist Proposes.—It is this situation which the bi-metallist has in view when he propounds his scheme. Accepting the existence of a large group of countries in which gold naturally circulates as money and another in which silver is so used, he proposes to create a league of states, some of which are what we may, for brevity, call silver states, and some, gold states, which shall, each for itself, but by simultaneous action, establish the free coinage † of the two

* If, for example, Germany were resolved into its constituent States, several would naturally gravitate towards the gold-using group; more, still, towards the silver-using group. In like manner, Northern Italy might go to the gold-using group, while Southern Italy would tend the other way.

† The distinction between free and gratuitous coinage is noted in par. 196.

metals, making the money of one metal to be legal-tender indifferently with money of the other metal, in payment of debts, at a certain ratio determined upon in advance by the consenting states. Say, for example, 15½ dwt. of silver to 1 dwt. of gold, the ratio adopted by the states of the Latin Union, viz., France, Italy, Belgium and Switzerland. The bi-metallist asserts that, if such league be formed between a considerable number of important commercial countries, even though it does not embrace all countries, the relative value of gold and silver will be kept close to the mint-ratio so established.

When asked what is the object in view in such an international arrangement; what advantage is anticipated of sufficient importance to make it worth while to endeavor to overcome the natural reluctance of nations to bind themselves to act in common respecting matters which touch their sovereignty, to make it worth while to resort to international conferences and congresses, the bi-metallist adduces two considerations which he alleges to be of vast importance to the world's trade and industry.

563. A Par of Exchange* Desired between Gold Countries and Silver Countries.—The first is the establishment of a par of exchange between silver-using and gold-using countries.

We saw (par. 543) that between two countries having the same money metal, a par of exchange exists. This par of exchange is realized whenever the sum of the payments to be made in one country by merchants of the other country, within a certain brief period, is equal to the sum of the payments to be made in the latter by the merchants of the former country, in which event a merchant paying down a certain amount, say 1,000 ounces, of the common money metal, say gold, in his own country, can thereby purchase the right to receive, himself, or through his agent or representative—his creditor, let us suppose—1,000 ounces of that metal in the country in

---

* The question of foreign exchanges has been treated under a preceding title.

question. Exchange will, in fact, fluctuate about this par of exchange, now above and now below, according to the movements of supply and demand, as these are determined by the relative amounts of debts to be paid and of payments to be received, respectively, in the course of trade between the two countries. The outside limits of these movements of exchange are, as we saw, fixed by the cost of exporting or importing specie.

But between two countries having money of different metals, say of gold in one country and of silver in the other, there is no par of exchange, irrespective of a bi-metallic league like that under consideration. Wholly in addition to the usual movements of exchange, the question, how much gold an Indian merchant can obtain the right to receive in London, by paying down a certain amount of silver in Calcutta, depends on the silver price of gold and the gold price of silver, at the time. And as the two metals have their separate sources of supply, and, to a certain extent, independent uses, whether in the arts or as money, their respective values are likely to fluctuate greatly.

564. It is a necessary result of this that much more uncertainty is involved in trade between a gold and a silver country than between two gold countries, or two silver countries: the chances of undeserved losses or unearned gains are greatly increased. No merchant in a silver country selling to a gold country, no merchant in a gold country selling to a silver country, can know for how much of the metal which forms the money of the country to which he exports his wares he must sell them, in order to make himself good for the metal which he has expended at home in producing or purchasing them.

The English merchant who sells to Calcutta or Hong Kong or Mexico, may do all that lies within him with the highest wisdom and skill; he may buy the right sort of goods and buy them at a bargain, ship them at the proper season to the best market, sell them at the highest ruling prices, and bring the proceeds safely home to Liverpool, yet a fall in silver, between the sale of the goods and the receipt of the proceeds, may strip him of all the profits of his venture, of all the fruits of the year's business, or even entail a heavy loss upon him.

It is true that, in one sense, what one merchant in an individual case loses, some other merchant, or some banker, or some speculator, may gain. But it is not true that unearned gains encourage industry to the extent to which undeserved losses discourage it. On the contrary, not only does the good done almost always fall far short of compensating for the evil wrought, but it often happens that, as mercy between man and man blesses both him that gives and him that takes, so the sums of wealth transferred by speculation or accident, not only leave the loser grieving and crippled, but curse and blight him whom they seemingly enrich.

565. Now this grievous disadvantage under which international trade suffers, the bi-metallist professes to be able to remove, through the scheme that has been described. It is not now the question whether this can, indeed, be done ; but whether the result be desirable, and, if so, whether desirable in a degree to justify a considerable effort, perhaps some sacrifice.

It is one of the accidents of the controversy over this question that the mono-metallist writers are estopped from denying that this result would, if practicable, be desirable in a very high degree. There are but few of those writers who have not, in discussion of the effects of inconvertible paper money, treated the loss of a par of exchange with foreign nations (par. 220) as a serious disaster. In dealing with such a case, for example, as that of France between 1871 and 1877, they have attributed most unfortunate consequences to the inconvertibility of the money of the Republic into that which was the money of the commercial world, even though the notes of the Bank of France were at a very slight, often hardly appreciable, discount. In the same way these writers, during the continuance of the American suspension, 1862 to 1879, were accustomed (and rightly) to attribute to the inconvertibility of the greenbacks most injurious effects upon the trade and production of the United States, and this, even after the premium on gold had sunk to a low average, and had ceased to fluctuate violently or rapidly. "Any degree of depreciation, however small, even the liability to depreciation, without its reality," to use Mr. Bagehot's phrase, was declared to be a cause of mischief, to be eradicated by the most heroic efforts of the suffering nation, at almost any sacrifice.

566. The Greater Stability of Value in Bi-metallic Money. —A second benefit which, according to the bi-metallist claim, would result from the establishment of an international league for the free coinage of both metals, as indifferent legal tender, at a certain fixed ratio, in payment of debts, is that the two metals, thus bound together, would constitute a better money than either metal by itself could be. The inequalities of mining production would tend in a degree to equalize each other, with the result of greater uniformity in the production of the compound mass, and hence of greater steadiness in the value of money.

Here, again, the mono-metallists are at a controversial disadvantage. In order to establish the impracticability of the bi-metallic scheme, they have dwelt strongly on the tendency of the two metals to vary widely in value, and this view is fully borne out by the facts of the last three or four centuries.* But this argument against the practicability of the bi-metallic scheme virtually amounts to an admission of the merits of that scheme, if found practicable.

---

* Take the present century only, for illustration. When the century opened, silver was in course of rapid production. Three dollars' worth of silver was taken out, where one dollar's worth of gold was produced. Then came the series of South American and Mexican revolts and revolutions, between 1809 and 1829, by which mining machinery was destroyed, mining populations scattered, and the most prolific mines of the world closed. Mr. Jacob estimates that the stock of the precious metals in civilized hands fell off one-sixth in those twenty years. But gold now came in to fill the void. In 1823, the mines of the Oural began to yield largely, while about 1830 the gold sands of Siberia became known. And now only 68 cents' worth of silver was produced to a dollar's worth of gold.

In 1848 and 1851 came the gold discoveries of California and Australia, and so altered was the relative production of the two metals that only 27 cents' worth of silver was taken out, to a dollar's worth of gold! After 1861, however, the facts of production became more favorable to silver.

I think it must be conceded, on this statement, that the bi-metallic scheme, if it could be carried out so as to realize the expectations of its advocates, would confer very great benefits upon international trade, and, by consequence, upon the production of wealth.*

567. Is it Practicable?—Let us, then, inquire what are the economic conditions of the case ; how far it is reasonable to believe that this scheme could be successfully established.

What is the force to which the bi-metallist looks to restrain the tendency to divergence between the values of the two money metals, silver and gold ? It is evident that any rational scheme to influence value must aim at affecting either supply or demand. Can, then, government influence the supply of or the demand for a money metal ? Clearly, unmistakably, yes. Government can in a very great degree influence the demand for either of the money metals by coining it into money and conferring on the coin legal tender power.

In 1873 began a still further movement in the same direction. The director of the United States mint estimated the world's production of gold in 1884 at one hundred and two million dollars, and of silver (at 16 : 1 of gold) at one hundred and sixteen million dollars.

* I do not here present *the argument from the* STATUS in favor of the remonetization of silver in Europe and America, as money of full legal tender power, at a certain ratio to money of gold, under free coinage. That argument has respect to the vast bodies of debts and fixed charges, both public and private, contracted before the German demonetization of silver (say, 1873). It is urged that to require these debts, whether interest or principal, or both, to be paid in money whose purchasing power has been enhanced by the diminution of its volume through the extrusion of silver (except as small change) from the money system of Europe and America, will prove both a grievous injustice, as between debtor and creditor, and a great source of injury to trade and production. The English economic statisticians are generally agreed that the purchasing power of gold has largely increased since the German demonetization. How far this has been in consequence of that demonetization, is matter of dispute. The aggregate amount of national debts is now stated at $27,000,000,000. There are, in addition, vast bodies of public or political indebtedness, on the part of counties, cities and towns. Then we have the enormous mass of corporate (industrial), and private debts, the burden of which (at any time) depends primarily upon the purchasing power of the money in which interest or principal is to be paid.

To illustrate this, let us suppose that, in any country, both gold and silver are made legal tender in payment of debts, at the ratio of 15½ of silver to 1 of gold : that is, the law decrees that a debtor may extinguish an obligation by the payment of coins containing a certain number of ounces of gold, or, at his option, coins containing fifteen and a half times that number of ounces of silver. Let it be assumed that, at the moment of the decree, this was the actual market ratio between the metals.

Let it now be supposed that causes, natural or commercial, that is, affecting the supply of one metal or the other, or affecting the demand for the one or the other, begin to operate to produce a divergence from this ratio : say, to make an ounce of gold worth 15.60 ounces of silver, what will occur? The bi-metallic principle will at once begin to act in restraint of this movement toward divergence. How will it operate? Through the desire of every debtor to meet his maturing obligations in the cheapening metal. All debtors will, in the case supposed, seek silver. This extension of demand acts directly in contravention of the force which is lowering its value. On the other hand, the metal—gold—which is tending to become dearer, from that fact falls out of demand. No debtor seeks it as the means of paying his debts. This diminution of demand at once operates in counteraction of the forces tending to raise the value of gold.

568. The Opinion of Mono-Metallic Writers.—Now, is this a purely fanciful view of the subject, taken only by advocates of the bi-metallic scheme? On the contrary, it has been seen in operation over extensive countries, of great commercial importance, through long periods of time ; and the validity of the cause is fully confessed by mono-metallic writers of the highest reputation.

M. Chevalier, the eminent French economist, writing of this system as it prevailed in his own country in 1857, when, in consequence of the great gold discoveries in California and Australia, gold was tending to fall and silver to rise, and thus to pull away from the mint ratio of 15½ : 1, then established in France, speaks thus emphatically: "Whilst this state of things lasts, it will be *impossible* at London, Brussels, Hamburg, or even at New York, or at any other great center of commerce, for gold to fall much below $15\frac{1}{2}$ times its weight in silver." And Prof. Cairnes, writing of the same period, said: "The crop of gold has been unusually large; the increase in the supply has caused a fall in its value; the fall in its value has led to its being substituted for silver; a mass of silver has thus been disengaged from purposes which it was formerly employed to serve; and the result has been that *the two metals have fallen in value together.*"

Mr. Bagehot wrote in the London *Economist:* "Whenever the values of the two metals altered, these [bi-metallic] countries acted as equalizing machines; they took the metal which fell, they sold the metal which rose; and thus the relative value of the two was kept at its old point."

And the late Prof. Jevons, writing in 1874, under the title, the Equivalence of Commodities (see par. 142), says: "It is upon this principle that we must explain the extraordinary permanence of the ratio of exchange of gold and silver: that *this fixedness of ratio does not depend upon the amount and cost of production* is proved by the very slight effect of the Australian or Californian discoveries."

And elsewhere Prof. Jevons thus illustrates the compensatory action of the two metals: "Imagine two reservoirs of water, each subject to independent variations of supply and demand. In the absence of any connecting pipe, the level of the water in each reservoir will be subject to its own fluctuations only. But, if we open a connection, the water in both will assume a certain mean level, and the effects of any excessive supply or demand will be distributed over the whole area of both reservoirs.

"The mass of the metals, gold and silver, circulating in Western Europe in late years, is exactly represented by the water in these reservoirs, and the connecting pipe is the law of the 7th Germinal an XI,* which enables one metal to take the place of the other as an unlimited legal tender."

---

* French revolutionary style for the year 1803, the date commonly assigned to the establishment of the bi-metallic system in France.

569. Bi-Metallism not a Chimera.—We see, thus, that the bi-metallic scheme is based upon economic principles which are incontestable. If it be worth while for any nation to undertake this work of holding silver and gold together, it can do so just as long as it has any considerable quantity of the metal which at the time tends to become dearer, to dispose of. If it be worth while for any group of nations to undertake this, they can maintain the approximate equivalency of the two metals just as long as their joint stock of the metal which at that time tends to become dearer remains unexhausted. Every additional state that joins the bi-metallic group strengthens the system in two ways, first, by contributing to the supply of the metal which may, under the natural or commercial conditions prevailing at the time, tend to become dearer, and, secondly, by withdrawing itself from the list of States which may possibly contribute to the demand for that metal.

570. The Operation Illustrated.—We may suppose the commercial world to be divided into sixteen states, A to P, the first six having the single gold standard; four, G to J, the so-called double standard of gold and silver, under the bi-metallic system: say at $15\frac{1}{2}:1$; the remaining states having the single standard of silver, thus:

A, B, C, D, E, F, (G, H, I, J,) K, L, M, N, O, P.

It is evident that, in the event of a change in the conditions of supply tending to cheapen silver relatively to gold, the new silver would pass into the countries of the double standard, G to J, and be there exchanged for gold, at the rate of $15\frac{1}{2}:1$, with some small premium as the profit of the transaction, and, as a result, the gold displaced from the circulation would be exported to the gold countries, A to F, in settlement of trade balances.

The rapidity with which this substitution of silver for gold in the bi-metallic states will proceed must depend, first, on the force of the natural causes operating to cheapen silver; and, secondly, on the force of the commercial causes operating to maintain or advance the value of gold. The length of time during which the drain of the dearer metal can be sustained without exhaustion, will (given the rate of movement) depend solely upon the stock of that metal existing in the bi-metallic states when the drain begins.

But chief among the causes operating to advance the value of gold, is the exclusive power with which gold is invested by law to pay debts in states A to F; while the stock of the dearer metal available to sustain the drain described, is made up, not of all the gold in the sixteen states A to P, or in the ten states A to J, but only of the gold in the four bi-metallic states, G to J.

Now, let us suppose the sixteen commercial states to be somewhat differently divided, as follows:

A, B, C, D, (E, F, G, H, I, J, K, L,) M, N, O, P.

The bi-metallic system is now not twice merely, but many times as strong, since not only is the amount of the dearer metal subject to drain increased, but the demand for that metal, in preference to silver at 15½ : 1, now comes from four countries only, instead of six, as formerly.

The transfer of still another state from each of the two single-standard groups, would vastly increase the stability of the bi-metallic system.

A, B, C, (D, E, F, G, H, I, J, K, L, M,) N, O, P. Not only would the base of the system be broadened by bringing the dearer metal of ten states, D to M, under tribute, in the event of changes operating on the supply of either metal; but the force threatening the equilibrium of the system would be reduced, since the demand for the dearer metal would now come from only three states: A, B, C, in the case of a cheapening of silver relatively to gold; N, O, P, in the case of a cheapening of gold relatively to silver. Those three states can not take the dearer metal indefinitely. They would soon be surfeited. A further increase of money in them would be followed by a fall in its value, which would soon proceed so far as to bring the metals together again.

And it is to be noted that, with a bi-metallic league embracing so many states, those which tended naturally to the use of silver as money would continue to use silver predominantly; those which tended to use gold would still use gold as their main money of circulation. Whenever causes began to operate to cheapen silver relatively to gold (at the mint ratio between the two metals established by the league), the gold using countries would take some additional silver and discard some gold ; but this increase of demand for silver and diminution of demand for gold would check the movement to divergence before the character of the circulating medium became greatly changed. In the event of a cheapening of gold relatively to silver, the substitution of gold for silver, in the silver-using states, to the extent only of a small fraction of their circulation, would suffice to put a stop to the movement.

571. This is the bi-metallic scheme. The question of securing the co-operation of independent states to any end, is a political, not an economic question : that is, the desired end is to be obtained by the action of governments, moved by various considerations and interests, and not by the laws of trade.

Our limits will not permit us to enter into a discussion of the causes which have, since 1874, suspended the bi-metallic policy of the Latin Union, or of the probabilities of the future respecting the indifferent use of gold and silver as money.

XV.

THE REVENUE OF THE STATE.

572. The revenue of the State may be derived from :

I. Voluntary Contributions.*

It is, to most of us, difficult to conceive a state of society where the expenses of government should be met through spontaneous self-assessment ; yet, in a more primitive condition, such a state of things has existed widely, † and in a few happy instances has come down nearly to our day.

* Voluntary Taxation, says Emile de Girardin, it is the State stimulated ; it is the State economical ; it is the State Republican and Democratic.

† The words Dona, Benevolences, etc., in the history of revenue, testify to the original assumption that contribution was voluntary.

The papal revenues* may perhaps be brought under this title. Adam Smith cites Hamburg, Basle, Zurich, Underwald, Holland, and other communities, where the self-valuation of the citizen was accepted.

An American,† long resident in Europe, thus describes his experience in a community where the principle of self-assessment still survived:

"For four years it was the good fortune of the present writer to be domiciled in one of these communities. Incredible as it may seem to believers in the necessity of a legal enforcement of taxes by pains and penalties, he was, for that period, by law and usage, in the strictest sense of the term, his own assessor and his own tax gatherer. In common with the other citizens, he was invited, without sworn statement or declaration, to make such contribution to the public charges as seemed to him just and equal. That sum, uncounted by any official, unknown to any but himself, he was asked to drop, with his own hand, into a strong public chest; on doing which, his name was checked off the list of contributors, his duty done."

573. II. Lucrative Prerogatives, Public Property, and State Enterprise.

The following may be named as the chief sources of revenue under this head:

(1.) Rent-charges in favor of the state as the proprietor of all lands. This has been fully discussed under the title: the Nationalization of the Land (pars. 496–505).

(2.) Escheat: the principle that the state is the proprietor of all property to which individual titles or claims are lost. This principle was early established in all countries whose legal or fiscal history we know.

It is evident that the scope of this principle will widen or

---

* The Pope was the greatest capitalist of the Middle Ages. The British Parliament at one time declared the revenues derived from the people of that Kingdom by the Pope to be five times as great as those obtained by the Crown.

† Rev. Dr. Warren, President of Boston University.

contract in correspondence with the laws regulating the descent and bequest of property and prescribing the times and modes of proving claims. Under the feudal system, escheat constituted a most important source of revenue. In England, the right of devising real property did not exist after the Conquest, until the time of Henry VIII. Modern society, however, has given continually wider extension to the power of bequest and the principle of inheritance, until escheat has ceased to be of much importance.

In 1795, the great English law reformer, Jeremy Bentham, in a pamphlet entitled, "Escheat *vice* Taxation," propounded a scheme by which the entire revenue of the state should be derived from this source.

Bentham proposed an extension of the existing law of escheat, "a law coeval with the very first elements of the Constitution," and a corresponding limitation of the power of bequest. The effect intended was to be "the appropriating to the use of the public all vacant successions, property of every denomination included, on the failure of near relations, will or no will, subject only to the power of bequest, as hereinafter limited."

By near relations, he means "such relations as stand within the degrees termed prohibited with reference to marriage."

Further, in the case of "such relations within the pale as are not only childless, but without prospect of children," he proposes, that, instead of taking their share in money, they should take only the interest of it for life.

"As to the latitude to be left to the power of bequest," he writes, "I should propose it to be continued in respect to the half of whatever property would be at present subject to that power."

Bentham argues that in the distribution of property there is no sense of hardship but in proportion to disappointment: expectation thwarted. "Hardship," he says, "depends upon disappointment; disappointment upon expectation; expectation upon the dispensations, meaning the *known* dispensations, of the law."

If, therefore, the law were so framed, distant relations* would not expect to succeed; would consequently not be disappointed; and would consequently suffer no hardship.

574. (3.) Fines and forfeitures for Criminality and Delinquency. Since government exists largely for the protection of life, property and labor, the cost of maintaining government and administering justice might properly be drawn, if it were found possible, from the delinquent and criminal class.

In feudal times, fines and forfeitures constituted a very important source of revenue to the crown.

(*a*) The relation of the tenant to the lord was a personal one, and any failure in personal loyalty, though it did not become a crime against society, was punished by heavy fines or by total forfeiture.

(*b*) The crimes of those days were largely political, and political offenders are likely to be men of wealth and position. The Wars of the Roses were so fruitful of forfeitures that a large proportion of the land became the property of the crown.

In the present age political crimes have become comparatively infrequent, and the criminal class are now mainly drawn from the poor, who are not proper, perhaps not possible, subjects for pecuniary exaction.

Hence this branch of public revenue has shrunk into comparative insignificance. Fines and forfeitures pay a part of the expense of strictly judicial establishments, especially of the lower or police courts; but they add little to the general receipts of the state.

(4.) Tributes from colonies, dependencies and conquered nations, including war fines, requisitions and indemnities.

The subject is a fascinating one; † but I must resist the temptation to enlarge upon it.

---

* The principle of Bentham's proposal is sanctioned by the legacy and succession duties of England, which exact ten per cent. from strangers, and only one per cent. from children.

† It would be specially interesting to compare the system of exaction practiced by the Greeks, Carthaginians and Romans, in ancient times, and by the Dutch and Portuguese, in modern times, with the English sys-

575. (5.) The sale of offices, honors and titles.

This source of revenue makes a very prominent figure in the history of finance ; but has, at present, mainly a curious interest.

The sale of offices, titles, etc., by the state, may fall into several different categories.

(*a*) The sale of offices of dignity and honor, as in the case of the patents of nobility, granted by James I.* of England, the effect of which merely is to lower the real honor and dignity of such offices, perhaps with only a political and social retribution.

(*b*) The sale of offices, as under many of the Popes, which carry salaries in the nature of annuities terminable by death, the price paid representing, more or less exactly from the actuarial point of view, the capitalized value of the annuity.

(*c*) The sale of offices, as once practiced largely in France, which carry exemptions from political burdens and from taxes. This amounts simply to a sale of the rights of the state in respect to taxation, and is, in effect, an anticipation of revenue. A government which was in such straits as to resort to practices like these would be likely to make a very bad bargain for itself ; and so in France it proved.

"As the finances became more embarrassed," says M. de

---

tem of seeking the interest of the mother country, or the conquering country, in the right to impose navigation laws and commercial restrictions, and in the benefits of patronage in officering the public service of colonies and dependencies.

* The sum paid to constitute a Baron was £10,000 ; a viscount, £15,000, an Earl, £20,000.—Taylor, Hist. of Taxation in England.

"The price of the dignity of a Baronet," says Taylor, "was equivalent to £1095, ninety-three of whom were created."

These are instances of the sale of offices to willing purchasers. James' son, Charles I., undertook the sale of his offices to his subjects, *willy nilly*. He revived the feudal practice of "Knight's Fee," and compelled persons holding land of a certain yearly value to come up and be knighted, or submit to a fine for contumacy. Brodie says, "Charles did not restrict it to men of landed property, but included lessees, merchants, and others."—*Hist. Br. Empire.*

Tocqueville, "new offices were created, with exemptions from taxation or privileges by way of salary; and as they were created to supply the wants of the treasury and not the requirements of the public service, an immense number of them were useless or positively mischievous.

"As early as 1664, when Colbert instituted an inquiry into the subject, it was discovered that the capital invested in this miserable business nearly amounted to 500,000,000 livres. It is said that Richelieu abolished 100,000 offices. They rose anew, under fresh names. For a trifle of money, the state bartered away the right of directing and controlling its own servants. The net result of this system was a government machine, so vast, so complicated, so cumbrous, and so inefficient that it was actually found necessary to let it stand idle, while a new instrument, constructed with more simplicity and better adapted for use, performed the work which these countless functionaries were supposed to do."

It was Louis XII. who systematized the sale of offices, and Henry IV. who first sold hereditary ones.

(*d*) The sale of offices, as notably under the Roman Empire, which carry rights, privileges and exclusive opportunities by which the purchaser may reimburse himself for his outlay, either through a monopoly or through the collection and disbursement of the public revenue.

576. (6.) Domains (L'Etat Capitaliste.)

Even under the modern European principle of the private ownership of land, the state is, in all countries, the possessor of larger or smaller domains from which a revenue may be derived.

It is the habit of writers on finance to speak, and perhaps justly, in the most disparaging tone of the administration of public estates, for productive uses.* Adam Smith expresses

---

*M. Leroy Beaulieu dwells upon the distinction between the property of the State, which is left to the enjoyment of the community, or which is devoted to government uses, and that which is sought to be administered productively. The former he terms *domaine public*; the latter *domaine privé de l' Etat.*

himself in the strongest terms. "The servants of the most negligent master are better superintended than the servants of the most vigilant sovereign." Referring to his own country, he says: "The crown-lands of Great Britain * do not, at present, afford the fourth part of the rent which could probably be drawn from them, if they were the property of private persons. If the crown-lands were more extensive, it is probable they would be still worse managed." And, not to disparage English administration too greatly, he adds: "In the present state of the greater part of the civilized monarchies of Europe, the rent of all lands in the country, managed as they would probably be if they all belonged to one proprietor, would scarce amount, perhaps, to the ordinary revenue which they levy upon the people, even in peaceful times."

However much this statement might require to be modified with respect to the management of government property in a country like Germany, with its admirable civil service and its systematic administration of public trusts, no one would think of questioning the full literal truth of Adam Smith's declaration if applied to our own country, with its civil service based upon the principles of rotation in office and appointment as the reward of partisan activity.

Of the present Enropean States, Russia, Prussia, Bavaria, Sweden, and Hanover, derive considerable revenue from pub-

---

* Did our space allow, it would be interesting to refer to the alienations and resumptions and renewed alienations of the Crown-lands, through the reigns of the Tudors and the Stuarts. Strangely enough, it was that model financier, William III., who effected the greatest havoc among the royal domains. One can scarcely read of the wholesale squandering of the property of the Crown by this monarch, without the suspicion that he clearly saw the coming on of the modern system of finance, when the necessities of the state should be met, no longer by rents and fines and forfeitures and escheats and purveyance, but by systematic taxation; and that, in something like contempt for the feudal sources of revenue, he purposely chose to dissipate the patrimony on which his predecessors had relied. "At the end of William's reign," says Sir E. May, "Parliament, having obtained accounts of the state of the land revenues, found that they had been reduced by grants, alienations, incumbrances, reversions, and pensions, until they scarcely exceeded the rent-roll of a squire."

lic domains, the first named being so pre-eminent in this respect that M. Cherbuliez * mentions it as almost the only state which draws a notable proportion of its revenue from such a source.

577. (7) State Enterprise (L'Etat Entrepreneur).—Whatever the disabilities of the state in acquiring a revenue from the rental or sale of property, whether that consist of agricultural lands, or mines, or forests, or fisheries, or phosphate deposits, those disabilities are greatly increased when the state undertakes the management of commercial or manufacturing business.† The state as capitalist is at no small disadvantage; as entrepreneur, that disadvantage is vastly aggravated.

Yet the rule of failure, on this side of governmental agency, is not unbroken. Dr. Smith mentions the republic of Hamburg as deriving a considerable revenue from a public wine cellar and from an apothecary's shop. The profits of banking ‡ have been realized in a notable degree by several cities, among them Hamburg, Venice and Amsterdam. The post-office can be made, and has been made, "to pay," and that handsomely. If the post-office in the United States is not a source of revenue, it is because our people have chosen to make it an agency for promoting the settlement of the country. The business of distilling in Russia, of sugar refining in Egypt, and of opium manufacture in British India, have been made the subject of no inconsiderable profit to government,

* Science Economique. Worth mentioning in this connection are the sugar plantations, private property of the Khedive of Egypt, the guano deposits of Peru and Chili, and the mahogany forests of Honduras, on the credit of which vast loans have been obtained, within recent years, in the London market.

† Adam Smith remarks that no two characters are more inconsistent than those of trader and sovereign. "If the trading spirit of the English East India Company rendered them very bad sovereigns, the spirit of sovereignty seems to have rendered them equally bad traders."

‡ The Prussian Bank in 1874 declared dividends of 12 3-4 per cent. One-half the net gains of the bank go to the state. The United States was a partner to the extent of one-fifth in the bank of 1791–1811, and again in that of 1816–1836.

The supply of towns in the matter of water, and, in a smaller number of instances, of gas, has been attempted, not unsuccessfully, by municipal governments.

The instance which goes furthest to contradict the generally received opinion of the hopeless incapacity of the state to conduct industrial enterprises, is afforded by the railways of Germany.

578. III. Quasi Taxes.—The following may be named as sources of revenue under this head:

(1.) Monopolies conferred upon individuals or corporations, in consideration of a capital sum paid down, or of a share in the resulting profits.

Monopolies have played a conspicuous part in the history of public revenues; and, in spite of the spirit of the age which is, in general, strongly opposed to exclusive privileges of manufacture and sale, they still form a prominent feature in the budget of many countries of Europe.

Monopolies may be commercial, industrial or financial. The distinction between the monopolies of the past and those of the present day is marked. Formerly monopolies were granted, for the profit of the government, to persons and corporations to carry on a vast variety of operations,* great and small alike, most of which were susceptible of private management.

---

* The story of the rapid extension of monopolies in England under Elizabeth, of the indignation aroused thereby throughout the realm, and of the submission of the haughty Tudor to the rising storm, is familiar to every school-boy. Hume remarked that, had Elizabeth's system of monopolies been continued, the England of his day would have contained as little industry as Morocco or the coast of Barbary.

Charles I. played the same game as Elizabeth, and aroused an equal popular indignation, until even the subservient judges kicked at the restraints everywhere imposed upon trade.

Says Brodie, after referring to the soap monopoly: "Almost every article of ordinary consumption, whether of manufacture or not, was exposed to a similar abuse; salt, starch, coals, iron, wine, pens, cards and dice, beavers, felts, bone-lace, etc., meat dressed in taverns, tobacco, wine casks, brewing and distilling, lamprons, weighing of hay and straw in London and Westminster, gauging of red herrings, butter-casks,

Such were the monopolies of the 17th and 18th centuries. To-day, under the light of political economy, all prudent governments restrict the principle of monopoly to a very few highly important interests, and, by preference, to those which in their nature tend toward monopoly. Thus Bentham, that arch enemy of monopolies, proposed the collection of large revenues from bankers, who were to be compensated by a monopoly within their several districts, on the ground that banking was a business tending to monopoly.

In the same way, taxes on railway goods and passenger traffic in England and France have been defended, even by free-traders, on the ground that railway transportation is necessarily very much of a monopoly; that full and effective competition can rarely be introduced and never long maintained ; and that the state may, therefore, accepting the fact of a substantial monopoly, properly derive a profit therefrom.

But there are also certain special interests of great commercial importance, in every way fitted for private management, which, on account of their high capability for yielding revenue, some enlightened nations still constitute exceptions to the principle of open public competition.

Among the subjects thus specially excepted from the principle of competition, are opium, salt, tobacco and matches.

579.—(2.) Lotteries. This needs only to be mentioned as a source of revenue largely made use of, in the past, and still forming an important feature in the budgets of many civilized countries. Of the moral and social objections* to this system of raising money, we are not called to speak here. Economically speaking, there can be no doubt that, while lotteries afford a most effective means of securing a present revenue,

---

kelp and seaweed, linen cloth, rags, hops, buttons, hats, gutstring, spectacles, combs, tobacco, pipes, etc., saltpeter, gunpowder, in short, articles down to the sole gathering of rags, were all under the fetters of monopolies, and consequently deeply taxed."

* It is to be noted that the laws against private lotteries which, doubtless, did much to educate that public sentiment which now makes even public lotteries impossible in many countries, originated in the desire to secure to the state the profits of this source of gain.

appealing, as they do, to one of the strongest passions of human nature, they yet, in their ultimate effect, weaken the state by discouraging patient industry, and thus impair the revenue capabilities of any people among whom they come to be extensively employed. In two of the states of the American union, lotteries are still conducted under government patronage. Every one is familiar with them as agencies for collecting money for charitable and religious associations.

580.—(3.) Purveyance.—The right of buying provisions and other necessaries for the use of the royal household, at an appraised valuation, in preference to all other purchasers and even without the consent of the owner, might have been included among the "lucrative prerogatives" mentioned under a former head, or may indifferently be regarded as a quasi tax. Once extensively practiced, purveyance is now greatly restrained and confined, and in almost all highly civilized countries is wholly discontinued—except during actual war, or in the case of a royal progress.

581.—(4.) Fees.—A fourth mode of raising revenue, which partakes largely of the nature of a tax, without bearing its form, is through the exaction of fees for stated or occasional services performed by the agents of the State.

So far as fees are, in the phrase of Garnier, not *fiscal*, that is, so far as they constitute merely a return for the expense to which the individual receiving the benefit has put the state, on his own behalf, they do not come under the present title. We are only concerned here with fees exacted by the state as a means of revenue, in excess of the expense to which the state is put by the performance of the service, and where, perhaps, the so-called service is itself interposed only as an occasion for the imposition of a tax, as in the case of many custom-house services.

Into the same category would properly fall all the fees exacted from individuals where the main benefit is received by the community, even though the aggregate of such receipts should not equal the expense to the state of maintaining some necessary service. Judicial fees are often of this nature, the cost of obtaining the adjudication of a great principle having been formerly thrown upon single individuals, who were frequently less benefited than thousands of others by the decisions reached. This system was fiercely attacked by Bentham. "Who goeth to warfare at any time at his own charges? saith St. Paul. It is the poor litigant who makes war upon injustice."

It is also fairly a question whether the maintenance of the ordinary roads of a country is not, in such a sense and in so far, a general charge, that fees, under the name of tolls, constitute a *quasi tax*, instead of being, according to the assumption on which they are collected, the price paid by the individual for a service rendered to himself directly and exclusively.

Of other forms of quasi taxes (5) seigniorage on the coin, and (6) the issue of paper money, enough has been said in Part III.

582. IV. Taxation in its Various Forms.—Taxation may be considered (*a*) according to its ultimate Bases, which may be Rent-bearing land, Wealth, Revenue, Faculty, or Expenditure, one or all of these.

The first we have already discussed under the title "The Nationalization of the Land." A tax on rent, we have seen, is not a general tax. It does not fall upon those members of the community who do not own land. It does not affect the price of produce. It amounts merely to the assumption, or usurpation, as one is disposed to regard it, by the state, of the surplus of produce above the cost of cultivating the no-rent lands.

A tax upon the no-rent lands, either by themselves, or in common with other lands, is a tax on produce.

583. Again, taxation may be considered (*b*) with reference to the equities of contribution. In this connection we might discuss:

(1.) The Physiocratic theory of Taxation. The French Physiocrats (par. 48) holding, as they did, that land, alone of all agencies of production, yields a return above the cost of production, proposed, thereupon, to make land yield all the revenue of the state, as a measure both of justice and of political expediency.*

This tax is to be distinguished from the assumption by the state of the Unearned Increment of Land, as proposed by Mr. Mill and his associates. The latter, as we have seen, would not raise the price of produce. The former would do so, and was intended to do so.

But, with the complete refutation of the physiocratic theory of production fell the physiocratic scheme of taxation.

(2.) The Social Dividend Theory of Taxation, which is, in effect, that the members of the community should contribute to the public support in proportion to the benefits they derive from the protection of the state, or according as the services they receive cost the state more or cost it less.

(3.) A group of theories respecting the equities of taxation, differing not greatly among themselves, which give rise, respectively, to what we may call the-equality-of-sacrifice rule; the rule of contribution-according-to-ability, and the leave-them-as-you-find-them rule.

It is in discussing the theories of this group that the question of progressive taxation arises. That question is common to all the theories of this group.

(4.) We have the view taken by Mr. McCulloch,† in despair of reaching the equities of the case, which may be called the purely economic theory of taxation. The discussion of this theory brings up the whole question of the diffusion or "repercussion" of taxes.

---

* "Ils établissent d'abord que la terre seule donne un revenu net, c'est-à-dire, un revenu qui excède les dépenses nécessaires pour l'entretien des cultures et des cultivateurs ; ils établissent ensuite que ce revenu net est la source qui alimente tous les autres revenus ; ils en concluent qu'il est inutile de poursuivre les revenus mobiliers à travers les mille canaux où ils circulent : qu'il est plus commode et plus juste de les atteindre à leur source, et ils aboutissent à la théorie de l'impôt unique sur le revenu foncier."—Clamageran: Hist. de l'Impôt en France.

† "The distinguishing feature of the best tax is, not that it is most nearly proportioned to the means of individuals, but that it is easily assessed and collected, and is, at the same time, most conducive to the public interests."

584. (c.) The foregoing discussions are introductory to the consideration of any specific tax or group of taxes, or existing tax system, respecting which we may inquire how far it answers the requirements of equitable contribution, or, on the other hand, if we abandon the rule of equity altogether —as did Mr. McCulloch—how far it secures to the state the needed revenue, with a minimum of irritation to the public mind, with a minimum of expense and loss in collection, and with a minimum disturbance to trade and industry.

XVI.

THE PRINCIPLES OF TAXATION.

585. Inadequacy of the Literature of Taxation.—According to an eminent German financier, Hoffmann, it would be difficult to find, in the whole realm of political economy, a subject more generally misconceived, more disfigured by false views, more degraded by a partial study, than Taxation. "If," adds M. de Parieu, author of the ablest French work on the subject, "this proposition appeared true in a country where the problem of instruction in administration has for a long time been studied, it is probably still more so in France, where the practice is even further separated from the science of administration."

586. The body of English literature in finance is extremely unsatisfactory.* Adam Smith, indeed, gave to taxation about one-fourth of his Wealth of Nations; but his treatment shows little grasp of the subject, at any point; while his ignorance of the law of rent goes far to vitiate his general views. Ricardo dealt with taxation, at great length; and as a study of the

* I have been severely blamed for using language even stronger than this, in former editions of this work. I dare say my statements were too sweeping. Mr. Newmarch's papers on public debts and Mr. Gladstone's Budget speeches are never to be mentioned without honor. Mr. Robert Giffen, Prof. Cliffe Leslie, Mr. Inglis Palgrave, and Prof. Thorold Rogers have made important contributions to many questions touching local or imperial taxation.

propagation of an economic impulse from object to object, and from class to class, his discussion is masterly. But Ricardo's underlying assumption of perfect competition has necessarily resulted in conclusions which are widely inconsistent with the facts of industrial society. J. R. McCulloch discussed taxation and the funding system in a distinct treatise, which is not without value. Later English contributions to finance have, with few exceptions, either been trivial in character or have been confined to single phases of the general subject. No great, comprehensive English work on Taxation exists.

587. Perhaps we shall get as good an idea of the inconsequence of the English literature in this department, as can be obtained in any other way, by referring to Adam Smith's maxims respecting taxation. Dr. Smith proposed four maxims,* or principles, "which," says Mr. Mill, "having been generally concurred in by subsequent writers, may be said to have become classical." A vast deal of importance has been assigned by English economists to these maxims. They have been quoted over and over again, as if they contained truths of great moment; yet if one examines them, he finds them, at the best, trivial; while the first and most famous of these can not be subjected to the slightest test without going all to pieces.

588. The Social Dividend Theory of Taxation.—"The subjects of every state," says Dr. Smith, "ought to contribute

* "I. The subjects of every state ought to contribute towards the support of the government as nearly as possible in proportion to their respective abilities; that is, in proportion to the revenue which they respectively enjoy under the protection of the state.

"II. The tax which each individual is bound to pay ought to be certain and not arbitrary. The time of payment, the manner of payment, the quantity to be paid, ought all to be clear and plain to the contributor, and to every other person.

"III. Every tax ought to be levied at the time, or in the manner, in which it is most likely to be convenient for the contributor to pay it.

"IV. Every tax ought to be so contrived as both to take out and to keep out of the pockets of the people as little as possible over and above what it brings into the public treasury of the state."

towards the support of the government as nearly as possible in proportion to their respective abilities; that is, in proportion to the revenue which they respectively enjoy under the protection of the state."

This maxim, though it sounds fairly, will not bear examination. What mean those last words, "under the protection of the state"? They are either irrelevant, or else they mean that the protection enjoyed affords the measure of the duty to contribute. But the doctrine that the members of the community ought to contribute in proportion to the benefits they derive from the protection of the state, or according as the services performed in their behalf cost less or cost more to the state, involves the grossest practical absurdities. Those who derive the greatest benefit from the protection of the state are the poor and the weak—women and children and the aged; the infirm, the ignorant, the indigent.

Even as among the well-to-do and wealthy classes of the community, does the protection enjoyed furnish a measure of the duty to contribute? If so, the richer the subject or citizen is, the less, proportionally, should he pay. A man who buys protection in large quantities should get it at wholesale prices, like the man who buys flour and meat by the car-load. Moreover, it costs the state less to collect a given amount from one taxpayer than from many.

Returning to the maxim of Dr. Smith, I ask, does it put forward ability to contribute, or protection enjoyed, as affording the true basis of taxation? Which? If both, on what principles and by what means are the two to be combined in practice?

589. Taxation According to Ability.—But if we take the last six words as merely a half-conscious recognition of the social-dividend theory of taxation, and throw them aside, we shall still find this much-quoted maxim far from satisfactory: "The subjects of every state ought to contribute towards the support of the government as nearly as possible in proportion to their respective abilities; that is, in proportion to the revenue which they respectively enjoy."

But is the ability of two persons to contribute necessarily in proportion to their respective revenues? Take the case of the head of a family having an income of $500 a year, of which $400 is absolutely essential to the maintenance of himself and wife and children in health and strength to labor. Is the ability of such a person, who has only $100 which could possibly be taken for public uses, one half as great as that of another head of a family similarly situated in all respects except that his income amounts to $1000, and who has therefore $600 which could conceivably be brought under contribution? Manifestly not.

We shall, then, still further improve Dr. Smith's maxim if we cut away all after the first clause: "The subjects of every state ought to contribute towards the support of the government as nearly as possible in proportion to their respective abilities." The maxim as it stands is unexceptionable, but does not shed much light on the difficult question of assessment.

590. The Leave-them-as-you-find-them Rule of Taxation.—The best statement I have met of the principle of contribution based on ability is contained in an article in the *Edinburgh Review* of 1833: "No tax is a just tax unless it leaves individuals in the same relative condition in which it finds them." What does the precept, which we may call the leave-them-as-you-find-them rule of taxation, demand? In seeking an answer to this question, let us inquire, historically, what bases have been taken for assessment. Leaving out Rent-Bearing Land, whose fiscal relations have been sufficiently dwelt upon, we note four:

1. Contribution has been exacted on the basis of Realized Wealth, commonly spoken of as Capital.
2. On the basis of Annual Income, or Revenue.
3. On the basis of Faculty, or native and acquired power of production.
4. On the basis of Expenditure, or the individual consumption of wealth.

These are the four historical bases of taxation. Let us see how far each in turn answers the requirement of the Edinburgh Reviewer's maxim that the tax ought to leave the members of the community in the same relative condition in which it finds them.

And, first, of Realized Wealth. Wealth is accumulated by savings out of revenue. If, then, wealth alone is to be taxed, it is saving, not production, which contributes to the support of the state. Economically there can not be a moment's doubt that for government thus to draw its revenue from only that part of the produced wealth of the community which is reserved from immediate expenditure, must be prejudicial. The question also arises, where is the political or social justice of such a rule of contribution? *If my income belongs to me, to spend for my own comfort and gratification, without any deduction for the uses of the state, why should I lose my right to any part of it because I save it?* To tax realized wealth is to punish men for not consuming their earnings as they receive them. Yet it is eminently for the public interest that men should save of their means to increase the capital of the country.

591. Revenue as the Basis of Taxation.—Turning to Revenue, it would seem, on the first thought, that we had reached a rule of equitable contribution. Yet the rule of contribution according to revenue is subject to grave impeachment.

Here are two men of equal natural powers. One is active, energetic, industrious; he toils early and late and realizes a considerable revenue, on a portion of which the state lays its hand. The other lets his natural powers run to waste; trifles with life, lounges, hunts, fishes, gambles, and is content with a bare and mean subsistence. *Was his duty to contribute to the support of the state different in kind or degree from that of the other? If not, how has his idleness, shiftlessness, worthlessness, forfeited the state's right to a contribution from him in proportion to his abilities?*

We must, I think, conclude that, while to tax wealth instead of revenue is to put a premium upon self-indulgence in the expenditure of wealth for present enjoyment, to tax revenue instead of faculty is to put a premium upon self-indulgence in the form of indolence, the waste of opportunities, and the abuse of natural powers.

592. Expenditure as the Basis of Taxation.—Passing for the moment by our third title, we find that the fourth basis taken for taxation has been Expenditure. This must not be confounded with taxes on consumption, as constituting a part of a tax system in which taxes on realized wealth, taxes on revenue, taxes on faculty, one or all of these, also appear. Nor do we speak here of taxes on expenditure imposed in practical despair of an equitable distribution of the burdens of government. We are now concerned with expenditure only as the single basis of taxation, in the interest of political equity.

"It is generally allowed," wrote Sir William Petty, two hundred years ago, "that men should contribute to the public charge but according to the share and interest they have in the public peace ; that is, according to their estate or riches.

"Now, there are two sorts of riches, one actual and the other potential. A man is actually and truly rich according to what he eateth, drinketh, weareth, or in any other way really and actually enjoyeth. Others are but potentially and imaginatively rich, who, though they have power over much, make little use of it, these being *rather stewards and exchangers for the other sort than owners for themselves.*

"Concluding, therefore, that every man ought to contribute according to what he taketh to himself and actually enjoyeth, the first thing to be done is," etc., etc.

Arthur Young seems to have had the same view. After saying that every individual should contribute in proportion to his ability, he added in a note : "By ability must not be understood either capital or income, but that superlucration, as Davenant called it, which melts into consumption."

In this view, so far as any one possesses wealth in forms available for the future production of wealth, he is regarded as a trustee or guardian, in that respect and to that extent, of the public interests. Just this is said by Young—taxes "can reach with propriety the expenses of his living only. If they touch any other part of his expenditure, they deprive him of *those tools that are working the business of the state.*"

593. Fallacy of this Doctrine.—I do not see but that, if capital, or revenue in excess of personal expenditure, is to be exempted from taxation, on the plea that it has not yet become the subject of individual and exclusive appropriation, and is, therefore, presumably held and used in a way which primarily benefits society, the state has the right to inquire whether the use made or proposed to be made of wealth is such as will, in fact, benefit society, and benefit society, moreover, in the highest degree of which it is capable.

The citizen says to the state, "You must not tax this wealth because I have not yet appropriated it exclusively to myself. Indeed, I am going to use it for the benefit of society." The state rejoins: "Yes, but of that we must satisfy ourselves. We must be the judge whether your use of your wealth will benefit society. Pay your taxes, and you can do with your wealth as you like. Claim exemption on the ground of public service, and you rightfully come under state supervision and control."

The fallacy of the theory we are considering lies in the failure to recognize the fact that the selfish and exclusive appropriation and enjoyment of wealth are inseparable from its possession. The pride of ownership, the social distinction which attends great possessions, the power which wealth confers, are additional to the merely sensual enjoyment to be derived from personal expenditure. Would I resent the interference of the government, or of my neighbors, in the management of my property, upon the ground that it was not being used in the best way? What is that resentment but the proof of a personal appropriation, an exclusive appropriation, of that wealth? My resentment would spring out of the deeply seated feeling that my management of my own property is my right: and that he who should deprive me of it would take from me what is as truly mine as the right to eat, drink, wear, or otherwise consume and enjoy any portion of it; that, short of absolute mental incapacity, it is my prerogative to control my own estate, even though not to the highest advantage of the community, or even of myself: though not wisely or well. In other words, I am not a trustee, but a proprietor.

594. The Dangerous Nature of this Doctrine.—This doctrine of the Trusteeship of Capital is not more irrational than it is socially dangerous. It is held by men who are fierce in denouncing graded taxation as confiscation; yet it is, in its very essence, communistic. If the owner of wealth is but a trustee; if "his tools are working the business of the state," then the real beneficiary may enter and dispossess the trustee if any substantial reason for dissatisfaction as to the management of the property exists; the state may take the tools into its own hands and "work its business" for itself.

595. Faculty as the Basis of Taxation.—I reach, then, the conclusion that Faculty, the power of production, constitutes the only theoretically just basis of contribution; that men are bound to serve the state in the degree in which they have the ability to serve themselves.

I think we shall more clearly see Faculty to be the true natural basis of taxation if we contemplate a primitive community, where occupations are few, industries simple, realized wealth at a minimum, the members of the society nearly on a level, the wants of the state limited. Suppose, now, a work of general concern, perhaps of vital importance, requires to be constructed: a dyke against inundation, or a road, with occasional bridges, for communication with neighboring settlements. What would be the rule of contribution? Why, that all able-bodied persons should turn out and each man work according to his faculties, in the exact way in which he could be most useful.

In regard to a community thus for the time engaged, we note two things: first, no man would be held to be exempt because he took no interest in the work; he would not be allowed to escape contribution because he was willing to relinquish his share of the benefits to be derived, preferring to get a miserable subsistence for himself by hunting or fishing; secondly, between those working, a higher order of faculties, greater muscular power, or superior skill would make no distinction as to the time for which the individuals of the community should severally remain at work.

596. The Ideal Tax.—This is the ideal tax. It is the form of contribution to which all primitive communities instinctively resort. It is the tax which, but for purely practical difficulties, would afford a perfectly satisfactory measure of the obligation of every citizen to contribute to the sustentation and defense of the state. Any mode of taxation which departs in essence from this involves a greater or smaller sacrifice of the equities of contribution ; and any mode of taxation which departs from this in form is almost certain to involve a greater or smaller departure in essence.

And it deserves to be noted that the largest tax of modern times, even in the most highly organized societies of Europe, the obligation of compulsory military service, is assessed and collected on precisely this principle.

597. The Faculty Tax Impracticable.—But while the tax on Faculty is the ideal tax, it has usually been deemed impracticable, as the sole tax, in a complicated condition of industrial society. As occupations multiply and the forms of production become diversified, the state can not to advantage call upon each member, by turns, to serve in person for a definite portion of each day or of the year. Hence modern statesmanship has invented taxes on expenditure, on revenue, on capital, not as theoretically just, but with a view to reduce the aggregate burden on the community, and to save production and trade from vexation and obstruction.

598. We recur to the Tax on Revenue.—The politicians of the existing order, as we have seen, shrink from the effort involved in levying the public contributions entirely, or even chiefly, according to faculty. Next in point of political equity comes the tax on incomes, or the revenues of individuals. That tax, as we now contemplate it, is a tax on the revenues of all classes, with exception only of the amount requisite for the maintenance of the laborer and his family, after the simplest possible manner, in health and strength to labor. It is not a compensatory tax, constituting a part of a system in which realized wealth and various forms of expenditure are also brought under contribution, but the sole tax imposed by the state.

599. Exemption of the Actual Necessaries of Life.—It has been said that from such an income tax the necessary cost of subsistence must be exempted. Mr. D. A. Wells has, indeed, laid down two propositions: first, that "any income tax which permits of any exemption whatever is a graduated income tax;" and, secondly, that "a graduated income tax to the extent of its discrimination is an act of confiscation." But the exemption of a certain minimum annual revenue is a matter of sheer necessity, whether the state will or no. Economically speaking, it is not possible to tax an income of this class. A man in the receipt of such an income can not contribute to the expenses of government. Should the state, with one hand, take any thing from such a person as a taxpayer, it must, with the other, give it back to him as a pauper.

Conceding the exemption, on purely economic grounds, of the amount required for the maintenance of the laborer's family, one of the most vital questions in finance arises immediately thereupon, to wit: shall the excess above the minimum, shall the superfluity of revenue, which may be spent or saved at the will of the owner, be taxed at a uniform rate, or at rates rising with the increase of income?

600. The Question of Progressive Taxation.—The question of progressive taxation has always been one of great interest while the fiscal policy of states rested with the wealthy and well-to-do classes. It is certain to acquire vastly greater importance as political power passes more and more into the hands of the class of small incomes.

Upon the question of the equity of progressive taxation writers on finance are divided. One party holds that any recognition of this principle is sheer confiscation: the other admits that progressive taxation may be carried to a certain point without injury either to the sense of political justice or to the instincts of industry and frugality, some even holding with J. B. Say that "taxation can not be equitable unless its ratio is progressive." Both parties agree that there is great danger that, under popular impulse, progressive taxation may be carried so far as not only to violate all the equities of contribution but seriously to shock the habits of acquiring and saving property.

The system of progressive taxation prevailed at Athens. There were four Solonian classes of citizens, arranged according to wealth. Of these the first paid no taxes; the class next above them were entered on the tax-books at a sum equal to five times their income; the next class at ten times their income; the richest class at twelve times their income.

The principle of graduation, or progressive taxation, was a favorite one with the statesmen of the French Revolution. It was for a time adopted by the Convention in 1793. In consequence, perhaps, of the appetite thus created among the people for laying the burdens of government mainly on the rich, many of the later French writers on finance have been very strenuous in denouncing the principle.

Yet this system was approved, as we saw, by Say, and also by Montesquieu. In the personal tax, wrote the latter, "the unjust proportion would be that which should follow exactly the proportion of goods." Referring to the Solonian Categories at Athens, he said: "The tax was just, though it was not proportional. If it did not follow the proportion of goods, it did follow the proportion of needs. It was judged that each had equal physical necessities, and that those necessities ought not to be taxed; that the useful came next, and that it ought to be taxed, but less than what was superfluous; and lastly, that the greatness of the tax on the superfluity should repress the superfluity."

In 1848, at the Revolution, the idea of progressivity was revived. The provisional government in a decree, said: "Before the Revolution taxation was proportional; then it was unjust. To be truly equitable, taxation must be progressive."

M. Joseph Garnier, editor of the *Journal des Economistes*, makes a distinction between progressive taxation, properly so called, and progressional taxation. It is, he says, against the first that all the objections are directed which we find in writers who declare that progressive taxation is a species of confiscation, tending to the absorption of great fortunes by the state, to the leveling of conditions, to the destruction of property, to the discouragement of frugality and industry, to the emigration of capital. There is, M. Garnier holds, a species of increasing taxation which is rational and discreet, to which he applies the term progressional, which is held within moderate limits, which is collected by virtue of a tariff of duties slowly progressive, and which, at the maximum, can not pass beyond a definite portion of the income of the individual.

In Prussia the tax on small incomes, known as the *Klassensteuer*, is levied on a scale of twelve degrees.

In England the principle of progression has never been admitted into the income tax further than is involved in the exemption of a certain minimum. How the subtraction of a constant amount from all incomes, and the taxation of the excess at a uniform rate, causes the rate on the total incomes to rise, from lowest to highest, will appear from the following table.

601. The Effect of Exemptions.—If we suppose the constant amount exempted to be $1,000, and the rate of taxation on the excess to be ten per cent., incomes of different amounts will in effect be taxed as follows :

Income.	Income subject to Taxation.	Amount of Tax.	Rate of Taxation on Total Income.
$1500	$ 500	$ 50	3.33 + per cent.
2000	1000	100	5 "
2500	1500	150	6 "
3000	2000	200	6.66 + "
3500	2500	250	7.14 + "
4000	3000	300	7.5 "
4500	3500	350	7.77 + "

But while the principle of progressivity has never been admitted into the income tax of England, it has been extensively applied to the so-called "Assessed Taxes ;" that is, taxes on carriages, horses, servants, etc.

602. The question of progressive taxation is a nice one in theory, while in its practical application it is beset with the gravest difficulty, arising out of the instincts of spoliation which are deeply rooted in the human breast, an inheritance from ages of universal warfare and robbery. The appetite for plundering the accumulated stock of wealth, once aroused, may become a formidable social and political evil.

Were the highest human wisdom, with perfect disinterestedness, to frame a scheme of contribution, I must believe that the progressive principle would in some degree be admitted; but in what degree, and by what means, I am at a loss to suggest.

That progressive taxation would be the demand of triumphant socialism, as it was of the Revolutionists of 1793 and 1848, we already know. That progressive taxation will be urged in the spirit of spoliation and confiscation, is most probable. The friends of the existing order will do well to be prepared to take their ground intelligently and maintain it with firmness and temper.

603. A Tax on Revenue Impracticable as the Sole Tax.—While, as the sole tax, the tax on revenue has been approved, on grounds of political justice, by many, perhaps most, writers on finance, it has, like the tax on faculty, generally been rejected as impracticable, in view of difficulties in assessment, affecting incomes both high and low, more indeed the higher than the lower, and difficulties of collection, affecting especially incomes of the lowest class. Few writers of reputation, have, without qualification, advocated such an income tax as both politically expedient and economically advantageous. Fewer statesmen have had the courage to propose it to the legislature.

Revenue, or income, having, then, been abandoned generally throughout modern society as the sole basis of taxation, and only in exceptional cases forming even an important feature of existing tax systems, Expenditure has been resorted to increasingly, in the past and present century, from considerations not so much of political equity as of political and fiscal expediency. By far the greater portion of the revenue of the most advanced states is derived from taxes on consumption, as they are called; and every new demand of the treasury is met mainly from this source.

Yet even now Wealth is still employed in many communities

as the sole basis of taxation, the measure of the obligation to contribute to the support of government. It was the preferred form of taxation throughout the American colonies. It is still the principal form of non-federal taxation in the United States, as the Grand Lists of townships, cities and counties testify.

604. Is a Tax on Capital Equitable?—How can a tax on realized wealth or capital be justified?

Let us take two cases: first, when income is not taxed; secondly, when income is taxed.

First, when income is not taxed. It is claimed that the result of realized wealth affords the best practical measure of income or of productive faculty. Now, that such a claim in behalf of a property-tax should be conceded, or even seriously considered, clearly requires two things: first, that the ne'er-do-weels shall be comparatively few in number; and secondly, that the disposition to save out of income, for the accumulation of wealth, shall be the general rule in the community. These requirements were met in the American colonies generally. Barring the effects of intemperance, it was a rule with few exceptions that Americans in those times were disposed to labor, and to labor hard, that they might produce wealth; while, so general was the desire of wealth, so stalwart the manhood of those times, so simple the habits of the people, so high the social importance attributed to the possession of capital, that all the surplus above decent, wholesome subsistence, after adequate provision for intellectual and religious culture, was likely to go towards accumulation.

The mere statement of these elements of the case suffices to show the difficulties besetting such a principle of taxation, in its application to communities like those of the present day, with a less stringent public sentiment, with more extravagant modes of living, with a less general elevation of tastes and ambitions, with greater proneness to self-indulgence, with vast classes that do not even try to save. In such a state of society, to tax only that part of revenue which is laid by for future consumption, or to assist in the further production of wealth, is both politically unjust and economically vicious, exciting to extravagance and discouraging frugality.

Secondly. But if a tax be imposed on income, how can a property-tax be justified at all? Have not the whole community been once taxed upon income, as affording a measure of the ability to contribute to the public service, and shall now a portion of the wealth so excised be again subject to deduction, on no other ground than that it has been saved, presumably to assist in future production?

605. The Purely Economic Theory of Taxation.—Mr. McCulloch, the author of one of the few works of value in the English literature of Taxation, boldly proposed to abandon altogether the attempt to follow out the equities of contribution. I have already quoted his statement: "The distinguishing feature of the best tax, is, not that it is most nearly proportioned to the means of individuals, but that it is easily assessed and collected, and is, at the same time, most conducive to the public interests."

The line of reasoning which leads up to Mr. McCulloch's conclusions may be stated as follows: Government springs from injustice, and, in the constitution of things, must commit more or less injustice. It is of no use to attempt to pursue the equities of contribution; they will elude you. It is admitted that it is impossible to distribute equally the benefits of government; why make the hopeless effort to apportion its burdens with absolute justice? Get the best government you can; maintain it at the least expense consistently with efficiency; collect the revenue for the service by the most convenient, simple and inexpensive means. By undertaking to effect an equitable apportionment of the burden, through complicated methods or by personal assessment, you are not only likely to fail; you are certain, at the best, to add to the aggregate cost of the service, and are in great danger of generating new and distinct evils by disturbing economic relations and obstructing the processes of production and exchange.

606. The Theory of the Repercussion or Diffusion of Taxes.—While writers on finance have commonly insisted that the equities of contribution should govern in assessment, a belief in the so-called Repercussion, or diffusion, of taxes has led economists very generally to give their approval to the system of indirect taxation, the growth of which forms the most marked feature of the fiscal history of the present century.

Let the state, it is said, levy its contribution on such articles of general consumption as are most easily reached, or on such of the processes of production or exchange as lie most open to view, trusting to the laws of trade to distribute the burden over the whole body of the population.

This plea raises the question of the Incidence, the ultimate incidence, of taxation. "I hold it to be true," said Lord Mansfield in his speech on taxing the Colonies, "that a tax laid in any place is like a pebble falling into and making a circle in a lake, till one circle produces and gives motion to another, and the whole circumference is agitated from the center." Taxes uniformly advanced on all like competing property," says Mr. Wells, "will always tend to equate themselves, and will never be a special burden to those who originally made the advances to the government."

607. How do Taxes Tend to Diffusion?—This, which may be called the Diffusion-theory of taxation, rests upon the assumption of perfect competition. It is true, to the full extent, only under conditions which secure the complete mobility of all economic agents. As far as members of the community are impeded in their resort to their best market by ignorance, poverty, fear, superstition, misapprehension, inertia, just so far is it possible that the burden of taxation may rest where it first falls. It requires, as Prof. Thorold Rogers has said, an effort on the part of the person who is assessed to shift the burden on to the shoulders of others. Not only is that effort made with varying degrees of ease or difficulty; but the resistance offered may be of any degree of effectiveness: powerful, intelligent, tenacious, or weak, ignorant, spasmodic. The result of the struggle thus provoked will depend on the relative strength of the two parties; and as the two parties are never precisely the same in the case of two taxes, or two forms of the same tax, it must make a difference upon what subjects duties are laid, what is the severity of the imposition, and at what stage of production or exchange the contribution is exacted. It is not, it never can be, a matter of indifference when, where, and how taxes are imposed. "The ability to evade taxation," writes M. Say, "is infinitely varied, according to the form of assessment and the position of each individual in the social system. Nay, more, it varies at different times. There are few things so unsteady and fluctuating as the ratio of the pressure of taxation upon each class, by turns, in the community."

608. M. Say's Views.—It has always seemed to me strange that J. B. Say should be cited, as he so often is, as an authority on the side of the Diffusion-theory of taxation. Not only in the paragraph from which I have quoted does he recognize the vital importance of the right "seating" of taxes; but in his references to the essay of Canard, which had been crowned by the Academy (1802), he is even more pronounced. Canard had said that it is of little importance whether a tax press upon one branch of revenue or another, provided it be of long standing, because every tax in the end affects every class of revenue proportionally, as bleeding in the arm reduces the circulating blood in every portion of the human frame. To this M. Say rejoins that the object taken for comparison has no analogy with taxation. The wealth of society is not a fluid, tending continually to a level. It is, the rather, an organism, like a tree or a man, no part of which can be lopped off without permanently disfiguring and crippling the whole.

609. M. de Parieu's Views.—M. de Parieu has given a chapter of his great work to the Incidence of Taxation. In respect to what he calls taxes levied upon the conditions of every human existence, he reaches the result that they have effects very obscure, and in a still greater degree subject to dispute. Where taxes are levied in cities upon the necessaries of life, he finds no considerable danger of evil effects, since there is a constant intercommunication between the laborers of towns and those of rural districts, and migration will soon restore the equilibrium after the disturbance created by the new impost. It is otherwise when a new tax is imposed throughout the whole extent of a country. The emigration of laborers to foreign parts is only accomplished against a certain resistance, arising out of their habitudes and affections. It is always, moreover, accomplished at a definite loss and an indefinite risk. To throw taxes on consumption back upon the capitalist or the employer becomes, in M. de Parieu's judgment, a task very difficult and often wholly impracticable.

610. Conclusion.—I reach the conclusion that, in a condition of imperfect competition, we have no assurance that indirect taxes will be diffused equably over the whole community, leaving each class and each individual in the same relative condition as before the imposition. Something less, it may be much less, than a proportional contribution must result from the differing strength and opportunities of the several classes and individuals. The legislator can not, then, adopt the comfortable doctrine of the indifference of the place and the person where and on whom the burden shall be laid. His responsibility abides for the ultimate effects of the taxes he imposes. Whether with reference to the equities of contribution or to the general interests of trade and production, he is bound carefully to consider the nature and probable tendencies of every projected impost.

XVII.

PROTECTION VS. FREEDOM OF PRODUCTION.

611. The Doctrine of Laissez-Faire.—The question of Protection, as against Freedom of Production—not, as it is commonly stated, against Freedom of Trade—is rarely discussed, on both sides, upon purely economic principles; perhaps has never been, in an actual instance, decided without the intermixture of political or social considerations.

The arguments of those who have favored the policy of so far limiting the territorial division of labor (see par. 83), as to constitute industrial entities corresponding to existing political entities (which I take to be the real intent of what is called Protection) have been of every degree of vagueness;

but it seems to me that the confusion of the public mind need not have existed, at least to so great an extent, had not the professional economists taken an unjustifiably lofty attitude on this subject, practically refusing to argue the question at all as one of national expediency, contenting themselves with occupying the high ground of *Laissez-Faire.*

Now, that doctrine, although established by the older economists to their own satisfaction, as containing a principle of universal application, and thus deemed by them a conclusive answer to all arguments specially directed to justify restrictions upon international trade, has never been accepted, in the fullness of significance by them given it, throughout any wide constituency, not by any large proportion of the educated classes, not even generally by publicists, or statesmen, or men of affairs.

612. Opposition of the Economists to Factory Legislation.—Thus, when factory legislation was first proposed in England, nearly the whole body of professional economists opposed any interference with the freedom of contract respecting labor. They asserted the entire competence of the laboring classes to protect their own interests. They declared that interference on behalf of the laboring classes could only be mischievous, in the long run, to the laborers themselves. They put themselves on record in the most formal manner against all measures of restriction upon factory and workshop labor. They cast in their lot with the opposition to this class of legislation, and staked the reputation and influence of political economy upon their being right in this matter.

Had they won upon that issue ; had the results of the factory acts been proven deleterious to the interests of the working classes themselves, or even to the industrial power of the kingdom, it would have been a rare triumph for the economists, and their influence would have been greatly strengthened. But it did not turn out so. Although in the first instance, that of the act of 1802, Sir Robert Peel, the elder, had been so solicitous not to violate the principle of the self-sufficiency of labor that he made the bill apply only to apprentices, the wards of the state, the political rightfulness and the economic expediency of regulating the contract for labor so grew upon the public mind of England, that act after act extended the supervision of the state over factory and workshop until the policy of restriction had vindicated itself to the complete satisfaction of the working-classes, even, in the main, of the master class, themselves, and of the statesmen of the kingdom and publicists almost without exception.

613. Freedom the Rule: Restraint the Exception.— The fact that in the controversy over the factory acts the economists of the *laissez-faire** school are proved to have been in the wrong, does not show, or go to show, that they are wrong in their opposition to laws in restraint of international commerce. It does not even create a presumption to that effect.

Although the necessity of making exceptions to the rule of freedom of individual action has been established as completely in respect to industry as in respect to politics, freedom of action is yet so far the condition of health and power and growth in the field alike of politics and of industry, that those who propose to make exceptions in either are bound to show cause for every such exception. A heavy burden of proof rests upon them. Their case is to be made, and made against a powerful presumption in favor of liberty, as that condition which hath the promise not only of that which now is, but, in a higher degree, of that which is to come. There is not and

* "Now I beg you to remark the strange assumptions that underlie this reasoning. Human interests are naturally harmonious; therefore we have only to leave people free, and social harmony must result; as if it were an obvious thing that people knew their interests in the sense in which they coincide with the interests of others, and that, knowing them, they must follow them; as if there were no such things in the world as passion, prejudice, custom, *esprit de corps*, class interest, to draw people aside from the pursuit of their interests in the largest and highest sense. Nothing is easier than to show that people follow their interest, in the sense in which they understand their interest. But between this and following their interest in the sense in which it is coincident with that of other people, a chasm yawns. *That chasm in the argument of the laissez-faire school has never been bridged. The advocates of the doctrine shut their eyes and leap over it.*"—Prof. John E. Cairnes.

there can never be any positive virtue in restraint. Its only office for good is to prevent waste and save the misdirection of energy. There is no life in it, and no force can come out of it.

That which is called "protection" operates only by restraint; it has and can have neither creative power nor healing efficacy. All the energy that is to produce wealth exists before it and without respect to it ; and just to the extent to which protection operates at all, it operates by impairing that energy, and reducing the sum of wealth that might be produced if protection did not exist.

I say, that might be produced, not that *would* be produced. The latter point may fairly be disputed between the free-trader, who should rather be called the free-producer, and the advocate of the system of restricted production. The force of the steam at the piston-head is less than the force of the steam in the boiler, less by all that is necessary to conduct it thither from the boiler ; yet it is the force of the steam at the piston-head, and not where it is generated, which moves the wheels of the engine. The harness hampers the movements of the horse ; but it is the harnessed horse that draws the load. Discipline operates directly to reduce the sum of the impulses by which soldiers are actuated, and, by consequence to reduce their individual energy; but a disciplined army will defeat a mob of many times its own numbers.

614. What the Protectionist Has to Prove.—If the protectionist can show that restraints imposed by law upon the industrial action of his countrymen, or the men of any country he chooses to take for the purposes of the debate, have the effect, not, indeed, to generate productive force, but to direct the productive force generated by human wants setting in motion human labor with a better actual result* than under

*Much as I admire the pithiness and vigor of Prof. Sumner's argument before the Tariff Commission, in 1883, I can not but think that he unduly disparages the losses to production which occur under the regime of free-exchange. I have in another place (pars. 99–109, and again 236 to 243) adduced considerations which seem to me to justify a very serious view of the extent and importance of these losses. Let the protectionist, if he can, show good grounds for believing that under the system he proposes there would be a better outcome.

the rule of freedom, he will make his case. But this is to be proved, not taken for granted ; and it is to be proved only by sound and serious argument, not by strenuous assertion and senseless clamor.

615. Why Should Industrial Correspond to Political Entities?—In proceeding to establish the importance of checking the extension of the territorial division of labor at the boundary lines of nationalities, the protectionist writers have been seriously embarrassed from the lack of reasons to give why industrial entities ought to correspond to political entities. Had they undertaken to show that every million or five millions of people might advantageously be organized into a separate industrial entity, having either no commercial intercourse at all with communities on the outside, or a commercial intercourse much reduced and retarded ; or had the protectionist writers undertaken to show that every ten or twenty square degrees upon the earth's surface, whatever the number of inhabitants, should become an industrial entity, trade within the limiting parallels and meridians being unrestrained and even encouraged, while trade across those lines should be deemed in a higher or lower degree mischievous ; or had these writers undertaken to show that every important river basin or drainage system should be constituted an industrial entity, in as great a degree as possible independent of others, they would have had a much less difficult task. A good deal might be said upon the theme that the world-wide extension of the principle of the division of labor needs to be crossed and checked by artificial obstructions to prevent certain economic and social evils.

We have shown (par. 227 to 243) that grave industrial mischiefs may originate in this principle, though which producer and consumer are set apart, often by a vast distance, sometimes by half the circumference of the globe ; that misunderstandings may arise between producer and consumer which will result in a smaller production of wealth, a lower satisfaction of human wants, and that these misunderstandings are sometimes aggravated by suspicion or panic with the most deplorable consequences. The fact is incontestable, and it would be easy to exaggerate its importance.

But when the attempt is to prove that the principle of the division of labor should be allowed to extend itself freely within the bounds of nationality but not beyond them, additional difficulties of a grave character are encountered at the outset, in the great and, from the economic point of view, unaccountable irregularity and whimsicalness with which the surface of the earth is divided among independent sovereignties. One nation comprises two millions of inhabitants, like Denmark, Greece or Chili ; another ten, like Mexico, Brazil or Siam ; another thirty, like Italy or Japan ; another sixty, like the United States ; another eighty, like Russia ; another three hundred and fifty, like China. The territory occupied by one nation crosses and includes two, three or five great river systems ; in other cases, one river system embraces the territory of two, three or five nations. A stream which a boy can wade may form the dividing line of two independent states ; a third state may collect its revenues across the Atlantic and the Pacific oceans, and its magistracy send their warrants alike to Hudson's Bay and into the South Sea. One people may stretch from North to South across sixty degrees of latitude ; another from East to West, through half the daily journey of the sun. One country may be occupied by a population as homogeneous as the inhabitants of some old city ; while under the same flag, and subject to the same laws, may live the representatives of many races : some dressed in the latest Paris fashion, others tattooed upon the naked skin ; some using the telephone, others the assegai ; some finding their choicest amusement in the Wagnerian opera, others in the war dance that opens the feast of human flesh.

616. The United States as an Instance.—It will readily appear that the protectionist writers have a difficult task in establishing the necessity of drawing the lines of industrial circumvallation along the boundaries of empire.

Take the United States for example. Here are thirty-eight states trading among themselves with the utmost activity, the exchange of commodities and services being as free as the movements of the air ; and in this freedom all good citizens rejoice.* But this condition of things is made, by the doctrine under examination, to be dependent entirely upon the political relations of these states. Were they under different governments, the exchange of commodities and services which now promotes the general wealth and the general welfare would be fraught with mischief and possible ruin.

It is, of course, possible that some new analysis of the conditions of production may yet disclose the law which thus makes trade within the limits of sovereignty beneficial, and trade across the boundaries of separate states deleterious to one or both parties; but thus far assertion coupled with vituperation has taken the place of the analysis required.

617. Protecting the Strong against the Weak.—In the old world, the argument for protection is based on the importance of protecting the industrially weak against the industrially strong; and I am not certain that something might not be said for this. Russia strives to protect her labor against the better paid labor of Germany; Germany, in turn, strives to protect her labor against the vastly better paid labor of England. Among all fully settled countries, the rule, without exception so far as I am aware, is that that country in which the higher wages are paid offers its products at lower prices than the

---

* "If it be asserted that states which pursue different industries can not afford to trade freely with one another, here we have them, New York and Pennsylvania, Massachusetts and Minnesota, Maine and Louisiana. If it be asserted that states with like industries can not afford to trade freely with one another, here we have them, Indiana and Illinois, Iowa and Minnesota, Massachusetts and Rhode Island, Alabama and Mississippi. If it be said that small states can not afford to trade freely with great empires, here are New York and Connecticut, Pennsylvania and Delaware. Why do not the great states suck the life out of the small ones? If it be said that new states, with little capital, and on the first stage of culture, can not afford to exchange freely with old states having large capital and advanced social organization, here are New York and Oregon, Massachusetts and Idaho. How can any territories ever grow into states under the pressure? If it be said that a state which relies on one industry can not afford to exchange freely with one which has a diversified industry, here are Pennsylvania and Colorado, California and Nevada, any of the cotton states and any of the Northeastern states."—*W. G. Sumner*, "*Protection in the United States.*"

competing products of countries where the lower wages are paid.

In the United States, however, the argument for protection has based itself on the assumed necessity of protecting the strong against the weak. In Australia and Canada it is the same. It is alleged to be essential to the maintenance of the high wages prevailing in these countries, that the products of the "pauper labor of Europe" shall not be sold freely in their markets.

Why is it that the plea of those who desire to check the extension of the division of labor on the lines of nationality, suddenly changes as they pass from old and fully settled countries, to countries but recently, and perhaps still but partially, occupied and cultivated?

618. Why Wages are High in New Countries.—The explanation is found in the fact that the populations of what we call "new countries," that is, countries where an inadequate population is applying progressively to fresh fields advanced methods and machinery, possess an immense advantage in the conditions of living over the populations of "old countries," where the land has long been fully occupied, where the capabilities of the soil, even on fields of small natural productiveness, are heavily taxed to furnish subsistence to the inhabitants, and where systematic, continuous manuring has to be practiced in order to keep the land in condition.

The enomous profit of cultivating a virgin soil without the need of artificial fertilization, and the abundance of food and other necessaries of life enjoyed by the agricultural class have tended continually to disparage mechanical industries in the eyes alike of the American capitalist and of the American laborer.

619. The Competition of the Farm with the Shop.—It has been the competition of the farm with the shop which has, from the first, most effectually retarded the growth of manufactures in the United States. A population which is privileged to live upon a virgin soil, cultivating only the choicest fields and cropping these through a succession of years without returning any thing to the land, can live in plenty. If that population possess the added advantage of great skill in the use of tools and great adroitness in meeting the large and the little exigencies of the occupation and cultivation of the soil, the fruits of agriculture will still further be greatly increased. The dietary of an American farmer, cultivating his own land with the aid of his growing sons, would amaze a peasant from any portion of Europe. An abundance of nutritious food is and has been, ever since the revolutionary period, the sure condition of the life of the agriculturist in the United States. It was not with our fathers, even in New England, a struggle for the necessaries of life, but for social decencies and what, in any old country, would have been called luxuries.

Now, the mode of living on the part of the agricultural population has necessarily set a minimum standard of wages for mechanical labor. With an abundance of cheap land, with a population facile to the last degree in making change of avocation and of residence, few able-bodied men are likely to be drawn into factories and shops on terms which imply a meaner subsistence than that secured in the cultivation of the soil.

620. The Hand Trades.—There are certain classes of mechanical pursuits, however, which, by their nature, secure to those who follow them a minimum remuneration fully up to the standard of the agricultural wages of the region. Such, for instance, are the trades of carpenter, blacksmith and mason, in which the work is of a kind which can only be done upon the spot. The house can not be built abroad and imported for the farmer's use ; the wagon must be mended near the place where it broke down ; the horse must be shod, the tools sharpened, by the artisans of the neighborhood. If, then, the farmer will have such services performed, he must admit those who perform them to share his own abundance ; he must pay wages or prices which will attract men, and those, by necessity, men exceptionally intelligent and skillful, into those trades. Hence we find the mason, the blacksmith, the plumber, the carpenter, the house painter, the cobbler, in every part of the United States, receiving wages which bear no relation whatever to the wages paid for the same class of services in other countries, but which stand in a very exact relation to the rewards of agricultural labor here.

Nor has it ever been found necessary to encourage or stimulate these trades for the good of the country. What statesman ever introduced into Congress a bill intended to increase the number of carpenters or blacksmiths, or to enhance their wages?

621. Personal and Professional Service.—But, again, there are certain classes of services, of a personal or professional nature, which have also secured for those rendering them a participation in the abundance enjoyed by the tillers of the soil in the same region. The remuneration received by the members of these classes, whether called the wages of domestic servants, or the fees of physicians and lawyers, or the salaries of schoolmasters and clergymen, or the profits of retail trade, has been out of all relation to the remuneration of similar services in other countries, and has amounted to just what I have termed it, *a participation in the abundance enjoyed by the agricultural population.* Since these services could only be performed upon the spot, the agriculturists have been obliged, if they would have the services rendered, to pay for them, out of the large surplus of their own produce, at least enough to make these professions and avocations equally desirable with their own, uncertainty of result, loss of time in preparation, expense of education and training, healthfulness and agreeableness of work, etc., being taken into account; and, since the agricultural classes have desired that these services should be performed, and have been willing to pay for them on the scale indicated, there has never been any call for Congressional action to secure the requisite number of lawyers, physicians, clergymen, schoolmasters, domestic servants or retail tradesmen.

622. The Factory Industries.—But now we note that there are still other important classes of services to be rendered, respecting which the rule changes. The remuneration of the persons rendering these services no longer has reference to the abundance of agricultural production in the several sections of the United States; is no longer irrespective of the remuneration of similar classes elsewhere. These persons are not, necessarily, admitted to a participation in the fruits of American agriculture.

The services referred to are such as can be performed without respect to the location of the consumer of the product. They are nearly identical with what we call, in the technical sense of the term, manufactures.

Whenever the American farmer wants a pane of glass set, or a pair of boots mended, or a horse shod, he must pay some one, his neighbor, enough for doing the job to keep him in his trade and to keep him out of agriculture, in the face of the great advantages of tilling the soil in New York, or Ohio or Dakota, or wherever else the farmer in question may live; but how much he shall pay the man who makes the pane of glass, or the pair of boots, or the set of horseshoes, will depend upon the advantages of tilling the soil, not where he himself lives, but where the maker of the horseshoes, the boots, or the glass may live.

If he will have the work done he must pay some one, somewhere, enough to keep him in his trade and out of agriculture; but not necessarily out of New York agriculture, or Ohio agriculture, or Dakota agriculture; but, perhaps, out of English agriculture, or French agriculture, or Norwegian agriculture, under the the requirements of constant fertilization, deep plowing and thorough drainage, and subject to that stringent necessity which economists express by the term, "the law of Diminishing Returns."

Now, to offset and overcome the inducements to engage in agriculture, even in Merry England, is a different thing, a very different thing, from keeping a man in his trade and out of agriculture in the United States.

The American agriculturist, having large quantities of grain and meat, or cotton and tobacco, left on his hands, after providing ample subsistence for his family, and even after hiring the carpenter, mason and blacksmith, the schoolmaster, lawyer and doctor, for as much time as he requires their respective services, and still further, after putting a good deal into farm implements and increase of stock, is desirous of obtaining with the remainder sundry articles more or less necessary to health, comfort and decency. To him it makes no difference whether the articles he requires are made on one side of the Atlantic or on the other ; but it makes a great difference what he is obliged to pay for them ; how much of his surplus grain and meat, tobacco and cotton must go to secure a certain definite satisfaction of his urgent and oft-recurring wants. If he must needs pay some one to stay out of American agriculture and do this work, his surplus will not go so far as if he were allowed to pay some one to stay out of English agriculture to do it.

623. What the State Can Do.—But here the State enters and declares that it is socially or politically necessary that these articles, these nails, these horseshoes, this cotton or woolen cloth, or what not, shall be made on this side of the Atlantic. That necessity the agriculturist, as consumer, can not be expected to feel ; he does not care where the things were made ; he only wants them to use. He does not care who makes them ; he does not even care whether they are made at all ; they would answer his purpose just as well were they the gratuitous gifts of nature, spontaneous fruits of the soil, or the sea, or the sky. Whatever his own economic theories may be, he will, as purchaser, every time select the cheapest article which will precisely answer his need. He will not, of his own motion, pay more for an article because it is made on his side of the Atlantic than he could get an equally good article for, bearing the brand of Sheffield or Birmingham or Manchester. But if the State says he must, he must ; and consequently the American maker of this article is by force of law admitted to a participation in the abundance enjoyed by the American agricultural class. The tiller of the soil is now compelled, by the ordinance of the State, to share his bread and meat with the maker of nails or of horseshoes, of cotton or of woolen cloth, just as he was before compelled by the ordinance of Nature to share his bread and meat with the blacksmith, carpenter and mason, the schoolmaster, lawyer and doctor.

It is perfectly true, therefore, as the protectionist asserts, that a tariff of customs duties upon foreign goods imported into new countries tends to create and maintain high rates of wages in the factory industries. But for protective duties, those articles which, in their nature, can be readily and cheaply transported will be produced predominantly in countries where the minimum standard of mechanical wages is set by agricultural conditions far less favorable than those which obtain in the United States, in Canada, or in Australia.

But while the law thus can and does create high rates of wages in factory industries, it does not and it can not create the wealth out of which that excess of manufacturing wages over those of older countries is paid. That wealth is created by the labor and capital employed in the cultivation of the soil.

XVIII.

SOCIALISM.

624. Difficulty of Defining Socialism.—It is not easy to define the word socialism, for the purposes either of controversy or of description. It is, perhaps, impossible to give a definition which shall be satisfactory to all. One man invidiously calls another a socialist, only to receive the same appellation himself from a third person differing from him in political opinion. Let us, however, do the best we can, in the confusion which prevails on this subject, to characterize socialism.

We find that term applied to a great variety of political schemes, in all of which is present one quality, in higher or lower degree. This quality is the essence of socialism; and, as it is found more and more fully developed, the socialist character of any political scheme becomes more and more distinctly pronounced. We may apply the term, socialistic, to this quality.

625. Meaning of the Word Socialistic.—What then does the word socialistic signify? I answer, it is properly applied to an unconscious tendency or a conscious purpose to extend the powers of the state beyond a certain necessary, minimum, line of duties, for a supposed public good, under popular impulse. It may be added, though rather in explanation than in qualification of our definition, that the supposed public good in view generally involves a greater or a smaller change in the distribution of wealth, as effected under the rule of competition and individual initiative. This, however, is not always the case.

626. Anarchism.—We have spoken of extending the powers of government beyond a necessary, minimum, line of duties. What is that line? On this question opinions differ, but I deem it conducive to a clear understanding of our subject to conceive that line as drawn along the Police Powers of the state. Those, indeed, who call themselves Anarchists hold that government is not a necessary means of social existence; but that, on the contrary, government produces most of the very evils which are made the excuse for government. They profess to believe that government represses individual activities for good, at many points, and paralyzes forces which otherwise would continually operate to ameliorate the conditions of life, to harmonize social relations, and to give inspiration and impulse to human efforts seeking at once the good of the individual and of the community. The Anarchist even asserts that certain vicious and destructive appetites and passions, which have been held to be inherent in human nature and to place the necessity of government beyond the possibility of question, are, in fact, generated by government itself, and would soon disappear in a state where no man presumed to make a law for another or to place any restraint upon his actions.* Apart, however, from the small and as yet insignificant body of men known as Anarchists, it is held by all persons, of high or low degree, of much or little political experience, that government is at least a necessary evil; and most men cheerfully submit to whatever restraints or sacrifices are involved in its maintenance. There are certain func-

* The reader who may be interested to see the most and best that can be said in behalf of this strange doctrine of anarchy, is referred to an article by Prince Kropotkin in the *Nineteenth Century* for August, 1887.

tions known as the police powers, which are, with substantial unanimity, admitted to belong to government. These are, speaking in a very general way, the protection of life, person and property and the preservation of the civil peace. These powers clearly embrace the repression of obtrusive vice and the protection of the common air and the common water from pollution. The term socialistic can not be properly applied to any measure undertaken, in good faith, for the attainment of these objects. In a highly organized industrial or social state, the police powers will naturally be exercised through agencies and instrumentalities unknown in a more primitive condition; but these are not, on that account, to be considered in any degree socialistic, so long as they are directed toward the end indicated.

627. Examples of Socialistic Measures.—Whenever and wherever, for any supposed public good, measures are undertaken or proposed, from a popular impulse, or in obedience to a popular demand, which carry, or would carry, the functions of government beyond the line we have drawn, the term socialistic is properly to be used, not as a term of reproach or contumely, but as a strictly descriptive title. The line of the police powers may, in any given instance, be transcended by much or by little; the object sought may be thoroughly practicable or wildly fanciful; the results may be highly beneficial or deeply injurious to society; but every measure or proposal of the nature we have described is socialistic. Thus, public schools are distinctly socialistic. Education is a matter proper to individual initiative and enterprise, within the family or, by voluntary association, within larger groups. It is only during the last twenty years that this function has been assumed by government in a country so free, prosperous and enlightened as England. When this great step was taken it was distinctly and unmistakably socialistic, yet not the less meritorious and beneficial. That step had been taken, generations before, in the United States, with the consent of all parties and all classes, and with the happiest results in peace, order and prosperity. On the other hand, the government in England owns and operates the telegraph, a policy from which we in the United States shrink with reluctance as dangerously socialistic.

628. Public roads and bridges also exhibit the socialistic character in a highly marked degree. In a very primitive state of society, where, yet, all the police powers are fully exercised, each man looks out for his own paths of travel or transport, and maintains his own communications with friends and neighbors, across the commons or through the forest. Even after roads are laid out, and, later still, are graded, drained and perhaps paved, at great expense, and streams and ravines are bridged, this work continues to be regarded as altogether a matter for private enterprise. Individuals or associations lay out the roads and build the bridges, collecting toll from every one who passes over them. Those who use the roads much pay much; those who use them little pay little; those who stay at home pay nothing at all. At last* there comes a time when it is seen that, though this function naturally belongs to individuals, and has indeed been exercised by individuals with a reasonable degree of success, yet a great public advantage will result from making these avenues of communication free to all and supporting them thereafter at the public expense. The step thus taken is purely, highly socialistic. The responsibility, the labor, the expenditure involved in these undertakings pass from private citizens to public officials. Individuals no longer pay for this service according to the proportion in which they enjoy it. Each contributes, whether he will or not, to the construction and maintenance of roads and bridges, which he may use much or may not use at all.

629. Protectionism is purely and highly socialistic. Its purpose is so to operate upon individual choices and aims, so to influence private enterprise and the investments of capital, as to secure the building up, within the country concerned, of certain branches of production which could not be carried on,

* The general movement by which roads and bridges have almost universally been made free, began, even in the most enlightened countries, only sixty or seventy years ago.

or would grow but slowly, under the rule of competition and individual initiative. With this object in view, government begins by preventing the citizen from buying where he can buy cheapest ; it compels him to pay ten, thirty or fifty per cent. advance, it may be, upon the prices at which he could otherwise purchase ; it even assumes the right to make existing industries support the industries which are thus to be called into being. Not incidentally, but primarily and of purpose, it affects vitally every man's industrial conditions and relations. It does this for a supposed public good.

630. The Socialists.—We have, perhaps, sufficiently illustrated the significance of the word socialistic. What then is socialism? Perhaps we had better first ask, who is a socialist? Under our definition, the advocacy of a socialistic act or measure will not necessarily characterize a socialist. Thus, protection, as we have said, is socialistic. Yet the protectionist is not, as such, a socialist. Most protectionists are not socialists. Many protectionists are, in their general views, as strongly anti-socialist as men can well be.

The socialist is one who, in general, distrusts the effects of individual initiative and enterprise ; who is readily convinced of the necessity or utility of the assumption, by the State, of functions which have hitherto been left to personal choices and personal aims ; and who, in fact, approves and advocates many and large schemes of this character.

The person of whom all this could be said might properly be called a socialist ; yet there are many such persons who would wish, after enlarging the powers of government at many points, correcting, as they conceive it, many of the infirmities and evil liabilities of society by force of law, and introducing incentives and impulses which, as they believe, can only be administered by the organized power of the State, still to leave individual initiative and enterprise the general rule of life. The extreme socialist is he who would make the State all in all : private enterprise, personal choices and aims being lost in the general movement of a society dominated and directed by a majority vote. In the view of the extreme socialist, the powers and the rights of the State are the sum of all the powers and all the rights of the individuals who compose it; and government becomes the organ of society in respect to all its interests and all its acts.

631. Socialism.—The term "socialism" may, then, properly be applied (1) to the aggregate of many and large schemes for the extension of the powers of the State, actually urged for present or early adoption; or (2) to a programme contemplated, at whatever distance, for the gradual replacement of private by public activity; or (3) to an observed movement or tendency of a highly marked character in the direction indicated.

It will be seen that socialism and anarchism are in theory absolutely antipodal. The former would proceed by magnifying the powers of the State and enlarging the sphere of its operation, until personal choices and aims should wholly disappear in respect to all matters in which others, or the community as a whole, could possibly be interested. The complete establishment of socialism would, therefore, involve a tyranny more far-reaching and searching than that of the most absolute despotism ever founded among men. Anarchism, on the contrary, aims at the complete abolition of government: the removal of every form of restraint, leaving personal aims and choices wholly unchecked by law or authority, subject only to moral influences, to persuasion and to the force of public sentiment.

632. Socialism vs. Communism.—The distinction between Socialism and Communism is not to be drawn so easily. The two schemes have, necessarily, much in common; while the boundaries of that which, theoretically, each has to itself have been much confused by vague or passionate treatment. In a previous publication,* I have sought to express as clearly as the nature of the case would allow, the essential differences between Socialism and Communism, as follows:

1st. Communism confines itself mainly, if not exclusively, to the one subject matter—wealth. On the other hand, Socialism, conspicuously, in all its manifestations, in all lands

* Scribner's Magazine. January, 1887.

where it has appeared, asserts its claim to control every interest of human society, to enlist for its purposes every form of energy.

2nd. So far as wealth becomes the subject matter both of Communism, on the one hand, and of Socialism, on the other, we note a difference of treatment. Communism, in general, regards wealth as produced, and confines itself to effecting an equal, or what it esteems an equitable distribution.

Socialism, on the other hand, gives its first and chief attention to the production of wealth; and, passing lightly over the questions of distribution, with or without assent to the doctrine of an equal division among producers, it asserts the right to inquire into and control the consumption of wealth for the general good, whether through sumptuary laws and regulations, or through taxation for public expenditure.

3rd. Communism is essentially negative, confined to the prohibition that one shall not have more than another. Socialism is positive and aggressive, declaring that each man shall have enough. It purposes to introduce new forces into society and industry, to put a stop to the idleness, the waste of resources, the misdirection of force, inseparable, in some large proportion of instances, from individual initiative; and to drive the whole mass forward in the direction determined by the intelligence of its better half.

4th. While communism might conceivably be established upon the largest scale, and has, in a hundred experiments, been upon a small scale established, by voluntary consent, Socialism begins with the use of the powers of the State, and proceeds and operates through them alone. It is by the force of law that the Socialist purposes to whip up the laggards and the delinquents in the social and industrial order. It is by the public treasurer, armed with powers of assessment and sale, that he plans to gather the means for carrying on enterprises to which individual resources would be inadequate. It is through penalties that he would check wasteful or mischievous expenditures.

If what has been said above would be found true, were one studying Communism and Socialism as a philosophical critic, much more important will be the distinction between them to the eyes of the politician or the statesman. Communism is, if not moribund, at the best everywhere at a stand-still, generally on the wane ; nor does it show any sign of returning vitality. On the other hand, Socialism was never more full of lusty vigor, more rich in the promise of things to come, than now.

633. It seems only needful to add, that, while the doctrines of Anarchism, Socialism and Communism are respectively held by not a few sincere and disinterested men, of a high order of intelligence, large numbers of those who embrace one or the other of these systems do so with no appreciation of the differences between them, being influenced wholly by a general discontent with the results of the existing social and industrial order, either as affecting themselves or as controlling the fortunes of their class. In addition to these, every public demonstration of socialistic or communistic organizations almost inevitably draws out a swarm of "lewd fellows of the baser sort," who for the time attach themselves to that party, out of a general hatred of law and order, or in the hope of plunder, or from a delight in riot and mischief.

INDEX.

☞ THE REFERENCES ARE TO SECTIONS, NOT TO PAGES.

Argyle, Duke of: restrictions on the contract for labor, 248
Anarchism, 626
Arithmetical *vs.* Geometrical progression, 392-3
Art: Political Economy as an art (a branch of statesmanship) distinguished from political economy as a science, 27-31
Assignats, so called, of French Revolutionary period, 219, 445
Athens, progressive taxation in, 600
Austria, paper money, 443
Authority, legal, excluded from our definition of value, 8
Ability, as the rule of taxation, 595-7, [See, also, Faculty]
Abstinence, the creator of capital, 87-93; interest, the reward of abstinence, 288
Accumulation, how influenced by the rate of interest, 288
Agriculture—deemed by the physiocrats the sole source of wealth, 48; subject to the condition of "diminishing returns," 49-53; plea that manufactures should be built up artificially to save exportation of the properties of the soil, 56-9; follows the pastoral condition in natural order of development, 63; the fluctuations in agricultural products render them a defective standard for deferred payments, 188-90; competition of agriculture with manufactures in new countries, 618-23
Alcoholic beverages, English expenditure upon, 406n
Alison, Sir A.; the potato, 404n
Amsterdam, Bank of, 523
Andersen, J., announces law of rent, 265
Babbage, Charles: cost of the materials of the iron manufactures, 53
Bacon, Lord: the true labor of philosophy, 24; the burden of taxation, 414; on usury, 419, 423n
Bagehot, Walter: influence of inconvertible paper money on foreign exchanges, 220, 565; the early Italian banks, 522; bimetallism, 568
Balance of Trade, 545-53
Banking Functions, the, 522-8; the banking agencies, 529; the State participating in the profits of banking, 577
Banking principle, the, so-called, *vs.* the currency principle, 225-6
Bank Money, Chap. 6, Part III
Bank of England, 222, 225; its foundation, 522
Bases of Taxation, 590
Bastiat, F.: confuses ethical and economical reasoning, 37; the economical harmonies, 346; the story of Jacques Bonhomme, 412
Barter, the primitive form of exchange, 161-2
Beaulieu, Leroy, domains, 576n
Belgium, underfed laborers, 68
Bentham, Jeremy: escheat *vice* taxation, 573; approves banking monopolies, 578; attacks judicial fees, 581
Bequest, [See Successions]
Bi-Metallism, 559-71
Birth-rate, diminished by increase of economic desires, 397-401
Bowen, Francis: the value denominator, 183n
Brabazon, Lord: inadequate food of French factory hands, 68
Brassage, 196

Brassey, Thomas, Sir: superiority of English labor in railway construction, 79
Brodie, George: sale of offices by Charles I., 575n; monopolies, 578
Building lots, rent of, 280
Bullion, its relation to coin, 193-200, [See Seigniorage]
Burke, Edmund: nothing so great an enemy to accuracy of judgment as want of classification and distribution, 44; the fiscal motive to paper money issues, 444
Cairnes, John E.: The character and logical method of Political Economy, 18-20; asserts for it the dignity of a science, 25; importance of the law of "diminishing returns," 48; the friction of retail trade, 149; relief of overcrowded occupations, 342; indifference of the rate of profits, 373; *laissez faire*, 613; co-operation, 428; bi-metallism, 568
Calvin, John, on usury, 418
Cameralistic science, its subject matter, 359
Canard, N. F.: the diffusion of taxes, 608
Cancellation of indebtedness, by banks and clearing houses, 524
Capability, productive, of a community, Chap. 4, Part II
Capital, Chap. 3, Part II; partial immobility of capital, 104; the remuneration for its use, *i. e.*, interest, Chap. 3, Part IV.; relation of capital to the scheme of co-operation, 426-8; relation of capital to wages, 320, 334-6 [With reference to taxation, see Wealth]
Carey, H. C.: his attacks upon the doctrine of rent, 484-92
Catallactics, the word offered by Archbishop Whately, as a substitute for political economy, 43
Celibacy, [See Marriage]
Chadwick, Edwin: the cellar populations of the English cities, 71
Charles I., of England; sale of offices, 575; of monopolies, 578
Chastity, female, how affected by the provisions of the English poor laws, 450
Cheap *vs.* Dear Food, 404
Cheap money, is inconvertible paper money cheap? 214-6
Cheerfulness, as contributing to labor power, 76-8
Cherbuliez, A. E.: domains, 576
Chevalier, Michel; money economizes labor, 164; applies the term *Brassage* to the actual cost of coinage, 196n; industrial effects of an increase of the money supply, 445n; bi-metallism, 568
Child, the, its relation to the subsistence of the family, 387-8
Civilization tends to diminish the sum of values, 12; effects of money in promoting civilization, 164
Clamageran, J. J.: the physiocratic theory of taxation, 583n
Clearing-house, the bankers' bank, 524
Climate: a good climate is not capital but a favorable condition of production, 86
Clothing, its relation to subsistence, 384
Cobden, Richard: the commutation of the feudal burdens upon land in England, 500
Coinage, 168, 179-80; cost of, *i. e.*, seigniorage, Chap. 4, Part III
Coin basis of bank money, [See Reserve, Specie]
Coin, debasement of; seigniorage, Chapter 4, Part III
Combination, in economics opposed to competition, 129
Comfort, ideas of, developed in the progress of society, 19, 395-9
Commerce, the old time theory that it could be beneficial to but one party, 3 [See also Exchange and International Trade]
Commodities, distinguished from services, 247-9
Communism, 632
Community of goods, what would become of wealth? 11
Competition defined, 129; relation of competition to the doctrine of rent, 268-76; relation of competition to the doctrine of interest, 298; to the doctrine of wages, Chap. 6, Part IV, also 465-73

Comte, Aug.: denies to political economy the character of a science, 25-6
Consumers and producers, possible misunderstandings between, Chap. 7, Part III
Consumption of wealth: Prof. Leslie holds that the neglect of this department of inquiry is due to the assumption of a beneficent order of nature, 35; consumption as a department of political economy, 381-2, Part V, *passim*
Consumptive *vs.* productive co-operation, 432-3
Continental currency, so-called, of the American revolution, 207, 209, 219
Contributions to the treasury of the State, 572; (compulsory: see Revenue of the State and Taxation)
Co-operation: an effort to get rid of the entrepreneur, 108; erroneous conceptions of many economists, 316-7, 426-8; anticipated benefits of, 429-31; practical difficulties, 432-6
Corn rents, 188-90
"Corn Laws" (English), 83
Corners, so-called, as a tool of the speculating class, 140, 364
Courcelle-Seneuil, J. G.: depreciation not a necessary result of inconvertibility, 213n; the theory of bank money, 224
Creasy, Sir Edward, the feudal burdens on land, 498
Credit sales, the characteristic, 186; their great importance in modern exchange, 187; the multiple standard of deferred payments, 459-64
Crises, [See Panics]
Cultivation, descending to inferior soils, [See Diminishing Returns]
Currency principle, the so-called *vs.* the banking principle, 224-6
Custom, its influence in modifying law or competition, 19; is always, in theory, opposed to competition, 129; its effects on price, 145-6
Darwin, Charles: the power of geometrical increase, 393
Dear *vs.* Cheap Food, 404
Debasement of the coin, Chap. 3, Part III
Debtor class, their demand for paper money issues, 445
Decency, ideas of, developed in the progress of society, 19; power to check population, 394, 400-1
Deferred payments, standard for, [See Standard, etc.]
Definitions, in economics, not less valuable because certain objects may fall across the lines of demarkation, 6; difficulty which political economy encounters from the use of terms taken from common speech, 42-3
Degradation of the laboring class, through unequal competition, 339-47, 466
Demand and supply, defined, 125; desire is not demand, 126; operation of demand and supply illustrated, 125-40; (Money), 170
Demand, international, equation, of, 153
Denominator of value, 182-3; how about paper money? 210
Departments, the four departments of political economy, 44; reasons for their retention, 111, 247-9
Deposits, fictitious, as a means of evading usury laws, 422 [See Safe Deposit]
Deposit and discount, the great banking function, 526
Depreciation, not a necessary result of debasement of coin, 197, 201; or of inconvertibility of paper, 213
DeQuincey, Thomas: "Profits are the leavings of wages," 327
Desire is not demand, 126
Desires, economic, tend to multiply as fast as gratuity replaces value in the case of articles which were the subject of former desires, 13-4, 63, 66-7, 92-3, Chap. 2 and 3, Part V
Destruction of wealth, keeping down accumulations of capital, 110; popular notion that it stimulates production, 411-3
Deterioration, liability to, as affecting price, 143

Devon, Earl: Irish Commission of, 1844, 394
Diet, diversified, taste for, as antagonizing the procreative force, 398
Difference, economic, what constitutes an economic difference? 133
Diffusion of taxes, 606-10
Diminishing returns in agriculture, 51-4, 257
Discipline creates no force, but may prevent waste, 348-51
Discount and deposit, the great banking function, 526
Discredit of money, its influence on the money demand, 200-1
Distribution, as a department in political economy, Chap. 1, Part IV
Division of Labor [See, also, Territorial Div. of Lab.], how it originates, 80; how it becomes a source of productive power, 81-3; gives rise to exchange, 112; evil possibilities attendant upon, Chap. 7, Part III
Domains, as a source of revenue to the State, 576
Douglass, William: the debtor class in early Massachusetts, 445
Dress, as a form of consumption, 384
Dynamics of wealth, found in consumption, 382
Economics, [See Political Economy]
Efficiency of the individual laborer, dependent on several causes, 65-78; varying efficiency of labor in different countries, 79; relation to wages, 456
Emigration of capital, 299; of labor, 298-9
Employer, the, [See Entrepreneur]
Employment, regularity of, as an element of wages, 320
Employed laborer, [See Laborer]
England, insufficient food of agricultural laborers, 68; contrasted with India and Russia as to the efficiency of its laboring population, 79; its industrial organization, 252; rents kept down by public sentiment, 269; its usury laws, 419; poor laws, 447-51; relation of wages to capital, 454; factory legislation, 467; its strikes, 467; progressivity in taxation, 601
English School of Political Economy, so called, 17; erroneous views of English economists regarding the relation of wages to the product of industry, 326
Entrepreneur class, the, their function, 85, 231, 245; as claimants to a share of the product of industry, 252, 330-2, Chap. 4, Part IV, also 474-82; the State as entrepreneur, 577
Equation of international demand, 153
Equity, political, its relation to political economy, 36
Equities of contribution to the State, 583 [See also Taxation]
Escheat, as a source of State revenue, 573
Esprit de corps in industry, 84
Ethics, relation to economics, 19, 36
Exemptions from income, prior to taxation, 600-1
Exchange, the old-time theory that it could be beneficial to but one party, 3; arises from the division of labor, 112, 236-7; its reaction upon production, Chap. 7, Part III
Exchange, the science of, this term offered as a substitute for Political Economy, 5-6
Exchange, as a department of Political Economy, Part III; how distinguished from distribution, 247-9
Exchange, (Trade) International, Chap. 2, Part III
Exchanges, Foreign, 541-58; relation to Bi-metallism, 563-5
Exhaustion of the soil, 56-8
Expenditure, as the basis of taxation, 592-4
Factory laws, 471-3
Faculty, as the basis of taxation, 595-7
Family, the formation of, 386-7; solidarity of, 390
Fawcett, H.: insufficient food of West of England laborers, 68,

Cottier rents in Ireland, 273n; differing wages in different localities, 273; the doctrine of the Wage Fund, 458n.
Fecundity, made by M. Comte a test of a true science: does political economy bear this test? 25
Fees, as a means of revenue, 581:
Feudal burdens on land, how commuted? 498
Fiat money, [See Inconvertible Paper Money]
Final utility, 131, 139
Financiering, as a banking function, 522
Fines and forfeitures, as a source of revenue to the State, 574
Fittest, survival of, [See Survival]
Fixed incomes, relation to the multiple standard, 464
Food, [See, also, Subsistence]: its relation to labor power, 66; the primary form of capital, 87, 97.
Force, productive, can not be lost out of nature, but may be lost out of man's reach, 56
Forced circulation, generally a characteristic of government paper money, 207
Forced sales, sometimes caused by usury laws, 423
Form-value, 46
France: underfed factory hands, 68; repression of population, 401; progressivity in taxation, 600-2
Francis, John: the city banks of London, 526
Free, distinguished from gratuitous coinage, 195
Free trade and exhaustion of the soil, 56; and the territorial division of labor, 57, 613-23 [See Protection *vs.* Freedom of Production, Part VI.]
French economists apt to confuse ethical and economic reasoning, 37: right in their views of the relation of wages to the product of industry, 326n
Fullarton, J.: the theory of bank money, 224
Gallatin, Albert: bank money becomes a sort of legal tender, 223n
Gangs, agricultural, so-called, in England (children), 342
Garnier, Joseph: progressivity in taxation, 600
Genoa, bank of (St. George), 522
Geometrical *vs* arithmetical progression, 392-4
George, Henry, his "Progress and Poverty," 506-21
Germany, its railroad system, 577
German school of political economy, so-called, 17
Gibbon, E., likens money to letters, 164
Gilbert's Act (English Poor Laws), 448-9
Girdlestone, Canon: the diet of the laborers of Devonshire, 68
Girardin, Emile de: voluntary contributions, 572n
Gladstone, Wm. E.: his Budget Speeches, 586n
Glut, [See Overproduction]
Gluttony: regarded by Mr. Mill as a perpetually antagonizing principle to the desire of wealth, 21
Gold [See Precious Metals; in its relations to Silver, see also Bimetallism]
Gouge, Wm. M.: the theory of bank money, 225
Government, as producer and consumer, 357-60, 414-6; its revenue, and the means of obtaining it, 572-84
Government administration of productive property, 505, 576-7
Grain, as money, 189-90
Gratuity, relation to value, 12-3
Gratuitous, distinguished from free, coinage, 195
Greed, often antagonistic to the enlightened pursuit of wealth, 23, 378
Greenbacks, so-called, of the United States, 209, 211, 444
Gresham's Law, 181
Ground rents, 283
Hallam, H.: the penal code of Ireland, 271
Hamilton, Alex.: the danger of paper money issues, 444n
Hard times, so-called, their cause, 235-42
Harmonies, the economic, 344-6

Harrison, Fred'k; the small success of productive co-operation, 434
Harvesting, subject to the condition of diminishing returns, 53n
Hastings, George W.: necessity of the workhouse test, 452
Hazardous risks of capital, how compensated, 293-7
Health is not wealth, though perhaps better than wealth, 10
Hearn, Wm. E.: substitutes the term Plutology for Political Economy, 43; explains the former idleness of the Scottish people, 78
Hebrews, ancient, usury forbidden, 417-8
Higgling in the market, 149-50
Hoffmann, J. G.: the literature of taxation, 585
Holland, underfed laborers, 68
Hopefulness in labor, as an element of productive power, 76-8
Hunter state, the, 60
Huskisson, Wm.: repeal of the laws against combinations, 467
Immobility of capital and labor [See Mobility, etc.]
Income as the base of taxation, [See Revenue]
Inconvertible Paper Money, Chap. 5, Part III
Increment, the unearned, of land, 257, 265, 493, *et seq.*
India—the efficiency of its laboring population contrasted with that of England, 79; increase of population and condition of the people, 394; possible relation of taxation to production, 415
Indifference of the rate of profits, a doctrine, 373-80
Indolence, regarded by Mr. Mill as a perpetually antagonizing principle to the desire of wealth, 21
Inflation (money), 198-204, 213, 219-20, 441-5; tendency to inflation inhering in political money, 439-45
Inglis, H.: the city houses of Ireland in 1834, 70
Injuries, economic, tend to remain, 346-7
Injustice, only becomes a subject for the consideration of the economist when it issues as an economic force influencing the actions of men with respect to wealth, 36
Institutions, how far shall they be considered by the economist? 19
Insurance of the principal, an important element of interest, 293
Intellectual elements of supply and demand, 147
Intelligence, not wealth, 9-10; as a source of productive power, 72-4
Interest, as a share in the product of industry, 252, 332-6, 368-9; Chap. 3, Part IV [See Usury Laws]
International Trade: international values, 151-8
International distribution of money, 176
International division of labor [See Territorial, etc.]
Invention facilitated by the division of labor, 82
Ireland, the economic mischiefs of its land tenure almost irrespective of considerations of political equity, 36; inadequate shelter of the laboring population, 70; the "starving season," 94; rents: relation of the landlord and tenant class, 271-4; increase of population and state of the peasantry prior to the famine, 394
Irish, their traditional idleness at home due to unfair laws, 78
Jarvis, Edward: varying viability of the several nations of Europe, 320
Jevons, W. S.: illustration of the descending scale of utility, 131; but one price for a commodity, 132-3; substitution of one commodity for another, in use, as affecting price, 142n; the British coin, 180; the denominator of value, 182; advocates a tabular or multiple standard, 191, 463; repudiates the doctrine of the wages fund, 326; the *laissez faire* doctrine, 380; the law of wages, 326; the dynamics of wealth, 382n; his Money and the

Mechanism of Exchange, 524n; government interference with labor, 349, 352, 471; fluctuations in the value of gold, 1789–1874, 440; bi-metallism, 568
Johnson, S. W. Prof.: on the renewal of the soil by "weathering" and nitrification, 59
Johnston, J. F. W. Prof.: the constituents of the soil taken away in the crop, 56
Knies, Prof.: his classification of values, as time-value, place-value and form-value, 46
Knights of Labor, Part VI
Kropotkin, Prince: on Anarchy, 626
Labor: employed in agriculture subject to the condition of diminishing returns, 49-52; not so when employed in mechanical industries, 53-4; as one of the three primary agents of production, Chap. 2, Part II; varying efficiency of labor, 65-79; division of, 80-4; partial immobility of labor, 104; relation of labor to value, 119-24
Laborer, the, as a claimant to a share of the product of industry, 252; Chaps. 5 and 6, Part IV; the residual claimant upon the product of industry, 322-36
Laissez faire, the doctrine, 344-52, 380
Land, its tenure, how far of consequence to the economist? 19, 36; one of the three primary agents of production, 47-8; its capability of increased production, 49-54; influence of a popular tenure upon population, 401 [See building lots, pastures, water privileges, wood lots, mines; see also, Nationalization of the Land; see, also, Chapter on Rent, Part IV, and Attacks on the Doctrine of Rent, Part VI]
Landlord, the, as a claimant to a share in the product of industry, 252, Chap. 2, Part IV, 328-34, 368-70
Latin-Union, so-called, its monetary league, 195, 571
Laws, how far shall they be considered by the economist, 19
Leave-them-as-you-find-them rule of taxation, 590
Leslie, T. E. Cliffe: influence of natural theology on political economy, 35; influence of a popular tenure of the soil upon population, in France, 401
Liverpool, Lord: ancient bankers, 522
Loans, [See Interest and Usury Laws]
Locke, John, on usury, 424
Lotteries, as a means of revenue to the State, 579
Luxury, ideas of, developed in the progress of society, 19; its appearance in human societies, 398-9
Machinery: great differences among different peoples in the capacity of using it, 73-4; introduction of machinery as tending to set producers and consumers apart, 231-6
Malthus, T. R.: the law of population, 391, 395, 402
Man, the economic, 21
Manchester, or *Laissez Faire*, school of economists, 348
Mansfield, Lord: diffusion of taxes, 606
Manufactures: not subject to the condition of diminishing returns, 53-4; plea for building up local manufactures to prevent waste of soil, 56-9; relation to agriculture, in new countries, 618–23
Market, what is it? 134
Market price, its relation to normal price, 139
Marriage: early marriages in Ireland, 394; discouraged by economic desires, 397
Marshall, Alfred and Mary Paley, *Economics of Industry*: honesty, a part of the "personal wealth" of a country, 9; possible savings of Asia and England contrasted, 93n; influence of "plant" on the prices of commodities, 144n; the course of speculation and the cause of panics, 232; effect upon accumulation of a low rate of interest, 288n; origin of business profits, 311

Martineau, Harriet: effects of a premium on illegitimacy, 450
Massachusetts paper money, 443
Mastership in production, 85, 105-9, 231, 239 [See chapter on Profits in Part IV; also article Co-operation in Part VI]
Materials, the third form of capital, 96-7
May, Sir E: the English Crown lands, 576n
McCulloch, J. R.: varying fertility of soils, 254; relation of wages to profits, 327n; wages and cheap food, 404; governmental expenditure, 414; effects of an increase of the money supply, 445n; proposes the purely economic theory of taxation, 583, 605; his treatise on taxation and the funding system, 586
Measure of value, so-called, [See Denominator of Value]
Mechanical industry, not subject to the condition of diminishing returns, 53-4
Medium of exchange, money serves as the, 162; how about paper money? 209
Metals as money, 166
Metals, the precious, as money, 167; the irregularity of their production, 188-9, 440, [See also Bi-metallism and Multiple Standard]
Middlemen in Ireland, 272
Mill, John Stuart: correctness of the popular conception of wealth, 6; fails to observe distinction between wealth and property, 15; his statement of the premises of the Ricardian school, 21; he replies to Comte's criticism founded on the *consensus* of the social phenomena, 39; recognizes exchange as a department of political economy, 111n; the friction of retail trade, 149; the equation of international demand, 153; the unearned increment of land, 284, 497-500; doctrine of the wage fund, 453
Mines, rental of, 281
Mints, of various countries, 180n
Mobility of capital and labor, how far secured, 104, 339-45
Money, Chaps. 3, 4, 5 and 6, Part III; interest paid, in general, not for the use of money, but of other forms of capital, 286 [See, also, Bank Money, Inconvertible Paper Money, Political Money, Bi-metallism]
Monometallism [See Bi-metallism]
Monopolies, as a source of revenue to the State, 578
Monopoly value, 121
Moral considerations, how far do they concern the economist? 19, 36
Moral elements of supply and demand, 147
Mosaical code, prohibits usury, 417
Mortgages, are they wealth, or only property? 15
Motives, economic, shall all be taken by the economist, or only a few leading motives? 16-22
Multiple standard, for deferred payments, 191, 459-64
Napoleon, avoided the use of paper money, 214
"National" Political Economy, so-called, 32; why should industrial correspond to political entities? 615-6
Nationalization of the Land, 493-505
Natural Theology: its relation to political economy, 35
Nature, the assumption of a beneficent constitution of, as influencing the pursuit of political economy, 35
Nature, human: how far shall the economist seek to comprehend it, and include it in the premises of his reasoning? 16-22
Neison, Dr.: varying mortality of the several trades and professions, 320
New countries, so-called, why wages are high in them, 618-23
Nicholls, Sir George: effects of Gilbert's act, 449
Nitrification, so-called, as a means of renewing the soil subject to culture, 59
Nominal *vs.* real wages, 321
Nominal *vs.* real cost of labor, 321

Normal price: its relation to market price, 137-8
Norman, Geo. Warde: the theory of bank money, 225
North, Dudley: free coinage, 195
Occupation, change of, as a means of relieving the labor market, 342
Offices, sale of, 575
One price only for a commodity, 132
Opinion, public: influence on wages, 353-4
Organization of industry, 84-5; as affecting price, 144
Ortes, G.: intimates the laws of population, 395
Over-production, what the term means, 408-10
Overstone, Lord: the theory of bank money, 225; the course of speculation and over trading, 232; fictitious deposits, 422
Panics, the causes of, 232-3, 239; in the United States, 243
Paper money [See Bank Money and Inconvertible Paper Money]
Par of exchange: what it is, 543; between gold-using and silver-using countries, 561
Parieu, E. de: the literature of taxation, 585; the diffusion of taxes, 609
Pastures: relation to arable lands, 277
Pastoral state, the, 61
Pauperism, 446-52
Perry, A. L. Prof.: doctrine of the indifference of the rate of profits, 373, 379; doctrine of the wage fund, 453
Petty, Sir Wm.: his theory of taxation, 592
Physiocrats, the French, treated political economy as an art, 29; deemed agriculture the sole source of wealth, 48; their theory of taxation, 583
Physiology of man, how far of consequence to the economist? 16-20
Picking, or selecting, the coin, 179
Place-value, 46
Plant, so-called, its existence as affecting price, 144
Plutology, the term offered by Prof. Hearn as a substitute for political economy, 43
Political economy, its character and logical method, Part I
Political money, 439-45; [See also, Inconvertible Paper Money]
Politics, and economics, 349
Polo, Marco: the Chinese paper money, 206
Poor laws, [See Pauperism]
Pope, the, as a capitalist, 572
Population increases as tribes pass from the hunter to the pastoral state, and again as they initiate agriculture, 60-3; relation of subsistence to population, Chap. 1-3, Part V; effect of the increase of population in driving cultivation down to inferior soils, 51-4, 99, 257, 271-4; [See, also, The Nationalization of the Land, Part VI
Potato philosophy of wages, 404
Practical men, so-called or self-called, their readiness to assert their opinions on economic questions, 41
Prediction, capability of, made by M. Comte a test of a true science, 25
Prejudices, popular, their influence on political economy, 40
Premises of political economy, 16-23
Price, relation to value, 115; but one price for a commodity, 132; normal and market price, 137-9; price the agent in the international distribution of money, 176; relation of rent to the price of land, 261; to the price of agricultural produce, 262; relation of profits to the price of manufactured produce, 311
Price-current, need of, 182-3; how about paper money? 210
Price, Bonamy, objects to dropping the word wealth, 5; depreciation not a necessary result of inconvertibility, 213
Procreative force, the, its capabilities, 391-3; its persistence, 394; antagonized by economic desires, 397-401
Production of wealth, 44; Part II; modes of production, 46;

agents of production, 47; productive capability of a community, Chap. 4, Part II; reaction of exchange upon production, Chap. 7, Part III; reaction of distribution upon production, Chap. 8, Part IV
Producers and consumers, their relations and possible misunderstandings, Chap. 7, Part III
Productive co-operation, [See Co-operation]
Production, cost of, how related to value, 119-124, 151-8
Profits, of the entrepreneur, his motive in production, 231,239; profits, a share of the product of industry, 252, Chap. 4, Part IV; profits and rent are species of the same genus, 307-10; profits do not form a part of the price of manufactured products, 311; are not obtained by deduction from wages, 312; doctrine of the indifference of the rate of profits, 373,379; in co-operation the laborers aim to secure the entrepreneur's profits, 376-7
Progressive taxation, 600-2
Property, relation to wealth, 15
Protection *vs.* freedom of production, 611-23
Protectionist writers, hold that each country has a political economy of its own, 32; make much of the exhaustion of the soil, 56-8 [See, also, Protection *vs.* Freedom of Production]
Purdy, Fred.: variations in wages throughout England, 356n
Purveyance, as a means of revenue, 580
Quasi taxes, 578-81
Quesnay, M., his school of economists, 29, 48
Raguet, Condy: bank money in the United States, 223, 225
Railways of Germany, 577
Real *vs.* nominal wages, 319-20
Real *vs.* nominal cost of labor, 321
Realized wealth, (taxation) [See Wealth]
Redeemability of paper money, what it implies, Chaps. 5 and 6, Part III
Registration of land, the requirement adds virtually to the facility of transfers, 351
Rent, as a share in the distribution of the product of industry, 252, Chap. 2, Part IV; its relation to the price of land, 261; its relation to the price of agricultural produce, 262; tends to rise with growth of population, 257, 289, 497; rent and profits are species of the same genus, 307-10; does rent belong in equity to the community? 284 [See also Nationalization of the Land, and Attacks upon the Doctrine of Rent, Part VI]
Repercussion of taxes, [See Diffusion, etc.]
Reserve, specie, of bank money, 223
Restriction, so-called, the English, 207, 444
Retail trade, the friction of, 148-9
Revenue (individual), as the basis of taxation, 589, 591, 598
Revenue of the State, 572-84
Ricardo, David: his school of political economy, 22; treats political economy as a science, not as an art, 30; his views on seigniorage, 197-200; depreciation not a necessary result of inconvertibility, 213n; his relation to the doctrine of rent, 265; [See also, Attacks on the Doctrine of rent, Part VI] relation of wages and profits, 327; the incidence of a land tax, or tax on rents, 499
Rogers, J. E. T.: rents in England, 269; wages and cheap food, 427n; co-operation, 427n; the insurrection of the peasantry under Richard II, 469; the diffusion of taxes, 607
Roscher, Wm.: definition of capital, 87n; proportion of produce consumed upon the farm, 112n; advocates tabular or multiple standard, 191; the variety of man's economic wants, 395n; his reference to H. C. Carey, 487
Russia, the efficiency of its laboring population contrasted with that of the English, 76; paper money, 443

Safe deposit, as a banking function, 526
Sanitary conditions, as affecting the efficiency of labor, 69, 70
Saving [See Abstinence]
Say, J. B.: progressive taxation, 600 ; diffusion of taxes, 607-8
Scarcity value, 121
Schools of political economy, 16-23
Science, does political economy attain this dignity ? 25 ; distinction between political economy as a science and as an art, 27-8
Scotch, once an idle people, 78
Scotland, inadequate shelter of the laboring population, 70
Seasons, their influence on regularity of employment, 320
Seigniorage, Chap. 4, Part III
Selecting, or picking, the coin, 179
Senior, N.W.: relation of value to wealth, 7 ; relation of gratuity to value, 12 ; relation of rights or credits to wealth, 15 ; distinction between political economy as a science and as an art, 29 ; labor not essential to value, 120 ; money is " abstract wealth," 184; opportunities for extra earnings, 319 ; the consumption of wealth, 381 ; relation of famine to war, 395n ; the order of succession of human desires, 396 ; what is a luxury ? 399 ; his statement of the law of population, 395
Sentiment, personal, excluded from definition of value, 7 ; sentiment and political economy, 38 ; sentiment as modifying the influence of competition, 129
Services, distinguished from commodities, 247 ; services of the possessors of health, skill, strength and intelligence may be the subjects of exchange, though those qualities can not be, 9-10
Settlement, (parochial), English law of, 451
Shelter, its relation to subsistence, 384
Shocks, economic, their propagation through the industrial and commercial body, 237-43
Silver, [See Precious Metals ; in its relation to Gold, see, also, Bimetallism]
Sismondi, M. : rents in Tuscany, 270 ; influence of a popular tenure of the soil upon population, 401
Skill is not wealth, though it may become the means of acquiring wealth, 9-10
Slave labor, the cause of its inefficiency, 77
Smith, Adam : his Wealth of Nations, effect upon the relations of States, 3 ; treated political economy mainly as an art, 30 ; his economic writings influenced by his views as a professor of natural theology, 35 ; bank money, 223 ; the immobility of labor, 340 ; masters always in a combination not to raise wages, 468n ; the bank of Amsterdam, 523 ; voluntary contributions to the State, 572 ; inefficiency of government administration of productive property, 576 ; his maxims regarding taxation, 586-9
Social dividend theory of taxation, 588
Socialism, 624-33
Sociology : its relation to political economy, 39
Soil, the, a fund for the endowment of the human race, 55
Soldiers, their services economic in England, non-economic in Germany, 8
Solidarity of the family, as related to natural selection, 390
Specie reserve of bank money, [See Reserve]
Speculation, the course of, 232-3 ; the speculating class and their gains, 361-4
Steuart, Sir James, treated political economy as an art, 30
Standard of deferred payments, usually called standard of value, 184-90 ; how about paper money ? 218-9 ; how about bi-metallic money ? 440-5, [See also Multiple Standard]
Statistician, the economic, to be distinguished from the economist, 34

Stock, influence of a stock of a commodity on its price, 139-43
Storage, necessity of, as affecting price, 143
Strikes, 352, 468-70; co-operation would abolish strikes, 430
Structure in industry, 103-9
Subsistence: 86-7, 94, 97, 453-5; in its relation to population, Chapters 1-3, Part V
Substitution of one commodity for another in use, as affecting price, 142
Successions, limitations upon and taxation of, 573
Sumner, W. G. Prof.: the doctrine of protection, 614, 616
Supply and demand, 125-140; (Money) 174
Supply is not equivalent to stock, 140
Survival of the fittest, how far carried out in the human family, 390
Sympathy with labor, [See Opinion, Public]
Tabular standard, for deferred payments, [See Multiple Standard]
Taxation, its place in political economy, 357-60; Bentham's and McCulloch's view of taxation as stimulating production, 414-6; how taxation may be considered, 582-4; the principles of, 585-610 [See, also, Quasi Taxes]
Territorial division of labor, 83; the protectionist argument for limiting it, 611-6
Theology, natural: the proper attitude of the economist towards it, 35
Thompson, Prof. R. E.: exhaustion of the soil, 56
Thornton, Henry: the country banks of England, 525
Thünen, J. H. von: the principle of diminishing returns applies even to the harvesting of crops, 53n
Titles, sale of, 575
Time-value, 46
Tocqueville, A. de: sale of offices in France, 575
Tooke, Thomas: depreciation not a necessary result of inconvertibility of paper money, 213n; the theory of bank money, 224
Tools, the second form of capital, 95; their importance in production, 98
Torrens, Robert: the theory of bank money, 225
Trades-Unions, 465-6 [See, also, Knights of Labor, Part VI]
Transportation, in its relation to rent, 259-60; in its relation to prices, 176
Tributes from colonies, dependencies and conquered nations, 574
Truck, 473
Turgot, A. R. G.: the only physiocrat who treated political economy as a science; his strictly scientific method, 29
Twiss, Travers: the potato in Ireland, 404n
Under-production, what it results from, 407-10
Under-consumption, so-called, 409
Unearned increment of land [See, Increment, etc.]
United States: the laboring population well fed and well sheltered, 68-70; capable of using delicate and intricate machinery, 75; its money, 223-5 [See; also, Greenbacks]; panics, 243; rents, 268; increase of population, 392; its usury laws, 419; its banking agencies, 528-9, [see, also, the National Banking System, Part VI]; considered with reference to the question of protection, 616-22
Usury and usury laws, 368-9, 417-25
Utility, how related to value, 116; useful, in economics, does not mean beneficial, 117 [See Final Utility]
Value: related to wealth as attribute to substance, 7; defined, 8-9, 114; relation to price, 115; to utility, 116-7; is it a momentary phenomenon? 118; how related to labor, 119-24; value is governed by the relation of demand and supply, 125; the value of money, 169, 197-203, 212
Voluntary contributions [See Contributions]

Wage fund theory, 327 [See, also, Part VI]

Wages: as a share of the product of industry, 252; are not diminished by the sums received by the landlord class as rent, 263, 323; or by the sums received by the employing class as profits, 312, 325; the law of wages, Chaps. 5 and 6, Part IV; why wages are high in new countries, 618-23

Walker, Amasa: the theory of bank money, 225; co-operation, 427n

Warren, W. F.: voluntary contributions to the State, 572

Waste of materials (avoidable) an important element in production, 72, 330-3

Waste of soil, 256; some degree inevitable, 58; its relation to rent, 278

Water privileges, rent of, 278

Wealth: the subject matter of political economy, 1-3; definition, 4; relation of wealth to value, 7; [See, also, throughout, Capital]; as the basis of taxation, 604

Weathering, so-called, as a means of renewing the soil subject to culture, 59

Welfare, human, not the subject matter of political economy, 10

Wells, D. A.: exemption in taxation is confiscation, 599

Whately, Richard: popular prejudices aroused by political economy, 40; substitutes the term catallactics for political economy, 43; profits a species of the same genus as rent, 306

Whewell, William: his definition of science, 25

Wife, the, relation to the subsistence of the family, 386

William III, of England, dissipates the estates of the crown, 576

Wilson, Dr.: on usury, 419

Wilson, James: depreciation not a necessary result of inconvertibility of paper money, 213n; the theory of bank money, 224

Wolowski, Louis: no paper money in Poland, 206

Wood lots, rent of, 282

Workhouse test of pauperism, 447-50

Young, Arthur: "the magic of property," 77; expenditure as the basis of taxation, 592